An Innocent Abroad

FLASHPOINTS

The FlashPoints series is devoted to books that consider literature beyond strictly national and disciplinary frameworks, and that are distinguished both by their historical grounding and by their theoretical and conceptual strength. Our books engage theory without losing touch with history and work historically without falling into uncritical positivism. FlashPoints aims for a broad audience within the humanities and the social sciences concerned with moments of cultural emergence and transformation. In a Benjaminian mode, FlashPoints is interested in how literature contributes to forming new constellations of culture and history and in how such formations function critically and politically in the present. Series titles are available online at http://escholarship.org/uc/flashpoints.

A complete list of titles begins on p. 306.

An Innocent Abroad

Lectures in China

J. Hillis Miller

NORTHWESTERN UNIVERSITY PRESS | EVANSTON, ILLINOIS

Northwestern University Press
www.nupress.northwestern.edu

Printed in the United States of America

10 9 8 7 6 5 4 3 2 1

Library of Congress Cataloging-in-Publication Data

Miller, J. Hillis (Joseph Hillis), 1928– author.
[Speeches. Selections.]
An innocent abroad : lectures in China / J. Hillis Miller.
pages cm.
Includes bibliographical references and index.
ISBN 978-0-8101-3162-0 (pbk. : alk. paper) — ISBN 978-0-8101-3258-0 (cloth : alk. paper) — ISBN 978-0-8101-3163-7 (ebook)
1. Criticism. 2. Literature—Study and teaching. 3. Literature and globalization. I. Title. II. Series: FlashPoints (Evanston, Ill.)
PN85.M485 2015
801.95—dc23

2015029410

For Shen Dan, Wang Fengzhen, Wang Ning, and Richard Terdiman

Contents

Acknowledgments

First, let me warmly and gratefully thank Richard Terdiman, my colleague in the University of California multicampus system, for suggesting that I contribute a book to the FlashPoints series, now published by Northwestern University Press. He has waited patiently for a good many years for me to get around to doing this book, only nudging me politely now and then to ask me to get on with it, as more and more "lectures in China" have accumulated. This book would never have appeared without his instigation. It is a great honor for me to have this book appear under such distinguished auspices.

My heartfelt gratitude goes to all those in China who have been so kind and courteous to me and have taken such good care of me in China over the years. I have warm feelings for them all, not only the senior scholars who have been my hosts but also the graduate students and young faculty who were given the somewhat thankless job of accompanying me from one place to another. I have been honored and treated courteously in every possible way in China, not only by being given the best bits (among them, fish eyes, boiled river-turtle shells, and other strange delicacies) at feasts in my honor but also by having been awarded many honorary guest professorships (I count ten over the years, plus an honorary professorship at Peking University all the way back in 1994). I have also been honored by being repeatedly interviewed by journalists for publications like the *Literature and Art Gazette*; none of those interviews have been included in this book, but they were often intellectually exigent dialogues in which I was asked penetrating and informed questions.

First I thank Wang Fengzhen, now retired from the Institute of Foreign Literature at the Chinese Academy of Social Sciences, whom I first met when he was a visiting scholar at Irvine, before I ever visited China. Then must come Shen Dan, now Changjiang Professor of English Language and Literature at Peking University. She is an internationally renowned scholar in narratology. I met her on my first visit to China, in 1988. Wang Fengzhen and Shen Dan are my oldest friends in China. Next I thank Wang Ning of Tsinghua University, a distinguished theorist with an international reputation, who has arranged so many invitations for me, not only at his own university or universities but also at conferences in many places in China. After them comes Guo Rong, now an old friend, who I am told on good authority is one of my best translators. Then Guo Yanjuan, the author of a dissertation in Chinese on my work. She helped me immeasurably with the putting together of this book (for example, by compiling the appendix, which condenses much factual information about my lectures in China that I never would have been able to recover or discover for myself). Guo Rong and Guo Yanjuan are kindly collaborating to prepare a Chinese version of this book to be published by Nanjing University Press. That is a great honor for me.

I thank finally a list, by no means complete, of other scholars, whose names are given in no particular order. Their names are the tip of an iceberg, as we say, since I have kept no comprehensive record over the years. These scholars have been kind and hospitable to me—for example, by inviting me to lecture, or by interviewing me, or by serving as my host, or by sponsoring me for a guest professorship appointment, or by translating one or more of my lectures or essays, or by writing a dissertation on my work, or by coming to Irvine as a visiting fellow under my sponsorship: Huimin Jin, Xia Yanhua, Xu Qin (Daniel), Tao Jiajun, Chen Aimin, Ning Yizhong, Sheng Anfeng, Sheng Ning, Lu Xiaohong, Li Yuan, Li Zuolin, Chen Yongguo, Zhang Yifan, Huang Dexian, Xuan Gong, Xialin Ding, Ming Don Gu, Shaobo Xie, Wang Yue, and Xiaoming Yi. I have watched with pleasure and admiration the professional development of these friends and colleagues. My association with them has been an important part of my own professional life since 1988.

I gratefully acknowledge some of the previous publication of versions of many of the lectures in this book. The manuscripts of many of the lectures have long since disappeared. The lectures I actually gave were often abbreviated versions of essays that were published later on, and all have been revised for this book—often, for example, with comments from the present included within brackets. For this book, I used the actual lectures I gave, whenever I still had them, but in some cases I have had to use the published versions, and these are usually somewhat longer than the original lectures. The appendix lists the dates and locations in China where the fifteen lectures were delivered before they became the essays in this book.

The lecture that became chapter 1 was originally presented at a plenary meeting, held in Beijing in May 1988, of the Chinese Academy of Social Sciences. It was published three years later in David Easton and Corinne S. Schelling, eds., *Divided Knowledge: Across Disciplines, Across Cultures* (Newbury Park, CA: Sage Publications, 1991), 118–38. The version used in the present volume is a revised version of the original lecture as it appeared in that book.

The lecture that became chapter 2 was originally presented in 1994 to the Institute of Foreign Literature at the Chinese Academy of Social Sciences, for publication in the institute's journal. The lecture was dedicated to the memory of William (Bill) Readings, a brilliant young Oxford-trained theorist and literary critic and associate professor of comparative literature at the University of Montreal who had died in a commuter plane crash in Indiana on 31 October 1994. It was my hope that this dedication would call attention to his work and give him the posthumous influence in the People's Republic of China that he deserved. The lecture was deeply indebted to his thinking, especially as reflected in a manuscript which he left nearly complete at his death, and which was published in 1996 as *The University in Ruins* by Harvard University Press. Bill Readings's book remains timely, both because it contains what is still the best discussion of the stages that led to the present research university in the West and because it is by far the best of the many books that have been published about the transformation of the Western university. As for the lecture, it was translated by Tung-jung Chen as "Black Holes in the Internet Galaxy: New Trends in Literary Study in the United States" and was published in *Chung-wai Literary Monthly* 24:1 (1995), 72–89. The version that appears in the present volume is adapted from J. Hillis Miller and Manuel Asensi, *Black Holes / J. Hillis Miller; or, Boustrophedonic Reading* (Stanford, CA: Stanford University Press, 1999), a book in which my portion, *Black Holes,* is arrayed on facing pages with my coauthor's portion, *J. Hillis Miller; or, Boustrophedonic Reading.*

Chapter 3 was originally a Wei Lun Lecture presented at the Chinese University of Hong Kong and published by Hong Kong University Press. In somewhat altered form, the lecture was presented twice more in China, at Peking University on 9 April 1997 and two days later at the Chinese Academy of Social Sciences in Beijing. In November of the following year, in Denmark, it was given as a talk at the University of Copenhagen and at the University of Aarhus. It was then published as a "working paper" pamphlet (*Arbejdspapirer*) by the Institut for Litteraturvidenskab at the University of Copenhagen and by the Department of Comparative Literature at the University of Aarhus, in both instances with the title *Effects of Globalization on Literary Study*. The version presented in Denmark largely formed the basis of the text that was revised to form chapter 3 of this book. A few passages of the chapter have also been adapted from my portion of J. Hillis Miller and Manuel Asensi, *Black Holes / J. Hillis Miller; or, Boustrophedonic Reading* (Stanford, CA: Stanford University Press, 1999).

Chapter 4 was originally a lecture given at the International Conference on the Future of Literary Theory: China and the World, held at Beijing Language and Culture University in July 2000. It was published as "Will Comparative Literature Survive the Globalization of the University and the New Regime of Telecommunications?" in *Tamkang Review* 31:1 (2000), 1–21, and in a different version in Lisa Block de Behar, ed., *Comparative Literature Worldwide: Issues and Methods*, vol. 2 (Montevideo: Fundación Fontaina Minelli, 2000), 245–66. It was then published again as "Will Literature Survive the Globalization of the University and the New Regime of Telecommunications?" in Q. S. Tong, Wang Shouren, and Douglas Kerr, eds., *Critical Zone 1: A Forum of Chinese and Western Knowledge* (Hong Kong/Nanjing: Hong Kong University Press/Nanjing University Press, 2004), 153–64.

Chapter 5 was originally presented as a lecture at the International Conference on Marxism and Aesthetics held in Guilin, China, 23–26 July 2000. It was published in Chinese and then in English as "Promises, Promises: Speech Act Theory, Literary Theory, and Politico-Economic Theory in Marx and de Man" in *Research on Marxist Aesthetics*, vol. 4 (Guilin: Guangxi Normal University Press, 2001), 24–34. It also appeared in *New Literary History* 33:1 (2002), 1–20.

The lecture that became chapter 6 was first presented on 17 April 2001 at Baylor University and was published as a pamphlet for local circulation by the university's department of literature. The lecture was presented again in China several months later, on the occasion of the

Third Sino-American Symposium on Comparative Literature, held 11–14 August 2001 at Tsinghua University in Beijing, and at Beijing Language and Culture University during the same visit. It subsequently appeared in English in *Lectures by Famous Teachers* (Tianjin: Tianjin People's Publishing House, 2003), 28–62, and then in Chinese translation in *Cultural Studies*, vol. 4 (Beijing: Central Compilation and Translation Press, 2003), 65–83.

Chapter 7 began as a lecture presented first at Tsinghua University on 4 September 2003, and again at Suzhou University later that month. It was published in Chinese in several versions; in one of these, it occupied the first fifteen pages of a large volume issued with a Chinese title by Peking University Press in 2003. I have not found a record of any version previously published in English.

A shorter version of the lecture that became chapter 8 was originally presented to the faculty and students of the department of foreign languages at Tsinghua University in Beijing on 9 September 2003. The lecture was presented again in 2004 at Zhengzhou University. It was published in Wang Fengzhen and Shaobo Xie, eds., *Globalization and Indigenous Cultures*, special issue, *ARIEL* 34:1 (2003), 31–52. Material from the lecture was then reworked and expanded for J. Hillis Miller, "Derrida Enisled," in W. J. T. Mitchell and Arnold I. Davidson, eds., *The Late Derrida*, special issue, *Critical Inquiry* 33:2 (2007), 248–76, as well as for J. Hillis Miller, *For Derrida* (New York: Fordham University Press, 2009), and for J. Hillis Miller, *The Conflagration of Community* (Chicago: University of Chicago Press, 2011).

Chapter 9 began as a lecture presented first at the International Conference on Globalization and Local Culture, held 5–9 June 2004 at Zhengzhou University, and again at the International Conference on Critical Inquiry, held 12–15 June 2004 at Tsinghua University in Beijing. It was given a Chinese translation by Yifan Zhang and Yingjian Guo and published in the *Journal of Zhengzhou University* 5 (2004), 127–30. The English version, with revisions, was incorporated into a chapter of J. Hillis Miller, *Communities in Fiction* (New York: Fordham University Press, 2015).

The lecture that became chapter 10, published here in English for the first time, was presented on 17 June 2006 at a conference on globalization held 16–22 June at Wuhan University. Globalization has by now come to be so much taken for granted as to be, unfortunately, no longer all that much the subject of thoughtful reflection. On that occasion, however, it was a pleasure to try out my ideas on a distinguished

Chinese audience. Globalization had been a topic of some of my earlier lectures, but this conference, explicitly dedicated to globalization, gave me a chance to think through my perspectives on the topic at greater length, in a different time, and in a different context.

Chapter 11 began as a lecture presented on 4 November 2008 at Nanjing Postal-Telecommunication University. It is published here in English for the first time, though the last section is adapted from J. Hillis Miller, "Reading (about) Modern Chinese Literature in a Time of Globalization," in Wang Ning, ed., *China in the Twentieth Century*, special issue, *Modern Language Quarterly* 69:1 (2008), 187–94.

Chapter 12 was originally a lecture presented at the Fifth Sino-American Symposium on Comparative Literature, held 11–15 August 2010 at Shanghai Jiaotong University, where Wang Ning, Chen Jing, and Sheng Anfeng extended many courtesies to me during my visit. At the time of this symposium, I had already expressed my concerns about so-called World Literature, not only in a lecture presented in 2003 at Tsinghua University in Beijing and again at Suzhou University (see chapter 7 of this book) but also in a second lecture, presented first at Tsinghua University in 2003 and again in 2004 at Zhengzhou University (see chapter 8). For chapter 12 of this volume, I used an augmented version of my symposium lecture; the additions are my responses to an admirable paper given at the symposium by Thomas Beebee. The augmented version appeared as "Challenges to World Literature" in the bilingual Chinese/English journal published by Shanghai International Studies University, *Comparative Literature in China* 4 (2010), 1–9. The following year, a revision of the augmented text was published as "Globalization and World Literature" in Ning Wang, ed., *Comparative Literature: Toward a (Re)construction of World Literature*, special issue, *Neohelicon* 38:2 (2011), 251–65 (this special issue of *Neohelicon* gathered papers from the 2010 symposium held in Shanghai).

The lecture that became chapter 13 was presented in September 2010 at the International Conference on Literature Reading and Research, held in Guangzhou (once called Canton) at the Guangdong University of Foreign Studies (Guangdong is the name of the province). I chose in my lecture to take Yeats's poem "The Cold Heaven" as a paradigmatic example of the difficulties involved in deciding whether we should read or teach literature now. The poem also exemplifies the difficulties of explaining such a text to students, at home and globally. It comes from Yeats's volume of 1916, *Responsibilities*. The text of the lecture was published in Paul Socken, ed., *The Edge of the Precipice: Why Read*

Literature in the Digital Age? (Montreal/Kingston: McGill-Queen's University Press, 2013), 140–55, and in Jakob Lothe and Jeremy Hawthorn, eds., *Narrative Ethics* (Amsterdam: Rodopi, 2013), 13–24.

Chapter 14, which began as a lecture presented in September 2012 at Beijing Language and Culture University, is published here in English for the first time.

Chapter 15 was originally a lecture titled "National Literatures in the Context of World Literature Today," presented first at Tsinghua University and again at Peking University during a visit to Beijing, 10–12 September 2012. In a different and much longer form, the lecture was published as "Literature Matters Today" in Ranjan Ghosh, ed., *Does Literature Matter?*, special issue, *SubStance* 42:2 (2013), 12–32; I am grateful to Professor Ghosh for agreeing to a translation of my essay into Chinese, and to the essay's adaptation and reuse for this book. A translation into Chinese, by Xialin Ding, of the first half of "Literature Matters Today" appeared in Beijing University's *Guo Wai Wen Xue (Foreign Literature)* 2 (2013), 3–8.

Editor's Note

Richard Terdiman

There are turning points. Things do change. *An Innocent Abroad* is the result and the register of a cluster of transformations—some local, some epochal, all challenging, interconnected, and consequential. The lectures given in China by J. Hillis Miller, and collected here, trace the attempt by a widely influential American literary critic, theorist, and scholar to reflect upon the cultural intersections between China and the United States, and upon the discipline of literary studies conceived in light of its global diversities and differences. At the same time, this book confirms an ongoing alteration in how knowledge circulates. By collecting lectures delivered outside the United States and making them available everywhere in the world, *An Innocent Abroad* also evokes the question of the book in a time of change.

Hillis Miller presented his first lecture in China in 1988, ten years after China and the United States normalized relations. The 1980s marked a liberalization of academic contacts, particularly after the 1985 reforms facilitating educational exchanges were adopted under Deng Xiaoping. This development increased the number of Chinese university students studying in the US and the number of Chinese invitations extended to US academics.

Hillis Miller was among the early cohort of American literary scholars invited to China, and one of the most influential. Fredric Jameson, whose illuminating foreword follows this note, first lectured there in 1985. Miller's initial China talk came three years later, when he spoke to a plenary meeting of the Chinese Academy of Social Sciences in Beijing. Thus began a series of lectures and conference participations that extended over more than two decades; the latest of the talks collected here is from 2012.

These talks trace a trajectory. Just as Miller's understanding of the context in which he was presenting his lectures—particularly his acquaintance with the culture in which they were given—deepened over time, so too do the texts in this volume provide an evolving symptomatic reading of their historical, disciplinary, and geographical location.

Miller's audiences included university faculty, students, scholars, and artists. He introduced Chinese listeners to US literary studies in a period of ferment characterized by emerging—and controversial—trends in theory and methodology. His lectures reflected on the political and cultural issues implicated by these transformations in the field. And they presented Miller's own compelling and influential interpretations, particularly in the area of deconstruction—all of this with Miller's customary grace, erudition, subtlety, and interpretive brio.

In the West, the "theory revolution" was applauded by some and decried by others, but it was intensely consequential for the discipline of literary studies. For Chinese scholars in literature, these innovations, coming from far away, may well have been even more startling. Chinese academics were generally producing positivist scholarship in literary history, dominated by ideologically determined readings of texts. The new perspectives brought to China by Western academics proved to have important implications.

Like all the other Westerners who appeared in China in those early years of renewed exchanges, Hillis Miller, in his lectures, had to negotiate a distance between the disciplinary assumptions he had brought along with him and what an audience of Chinese academics was familiar with. The talks collected in this volume never "level down." Rather, they take the disciplinary distance that produced them as a focus for their own reflection; they unpack their assumptions for scholars who cannot be presumed to share them. This leads Miller to a practice of explication and clarification remarkable for its insight and its originality, and to formulations that have the potential to clarify Western literary studies for Westerners as well as for scholars in China. One can wonder whether Miller's striking syntheses would have arisen without the distance he traveled to deliver them.

Globalization thus alters interpretation in ways this book can help us begin to understand. Yet the volume represents another transformation worth reflecting upon, this one in the technology and practice of the book. The materiality of the publishing process, and the means through which scholars communicate and readers read, have important consequences. These structures change, and today they are changing fast. The transformations in the dissemination of knowledge that have occurred over the period comprised by the lectures collected here have influenced the nature of scholarship as much as has the globalization of scholarly exchanges. Consider how this volume of Hillis Miller's China lectures came together as an artifact, and in what form it comes to you.

An Innocent Abroad: Hillis Miller's wry, sly, Mark Twainian title indicates how much, in this new world, we have all already been denaturalized. And so with books themselves. In the humanities, books are at the heart of our activity; scholarly communication takes a lot of saying. But this production is being transformed, not only in the area of advanced intellectual reflection but also in the grittier economics of the publishing industry. Scholarly communication doesn't go without saying anymore.

The history of these developments begins far from literary studies; it arises with increased costs for academic journals in the natural sciences. Over the period of these lectures, the library subscription costs of science journals were doubling every few years. These costs were increasing because commercial publishers had purchased science journals to turn them into profit centers. Libraries needed the journals because scientists needed them. The publishers charged as much as the traffic would bear, and the charges went up and up.

But over the past few decades, university library budgets have been inelastic. As the proportion of acquisition money paid to the likes of Elsevier (which publishes *Cell*) and Taylor & Francis (which publishes *Molecular Physics*) grew, the slice of the budget pie for humanities books shrank.

Consequently, academic libraries could buy fewer copies of books in humanities fields. Academic presses thus sold fewer copies of humanities titles, which soon became less economically viable. Fewer such books could be published at all, particularly first books by younger scholars. A number of academic presses simply dropped entire humanities disciplines from their "product lines." (An example drawn from the university where Hillis Miller taught for many years: in 2002, the University of California Press abruptly jettisoned literary studies from its acquisitions program; the press also dumped intellectual history and philosophy.)

The ground was shifting under humanities scholarship. But how can scholars function if they cannot circulate their work? High-level committees were formed to study the question. They made recommendations. But the heart of the problem was that they could not increase library or press budgets by very much. To save money, they advocated online publication in nonscience fields. A second innovation was the formation of nonprofit science journals like the *Public Library of Science* (*PLoS*), for which subscription costs were only a fraction of what libraries were paying for proprietary journals; in this way, a little of the pressure was taken off acquisitions budgets. Third, and most pertinent here, scholars and presses were urged to explore new paradigms for humanities publication.

The FlashPoints series in literary studies, in which this book appears, is among the earliest and probably the boldest of these new models. The series debuted in 2007 with a paradigm incorporating three innovative elements. First, to find the books it publishes, FlashPoints depends for acquisitions on an editorial group of university faculty members and their contacts within the profession of literary studies. Second, because "literary production" is increasingly influenced by forces beyond "the literary" (narrowly conceived), FlashPoints emphasizes the interdisciplinary and international (and thereby seeks to broaden readership for books in the series). Third, FlashPoints books appear simultaneously in paperback copies and—in an important innovation—in free worldwide open-access versions on the Internet. Both in their acquisition and in their distribution, books in the FlashPoints Series aim to be *world* scholarship.

FlashPoints sought this volume of Hillis Miller's China lectures because they epitomize the internationalist and interdisciplinary spirit of the series. They represent cultural intersections and explore cultural questions of exceptional moment. The series editors thought that it would be a gift to publish these lectures in a modality that makes it possible for anyone in the world with Internet access to read the book. And we thought that the idea of such open-access publication would intrigue a celebrated scholar like Hillis Miller. Happily, it did. That's how this book came into your hands—or onto your computer screen—wherever in the world you are. The exchanges continue.

Foreword

Fredric Jameson

Hillis Miller's trips to China over the years of the post-Mao era—from 1988 to 2012, in some of which trips I myself participated—have come to form a remarkably coherent statement, an apologia for literature and reading of a new and welcome, far less conventional, kind. It avoids the traditional systematic aesthetic of an Ingarden or a Käthe Hamburger—in any case, no longer possible in our present literary and philosophical situation. It also omits any attempt—in any case, equally impossible—to summarize his own rich and unclassifiable career, to which the usual account of a development from phenomenology to deconstruction scarcely does justice. It also eschews the reactionary ressentiment of the now defunct National Association of Scholars in its denunciations of theory, cultural studies, and even more pernicious "leftist" schools and interests, deplorable for any proper aesthete and calculated to distract us from eternal verities and great books.

What opens a new path for Miller's wide-ranging account of contemporary literary criticism and theory—what makes a new approach to the "defense" of literature possible—is the very crisis of both today. Nor is the situation of these lectures irrelevant to their persuasive strategy, for to lecture abroad is always a problem fraught with danger and misunderstanding; but to lecture in China—whose changes from year to year in these last decades are so vertiginous as to mislead the dizzied pedagogue into offering anachronistic (when not condescending) stale wisdom—is a special case indeed. The "theory," whose good tidings were brought to us from Europe, is, for Chinese literary scholars, American, or was when it was new; and we no longer have to serve as its missionaries. Miller's strategy, his measured rhetoric, unerringly finds the issues and dilemmas both scholarly communities face, in the brave new world of the Internet and of globalization, the two combining in that very mutation of reading itself, when texts of all kinds find their ultimate "publication" on the smartphone. Indeed, the latter is a kind of symbol of the absorption of language by a now essentially visual culture: a new kind of tension between the media and the senses (if indeed verbal literature addresses the senses as such), which Miller had tactfully and unforgettably dramatized in his little book *Illustration*, which I take to be his own statement on "cultural studies" as such.

The lectures, however, spell out Miller's assessment of the dangers to the literary in a vaster context, and they make it clear that the tensions and incompatibilities between visual consumption and verbal comprehension are only a small and relatively specialized (biological, neurocognitive) part of a larger and indeed material, institutional contradiction.

We may in this sense use these rich lectures as a kind of immense rhizome which explores the crisis in all kinds of directions, organized by Miller's own pedagogical and poetic ingenuity (one lecture starts with Derrida's love letters, for example) and enriched with a whole array of incidental but arresting and exemplary literary analyses (from Thomas Wyatt to James, from Marx and Proust to Conrad's *Nostromo*, not omitting Wallace Stevens on American regionality). We must not omit, from these bravura excursions, probing analyses of the philosophical and political problems of collectivity and of the self, as these have been debated in the most recent theoretical literature.

But the heart of the work remains the new and urgent, contemporary problem: not what literature is, but whether it can survive in any recognizable form in globalization, a problem that promises to tell us as much about globalization as it does about literature. Miller's wisdom and vast pedagogical experience, however, dictate the right form of the question: not whether people will be reading books in the future (if only on their smartphones), but what will survive of literary study as such in its traditional, modern, or even future forms. This is a problem which transcends institutional questions (without leaving them behind) as much as it ignores the distractions of "the scholars'" worries about the coming tide of cultural illiteracy. The "crisis of the humanities"—a quite proper professional and political anxiety—is here rewritten as a series of sober inquiries: into the contradictions of "world literature" in a situation in which English is the hegemonic language, but in which the surviving plurality of languages (and their literatures) cannot be mastered in any effective and functioning disciplinary way. Ironically, the increase in the number of books on these subjects has begun to displace the properly literary studies themselves (a development that no doubt only serves to reinforce the problem).

Miller's lectures give us a great deal of useful information on the history of literature programs and literary theory itself, on the debates about cultural studies and the inroads of telecommunications in general into reading and teaching, and on the comparative as well (for example, on the problems of assessing Chinese literary study by comparison with the various Western critical methods).

We may be thankful that Miller offers no solutions to these dilemmas: those always turn out to be somebody's mere opinion, if not sheer prejudice. Instead, in this wonderfully witty and readable book, Hillis Miller has *produced the problem* (as the Althusserians liked to put it); and it is from the problem itself, and from the new explorations of its sources and consequences, that new and productive thinking has to start. As for this volume, the only consolation it has to offer us—but it is, in my opinion, an energizing and not a defeatist one—is that literature and literary study were *always* in crisis: this seemingly new and novel one offers a renewed confrontation with History as such.

Introduction

This book collects fifteen of the more than thirty lectures I have given at many universities in the People's Republic of China from 1988 to 2012. The lectures I have chosen are of several sorts, and my choices were based on several criteria. I wanted the collection to be representative of the sorts of lectures I have given in China, to include lectures given at as many different universities as possible, and to trace the evolution of my own thinking and of the lectures' contexts in China as these have markedly changed over the years. Most of the lectures are my responses to specific charges from my hosts for given conference topics, but a few are lectures I gave of my own choice, in classes or before nonconference university audiences. Most were written for delivery in China, but some are modifications of lectures or essays that were written for Western occasions and that I wanted to try out in China. I call the book *An Innocent Abroad*, partly in allusion to Mark Twain's *Innocents Abroad*, partly with a pun on "abroad" as meaning, among other things, both "in a foreign country" and "not on target; astray; in error" (*American Heritage Dictionary*). Especially since I still do not know Chinese, to my shame, and am by no means an expert on China, I have often been abroad in the second sense. I have nevertheless, gradually over the years and through many visits, begun to get the hang of things there a little, at least in the area of humanities study and scholarship in Chinese universities. I have continually been amazed by the intelligence, knowledge, open-mindedness, and intellectual energy of Chinese academics and students. I am not quite so innocently "abroad" as not to know that there may be monitors in classrooms and at conferences in China, as well as constraints on Internet use in China, but I must say that these are pretty completely invisible, for example, in the kinds of questions I am asked in discussion periods after a lecture. These are pretty much like American ones, at least as sharp and challenging. This introduction attempts to account for my experiences in China and for my choice of lectures to reprint in this book. I have not kept careful records of what lectures were given where, and when, in China, again to my shame, mostly because I had no idea I would ever need, many years later, to know the details. But I give in the appendix a list—more or less complete, compiled by Guo Yanjuan—of the many universities and institutes in China where I have lectured, along with dates and lecture titles.[1]

More important than the details, however, are the striking changes over the years since 1988 in China, in the United States, in literary study worldwide, and in my own writing and thinking, not to speak of my changing role in lecturing in China. I have been, over the course of these lectures, especially focused on the shift from print to digital media and the effect of that shift on teaching and research in the humanities—literary study particularly. That is a lot of changes taking place at once. It is therefore hard to use them all in accounting for a given lecture and its immediate circumstances. I have been especially struck, in rereading these lectures, by the immense changes in digital technology since the first of these lectures. What I have to say about that technology in the second lecture ("Black Holes in the Internet Galaxy: New Trends in Literary Study in the United States," given in 1994; see chapter 2) now seems quaint, old-fashioned, and obsolete. No iPhones, iPads, Kindles, or even iPods in those days! I spoke then of transistor radios as being up-to-date and changing the world! Nevertheless, my lectures in China have, as might have been expected, come back from new perspectives to the same topics, as my views of them have changed over the years along with changes in my Chinese audiences. I have attempted, however, to find and cut passages in a given lecture that echo too closely, sometimes word for word for a paragraph or so, something from a previous lecture. I have also added cross-references calling attention to places where a given topic has been discussed in an earlier chapter. The reader who follows these lectures in sequence will see that my views about all their chief topics have modulated over the years under the impact of a triple change: change in the actual external situation (for example, in the role of the humanities in higher education in the United States);

change in the audiences in China to whom I presented these lectures; and change in my own understanding of what is at stake. An example of my response to this triple change has been my gradual loss of concern with the history of various critical theories in the United States and a corresponding gradual conviction that global climate change is the most urgent issue confronting human beings today everywhere in the world, even more urgent than the self-destructive madness of our return once more to involvement in Iraq, Afghanistan, and, now, Syria, or than the Pentagon's arming of our local police forces with armored vehicles, automatic rifles, full battle gear, body armor, and the other paraphernalia of military occupation. It is in these contexts that I now ask myself, in 2015, whether the study of literature, my lifelong vocation, still matters, and if so, how.

First, changes in China since 1988: as everyone knows, China has undergone spectacular changes since 1988. When I first visited, the smell of coal smoke in Beijing from cooking and heating devices was strong, and the streets were full of bicycles, with the odd automobile here and there. Water in hotel rooms had to be boiled, and the city was full of narrow streets lined with tiny shops for food, bicycle repair, and the like. Each time I have returned, even after only a year or two away, the whole city has seemed transformed overnight, with new sectors of high-rise apartments, modern hotels indistinguishable from American ones, more and more automobiles, and no more coal smoke, but increasing Los Angeles–like automobile and industrial smog. China now has long-distance high-speed rail service that is the envy of the world. Superhighways abound, even within the city of Beijing and in other cities like Shanghai. China is even trying to do something about global warming, a big challenge for the Chinese. During these nearly thirty years, the Chinese university system has been utterly transformed, and the number of universities has doubled, from one thousand to over two thousand, with up-to-date programs not only in the so-called STEM disciplines (science, technology, engineering, and math) but also in humanities departments like English and comparative literature. I remember lecturing at one university that had just been completed, with multistoried, handsome, modern academic buildings, all glass and steel or aluminum, though with construction debris still visible around the edges. "How many students?" I asked. "Oh, about fifty thousand already," I was told. Truly amazing!

The changes in the United States during the last fifteen years have not been so positive, as most people know. We have been involved in two disastrous and hideously expensive wars, in Iraq and Afghanistan. Our infrastructure (bridges, roads, water supply, and the like) is crumbling, with only feeble beginnings, for example, of high-speed railways. Little is being done to regulate the greed and outright fraud of our banks and financial institutions. The gap between the rich 1 percent and the rest of the population is huge and growing all the time as the United States rapidly moves toward becoming a postdemocracy, a plutocracy. Limitless contributions by billionaires and corporations, along with gerrymandered congressional districts, are essentially making it possible for the rich to buy control of our government and then manipulate it to make the rich richer and the poor poorer. I say nothing of the recent revelations about the way the National Security Agency in the United States is spying on all American citizens, not to speak of the rest of the world, by collecting universal "metadata" of phone calls, e-mails, Internet and credit card usage, and the like. Unemployment is still dangerously high. Little or nothing is being done to deal with climate change, which will soon lead to sea-level rise that will flood our coastal cities.[2] Global warming has already led to much larger storms, both in summer and in winter, as well as to record heat. Our health care system is disastrously expensive—twice as much of our gross domestic product (GDP) as in other first-world countries (19 percent of US GDP, and moving toward 25 percent). All other advanced countries have single-payer health care. The Affordable Care Act will bring health care to 30 or 40 million Americans who do not have it at the moment, but those affiliated with the Republican-allied Tea Party movement are doing everything they can to repeal or defund so-called Obamacare and to make sure, as best they can, that it does not work in states where they are in control. [At the moment I first wrote this (13 October 2013), the Tea Party–allied minority in the House of Representatives had succeeded in shutting down the federal government (the Centers for Disease Control, the Environmental Protection Agency, the National Institutes of Health, the National Park Service, and so on, but of course with no effect on the pay of senators and representatives) by making outrageous demands for budget changes (including the defunding of Obamacare). A default on the federal debt was scheduled to occur on the following Thursday if no agreement was reached on raising the debt ceiling. This would have plunged the United States and the rest of the world, too, back into recession.—JHM] Our federal government, in short, was and remains thoroughly and catastrophically dysfunctional, which is the way the Tea Party apparently wants it.

During the years these lectures were given, American colleges and universities have also been in decline. The recession has meant cutbacks in funding for higher education generally. Big rises in tuition costs have put higher education out of reach for many potential students, and many of those who do go to colleges or universities graduate deeply in debt because they have been forced to borrow $100,000 or more. A university or college degree is no longer a guarantee of a good job. The shift to making our colleges and universities more and more into vocational training institutes (primarily for technology jobs), in addition to the effects of digitalization and the new power of the mass media, has meant especially steep declines in the humanities, with many foreign-language departments closing, a big reduction in the percentage of English majors, and so on. Over 70 percent of teaching in all fields in US colleges and universities is now done by so-called adjuncts, who are ill paid and have neither security of employment nor many "benefits," such as health care, pension contributions, and the like. In Texas, the platform of the state's Republican Party has as one of its planks the intention to forbid the teaching of critical thinking, not to speak of prohibiting the teaching of evolution as a proven scientific truth.

China and the United States, in short, have gone in opposite directions in the last quarter of a century, China up and the United States down. Why, then, have so many universities in China gone on inviting me to lecture, either at conferences or in independent appearances? I do not think it is because of my beautiful blue eyes, nor because all Chinese academics want to become deconstructionists. The reason, rather, in my view, is that I am seen as a person of some authority from the United States in language and literature study and in "theory" generally. This means that, in the view of Chinese academics, I can help them in their quite deliberate and self-conscious aim of creating up-to-date programs in the humanities and devising specifically Chinese forms of such disciplines as comparative literature or cultural studies or World Literature or even, paradoxically, Marxist aesthetics.[3] They want to learn what we do, and then do it better and in a distinctively Chinese way. I was, for example, invited to the beautiful city of Guilin in July 2000 to give a paper at the big International Conference on Marxism and Aesthetics (eventually published as "Promises, Promises: Speech Act Theory, Literary Theory, and Politico-Economic Theory in Marx and de Man"; see chapter 5). I asked a Chinese attendee why Westerners (Fredric Jameson, for example, not to speak of a rank amateur in Marxism like me) had been invited to speak about Marxist aesthetics. He said, "Because we don't have any." I suppose that the topic of the conference had been for some reason taboo or seen as unnecessary in the years after the Cultural Revolution.

I have found fascinating the change in my role as a lecturer in China over the decades since 1988. At first it was a matter of informing Chinese academics about things of which they may have known little. An example is my first visit. I was the member representing literary studies among a group of fellows of the American Academy of Arts and Sciences in various humanities and social sciences fields (history, philosophy, sociology, and so on, as well as literary studies) who had been invited to give talks about the latest developments in our fields to a plenary meeting of the prestigious and powerful Beijing branch of the Chinese Academy of Social Sciences (CASS). The first lecture in this book ("The Role of Theory in the Development of Literary Studies in the United States"; see chapter 1) is the final revision for publication of the one I gave, in all innocence, on that occasion. It was innocent because I really had little idea about the nature of the people in my audience. They were at that time—to a considerable degree, but by no means universally—older scholars who had survived the Cultural Revolution and were holdovers from the old days of Soviet influence in China. If they knew any Western language, it was likely to be Russian. CASS is radically different now, with many younger scholars trained in the West or exposed to the West by frequent visits there. You may remember that fellows of CASS, just a year after my 1988 visit, played a considerable role in the freedom movement culminating in Tiananmen Square. They were punished for that in various ways; a few leaders of the movement were imprisoned, but more generally they were subjected to even more hours of Marxist indoctrination each week, and they remained under surveillance and under suspicion for months if they had been spotted in Western news videos, taking part in demonstrations. I remember catching a glimpse, during an American television news broadcast at the time, of the big CASS building with banners hanging out the windows in support of the demonstrators. Even now, that moment in Chinese modern history is little discussed in China. Out of tact and fear of going astray, I would not bring it up there.

As the years went by, however, I was more and more asked to participate not as a "native informant" but as a colleague assisting more or less as an equal in the development of distinctively Chinese forms of literary theory, comparative literature, or World Literature. This is evident in the titles of the conferences at which I lectured. Here are three examples: "International Conference on the Construction of 21st-Century Chinese Literary Theory," "The Third Sino-American Symposium on Comparative Literature," and "International Conference on Translating Global Cultures: Toward Interdisciplinary Reconstruction." China wants to be a world leader in these as in other fields. I have come more and more to learn from these conferences as much as or more than I have contributed to them.

As the years have gone by, I have more and more turned to the question of why studying literature still matters now that we are in the midst of an epochal transition from printed books to digital media. Though I have certainly spent a lot of time explaining Western theory to Chinese audiences, since they want that, I have also made a point of insinuating into my lectures, whenever I can, actual readings of literary works—for example, poems by Tennyson and Yeats and a novel by Conrad, *Nostromo*—among the lectures selected here. Reading actual works of literature is what I love best to do. I believe theory is ancillary to that. An example not included here is a presentation I made to the English Department at Peking University about the kiss at the end of Henry James's *The Portrait of a Lady*. I have described, in one of the lectures that *is* included here, my anxious consideration of whether it would be considered decent in China to discuss a kiss, since I had never, ever, seen anyone kissing in public in China, nor did I find a single kiss in Stephen Owen's big anthology of Chinese literature from the beginnings to 1919, though many of his selections are erotic.[4] This is another, and final, example of my situation as an innocent abroad—why do they never kiss in public in China?

I have immensely enjoyed and benefited from my "Chinese connection." Lecturing in China has been an important part of my intellectual and personal life over the last twenty-five years and more. Much of my recent thinking and writing has been instigated by my Chinese experiences. I hope readers of this book may enjoy the lectures as much as I enjoyed writing and giving them.

J. Hillis Miller
Deer Isle, Maine

An Innocent Abroad

CHAPTER I

The Role of Theory in the Development of Literary Studies in the United States

This is a brief account of the origins and subsequent development of the discipline of literary studies in the United States since the creation of departments of English and of other modern languages during the last quarter of the nineteenth century. I shall focus especially on the changing role of literary theory in this development and on the theories explicit and implicit in the actual practices of literary study. Let me begin by making three general points:

1. Because the United States is a large democratic country with a relatively small degree of centralization or prescriptive governmental control over education, and because one of our most precious freedoms is the freedom of the teacher in the classroom, any attempt, such as this one, to make an orderly narrative out of the development of literary studies in America will necessarily ignore many regional and local differences and many cases of brilliant and effective but, in one way or another, idiosyncratic teaching of literature or writing about literature in the United States. The institutionalization of literary studies in America, the organization of departments, the setting of curriculum, degree requirements,

and so on, have been to a considerable degree local and ad hoc, and therefore different from one college or university to another. An example is a form of literary study, practiced mostly at The Johns Hopkins University during the 1940s and 1950s, that was strongly influenced by the "history of ideas" as developed by two philosophers, A. O. Lovejoy and George Boas. Another example is the work of the so-called Chicago Aristoteleans active in the 1940s and 1950s at the University of Chicago under the leadership of R. S. Crane. This mode of literary study is still influential here and there in the work of younger scholars and teachers. Although both of these forms of literary study produced brilliant results, they were relatively local phenomena. They do not fit very well into the developmental paradigm I shall propose. That paradigm is roughly and on the whole true, but a closer look at the texture or grain of the phenomena in question would reveal many irregularities and anomalies that cannot be fully described and accounted for here.

2. In my account, the role of theory in American literary study is emphasized. All literary study is at least implicitly theoretical. From the beginning of literary studies in the United States, there has been a fair amount of theoretical reflection about the actual practices of teaching and scholarship, their nature and goals. On the other hand, one feature of literary study in the United States has been a strong antitheoretical bias. This has been partly an attempt to persuade readers and students that whatever is being done goes without saying and does not need overt theoretical justification. It is partly also the result of a pragmatic American suspicion of the abstractions of theory. Theory, we Americans tend to think, comes between the reader and direct experience of literature. Nevertheless, one useful way to tell the story of literary study in America is to focus on the changing role, over the years, of overt theoretical or methodological reflection.
3. Literary study in the United States has had a threefold and, to a considerable degree, contradictory historical origin. Literary study is, first, an outgrowth of the training of students in composition, oratory, and forensic rhetoric for the purpose of teaching them to write and speak well in professional and public life. Second, literary study is an adaptation to the study of vernacular literatures of the tradition of scientific philology developed originally for the investigation of the Bible and of the "classics" of Greek

> and Latin literature. Third, it is a development of the humanism especially associated with the nineteenth-century English poet and critic Matthew Arnold (1822–1888). Such humanism justifies the study of literature by seeing it as an acculturating power in education, making available knowledge of what Arnold called "the best which has been thought and said in the world."[1] The purpose of imparting this knowledge is to make students better persons and better citizens.

It is difficult to reconcile completely these three presuppositions about the nature and purpose of literary study. The historical development of the discipline of literary studies in the United States, as I shall show, has therefore been marked by the fissures among these presuppositions, as now one, now another, or a combination of all three presuppositions has been dominant. These fissures, however, have rarely been acknowledged openly, although, as Gerald Graff has argued, recognition of them not only is an important historical insight but also would have great heuristic value in teaching.[2] In this chapter, my contention is that all three of these theoretical justifications for the study of literature are still strongly active and operative today, that they remain still irreconcilable with one another, and that, in spite of their cogency and plausibility, in spite of the fact that so many intelligent people of goodwill have held one or another or some combination of them, they are not wholly appropriate for present circumstances in the United States.

In the place of these three rationales, in my conclusion I shall suggest another justification, another definition of the social, cultural, and personal function of literary study in the United States today. Literary study of certain kinds, I shall argue, is a powerful and indispensable means of the critique of ideology. To put it another way, literary study is a means of using the mind to protect us against the mind itself and against the baneful effects that confusing linguistic with natural reality can have in the real world. The great twentieth-century American poet Wallace Stevens puts this in the following way: "If the mind is the most terrible force in the world, it is also the only force that defends us against terror. Or, the mind is the most terrible force in the world principally in this, that it is the only force that can defend us against itself." Stevens goes on to say, "The poet represents the mind in the act of defending us against itself."[3] If this is true of poetry, the study of poetry can also be such a self-defense. It can extend and cooperate with the work of the poet. Before discussing twentieth-century developments and the present situation, however, I shall first say something more about each of the three historical origins or roots of American literary study.

Until the development of graduate education in the United States in the late decades of the nineteenth century, and the concurrent development of departments of English and other European languages and literatures, the study of literature in American colleges was primarily an ancillary part of the education of young men, primarily white affluent young men, in speaking and writing well in preparation for public life and the professions. This included the inculcation of Christian morals, often most explicitly in a required senior course in moral philosophy as well as in required chapel attendance.

Training in Greek and Latin languages, not in vernacular literature, was the central feature of the humanities curriculum in American colleges until the last decades of the nineteenth century. That training inevitably involved some reading of works of literature in those languages. The interpretation of these works that went on in the classroom, however, when it went on at all, would probably strike most people today as exceedingly unsophisticated. The teaching was mostly rote drill in getting the translations, grammar, and syntax right, with occasional pauses to see the stories as moral exempla. In fact, there seems to have been precious little of that, perhaps because the morality was taken for granted, as apparently were answers to all these questions about meaning that we have come to raise.

The implicit theory behind all these years of training in the minutiae of Greek and Latin grammar and syntax is so patently absurd that one is surprised that it was expressed as often as it was. The assumption was that all that hard labor of memorizing vocabulary and paradigms was good moral discipline, and, beyond this, that the spiritual essence of Greek and Roman culture was somehow embodied in the grammar, syntax, and etymologies of those languages so that the classical spirit would be absorbed through the rote learning of linguistic minutiae. It is all very well to say that this is absurd, but does not some such belief still lurk in the minds of those who justify some kinds of language study as "good mental training" and as somehow morally uplifting? Graff quotes a splendid attack on these assumptions by Charles Francis Adams in a Harvard Phi Beta Kappa address of 1883. Adams called these assumptions "the great-impalpable-essence-and-precious-residuum theory" of classical study, defining that theory as the assumption that "a knowledge of Greek grammar, and the having puzzled through the *Anabasis* and three books of the *Iliad*, infuses into the boy's nature the imperceptible spirit of Greek literature, which will appear in the results of his subsequent work, just as manure, spread upon a field, appears in the crop which that field bears."[4] All that drillwork in Greek and Latin presupposed a theory of *Bildung*, or the education of the mind and character of young American upper-class males in preparation for professional and public life.

As scholars have begun recently to demonstrate, the high value put on the study of Anglo-Saxon or Old English when departments of English were established was to a considerable degree based on a variant of this theory, namely, the notion that the study of Old English grammar would lead students to absorb the roots of the Germanic or Aryan or Indo-European way of thinking, including the political principles that were the foundation of American democracy.[5]

The second branch of the trifurcated root of American literary study is the establishment, in the late nineteenth century in the United States, of research universities modeled on the German university with its concept of universal *Wissenschaft*, or scientific, verifiable knowledge. The founding in 1876 of The Johns Hopkins University by Daniel Coit Gilman initiated this development and began serious graduate education in the United States. As Jacques Derrida has persuasively argued, the founding of the University of Berlin in the early nineteenth century, followed by the gradual reshaping of all universities in the West on that model, was the deliberate institutionalization of the university's mission as the universal accounting for everything according to the Leibnizian principle of reason.[6] This is the presupposition that everything has its reason, or, to put it in more exactly Leibnizian terms, "for any true proposition, reason can be rendered: *Omnis veritatis reddi ratio potest*."

Everything can be accounted for and should be accounted for—by the university. This obligation to account for everything tended to be tied to the nationalistic aspirations of the universities. Each great research university tended to think of itself as serving one particular nation-state in its aim for dominance; and, as a part of this nationalism, increasing importance was given to the study of the nation's vernacular literature. The modern research university is where this vast enterprise of inventory, investigation, and explanation takes place. This occurs most evidently in the sciences. Or, to put it another way, the gradual transformation in the nineteenth century of all the universities in the West, including those in the United States, into the great modern research-oriented technoscientific servants of society, government, and industry we know today took place as the institutionalization of the principle of reason. It was a response to the obligation to account for everything, to give everything its reason, to explain everything by its cause. No doubt Leibniz would be surprised, and perhaps dismayed, to see the historical course his principle of reason has taken.

One region of this enormous collective work of the new research university was the obligation to account for the languages and literatures of all countries and historical periods. The names of this humanistic branch of the universal accounting were "scholarship," "research," and especially "philology." When philology was introduced into American universities—in the late nineteenth century, at the same time that departments of Western vernacular languages were established—a procedure and a rationale for the study of vernacular literature, quite different from the older notion of the cultivation of the gentleman, were instituted. The new commitment to the principle of a universal accounting justified, as one part of the new research university, a vast collective scholarly enterprise of editing, annotating, collating, establishing of texts, biography, bibliography, source study, dictionary and concordance making, etymological research, discovery and verification of historical and linguistic facts, and writing of literary and intellectual history. The models for this development of English, Germanic, and Romance philology (the main forms) were the disciplines of biblical scholarship and classical philology. The latter, highly developed in the nineteenth century, especially in Germany and England, were then appropriated in the United States. Although the theory of *Bildung,* or moral formation, which I have already mentioned, was present as a justification for this work, as was humanistic theory, which I have not yet fully discussed, philology was more centrally justified in terms of a theory of "value-free" research. This was the assumption that it is good and, in fact, an obligation for the university to assemble, in a knowable and retrievable form, information about everything whatsoever. This must be done simply because it is knowable, because it can be compiled, recorded, and stored in the library archives, and just in case someone needs to use it later on. Values as such, on the other hand, are not amenable to such study and compilation; therefore, study and compilation have no place in values. The assimilation and storage of facts was, according to this rationale, implicitly the highest value, the raison d'être of the university professor.

The ideology behind this enormous enterprise is the assumption that the establishment of facts, and of the explanatory causes about anything whatever, is a good in itself. But though a distinguished philologist like James Wilson Bright of The Johns Hopkins University, in his presidential address of 1902 before the Modern Language Association, could assert that "the philological strength and sanity of a nation is the measure of its intellectual and spiritual vitality" and that the philologist must participate in "the work of guiding the destinies of the country," he was utterly unable, as Gerald Graff observes, to give any reasonable explanation of just how the philologist, *as* philologist, was going to guide America's destiny.[7] As has been pointed out over and over through the decades by the humanistic critics of "philology," the positivistic or scientific ideal of literary study has no intrinsic way of determining any social or personal use that may be made of its results, despite the vague assumption that to get the facts right is an ethical good. The philological ideal as such is as nearly without persuasive cogency in its claims for the cultural use of such study as is the notion that the study of the minutiae of Greek, Latin, Old English, or Middle High German grammar is good in itself and good moral training for young men. (Students in institutions of higher learning were almost all young men in those days except at a few coeducational colleges or women's colleges.) The cogent justification of the social and personal utility of literary study has to come, therefore, from some other source—for example, from present-day support for the study of "minor" works or works hitherto excluded from the canon, on the grounds that such works are an indispensable means of understanding our cultural history or of resisting the ideological presuppositions built into the choice of works in the traditional, mostly male, canons of the national literatures.

Among other such justifications, the one stemming from the humanism of Matthew Arnold—the third fork in the trifurcated root of literary studies in the United States—has had the most shaping influence. The ideas about the social function of literary study that Arnold expresses were widely diffused in the nineteenth century and have a complex history in our own century. The American version of these ideas, moreover, had many other sources besides Matthew Arnold (for example, Carlyle and Ruskin, Arnold's contemporaries in England, and America's own Ralph Waldo Emerson). This humanism has a complicated history before Arnold, a history that goes back, to name one important genetic line, through the concept of *Bildung* in Goethe and Schiller as well as in other German romantic writers (strong influences on Arnold), through Renaissance humanism, to the idea of *paideia* in the Greeks. Nevertheless, Arnold's particular way of formulating the claim that the study of literature plays a fundamental role in the cultural formation of the citizen has had enormous influence on literary study in the United States. Arnold twice visited the United States on lecture tours, in 1883–1884 and again in 1886. His admirable series of essays and books on culture and on the function of literary study perhaps best formulates these humanistic presuppositions about literary study. These assumptions were institutionalized in the teaching and writing of the long line of distinguished humanist professors—or, as Graff calls them, "generalists"[8]—who taught in the early twentieth century in American colleges and universities: William Lyon Phelps of Yale; Bliss Perry of Williams, Princeton, and Harvard; Robert Morss Lovett of the University of Chicago; Irving Babbitt of Harvard; Stuart P. Sherman of Illinois; and Lionel Trilling of Columbia, among many others. Trilling was the youngest of these humanist teachers. His superb book on Matthew Arnold can be taken as a kind of summing up of the ideals of Arnoldian literary culture as they were embodied, in one way or another, in the teaching of literature in hundreds of American colleges and universities during the first half of the twentieth century.[9] These ideals also provided college and university presidents, commencement speakers, and department chairmen with their defense of the social utility of literary study.

In essays like "The Study of Poetry" and "The Function of Criticism at the Present Time" as well as in his influential book of cultural criticism, *Culture and Anarchy,* Arnold proposed the notion that Western literature, from the Greeks on down to Goethe and Wordsworth, is the storage house of "the best which has been thought and said in the world." Arnold presupposed that he and his readers lived in a bad time, a time when the influence of traditional religion was waning, and a time when commercialism, anarchic individualism, industrialization, and the rise of a philistine middle class were weakening culture and making genuine education difficult. Only study of the classics of our tradition could save our culture. How often similar ideas about twentieth-century American culture have been expressed in our own time by teachers of literature and by administrators as well as by politicians who concern themselves with education! And how often the study of the great works of literature of the past, from the Greeks on down, has been put forward as the sovereign antidote to our cultural sickness! The study of literature, the argument goes, alone can maintain culture in such bad times, or, as Lionel Trilling put this, "great works of art and thought have a decisive part in shaping the life of a polity."[10]

In the decades from 1890 to the 1940s, professors of literature in the United States—with the assumptions eloquently expressed by Arnold so deeply embedded in their thinking about teaching and scholarship in the humanities that they were hardly aware of them as assumptions open to criticism—set about to create and maintain the departments, curricula, and programs in teaching and research in vernacular literature that are to a considerable degree still intact today, especially in departments of English. [By no means still true.—JHM] The institutionalization of Arnoldian humanism in American departments of English has meant the following: a commitment to "coverage" of all English literature from *Beowulf* to at least Hardy or Kipling, more recently including coverage of literature down to the present day, with American literature now also included; a primary focus on a list of canonical works, almost exclusively by male writers (Chaucer, Spenser, Shakespeare, Donne, Milton, Pope, Johnson, Wordsworth, Keats, Shelley, Tennyson, Browning, Dickens, and the Victorian prose writers Arnold, Huxley, Newman, and Ruskin); and an emphasis on a thematic rather than a formal or even a historically relativistic reading of these writers. This canon is a relatively recent invention. It was established at the same moment in history that the departments of English were instituted. What was stressed in teaching this canon was the supposed expression by these writers of timeless and universal values, virtues, and ideals.

When the so-called New Criticism entered American literary study in the 1940s, that study was still dominated by an uneasy mixture of the three sets of presuppositions I have described. The New Criticism rapidly took over the curricula and procedures of teaching in English departments almost everywhere in the United States, although as a strong overlay superimposed on the old "scholarly" ideals rather than as the complete displacement of those ideals. The New Criticism dominated American literary study for the next twenty years, displacing or redefining all three of the assumptions about literary study that had presided over the first fifty years of its development. The story of the New Criticism—its assumptions, practices, and main figures—has been often told, most authoritatively and fully by Murray Krieger, and most recently [At least in 1988.—JHM] in the chapter on the subject in Vincent Leitch's book.[11] Here I shall only name the chief critics, name one landmark book, identify the main assumptions of the New Critics, and suggest some reasons why the New Criticism was so successful in transforming literary study in America.

The immediate precursors of the American New Critics were I. A. Richards, William Empson, and T. S. Eliot in England, and the great

American critic Kenneth Burke, who transcends any school or movement. The major critics involved in the development and institutionalizing of the New Criticism in American colleges and universities were John Crowe Ransom, Allen Tate, R. P. Blackmur, Cleanth Brooks, Robert Penn Warren, René Wellek, and W. K. Wimsatt. The book most responsible for the triumphant institutionalization of the New Criticism was *Understanding Poetry*, the introductory textbook by Brooks and Warren.[12] This made available in teachable form the basic assumptions about reading literature that the New Critics were exemplifying in their various books—for example, Cleanth Brooks in *The Well Wrought Urn*.[13] But for every student who read *The Well Wrought Urn*, hundreds and probably thousands used *Understanding Poetry* as a basic textbook. We still have the somewhat battered copy that my wife used in a course at Oberlin College in 1944 or 1945.

The New Critics focused primarily on lyric poetry, especially modern poetry and metaphysical poetry. Poems by Donne or Eliot were taken as paradigmatic of literature in general. The "close reading" of poems was assumed to be the main business of literary study. The poem was read more or less in detachment from its historical and social context. The assumption was that no special knowledge beyond what could be found in the dictionary, especially in the *Oxford English Dictionary*, was necessary to read a poem. A good poem was assumed to be, as Leitch puts it, "an autonomous, ahistorical, spatial object."[14] A good poem, moreover, was assumed to be an "organic unity" bringing disparate materials together in a complex ironic harmony of opposites in tension. Metaphor was assumed to be the fundamental trope of poetry and therefore of literature in general. Metaphor was seen as the basic way in which heterogeneous materials could be yoked together. The reading of poetry was assumed to be a good in itself, an end in itself; and at the same time, somewhat implicitly and covertly, it was assumed that reading poems has personal and social utility by providing models for the kind of reconciliation of competing needs, desires, or values necessary for successful living in the real world of twentieth-century America. Or, as Graff has put this, reading poems provides a nonconceptual "embodied" knowledge of universal values transcending the flux of history.

The New Criticism was so successful in part because it made possible the teaching of poetry to the new kinds of young people who were getting a college and university education in America, especially after the return of veterans from service in World War II. These were middle- and working-class Americans without wide historical or cultural knowledge, students who were more or less starting from scratch in freshman or sophomore college courses in literature. For the most part they were ignorant of the Bible, of classical mythology, and of all the other sorts of knowledge that previously had been taken for granted in readers of poetry. *Understanding Poetry* made possible the teaching of literature in a democratic country committed as no great nation had ever been before to mass higher education, to the offering of a college or university degree to more or less anybody.

At the same time, *Understanding Poetry*, in its choice of poems to be read and in what was said of them in the commentaries in the book, more or less covertly smuggled in some presuppositions borrowed from T. S. Eliot and from the southern American heritage of many of the New Critics. These presuppositions were conservative politically, religiously, and culturally. The choice of poems in *Understanding Poetry*, for example, was a choice made primarily from the traditional canon established in the earlier decades of the century. Even the denigration of the English Romantics, although taken straight from Eliot, echoed similar reservations about Shelley (for example, in Matthew Arnold). The metaphysical poets were prized, at least implicitly, for their expression of a traditional Christian vision of human life.

The next and, so far, final phase in the development of literary study in the United States up to the present time [Again, please remember that this was written in 1988.—JHM] was the gradual importation and domestication, beginning in the 1950s, of continental literary theories. This importation occurred at the same time that the myth criticism of a Canadian scholar, Northrop Frye, was exerting a strong influence in the United States. The wide appeal of Frye's all-inclusive systematic typology of literature in his *Anatomy of Criticism* was evidence that teachers and students of literature were beginning to feel a need for an explicit theory of literature, a need not satisfied by the New Criticism.[15]

By the mid-1960s, partly as a result of political factors like the Vietnam War, student activism, women's liberation, and the Civil Rights movement, conventional approaches to literary studies seemed increasingly irrelevant. Those who deplore the gradual triumph of the new theoretical approaches should remember that they were a response to a widely felt sense of the detachment of literary studies from social or personal usefulness. Theoretical work imported from Europe responded to that need for "relevance." First existentialism and phenomenology began to be assimilated as the basis of a new kind of literary criticism, and then, in the 1960s, structuralism, Lacanian psychoanalysis, newer kinds of Marxist criticism, and so-called deconstruction were brought in. It is convenient to date the start of the second, more radical wave of this primarily French invasion as arriving in 1966, the date of a structuralist symposium held at The Johns Hopkins University and sponsored by the Ford Foundation. Papers from this symposium were published in *The Languages of Criticism and the Sciences of Man*.[16] This symposium was one of the earliest and most influential of the multitude of international conferences on literary theory that now have become commonplace almost everywhere in the world. The Hopkins symposium brought Jacques Lacan and Jacques Derrida to the United States to present papers for the first time (Derrida had studied for a year at Harvard in the 1950s) along with representatives of a somewhat older generation of phenomenological critics like Georges Poulet, and Marxist critics like Lucien Goldmann and the classicist Jean-Paul Vernant. American literary study since then has been increasingly dominated by these imported theories and by the assumption of a need to base literary study on explicit theoretical reflection.

This invasion of literary study by "theory" is a major example of the breaking open of a discipline's traditional boundaries that is one theme of this book.[17] [Recall that this essay originally appeared in *Divided Knowledge*; see the present volume's acknowledgments.—JHM] In the United States today, it is no longer possible to remain narrowly within the study of primary literary texts and of the commentaries on them. To remain at the frontier of research and teaching, the American student or teacher of literature is likely to feel the need to have expert knowledge of philosophy, social theory, psychoanalysis, anthropology, linguistics, and history. The present situation in the study of literature in the United States is, as I have elsewhere argued, characterized by the almost universal triumph of theory.[18] This is true [Hardly true now.—JHM] in spite of the continued active presence of what Paul de Man called "the resistance to theory."[19] I suggest that, paradoxically, the most effective form of the resistance to theory these days (in fact, at any time) is a certain form of the triumph of theory.

But, first, what do I mean by the "triumph of theory"? I mean what is evident on every side, not only in the development of a large number of powerful, competing theoretical discourses, each with its somewhat barbarous code name (hermeneutic, phenomenological, Lacanian, feminist, reader response, Marxist, Foucauldian, structuralist, semiotic, deconstructionist, new historicist, cultural critical, and so on), but also in the accompanying immense proliferation of courses, curricula, books, handbooks, dissertations, essays, lectures, new journals, symposia, study groups, centers, and institutes, all overtly concerned with theory or with what is called "cultural studies." Taken together, these form a "hidden university" crossing departmental, disciplinary, and institutional boundaries. Much of the frontier work in literary studies is taking place today in this part of the university. This is not the place to try to characterize each of the kinds of literary theory I have named; it takes Vincent Leitch over four hundred pages to sketch out the main modes and their presuppositions.[20]

What needs to be stressed here, however, is the large number of competing theories and their incoherence. They cannot be synthesized into one grand, all-inclusive theory of literature. The victory of theory has transformed the field of literary study from what it was when I entered it forty years ago. In those happy days, as I have said, we mostly studied primary works in the context of literary history, paying some overt attention in our teaching to the basic presuppositions of the so-called New Criticism (the primacy of metaphor, the universality of the principle of organic unity, and so on). Now we are called on to become acquainted with a large number of incompatible theories, each usually based in disciplines outside literature, and each claiming our allegiance.

The present-day triumph of theory is no doubt overdetermined. It has many and incompatible "causes," or, to avoid begging a question by slipping in the word "causes," it would be better to say "concomitant factors." The conflict of diverse assumptions among the different theories is itself one such factor. Their obvious incoherence forces theoretical reflection. If everyone shares the same assumptions, they can be taken for granted. Explicit theory does not then appear to be necessary. Among other factors are the demographic changes that are making the United States more and more a multilingual country. It makes less and less sense to base literary study exclusively on canonical works in English literature. Another factor reducing the importance of literature written in England is the rise of the United States as a major world power, accompanied by a decline in the importance of England. Another force for change is the women's movement, which has had and is having enormous effects on American culture. Technological innovations like the jet airplane (which can bring scholars and critics from all over the world together for a conference), computers, tape recorders, and copying machines have enormously speeded up the dissemination of new work from place to place within the United States, from Europe and other continents to the United States, and from the United States to the rest of the world.

One of the important factors associated with the turn to theory is its function as a response to a need generated by a widespread loss of confidence in the unequivocal value of studying primarily works in the traditional male-dominated canon of English literature, plus Homer, Virgil, Dante, Cervantes, and so on, in English translation. The traditional justification for the study of the canon—that such study transmits from the old to the young the fundamental values of our culture, the Arnoldian "best which has been thought and known in the world"—has also been put in doubt. It is not that defenses of study of the traditional canon on these grounds are not currently being made—far from it—but they are likely to be made in a way that makes their ideological motivation evident. Such defenses no longer go without saying. Our consciousnesses have been raised, in large part by the works of theory itself. We are likely to feel that no choice of books for a syllabus, for example, or no choice of ways to read those books, is politically innocent. Such choices are no longer easily justified by the appeal to a universal consensus or to universal standards valid for any time, place, institution, or particular classroom.

At the same time, it is important to remember that the traditional canon still forms [Once again, in 1988.—JHM] the backbone of English curricula in most American colleges and universities, as empirical studies by the Modem Language Association (MLA) of America have discovered.[21] Study of the traditional canon has by no means been weakened as much as some critics of the supposed degradation of literature teaching in our colleges and universities have claimed. Nevertheless, discussion of the justification of the canon *is* taking place. At the practical curricular and pedagogical level, however, the result is more a matter of new works, and new approaches to canonical works, being added to traditionally organized courses than anything like a radical overturning of the received canon. In a similar way, in spite of all the attention being paid to new forms of literary theory, an immense number, perhaps the majority, of courses are still taught according to the methods and assumptions of the New Criticism, as the MLA studies have found.

The triumph of theory is to a considerable degree defined as a response to the new social, demographic, and technological developments, and as an attempt to think one's way out of them. The teacher wants to be justified in what he or she does. Appealing to theory is one way of seeking that justification. To put it another way, one of the major functions of literary theory is as a critique of ideology, that is, a critique of the taking of a linguistic reality for a material one.[22] The ideology in question in this case includes the hidden (but ideology is by definition hidden) assumptions of our procedures of teaching literature and of the general institutionalization of literary study. The result of this appeal to theory is that, more and more in the United States, literary theory has become a subject of study for its own sake. This is most conspicuous in the widespread development of courses devoted to the explicit teaching of theoretical texts as such, not simply as ancillary to the study of primary literary texts. It is also present in the inclusion of works of theory within courses that are not overtly "theoretical." Such courses, it would seem, are all to the good insofar as they recognize the importance of reading and using the works of theory. Courses of both sorts make the study of theory "academically respectable," as the saying goes. They institutionalize theory within the normal curriculum but also marginalize it as one more field of study among others.

On the other hand, it is easy to see the danger to the effective functioning of theory inherent in such courses. They may be a subtle form of resistance to theory. This may be so even when such courses are taught, as they usually are, by scholars who are deeply interested in theory and do not intend to do it any harm. Literary theory or critical theory, paradoxically, is or ought to be praxis. In this case, at least, theory *is* praxis, thinking *is* action, rather than being its speculative opposite. To put this another way, the distinction between theory and praxis, in this case, breaks down into something that is self-divided in another way, or in other ways. It is self-divided, for example, in the by no means symmetrical reciprocity between theory and reading, or between pedagogical theory and the results of pedagogy. Literary theory, that is to say, is of little or no use unless it is "applied," used. Theory must be active, productive, performative.

What theory performs or produces is or ought to be new readings, in the broadest sense of the word. But these readings in their turn are performative rather than merely passive or cognitive. They make something happen. The readings in question would of course include new readings of the works of theory. They should be "readings" in a strong sense of the word—that is, active, critical, rhetorical, "interventionist" readings as opposed to mere summaries of the manifest thematic context of the texts read. Theory itself is of no use unless it is read in this strong sense. Only then will it facilitate readings of other texts, readings that, as Jacques Derrida says, are radically inaugural in the sense that they implicitly or explicitly propose a new "contract" with the university and with the society or the state that the university serves. "When, for example," says Derrida, "I read a given sentence in a given context in a seminar (a reply by Socrates, a fragment from *Capital* or *Finnegans Wake,* a paragraph from *The Conflict of the Faculties*), I am not fulfilling a prior contract: I can also write and prepare for the signature of a new contract with the institution, between the institution and the dominant forces of society. And this operation, as with any negotiation (precontractual, that is, continually transforming an old contract), is the moment for every imaginable ruse and strategic ploy."[23]

This impressive proliferation of theoretical reflection about literature is without doubt the most "transferable" aspect of literary study in the United States today. I have named some of the technological advances, especially the immense development of telecommunications and the ease of travel, that have made Western literary theory available in other countries around the world. Colleagues in the People's Republic of China are remarkably well informed about Western theory and are strongly interested in further translations of Western literary theory. The same can be said for other countries I have visited around the world.

Literary theory is much more exportable than the local institutions of literary study in the United States. But there would not be so much interest in Western literary theory around the world—in the People's Republic of China, for example—if it did not respond to some local social and cultural need in the countries that are translating it, writing about it, and making use of it in teaching and writing. I see this appropriation of literary theory as part of a rapid worldwide cultural change that results in part from technological innovations like the personal computer and the fax machine, but that has other components as well, such as the proliferation of multinational corporations. In this new world of a multilingual copresence that crosses all national boundaries, literary study will more and more become a new form of comparative literature, no longer the separate study of national literatures. Comparative study demands explicit theoretical reflection. The "triumph of theory" is not an accident. It is a response to profound cultural, social, and technological innovations that are transforming our world. Such intercommunication among countries and cultures is by no means incompatible with maintaining local specificities in language and institutional forms. As Western theory is translated and assimilated throughout the world, it will be transformed in ways that cannot be anticipated. It will be changed to fit the new language and the local needs. This is happening now in the People's Republic of China. It will be a matter of deep interest to watch the transformations that accompany the transfer of this particular aspect of Western academic study.

The most recent development in literary studies in the United States, a major change in focus currently going on, is the shift from language-based study to history-based study. This is most conspicuous in the work of the so-called new historicists (for example, Stephen Greenblatt and his colleagues at Berkeley, and their associates at many other colleges and universities). It should be remembered that the theoretical presuppositions of the various scholars sometimes grouped as new historicists are diverse and to some degree contradictory, as is the case with any strongly innovative and influential movement. Moreover, the renewed interest in the historical contexts of literature is present in many other sorts of critics, too—in Marxists, Foucauldians, and more traditional scholars interested in the historical backgrounds of literature—and it has been part of the work of the so-called deconstructionists all along. This new interest in the historical or cultural contexts of literature is rapidly producing a vigorous new discipline called "cultural critique" or "cultural studies." Sometimes this new enterprise is located within traditional departments of English, French, or German, sometimes in the many new centers or institutes of cultural studies appearing in colleges and universities around the country.

This renewed attention to history is all to the good if it does not return to naive assumptions about the way literature is determined by history or merely reflects it. To put this another way, part of the strength of the new turn to history comes from insights, learned from structuralism and "deconstruction," into the complexities of the rhetorical or figurative dimensions of texts, both "literary" in the usual sense and "extraliterary" in the sense of their being historical documents of one sort or another. The question of the actual relation between a given literary text (say, a play by Shakespeare) and its historical context (for example, sixteenth-century treatises about hermaphroditism) must itself be a topic of sophisticated theoretical reflection.[24] Simply placing the play in its context and asserting that the context explains or accounts for the text is not enough.

Identification of the actual ways in which literature and history are related is a major frontier of theory today as well as of critical practice.[25] Three acts of reading (in the strong sense of the word) are necessary to this: a reading of the historical documents, a reading of the literary work in "the light" of those documents, and a reading of the relation between the two. The latter involves an especially difficult and controversial theoretical topic: the text-to-text relation. None of these acts of reading goes without saying. The insights of language-oriented theories, most especially so-called deconstruction as practiced by Jacques Derrida, Paul de Man, and a large number of younger literary scholars, are indispensable to any serious investigation of the relations of literature to history. One of the most important of deconstruction's insights is a recognition of the perlocutionary or performative aspect of the act of reading or teaching a work of literature. Reading makes something happen. It is, to borrow J. L. Austin's phrase, a way of doing things with words, not just a reflection or representation of some state of affairs, imaginary or real.[26] Works of literature (as well as criticism and the reading of literature) have a performative role in making history. It is a matter of great importance that the new investigations into the historical relations of literature recognize this dimension of the role of literature in society. It is in this region of literary study that attention to what I have called "the ethics of reading" has importance. The ethics of reading involves questions of an obligation or responsibility incurred by the act of reading or teaching a work of literature—an obligation to the text read, to the students to whom one teaches it, and to those who may read an essay one publishes on the work. The ethical and the political effects of reading and teaching literature are not necessarily the same. Both need to be recognized and interrogated as parts of the new theoretical work relating literature to history and seeing literature as performative, as making something happen.[27]

The new historicism and rhetorical reading (or "deconstruction") can therefore cooperate in the work of what, at the beginning of this essay, I called "critique of ideology." Since this claim is controversial, although essential to the argument I am making for a social function of the study of literature, let me make it clear what I mean by "ideology." At the plenary meeting held at the Chinese Academy of Social Sciences in 1988, discussion of these ideas among my Chinese colleagues focused sharply on my argument that literary study can and should be a critique of ideology. Scholars in the literature institutes of CASS, it appeared, are accustomed to thinking of the social function of literature as reinforcement of a consciously promulgated ideology, not as criticism of it. I learned that the word "ideology" has, or had, a positive meaning in China, whereas we in the United States would not ordinarily use the word in a positive sense to name the primary values of our culture—the word, for us, generally has a negative connotation; it names either unconscious and prejudiced presuppositions or the conscious program of some group. Nevertheless, the word "ideology" is also a focus of controversy in the West. It has several contradictory meanings, both within Marxist thought and outside it. By "ideology" I do not mean the conscious values and concepts deliberately promulgated and enforced by what Louis Althusser, the French Marxist, calls "state apparatuses" but rather—as Althusser defines ideology, both in "Ideology and Ideological State Apparatuses (Notes towards an Investigation)" and elsewhere—a largely unconscious or taken-for-granted (but therefore all the more powerful) system of valuation and judgment.[28] Ideology, for Althusser, is an imaginary rewriting of the real material conditions under which men and women in a given society live their lives. "Ideology," says Althusser, "is a system (with its own logic and rigor) of representations (images, myths, ideas, or concepts, depending on the case) endowed with a historical existence and role within a given society."[29] Or, to cite another definition, I mean by "ideology" what Paul de Man means when he says, "What we call ideology is precisely the confusion of linguistic with natural reality, of reference with phenomenalism."[30]

To put what I mean by "critique of ideology" in another way, whatever the case in other countries, the study of literature in the United States, now and in the coming decades, should have as its primary goal the teaching of good reading. What social or ethical good, it may be asked, is that? Courses in rhetorical reading have an essential role in a democratic society, I answer, in teaching citizens the skills necessary to read all the signs with which they are surrounded and to resist being repressed or oppressed by imaginary formulations of their real relations to the material, social, gender, and class conditions of their existence. Ideological formulations, defined as I have defined them, are false, illusory. They bamboozle us. Although it may be true that there is no society without its ideology, the errors caused by mistaking a linguistic reality for a natural reality are always potentially dangerous. Such errors cause much social and personal suffering that could be avoided. It is better to know the truth. Unlike Friedrich Nietzsche, who thought there were some truths that mankind could not stand knowing, I hold, on the contrary, that the truth will make you free. The teaching and study of literature, seen as training in good reading, and thereby as critique of ideology, can make an indispensable contribution to that liberation.

CHAPTER 2

Black Holes in the Internet Galaxy

New Trends in Literary Study in the United States

I understand that questions about the role of studying a nation's own literature, as well as about studying the national literatures of foreign countries, have been an important topic of discussion at the Institute of Foreign Literature of CAAS. This essay may make a small contribution to that discussion, not because it deals with the Chinese situation (about which I know little) but because it treats mostly the situation in the United States. This may conceivably have some analogies with the Chinese situation. The main peculiarity of the situation in the United States, as I shall argue in detail in this essay, is that until recently the United States has based its literary culture, at least in the university, on the study of a foreign literature written in the dominant language of the United States—that is, on English literature. This is of course not the case in China, but insofar as the study of foreign literatures, along with their theories and methods of criticism, may have importance in China, this might be seen as somewhat analogous to the situation in the United States.

The research university in its modern form as an institution in the West originated with the founding in the early nineteenth century of the University of Berlin. It was established according to the plan devised by Wilhelm von Humboldt. Such universities had as their primary role service to the nation-state. The latter was conceived as an organically unified culture with a single set of ideals and values enshrined in a unified philosophical tradition and national literature (or in a certain way of appropriating Greek and Latin literature). The university was to serve the nation-state in two ways: as the place of critical thinking and research, finding out the truth about everything, giving everything its rationality, according to the Leibnizian formula that says, "Nothing is without reason, no effect is without cause"; and as the place of education, formation, or *Bildung,* where male citizens (they were all male then in the university) are inculcated with the basic values of a unified national culture. It was the business of the university to produce subjects of the state, in both senses of the word "subject": as subjectivities and as citizens accountable to state power and capable of promulgating it. For Humboldt and his colleagues, following Kant, the basis of *Bildung* was the study of philosophy. That is why we professors are all still called "doctors of philosophy," whatever the discipline in which we received a higher degree. This is almost an absurdity these days, if you think of it, since philosophy proper is an increasingly marginal part of the university, with many professors of philosophy engaged in arcane problems of logic, and many PhDs in other fields knowing little or nothing about philosophy.

With some support from Schiller's *Letters on Aesthetic Education,* Anglo-Saxon countries in the mid-nineteenth century, first England and then the United States, deflected this paradigm in an important way by substituting literature for philosophy as the center of cultural indoctrination. Grounds for this shift already existed, of course, in the centrality to literary education granted by many of the German theorists—the Schlegels, Schelling, and Hegel, for example. This shift occurred in England, and in the United States to a considerable degree, under the aegis of Matthew Arnold's formulations about culture and anarchy, about the study of poetry, and about the function of criticism. The modern American research university has inherited the double mission of the Humboldtian university, most conspicuously in the founding of The Johns Hopkins University in Baltimore in 1876. Johns Hopkins was based explicitly and self-consciously on the German university rather than on the English university model, though Thomas Henry Huxley, as a spokesperson for the new scientific English university, spoke at the inauguration of Johns Hopkins University. The admirable proliferation of public as well as private research universities in the United States followed soon after or was already taking place.

The combination of gathering scientific knowledge, or *Wissenschaft* (which includes knowledge of history, cultural history, and literary history, as well as other forms of the "human sciences"), and at the same time teaching a nation's unifying values seems coherent enough. Nevertheless, a tension has always existed between these two goals as charges to the department responsible for doing research in and teaching a country's national literature. On the one hand, the charge is to teach students, by way of literature, the central ideas and values of a national culture. For English literature, it is assumed that these are enshrined in unalterable fixity in the nation's canonical works—in *Beowulf*, Chaucer, Shakespeare, and the rest. On the other hand, scientific research is supposed to be critical and disinterested (Arnold's word), a search for truth independent of subjective bias. Research is value-free, *Wertfrei*. It is organized according to a universal methodology of research applicable, *mutatis mutandis*, to the human sciences as well as to the physical sciences and to the life sciences.

For a long time, a touching confidence that these two enterprises would achieve the same results made it possible for departments of national literatures to believe they were fulfilling both missions and reconciling the two contradictory charges the university had given them. A professor of English could simultaneously pursue research of the most positivistic kind into the minutiae of an author's life, or do the most mind-numbing bibliographical and editorial work, and at the same time teach undergraduate classes extolling the ethical virtues contained in works by Milton, Johnson, Browning, T. S. Eliot, and the rest. The first activity made him (professors were almost all male) feel he was doing something useful to aid his university's scientific devotion to truth seeking. He was adding to the archives of achieved knowledge. The second made him feel he was fulfilling his responsibility to *Bildung*.

The strange use of the literature of a foreign country as the basis of the national culture in the United States is a symptom, however, of a fundamental change in the Humboldtian model of the research university when it was institutionalized in the United States. William Readings is right when he says that the concept of a unified national culture in the United States has always been a promise or hope for the future, something always yet to be created by contractual agreement among the free citizens of a republic rather than something inherited as an inescapable tradition from the nation's historical past.[1] English literature was co-opted by American schools and universities as the basic tool for the creation of a national culture that always remains something evermore about to be. An unbridgeable gulf remains between the way an English man or woman reads Shakespeare and the way any American can read him. Think, for example, of the different resonance in each country of the patriotic speeches in Shakespeare's *Henry V*.

Shakespeare's ringing affirmation of England's island unity and of the glories of victory at Agincourt has a hollow sound in a country that established itself in a revolutionary war by defeating the British. "Lexington," "Bunker Hill," "Yorktown," and "Valley Forge," names of battles in our War of Independence, have more resonance for us than "Agincourt." It might be argued that over the past fifty years we citizens of the United States have come to recognize that we have an indigenous national literature that serves to unify us and make us all Americans. Nevertheless, the rise of American literature and American studies as separate disciplines in US universities demonstrates just the point I am making. The important books on American literature, from those by Mattheissen, Feidelson, Lewis, and Perry Miller down to later work by Pearce, Bercovitch, Fisher, and Harold Bloom, have been devoted not so much to describing as to attempting to create the unified national culture we do not in fact have. They characteristically do this by a complex performative scholarly ritual masked as objective scholarship and by the appeal to such general concepts as the frontier (*Go West, young man!*), the American Renaissance, the American Adam, a certain use of symbolism, a certain use of Romance, the Puritan ideal, the internal coherence of a canonical poetic tradition from Emerson and Whitman through Stevens to Ammons and Ashbery, and so on, in incoherent multiplicity. Readings is right again when he says that the interest in canon and canon formation in recent literary scholarship in the United States arises from the fact that we do not have an inherited traditional canon and must create one by fiat. This is another form of that future-anterior speech act characterizing United States culture generally. If you have a canon that can be taken for granted, as to a considerable degree they do in England, you do not need to worry about it or theorize about it.

The Humboldtian concept of the university and of the place of national-literature departments within the university lasted until quite recently, at least as an ideal, in the United States. It is now rapidly coming to an end. We are entering or have already entered an era in which new paradigms for the university will have to be found. The changes are occurring simultaneously from within and from without the university.

How, looked at from the inside, did departments of English come to evolve from a relatively coherent and comprehensible program of courses and research devoted to the major periods of English literature (with some additional courses in American literature) to the strange and not easily defensible hodgepodge that is now characteristic of many departments in the United States? The changes began just after World War II, in the 1940s. A number of distinct phases may be identified: from the triumph of the New Criticism in the fifties and sixties to the hegemony of theory in the seventies and eighties to the rapid rise to dominance of cultural studies in the late eighties and in the nineties. Each of these has been a stage in the dismantling of the old idea of the humanities as teaching the values of a unified culture.

Once upon a time, so the story goes, were those primitive days before World War II when the canon was firmly in place. People did biography, philology, literary history, intellectual history, character description, and evaluation without any conscious need for theory, or without much awareness of the theoretical presuppositions of what they were doing. It was a naive form of extrinsic criticism. It was also the American version of Humboldtian *Bildung* or the Arnoldian study of the best that has been thought and said in the world. At Oberlin College when I entered—in 1944, just before the end of World War II, and just before the introduction of the New Criticism—the required freshman course in English was a composition class, the textbook for which was a series of readings about the ideals of a liberal education by such nineteenth-century English authors as Newman, Arnold, Huxley, and others. The writings of these authors were not presented only as models of good prose. (Just try to write like Arnold or Newman! Almost impossible.) Reading them also provided that *Bildung*, that indoctrination in basic cultural ideas, that was still thought to be a primary function of higher education in the United States. I doubt that many such courses are taught anywhere in the United States today as a requirement for all undergraduates.

Then, after 1945, at least in the United States, came the epoch of the New Criticism. The New Criticism was in part a response to the need to teach literacy and literature to large numbers of veterans returning from the war who could now go to college because of the GI Bill, but who were almost wholly ignorant of the Western tradition. The New Criticism did not respond to this need as might have been expected—by devising crash courses in that tradition. Quite the contrary. The New Criticism presupposed that it is not necessary to have any special knowledge of literary or intellectual history in order to read a poem. You could be a good reader and a good citizen without ever learning that history. The poems in Brooks and Warren's *Understanding Poetry*, the basic text long used in colleges and universities for teaching New Critical methods, are pretty thoroughly detached from their surrounding contexts. They are given dates and authors, but that is about all. A good dictionary is assumed to be the only required tool of explication. Each poem is found by accident, so to speak, written on a loose sheet of paper blown by the wind, contextless. The poem is then given the powerful context of *Understanding Poetry* itself. The New Criticism was an extreme form of atheoretical intrinsic criticism, so we are told. It falsely claimed to be so commonsensical as not to need theoretical presuppositions, while insinuating into students' minds a whole set of theoretical presuppositions about the superiority of lyric poetry, the autonomy of the literary work, the organic unity of good works, the importance of metaphor over other figures, the superiority of the seventeenth-century English lyric over the English Romantic lyric, and so on. Shelley is a special target of *Understanding Poetry*, as the best example of all the ways not to do it.

The New Criticism also had, as its critics have observed, an implicit reactionary agenda that smuggled a good many conservative political and ethical ideas in by way of an apparent formalist objectivity. The New Criticism was a mode of what in more recent years has been called "aesthetic ideology." Aesthetic ideology means asserting for literature the sort of role in support of the organic nation-state that is claimed for it in Schiller's *Letters on Aesthetic Education*. In the case of the New Criticism, it also meant asserting a large degree of self-enclosed autonomy for literature. The "organic unity" of the good literary work justified cutting it off from its biographical and historical context and studying it as a self-enclosed, self-sufficient formal monad that could be "analyzed" and appreciated in isolation from all its contexts. Such a work is its own end and should be appreciated as such, in detachment from any vulgar instrumental use. It is no accident that John Crowe Ransom, one of the founders of the New Criticism, was a Kantian of sorts. This set of presumptions about literature explains why for the New Critics the short lyric was the paradigmatic example of a literary work. It is much more difficult to make claims of contextlessness for, say, the novel, or for its self-enclosed unified autonomy in which each minute element can be shown to contribute to the whole.

The account of the New Criticism as a reactionary formalism was distorted, however, by the failure to recognize that attention to how meaning is generated by language (as opposed to extraction and discussion of thematic meaning) is already a more than rudimentary theoretical move. It is a move that has far-reaching consequences.[2] The move subverts the conservative agenda of many of the originators of the New Criticism. The political effect of the New Criticism can by no means by summed up by identifying the politics of its founders. Whatever those founders intended, the New Criticism in its potentially subversive attention to "close reading" was already a stage in the dismantling of the traditional idea of the university as the guardian and transmitter of a single culture's eternal values. In place of that, the New Criticism put, more or less in spite of itself, technical training in the skills of close reading, skills that in themselves were detached from any fixed cultural values and could be applied to any text of any time. The New Critics asserted certain universal cultural values while at the same time teaching an ahistorical, technologized form of reading that was antipathetic to those values.

The New Criticism was superseded in the sixties, seventies, and early eighties by the heyday of theory—structuralist, semiological, phenomenological, reader response, Marxist, Lacanian, or Foucauldian, but especially and quintessentially deconstructionist theory. Deconstruction was the model of exigent and rigorous theory. Like the New Criticism, so the story goes (but in this case the story lies), deconstruction was a form of intrinsic criticism, but an intrinsic criticism supported by a sophisticated and subtle theoretical reflection. Deconstruction, so this false story goes, is apolitical and ahistorical, turns everything into language, and so on, according to a familiar apotropaic litany. Most educated people have encountered this story not only in journalism but also in academic discourse of both the right and the left.

Everything in this widely accepted account of deconstruction is distorted and wrong, often in asserting the exact opposite of what is actually the case. Jacques Derrida, not only in the manifest orientation of his work but also in patient argument in many interviews, has demonstrated repeatedly the error of each of these false characterizations. "Deconstruction," he says in "Mochlos ou le conflit des facultés," "is also, at least, a position taking [*une prise de position*], in the very work it does [*dans le travail même*], with regard to the politico-institutional structures that constitute and govern our practices, our competences, and our performances."[3] The important terms here are "work" and "position taking." Deconstruction is work. It works. It works by taking a position, by actively intervening in the institution and in the political field within which the institution is situated. In an interview with Richard Kearney published in 1984, Derrida responded sharply to the charge that deconstruction sees language as referring only to itself: "It is totally false to suggest that deconstruction is a suspension of reference. Deconstruction is always concerned with the 'other' of language. I never cease to be surprised by critics who see my work as a declaration that there is nothing beyond language, that we are imprisoned in language; it is, in fact, saying the exact opposite."[4] Paul de Man, in the 1983 interview with Stephano Rosso published in *The Resistance to Theory*, responded to Rosso's question about the "frequent recurrence of the terms 'ideology' and 'politics'" in his recent work: "I don't think I ever was away from these problems, they were always uppermost in my mind."[5] It can easily be demonstrated that this is the case. Paul de Man's work is always concerned with ideology, politics, and history—with the social effect of institutionalized ideological errors in literary study, for example, and with developing an alternative form of active intervention in history. But these forms of active intervention were no more compatible with fulfilling the mission of transmitting the fixed values of a national culture than was the New Criticism. The rise of theory was the next stage after the New Criticism in the dismantling of the traditional role of national-literature departments as the formation of subjects imbued with a national culture. Those who have seen theory as inimical to the traditional role of the humanities—that of forming citizens by inculcating in them a single national culture—are right, though it needs to be added that this model was, in the United States and in the West generally, already moribund at the time when theory became dominant. The rise of theory was more a symptom than a cause. The error has been to see it as causing what it simply responded to actively. It responded, moreover, by fulfilling with a clear conscience that other half of the university's mission—to understand everything rationally. Theory is intrinsically transnational. It is no accident that European theory, as transformed and extended within the American university, is being appropriated by universities all over the world in a way parallel to the global spread of Western technology and capitalist economic organization.

The theory of the sixties, seventies, and eighties goes on being carefully read, appropriated, and used in ever new and diverse ways. Moreover, it is constantly being extended in new theoretical work. Wherever the new forms of cultural studies are effective both in getting new knowledge and in making institutional or political change, they will have been so by appropriating or reinventing, whether consciously or not, the theory that they sometimes denigrate. Why that is so I shall explain later.

The mistaken characterization of deconstruction—as a synecdoche for "theory" generally—has nevertheless seemed to some necessary so as to clear a space for cultural studies. This is especially true wherever such studies are an antitheoretical return to extrinsic criticism. It was in reaction to the supposed dead end of formalist criticism in deconstruction, so the story goes, that around 1980, or even earlier, there was a swing back to extrinsic criticism, to a new desire to politicize and rehistoricize the study of literature, to make it socially useful, to make it an instrument of the liberation and intellectual enfranchisement of women, minorities, and the once colonized in a postcolonial, post-theoretical epoch. "Culture," "history," "context," "media," "gender," "class," "race," "the self," "moral agency," "multiculturalism," and "globalization" have now become, in different mixes, the watchwords of the new historicism, of neopragmatism, of cultural studies, of film and media studies, of women's studies and gender studies, of studies of various "minority discourses," and of studies in "postcolonialism." The list is by no means homogeneous.

A specific example of this proliferation of terms and subdisciplines is the addition of new entries for "imperialism/nationalism," "desire," "ethics," "diversity," "popular culture," and "class" to the second edition of *Critical Terms for Literary Study*.[6] In 1990, the date of the book's first edition, these were not yet "critical terms for literary study"; five years later, they were important enough to warrant the editors' having done the book over. The tendency to guide thinking by appeal to a list of slogans or "buzzwords" is characteristic of these new developments. Another example is the list of "terms for a new paradigm" that Antony Easthope gives in *Literary into Cultural Studies*: "institution; sign system; ideology; gender; subject position; the other." Easthope goes on to say of these abstractions that "others could be easily added to them if required."[7] They do not form a closed system but are just a list of what the field of cultural studies happens to be interested in. Easthope, like others in cultural studies, is anxious not to close the door on the inclusion of further topics. "Culture" in "cultural studies" becomes a term progressively emptied of meaning by coming more and more to include everything in human life. Another good example of this process is the last paragraph of a letter to the *New York Times* from Conrad Atkinson, written when Atkinson was a professor of art at the University of California at Davis. Defending a proposed Disney theme park to be built five miles from the site of a major Civil War battle at Manassas—Atkinson's defense is offered on the grounds that opposing the park would be the same kind of snobbism that attacked rock music and Elvis Presley, and on the grounds that visual experience can be as sophisticated and subtle as verbal meaning (with which I agree)—he says, "Remember: You never know where culture is gonna come from; you never know what culture is gonna look like; you never know when or where you're gonna need culture; you never know what culture is gonna do, and you never know what culture is for."[8] In this quite extraordinary statement, "culture" becomes a magic invisible elixir, an omnipotent cure-all—or, to put this another way, "culture" becomes, in its ubiquity, power, and invisibility, a synonym for "ideology." Culture is everywhere, and it is unknowable by definition. Cultural studies must then be the study of an object not open to study, since everything under the sun may be culture, and you can never know what it is, what it does, and what it is for. Or perhaps Atkinson means that you can never know beforehand what is going to turn out to be culture, so you should suspect everything of being culture and therefore study it. Anything in the world might be culture and is therefore worth study by cultural studies.

What we call "cultural studies" today is a heterogeneous and somewhat amorphous space of diverse institutional practices that can hardly be said to have a common methodology, goal, or institutional site. Every location in this space is fiercely contested—a good sign that something important may be at stake. Nevertheless, in spite of their diversity, all these new projects share an interest in the historical and social contexts of cultural artifacts. They tend to presume that the context is explanatory or determining. The author is back in. His or her death was prematurely announced. The subject, subjectivity, and the self are back in, along with personal agency, identity politics, responsibility, dialogue, and intersubjectivity. New or renewed interest has sprung up in biography and autobiography, in popular literature, in film, television, and advertising, in visual culture as opposed to linguistic culture, in the nature and role of "minority discourses" within the hegemonic discourse, and so on.

Though "theory" continues to play a subsidiary role in cultural studies, as in "film theory" or "queer theory," it has often been superseded by a return to precritical, pretheoretical, mimetic, referential, representational assumptions about the way literature and other arts mirror their historical and social contexts. The rejection of language-based theory, on the basis of the false characterization of it that I sketched earlier, has been for some scholars an essential part of this shift to a new form of extrinsic criticism. Why is this the case? Just why have some found it necessary to "abject" theory (as Tom Cohen often puts it)—to tell a false story about theory—in order to clear a space for these new developments?[9] How does this mistake about theory vitiate some work in cultural studies? Deconstruction never rejected the referentiality of language. Far from it. But it saw the inescapable referential vector of language as a problem to be interrogated, not as a solution that can be taken for granted. Insofar as the project of cultural studies has depended on the traditional idea of culture—that is, the production in a subject, or in a subjectivity, of an identity through indoctrination by a nation-state or its surrogate (for example, an ethnic or gender community, such as the presumed communities of African Americans, Chicanos/Chicanas, or gays and lesbians)—it has been necessary to resist deconstruction's questioning of the key concepts necessary to this idea of culture: the concepts of identity, of agency, of the unity of a given culture (whether hegemonic or minority), and of the definition of the individual by his or her participation in a nation or community. The questioning by theory of these concepts often needed to be sidestepped in order for the project of cultural studies and related new disciplines to get going and keep going. These key concepts are glued together (for example, the specular relation between a culture as a whole and any subject identity within it) by a reinstalled referentiality that can no longer afford to be put in question and remain a question. Hence the need—among some, at least, in cultural studies—to "abject" theory.

The term "cultural studies" itself suggests the degree to which this new discipline has, in its own self-definition, accepted one side of the traditional mission of the nation-state university that it would transform. That mission was, you will remember, double: to amass and archive critical knowledge, knowledge both of physical and biological nature and of culture (for example, knowledge of literary history as a key form of culture); and to form subjects of the state by inculcating in them the national culture through the process that the Germans called *Bildung*, and that we in the United States have traditionally called a "liberal education." The field of cultural studies has repudiated the second mission, since to fulfill it would be to fall into the hands of the conservatives who want a single canon and the values of a single national culture taught in schools and universities. But the field has embraced a form of the first mission by making culture itself an object of study, of understanding, and of archival storage, as the term "cultural *studies*" suggests.

Culture, rather than being what determines the subject as who he or she is after a lengthy process of education by the state's educational apparatus, is now, in all its diversity, an object of study like any other, like astrophysics and the human genome. The ease with which cultural studies has been institutionalized in American universities may be explained less by an eagerness to give minority cultures representation in the university than by a recognition that cultural studies can be so easily coopted for one of the quite traditional missions of the research university. Turning minority cultures into objects of university study, like elemental particles and chromosomes, may be a way of destroying those cultures, not preserving their vitality. Opposition to cultural studies might be stronger if it were understood that all these diverse cultures are going to be inculcated in students, not just studied. Where inculcation has really happened, the university has tended to respond with violence—by calling in the police, for example, as in the late sixties.

In any case, the university's project of *Bildung* depended on the notion of a nation-state with a single unified culture. It does not seem to make sense to teach students to be subjects of many cultures simultaneously. Or it makes sense only through a radical redefinition of culture along the lines of the global economy of consumerism that is reshaping the university these days as one more transnational corporation among others. Culture then becomes a superficial matter of fashion and dress, which is no doubt just the way the new global capitalism wants it—a whole world full of people in vestigial native costumes wearing blue jeans underneath and listening to transistor radios. [One would say now "using smartphones."—JHM] The question is how to live within the multicultural situation without succumbing to this superficiality.

The goals of all these new developments—cultural studies, women's studies, studies in various minority discourses, and so on—are laudable. Who could oppose giving a voice to the heretofore voiceless, to women and minorities, to gays and lesbians, to the economically disadvantaged? Who could oppose giving a place in the university to all the ethnic varieties that characterize both our national society (I speak of the United States, and from my "subject position" here and now) and the new global society that is more proximate every day? Who could oppose using such study to help create the democracy to come, that horizon of all our political and intellectual effort? Who could oppose the careful study of popular culture and of those media—television, video, cinema, blogs, social networks—that shape our minds and behavior far more than books do these days? A fundamental part of work in cultural studies has been descriptive and archival. Works in different media and from different cultures, works by women and minorities, need to be identified, categorized, edited, republished, brought into the open, and made available in the university and to the general public so they can be effective there.

Putting these neglected works in the classroom, in curricula and in books as well as in articles, conferences, and study groups, is only the beginning of the work, however. Knowledge is not enough. Archiving multiculturalism, as I have suggested, may even denature or negate the power that such works have to make cultural change. The university has a formidable power of recuperation and neutralization.

Why did the massive shift to cultural studies from language-based theory begin to occur just when it did—that is, around 1980? The shift was no doubt overdetermined. Many factors accompanied it. Nevertheless, one crucial force was the growing impact of new communications technologies. Of course these changes went on throughout the twentieth century, but they accelerated as we entered the electronic age. The younger scholars who have turned so spontaneously and so massively to cultural studies are the first generation of university teachers and critics who were brought up with television and with new forms of commercialized popular music. Many of them, as children and teenagers, spent more time watching television or listening to popular music than reading books. I do not say that these are necessarily bad activities. They are just different. Reading books can be bad for you, too, as Flaubert's Emma Bovary, Conrad's Lord Jim, and Cervantes's Don Quijote show. To a considerable degree, the critics who belong to this new generation have been formed as what they are by a new visual and aural culture that is fast replacing the culture of the book. It is not surprising that they should wish, in spite of their vestigial participation in the culture of the book, to study what has contributed so much to making them what they are.

At the same time, the new communications technologies are rapidly transforming the way research and teaching are carried on in the humanities. These transformations have accompanied and, to some degree, brought about the replacement of the Humboldtian university in the service of a single nation-state by the new technologized transnational university that serves the global economy. Since we are in the midst of these changes, it is difficult to see them clearly. Some of the claims for the revolutionary effect of computers on the humanities have clearly been exaggerated or wrongly formulated. Seen from a certain point of view, a computer, even one connected by modem or Ethernet to the World Wide Web, is, as many people would claim, no more than a glorified typewriter. One should not underestimate, however, the changes this glorification makes—the new ease of revision, for example, given the facility with which things can be added, deleted, or moved from one place to another in a computer file as opposed to a typed manuscript. Such ease gradually encourages the adept in computer composition to think of what he or she writes as never being in quite finished form. Whatever is printed is always just one stage in a potentially endless process of revision, deletion, addition, and rearrangement. Nothing, however, prevents using the computer for quite conventional or traditional work in humanities research or teaching. In fact, the configuration of certain types of database formats, hypertext and multimedia though they may be, may encourage traditional notions about the relation of a work to its author and to its historical and cultural contexts.[10] Brown University's Institute for Research in Information and Scholarship (IRIS) project in Victorian literature is to some degree an example of that. It presumes that a Victorian work like Tennyson's "The Lady of Shalott" is to be understood by more or less traditional placement of the poem in its socioeconomic and biographical context—by reference, for example, to the building of canals in England at the time.[11] The apparent freedom for the student to browse among various links may hide the imposition of predetermined connections. These may reinforce powerful ideological assumptions about the causal force of historical context on literary works. It depends on what links have been set up, or on the user's inventiveness in setting up new ones. Hypertext can be a powerful way to deploy what Kenneth Burke called "perspective by incongruity." In any case, hypertext files of whatever sort are powerful solvents of the assumption that proper meaning fits into the linear continuity of the traditional printed book. On the one hand, the significance of the computer, as of the typewriter, the Linotype machine, or any other technological device, depends on what use is made of it. On the other hand, neither the computer nor the typewriter nor the Linotype machine is just one technological device among others. Each belongs to that special class of such devices that serve as prostheses to the hand, voice, ears, and eyes in the generation, projection, reception, and exchange of signs. The computer, as one such device, is quite different from the typewriter. It imposes its own new matrix on the process of sign generation, reception, and exchange. It would be a mistake to minimize the changes it will make in the way humanists do research and teaching, and in the intellectual space within which humanists are rapidly coming to live.

It could be argued that hypertext does no more (though that is quite a lot) than make materially embodied, and more easily available in a new technological mechanism, what has always been the case about linguistic assemblages, and perhaps about the "life" with which they are intertwined. In a passage almost at the end of Proust's *À la recherche du temps perdu*, Marcel, meditating on the form the great work he is about to write will have to take, describes the way any encounter with a person involves everything else and can lead to it. Therefore, says Marcel, he realizes he needs a new technique of narration, a kind of three-dimensional technique not all that different from hypertext:

> I have said that it would be impossible to depict our relationship with anyone whom we have even slightly known without passing in review, one after another, the most different settings of our life. Each individual therefore—and I was myself one of these individuals—was a measure of duration for me, in virtue of the revolutions which like some heavenly body he had accomplished not only on his own axis but also around other bodies, in virtue, above all, of the successive positions which he had occupied in relation to myself. And surely the awareness of all these different planes within which, since in this last hour, at this party, I had recaptured it, Time seemed to dispose the different elements of my life, had, by making me reflect that in a book which tried to tell the story of a life it would be necessary to use not the two-dimensional psychology which we normally use but a quite different sort of three-dimensional psychology [*d'une sorte de psychologie dans l'espace*], added a new beauty to those resurrections of the past which my memory had effected while I was following my thoughts alone in the library, since memory by itself, when it introduces the past, unmodified, into the present—the past just as it was at the moment when it was itself the present—suppresses the mighty dimension of Time which is the dimension in which life is lived [*cette grande dimension du Temps suivant laquelle la vie se réalise*].[12]

À la recherche du temps perdu may be seen as a huge database of memories. Marcel treats his memories as though he had a hypertext program for moving around within those memories. Anywhere you begin will lead, ultimately, by a series of links, everywhere in that vast storage disk of recollections, but not according to any predetermined pathways. We readers must do the same. We readers of Proust are constantly coached into doing the same by the narrator's intricate system of cross-references. These are not entirely unlike hypertext links, though the reader must have stored the whole enormous text in his memory and do the work that hypertext does. Something of the same sort could be said of a more conventional work like Anthony Trollope's *Ayala's Angel* (1881). The good reader of this novel will connect whatever passage he or she is reading with earlier, similar passages and create a virtual hypertext version, without the aid of any machinery other than the printed pages and his or her own memory.

Nevertheless, in the period now coming to an end, when the printed book dominated as the chief means of storing and retrieving information, it was still possible to be beguiled into thinking of a work like *Ayala's Angel* or even like *À la recherche du temps perdu* as a stable and unmoving organic unity, on the model of a two-dimensional spatial array. Such a fixed text imposed on its readers a single unified meaning, generated by a linear reading from the first word through to the end—in Proust's case, more than three thousand pages later. The reader who accepted this model could think of the act of reading as a purely cognitive matter. I as reader do not create a meaning that did not exist before I actively engaged myself, "interactively," in the text. The meaning was there, waiting to be generated in me through an act of essentially passive reception. Hypertext that is overtly organized as such, on the other hand, offers the reader the necessity at every turn of choosing which path to follow through the text, or of letting chance choose for him or her. Nor is there any "right" choice, that is, one justified objectively by a pre-existing meaning. Hypertext demands that we choose at every turn and take responsibility for our choices. This is the ethics of hypertext. Hypertext brings into the open the way the generation of meaning in the act of reading is a speech act, not a passive cognitive reception. As such a "doing things with words," it is not fully authorized or justified by the text. The text makes a demand on me to read it. My reading is a response to that demand, a response to an irresistible sense of obligation to read all the books, and now all those texts on the Internet, too. But whether or not we have fulfilled this obligation in a given case can never be confirmed. The reader, in the end, is solely responsible for what he or she makes of a text.

Hypertext read on the computer screen brings this uneasy situation out into the open. It teaches us to see earlier works of literature in a different way, as already protohypertexts that invite or allow many different pathways of reading, since all reading, even the most linear, involves the constant to-and-fro of cross-referencing memory, inside the text and out, that Proust describes as the essential structure of human time. For this mobile, ungrounded, and unmasterable vibration, fixed visual-spatial images like "the Internet" are not adequate. They do not do justice to the linguistic, or semiotic, or sign-system structure that is possessed, each in its different way, by an interactive multimedia work on CD-ROM like *Myst* and by a novel from the age of the printed book like *À la recherche du temps perdu* or *Ayala's Angel*.[13] Works of literature are black holes in the Internet Galaxy.[14] The presence of literature and the literary on the Internet forbids thinking of the Internet as a transparent electronic highway system on which "information" passes back and forth freely and without interruption, as an open secret. There would be much more to say about this blocking of the transfer of information by what might be called the "literary" or "rhetorical" element in any sign system or text, even the most transparently "scientific," but I must postpone that for another time.

In this essay, I have attempted to say something about the changes since World War II in the study of national literatures in the United States. I have attempted also to relate some of the more recent changes to the increasing domination of US culture by cinema, radio, television, and video as well as by such newer communications technologies as fax machines, e-mail, and computers. These technologies have radically transformed not only the ways in which cultural expressions reach people (no longer so much by way of the printed book, more and more through visual media like cinema and television) but also the ways in which they are studied (more and more by way of computers, which are rapidly becoming more powerful as well as more able to mix pictures, movies, and audio with text). The rhythm of these developments is no doubt different in the People's Republic of China, but the new communications technologies will have a decisive influence here, too, both on cultural forms and on how they are studied. This essay may perhaps be helpful as a report on the ways in which these changes have occurred and are occurring in the United States.

CHAPTER 3

Effects of Globalization on Literary Study

Everyone hears on all sides these days about globalization and its effects. My topic is the effect of globalization on literary study. As Masao Miyoshi and others have pointed out, globalization is an uneven process. Millions of people all over the world are as yet relatively untouched by some of the globalizing forces I shall identify (for example, those who do not have access to a computer). Even so, hardly anyone has remained wholly detached from globalizing influences. Radios and VCRs are almost ubiquitous on remote Pacific islands, for example. Native Americans of northern Canada now use outboard motors and snowmobiles, not paddles and dogsleds. Most have radios. Airplanes come and go in extremely remote areas of northern Canada.

Three features of this immensely accelerated process of globalization today may be identified. The first is relatively low-tech. We have become so used to it as to take it for granted as part of the normal aspect of things. Nevertheless, it is of crucial importance, even in literary study. I refer to new means of rapid travel and shipping. If I had not been able to fly to China in a few hours, if I had had to take a slow boat and give weeks to the journey, it is unlikely I would have come here. Many academics, even those in the humanities, have become used to flying all over the world to do research, to attend conferences, and to lecture. This means that, rather than belonging to local or even national scholarly communities, many academics belong at least as much to transnational groups of scholars with common interests as they do to departments or research groups within their own universities. An unprecedented movement of scholars and researchers in all fields, including the humanities, defines our present situation. This is one thing that is meant by globalization.

A second feature is the globalization of economies. The companies and corporations that research universities increasingly serve and are paid by (as opposed to traditional service to the state, and funding by it) tend more and more to be transnational in scope. A transnational corporation may have offices in many different countries, be owned by investors from all over the world, manufacture goods in several countries (wherever labor is cheapest), and sell those goods all over the world. Such corporations do not owe primary loyalty to a single country or government. Orange County, California, where I live and work now, is full of such corporations. They are having an increasing influence on the University of California at Irvine, which is located in Orange County. The proliferation of transnational corporations means a major transformation in the nature and role of the contemporary research university. Rather than owing primary allegiance to state funding agencies (such as, in the United States, the National Science Foundation, the National Institutes of Health, or the National Endowment for the Humanities), university researchers are now often working for transnational pharmaceutical companies, computer companies, or other high-technology enterprises. This change is even happening in the humanities. My university has a new professorship of Korean studies funded by the Samsung Corporation. It would be hard to exaggerate the change in the US university being brought about by the shift in funding from government agencies to transnational corporations.

The proliferation of transnational corporations is one major feature of the decline of the nation-state, about which we hear so much. Bill Gates, the head of Microsoft, may have more actual power to determine what happens, on a global scale, than Bill Clinton, even though the latter is the president of the United States. [The former president is now attached to the Bill, Hillary & Chelsea Clinton Foundation. Bill Gates, cofounder and former CEO of Microsoft, and now a technology adviser to the company, is cofounder of the Bill & Melinda Gates Foundation and serves as the foundation's cochair.—JHM] New transnational trade organizations and arrangements, such as the North American Free Trade Agreement (NAFTA) or the European Union or Asia-Pacific Economic Cooperation (APEC), characterize this new transnational globalization of economies. The fierce resistance to this form of globalization—in my country, in the form of trade sanctions and counterproductive new immigration restrictions, not to speak of the unconstitutional provisions of the Communications Decency Act—indicates the anxiety produced by the new permeability and fragility of national boundaries. Nevertheless, that increasing vanishing of frontiers is an irresistible feature of our current situation.

The end of the Cold War brought a severe recession to California in the early 1990s as defense industries were radically cut. That greatly reduced state support for the nine-campus University of California—from over $2 billion down to $1.6 billion, a 20 percent reduction. The reduction was publicly justified by state revenue losses. The real reason was probably that, with the Cold War over, United States society no longer needed the university for the old reasons—that is, for military research and to be better than the Soviet Union in everything, including the humanities. Our National Endowment for the Humanities, the budget for which has now been substantially reduced, was originally founded with the specific intention of our being better than the Soviets in that area, too. We were told on all sides in the early 1990s that state support for the University of California would never again rise to the generous levels of the 1980s. Severe cutbacks in staff and programs were made. About two thousand professors were enticed into early retirement by the offer of a generous "golden handshake."

Now, just five or six years later, state funding is back to the old level. It took those in charge of the university only about five years to figure out a new mission for it. This change is strikingly clear in recent statements by Pete Wilson, governor of California, and Richard C. Atkinson, University of California president. In presenting his proposals for the California 1996–97 budget, Wilson said, "California universities and colleges have long been revered as the finest institutions in the world. Like the pioneers, entrepreneurs, and innovators who made California a land where any dream is possible, our institutions of higher learning are carrying on that tradition by preparing our students to compete and win in the global marketplace." Atkinson echoed Wilson almost word for word: "I applaud the governor's recognition of the important role higher education plays in preparing a skilled workforce for competition in the global marketplace and the important role UC plays in a healthy California economy."[1]

What, one might ask, will be the role of literary study in this new technological and instrumental university? This new economically oriented research university is radically different from the old Humboldtian research university, modeled on the University of Berlin. The latter was founded in the early nineteenth century. The Humboldtian research university was devoted to a combination of *Bildung*, or training in national values, and *Wissenschaft*, or the search for knowledge in all fields for its own sake, the attempt to find out the truth about everything.[2]

The third form of globalization is perhaps the most far-reaching in its transformative effects. I mean the rapid development of new communications technologies. These have been changing the texture of daily life by putting the close in touch with the far ever since the invention of the telegraph and the telephone in the nineteenth century. Recent technological developments have accelerated these changes geometrically. Everyone knows what those developments are: first cinema, then radio, then television, then records, tapes, VCRs, CD-ROMs, computers, fax machines, and now e-mail, the Internet, and the World Wide Web. These are bringing about, as many analysts have argued, a major paradigm shift in human life on the globe, a shift from the age of the book to the electronic age.[3] The new devices put anyone who has them in more or less instantaneous communication with other people anywhere in the world, thereby contributing with a vengeance to globalization in all its aspects.

The World Wide Web is the most radical and transformative of these innovations. It puts anyone with a connection to it in possession of an enormous incoherent multimedia database. Music, advertising, chat rooms of all kinds where people can exchange views online, weather information, the latest photographs from the Hubble Space Telescope, stock market quotations, computer games, and endlessly proliferating websites on every conceivable topic jostle side by side by with an increasing number of books online and digitized artworks. All these come from all over the world to my computer screen, where they are equally near (and far). A Vermeer website, for example, allows me to download facsimiles of any or all of Vermeer's paintings and to use them, if I like, as screen savers. Another website, in Danish, contains a wonderful assembly of wall paintings from medieval Danish churches. I discovered the other day a Henry James website that has a constantly increasing number of James's works online, including *The Ambassadors* and *The Golden Bowl*. Programs with strange names like "spiders," along with search engines such as Yahoo, Lycos, and WebCrawler, have been developed to help the browser find things in this immense and exponentially proliferating disorder. The people who have created and who use the

World Wide Web are, many of them at least, an irreverent and witty lot. They are inhabited by a new sense of democracy and freedom. They are immensely creative in ways that are truly inaugural. They are gifted in creating new and constantly shifting forms of assembly in cyberspace. [I need hardly stress the immense increase in the scope of the Internet since 1997, when this lecture was presented. Examples are that amazing search engine, Google, and that equally amazing digital encyclopedia, *Wikipedia*.—JHM]

I want to stress three important effects, among many others, of these concomitant forms of globalization.

First is the way they work to bring about a decline in the integrity and power of the nation-state, the dominant form of political and social organization since the eighteenth century.

Second is the way globalization is leading to many new forms of constructive and potentially powerful social organization, new kinds of communities. These include research and university communities. An example is the sense of lively and often contentious solidarity among those who interact with one or another website or chat group—those devoted, for example, to a theorist like Derrida, or to canonical writers like Shakespeare, Henry James, and Proust, or to groups like feminists or those in minority studies. The new forms of transnational organization by way of the Web are also creating new forms of political groupings. A recent essay by Jon Katz in *Wired*, one of the most important journals about these changes, describes and celebrates what is going on, in the United States at least, as not only "the slow death of the current political system" but also "the rise of postpolitics and the birth of the Digital Nation." Surfing the Net during the recent presidential election, Katz claims that he "saw the primordial stirrings of a new kind of nation—the Digital Nation—and the formation of a new postpolitical philosophy. This nascent ideology, fuzzy and difficult to define, suggests a blend of some of the best values rescued from the old dogmas—the humanism of liberalism, the economic opportunity of conservatism, plus a strong sense of personal responsibility and a passion for freedom." Whether this new postpolitical community will come to anything remains to be seen. I think Katz is right, however, to say that a new form of dynamic change or even a disquieting fluidity characterizes interaction on the Web. "Ideas," says Katz, "almost never remain static on the Web. They are launched like children into the world, where they are altered by the many different environments they pass through, almost never coming home in the same form in which they left." Katz is hopeful that these postpolitical communities can lead to a better world, if those belonging to them choose to use their power in the right way. "The ascending young citizens of the Digital Nation can, if they wish," he says, "construct a more civil society, a new politics based on rationalism, shared information, the pursuit of truth, and new kinds of community."[4] We shall see about that. It might go the other way. It all depends on many unpredictable factors. Certainly tremendous efforts of various sorts are now being made in the United States both to control and to censor the Web and, with conspicuous success, to commercialize it.

The third effect of globalization I want to discuss is even more problematic. It is also closer to accounting for the radical changes in literary study, and in humanistic study generally, that are currently occurring, at least in the United States. Walter Benjamin long ago argued that new technologies—new modes of production and consumption, all the changes made by nineteenth-century industrialization—had already created a radically new human sensibility and therefore a new way of living in the world: "As the entire way of being changes for human collectives over large historical periods, so also change their modes of sensual perception [*die Art und Weise ihrer Sinneswahrnehmung*]."[5] All the changes brought about by industrialization, the rise of great cities, and the development of new communications technologies like photography and cinema produced, according to Benjamin, a new way of being human: the nervous, solitary Baudelairean man of the crowd. This new kind of human being is hungry for immediate experience while at the same time obsessed with the sense of a faraway, unattainable horizon that undermines every immediacy. Benjamin's most often cited essay on this topic is "Das Kunstwerk im Zeitalter seiner technischen Reproduzierbarkeit" ("The Work of Art in the Age of Technical Reproducibility").[6] One would do well to be skeptical about such claims for a mutation in sensory experience. These claims are associated, in Benjamin's formulations, with the rise of new collectivities. We still have the same five senses that our ancestors had. Evolutionary mutations usually take thousands and thousands of years, not a mere two centuries. Nevertheless, the human sensory, emotional, and cognitive apparatus is unusually flexible among those possessed by different life forms. It may be that a man or woman today sitting before a computer screen or watching a film on a VCR or watching television has a radically different sense of being in the world from that once possessed by the inhabitant of an eighteenth-century village. Reading works of literature from the past is one way to find out about that. This is one strong defense of reading literature. The evidence, I must say, is ambiguous. Shakespeare's people, or even Chaucer's, seem in many ways more like us than radically different, in spite of the fact that they had no television. Nevertheless, the differences are important, too. They need to be studied carefully in order to be identified accurately.[7]

Jacques Derrida, in an eloquent passage from a recent seminar, stresses the strange combination of solitude and a new kind of being with others of the person using a computer to reach the World Wide Web. He also emphasizes the breakdown of traditional boundaries between inside and outside brought about by new communications technologies. We no longer dwell privately, sequestered in our homes. As the epochal cultural displacement from the book age to the hypertext age has accelerated, we have, in Derrida's view, been ushered ever more rapidly into a threatening living space. This new electronic space—the space of television, cinema, telephone, videos, fax, e-mail, hypertext, and the Internet—has profoundly altered the economies of the self, the home, the workplace, the university, and the nation-state's politics. These were traditionally ordered around the firm boundaries of an inside/outside dichotomy, whether those boundaries were the walls between the home's privacy and the world outside or the borders between the nation-state and its neighbors. The new technologies invade the home and confound all these inside/outside divisions. On the one hand, no one is so alone as when watching television, talking on the telephone, or sitting before a computer screen reading e-mail or searching an Internet database. On the other hand, that private space has been invaded and permeated by a vast simultaneous crowd of verbal, aural, and visual images existing in cyberspace's simulacrum of presence. Those images cross national and ethnic boundaries. They come from all over the world with a spurious immediacy that makes them all seem equally close and equally distant. The global village is not out there but in here; or, a clear distinction between inside and out no longer operates. The new technologies bring the *unheimlich,* "other," into the privacy of the home. They are a frightening threat to traditional ideas of the self as unified and as properly living rooted in one dear particular culture-bound place, participating in a single national culture, firmly protected from any alien otherness. They are threatening also to our assumption that political action is based in a single topographical location, a given nation-state with its firm boundaries, its ethnic and cultural unity.

The decline of the nation-state; the development of new electronic communities, communities in cyberspace; and the possible generation of a new human sensibility, leading to a mutation of perceptual experience and making new cyberspace persons—these are three effects of globalization. What is happening to literary study as a result of these changes? Can we still study literature today? Ought we or must we study it? Why? What purpose does literary study serve in the new globalized world? I want to make four points that will sketch out an answer to these questions, or at least circle around them.

The first thing to say is that, however we might wish it were not the case, the sad fact is that literature in the old-fashioned sense is playing a smaller and smaller role worldwide in the new globalized cultures. This fact is particularly distressing to me, since I have already spent fifty years in the study of literature and plan to go on studying it. It is painful to have a lifelong vocation for something that has diminishing importance. Nevertheless, the facts must be faced. If someone is watching television, or a movie on the VCR, or surfing the Internet, he or she cannot at the same time be reading Shakespeare or Emily Dickinson, though some schoolchildren and even some university students claim to be able to do both at once. All the statistics show that more and more people are spending more and more time watching television and cinema. Now there has been a rapid shift from those to the computer screen. The cultural function once served by novels—in nineteenth-century England, for example—is now being served by movies, by popular music, and by computer games. There may be nothing intrinsically wrong with this, unless you happen to have, as I do, a big investment in the old printed-book culture. Though many works of literature are available online, ready to be downloaded to anyone's computer, I believe relatively few people are using that wonderful new resource. Certainly the new "digital young" Jon Katz describes are not, except rarely, using the Internet to get access to Shakespeare.

One strong point made by Katz about the citizens, or "netizens," of the new Digital Nation is their commitment to popular culture and their disdain for those who still live outside it and want to lecture them about the shallowness of popular music, cinema, and so on. "The digital young," says Katz, ". . . share a passion for popular culture—perhaps their most common shared value, and the one most misperceived and mishandled by politicians and journalists. On Monday mornings when they saunter into work, they are much more likely to be talking about the movies they saw over the weekend than about Washington's issue of the week [or, I might add, about what a wonderful poem Milton's *Paradise Lost* is.—JHM]. Music, movies, magazines, some television shows, and some books are elementally important to them—not merely forms of entertainment but means of identity." Poems and novels used to be means of identity. Now it is the latest rap group. "As much as anything else," Katz continues, "the reflexive contempt for popular culture shared by so many elders of journalism and politics has alienated this group, causing its members to view the world in two basic categories: those who get it, and those who don't. For much of their lives these young people have been branded as ignorant, their culture malignant. The political leaders and pundits (one might add: the educators) who malign them haven't begun to grasp how destructive these perpetual assaults have been, how huge a cultural gap they've created."[8] The colophon page of *Wired* not only lists the "Zines [that is, magazines] of Choice" but also "Music that helped get this magazine out." The April 1997 issue lists, among others, Matthew Sweet, *100% Fun*; Arvo Pärt, "De Profundis (Psalm 130)"; Melvins, "Interstellar Overdrive"; Steven Jesse Bernstein, *Prison*; *Miami Vice*; and Mari Boine, *Radiant Warmth*. What this has to do with globalization is clear enough. This popular culture is disseminated all over the world through films, tapes, CDs, radio broadcasts, and, now, the Internet as the latter becomes more and more a multimedia operation. This media culture has immense power to drown out the quiet voice of the fading book culture, and also to drown out the specificities of local cultures everywhere, just as everyone everywhere now is coming to wear blue jeans and to carry a transistor radio or a portable tape or CD player. [Nowadays, an iPhone.—JHM]

A second effect of globalization on literary study is the transformation being wrought in it by the new electronic devices. Though few members of the new Digital Nation may make use of the computer and the World Wide Web for literary studies, the work of those who do continue such studies is being markedly changed by the new devices. Composition on the computer differs greatly from composition in longhand or on the typewriter. The possibilities for easy revision make a work of literary study seem never quite finished or able to be finished. It can so easily be expanded, rearranged, cut, given further footnote annotation, and so on. Moreover, it is already possible to produce hypertext versions of works in literary study, essays that contain pictures, film clips, audio clips, and buttons that when clicked on will transport the reader to other texts, graphics, video, or sounds. The peculiarity of such essays is that they can be read only on the computer screen. A proliferation of online journals is transforming the conditions of publication and dissemination in literary studies. I have already spoken of the way rapid transportation can make an individual scholar part of a transnational research group, not just a professor working locally in his or her own university. New communications media make those new communities even more active. Moreover, amazing research resources are being made available online—for example, the exponentially increasing number of digitized literary texts, or such resources as the Rossetti archive being assembled at the University of Virginia. They will give anyone who can reach the Internet access to all of Dante Gabriel Rossetti's paintings, drawings, and writings, in all their versions, with a large collection of ancillary scholarly materials. Another example is the ARTFL French database, available through a University of Chicago website. This database allows the user to search an enormous collection of major philosophical and literary works in French, from Montaigne and Descartes to Proust. All the places where Diderot, for example, uses certain words in close proximity may be called up in a minute to the researcher's computer screen. What you do with such data is up to you, but these resources give the researcher an improvised memory far more powerful than inert rows of books on the library shelf.[9] I have written elsewhere of the way all these changes fundamentally alter the way literary works of the past exist for the student or critic.[10] In the example I used, Anthony Trollope's *Ayala's Angel* in its digitized online form, brought down out of cyberspace in plain ASCII format from the Oxford Text Archive, is detached from the historical context that used to be brought with the material form of the printed book.[11] Now *Ayala's Angel* floats freely in cyberspace, juxtaposed in a strange new simultaneity to all the unimaginable complexity of other incongruous things on the World Wide Web.[12] This alteration in our sense of literary history is one of the most important effects of the new communications technologies on literary study.

The third effect of globalization on literary study is a concomitant of that decline of the nation-state I mentioned earlier. Literary study used to be organized chiefly as the separate study of national literatures (for example, in my case, the study of English, that is, primarily British literature, with a subordinate component of United States literature). Now such study is seen as a feature of imperialism. Each country—the United States, for example— is seen as multicultural and multilingual, and therefore as falsified by the study of a single nation's literature. This has been especially the case when, as with the institutionalization of English literature as a primary humanistic discipline in the United States, that literature has been the literature of a foreign country—a country, moreover, that we defeated over two hundred years ago in a war of independence.

The older separate study of national literatures is coming to be displaced by new forms of multilingual comparative literature, or by the study, for example, of global literature in English. The latter will place Canadian, Australian, New Zealand, African, Irish, United States, and Asian anglophone literatures side by side with British literature. The same thing is happening with worldwide francophone literature. Shakespeare will and should continue to be studied, but in a radically new context and historical perspective. Nevertheless, British literature should still and always be a major component of this transformed discipline of global literature in English, since British literature has had a decisive influence even on those writers (United States writers, for example) who want to contest its hegemony. You cannot understand the latter without knowing the former. You also cannot understand literature in English without knowing the literature in other languages that accompany it in different ways in each country where English is the predominant language.

The fourth effect of globalization, in the United States at least, has been the rapid rise of so-called cultural studies.[13] For cultural studies, literature is no longer the privileged expression of culture that it was, say, for Matthew Arnold, or for the United States university until recently. Literature is just one symptom or product of culture, among others, to be studied side by side not only with film, video, television, advertising, magazines, and so on, but also with the myriad habits of everyday life that ethnographers investigate in non-Western cultures or in our own culture. As Alan Liu observes, "literature" is "a category that has increasingly lost its distinction on the unbounded plane of cultural 'discourse,' 'textuality,' 'information,' 'phrase regimes,' and 'general literature.' " The field of cultural studies, as Liu puts it, "make[s] literature seem just one of many equipollent registers of culture and multiculture—no more or less splendid, say, than the everyday practices of dressing, walking, cooking, or quilting."[14]

Though people in this new field tend to be defensive about the relation of cultural studies to the social sciences, it seems evident that as the domain of cultural studies becomes more and more dominant in the humanities, the humanities will approach closer and closer to a merger with the social sciences, especially with anthropology and sociology. Just as anthropologists have learned much from colleagues in the humanities, so training at the graduate level in protocols of anthropology and sociology would be helpful for those going into cultural studies (for example, training in statistical analysis; in the relation between data and generalization; in the university's obligations when human subjects are used; in the need to learn, by hook or by crook, the languages necessary for the work undertaken; and so on). A traditional Eurocentric literary education is not much help for many of the projects of cultural studies.

The displacement of language-based theory by cultural studies is evident everywhere in the humanities departments of Western universities. One place where it can be clearly seen is in the so-called Bernheimer Report of the American Comparative Literature Association.[15] This report proposes that a new discipline of comparative literature should replace not only the old-fashioned, Eurocentric, pre-1975 form of comparative literature, which set canonical works from European and American national literatures side by side to "compare" them, but also the theory-based and reading-based comparative literature of the 1970s and 1980s. For these should be substituted a form of cultural studies that will compare cultures by juxtaposing many kinds of artifacts and forms of behavior—works verbal, visual, and aural as well as dress, habits of walking, and so on. Comparative literature will now study film, popular literature, popular music, advertising, and so on, alongside examples of what has traditionally been thought of as "literature." The Bernheimer Report has accepted so completely the current project of cultural studies that it might be taken as an authoritative description of that project, with a slight emphasis on the comparative aspect. Comparison, however, is always a part of cultural studies, even outside comparative literature departments. Here is what the report says about "the space of comparison today":

> The space of comparison today involves comparisons between artistic productions usually studied by different disciplines; between various cultural constructions of those disciplines; between Western cultural traditions, both high and popular, and those of non-Western cultures; between the pre- and post-contact cultural productions of colonized peoples; between gender constructions defined as feminine and those defined as masculine, or between sexual orientations defined as straight and those defined as gay; between racial and ethnic modes of signifying; between hermeneutic articulations of meaning and materialist analyses of its modes of production and circulation; and much more. These ways of contextualizing literature in the expanded fields of discourse, culture, ideology, race, and gender are so different from the old models of literary study according to authors,

nations, periods, and genres that the term "literature" may no longer adequately describe our object of study.[16]

"The term 'literature' may no longer adequately describe our object of study." You can say that again! This explosion of the discipline of comparative literature, leaving it commissioned to study just about everything human, and therefore nothing definite, parallels the similar explosion of English departments. By including everything listed here ("and much more"), the new comparative literature will marginalize literature, to say the least. It will compare everything that can be labeled "culture," in a self-enclosed circling, just as Diogenes Teufelsdröckh, in Carlyle's *Sartor Resanus*, was, in Carlyle's quaint spelling, a professor of *Allerley-Wissenschaft* at the University of Weissnichtwo.[17]

What is disappearing in the new comparative literature, as in many other forms of cultural studies, is the emphasis on reading that was so important a feature in theory of the 1970s and 1980s. In place of an exigent theoretical attention to reading is put an assumption of the "translatability," without significant loss, of cultural meanings from one language to another, one medium to another, one discipline to another. A strenuous rejection of translation was a keystone of the older comparative literature. This was the case even though the rejection of translation was to a considerable degree bogus. Comparative literature as a discipline has tended to express the linguistic imperialism of one or another single language—American English, for example, in the United States, or French in the case of the comparative literature of René Étiemble in Paris. The comparatist knows many languages but can translate them all into the dominant language he or she uses. This is the case, for example, with René Wellek's "monumental" history of modern criticism.[18] The implicit claim is this: "Trust me. I know all these languages and can translate texts from all of them into English for you. You can forget that they were originally written in German, Russian, Polish, Czech, or whatever. I have given the originals in a subordinate place, in case you want to look them up, but problems of untranslatability have largely been circumvented by my own mastery of all these languages. I am the relay station within which all these other languages are turned into English."

For the new "cultural studies" form of comparative literature, however, translation has a new meaning. It has to do not so much with finding equivalents in one language for expression in another but rather with the carrying over of an entire other culture or discipline into one's own. About turning the other into the same I shall say more later; here is what the Bernheimer Report says about translation:

> While the necessity and unique benefits of a deep knowledge of foreign languages must continue to be stressed, the old hostilities toward translation should be mitigated. In fact, translation can well be seen as a paradigm for larger problems of understanding and interpretation across different discursive traditions. Comparative literature, it could be said, aims to explain both what is lost and what is gained in translations between the distinct value systems of different cultures, media, disciplines, and institutions. Moreover, the comparatist should accept the responsibility of locating the particular place and time at which he or she studies these practices. Where do I speak from, and from what tradition(s), or countertraditions? How do I translate Europe or South America or Africa into a North American cultural reality, or, indeed, North America into another cultural context?[19]

Just by being who and where we are, the Bernheimer Report assumes, we translate all the time. Remembering vigilantly my own "subject position" will more or less handle whatever lingering problems of translation may remain.

Comparative Literature in the Age of Multiculturalism, the volume that contains the Bernheimer Report and a series of essays in response to it, registers the agony, in the sense of death throes, of the traditional discipline of comparative literature as it melts into being just another form of cultural studies. I doubt that this process can or should be stopped. It constitutes a necessary moment of evolution in the US university. It testifies to worldwide changes that prohibit a return to older forms of literary study. The old Eurocentric comparative literature, like the traditional separate study of European national literatures, will continue for a time, overlapping with the new work in cultural studies and with the various regional-studies disciplines into which cultural studies may and ought to evolve; but its death knell is ringing. The Bernheimer Report is an obituary only slightly premature. Nostalgia for the old privileged place of literature is expressed in some of the essays in the volume containing the Bernheimer Report—those, for example, by Peter Brooks, Michael Riffaterre, and Jonathan Culler, all older white males, like me. Nostalgia, however, will in this case butter no parsnips.

This new situation of literary studies is remarkably fluid and changing with dizzying rapidity. In this new context, what defense can be made for literary study? I make in conclusion three claims for its indispensable value.

First, whatever the situation may now be of a diminishing role for literature in the new global cultures, literature during the age of the book was a major way in which a culture expressed itself and constituted itself. Those who do not understand the past are condemned to repeat it. An absolutely indispensable means of understanding our pasts is the study of those pasts' literatures, not just the study of language as such. This even has a commercial or economic value. We citizens of California will not achieve that competitiveness in global economy for which Governor Wilson calls unless we learn not just the languages of our own country, and of those countries with which we trade and compete, but also their literatures. The study of literature gives an unparalleled ability to feel what it might have been like to live in Chaucer's time, in Shakespeare's time, or in Emily Dickinson's time, or what it might be like to live now within one or another East Asian culture, or within one of the minority cultures within one's own culture. In the United States, these would include Native American, Chicano, Asian American, and African American cultures, among others.

Second, for better or for worse, language is and will remain one of our chief means of communication, in solidarity or in dissensus. Literary study will remain an indispensable means of understanding the rhetorical, figurative, and storytelling possibilities of language as these language uses have shaped our lives.

Third, and perhaps most important, the close study of literature—I mean the actual words on all those pages—is an indispensable means of access to a confrontation with what I call the strangeness or irreducible otherness of others, not only those belonging to different cultures but even those within one's own culture. As opposed to the homogenizing implications of cultural studies, where the assumption tends to be that all cultures are variants of the same universal human culture, I propose the hypothesis that each work may be "other" to all the rationalizing apparatus we have constructed to make it the same, whether biographical, historical, cultural, or technological modes of analysis. This is as true for the great works in the Western tradition, from Plato and Sophocles to Faulkner, as it is for those more obviously exotic or alien works, such as writings in English by Native Americans in the United States or by Maori in New Zealand or by recently enfranchised black citizens of

South Africa, or such as francophone novels by North African Muslims. Putting Plato or Sophocles or Faulkner in the context of these, as the new curricula increasingly will do, is a way of showing how strange, how "other," these, too, are. This encounter with otherness will occur only through what used to be called "close reading," supported by most vigilant theoretical reflection. Many assert today that rhetorical reading is old-fashioned, reactionary, and no longer necessary or desirable. In the face of such assertions, I conclude with a stubborn, recalcitrant, and defiant plea for close reading in the original languages. Such reading is still essential to university study, even in the new globalized situation.

CHAPTER 4

Will Literary Study Survive the Globalization of the University and the New Regime of Telecommunications?

Jacques Derrida, in striking passages written by one or another of the protagonists of *La carte postale* (*The Post Card*), says the following:

> . . . an entire epoch of so-called literature, if not all of it, cannot survive a certain technological regime of telecommunications (in this respect the political regime is secondary). Neither can philosophy, or psychoanalysis. Or love letters. . . .
>
> Refound here the American student with whom we had coffee last Saturday, the one who was looking for a thesis subject (comparative literature). I suggested to her something on the telephone in the literature of the 20th century (and beyond), starting with, for example, the telephone lady in Proust or the figure of the American operator, and then asking the question of the effects of the most advanced telematics [*la télématique la plus avancée*] on whatever would still remain of literature. I spoke to her about microprocessors and computer terminals, she seemed somewhat disgusted [*avait l'air un peu dégoûté*]. She told me that she still loved

> literature (me too, I answered her, *mais si, mais si*). Curious to know what she understood by this.[1]

What Derrida, or rather his protagonist, in *La carte postale* says in the citation I have made is truly frightening, at least to a lover of literature like me, or like the protagonist's hapless acquaintance: the American graduate student in comparative literature who was looking for a dissertation topic. What the protagonist says arouses in me the passions of anxiety, dubiety, fear, disgust, and perhaps a little secret desire to see what it would be like to live beyond the end of literature, love letters, philosophy, and psychoanalysis, all prime examples of "humanistic discourse." To live beyond their end would be like living beyond the end of the world.

Derrida's words in *The Post Card* also perhaps generate in most readers the passions of disbelief and even scorn. What a ridiculous idea! We passionately and instinctively resist the statement that Derrida makes in such a casual and offhand way, as though it goes without saying. How could a change in something so superficial, mechanical, or contingent as the dominant means of preservation and dissemination of information—the change, to be precise, from a manuscript and print culture to a digital culture—actually bring to an end things that seem so universal in any civilized society as literature, philosophy, psychoanalysis, and love letters? Surely these will survive any change in the regime of telecommunications? Surely I can write love letters by e-mail? Surely I can compose and transmit literature or philosophy or even a love letter on a computer connected to the Internet just as well as I can with handwriting or with a typewriter or through a printed book? How is psychoanalysis, based as it is on face-to face-interlocution (it's called "the talking cure"), and tied to the regime of print, to be brought to an end by a shift to digital culture?

Derrida's curt and even insolent words arouse in me a passion of disgust like that in the graduate student to whom Derrida gave such strange advice. This advice, by the way, was taken by Avital Ronell in her own way, and no doubt not as a response to any direct solicitation from Derrida. Both Proust on the telephone and Derrida's *The Post Card* figure in Ronell's admirable *The Telephone Book*, itself in its format an anticipation of the new regime of telecommunications coming into being. Laurence Rickels had also already written brilliantly on the telephone in modern literature, psychoanalysis, and culture generally, as has Friedrich Kittler.[2]

Nevertheless, that is what Derrida is claiming: the change in the "regime of telecommunications" does not simply transform but absolutely brings to an end literature, philosophy, psychoanalysis, and even love letters. It does this by a kind of death-dealing performative fiat: "Let there be no more love letters!" How in the world could this be? Insofar as Derrida's words, either those he (or one protagonist of *The Post Card*) said to the graduate student or the words you or I read now in that book, generate the passions of fear, anxiety, disgust, incredulity, and secret desire, those words are a "felicitous" performative utterance. They do what they say and help bring about the end of literature, love letters, and so on, just as saying, "Je t'aime" ("I love you"), as Derrida argued in a recent seminar, not only creates love in the speaker but may generate belief and reciprocal love in the addressee, the one to whom the words are spoken.

In spite of all his love for literature, Derrida's writings—for example, *Glas* or *La carte postale* itself—have certainly contributed to the end of literature as we have known it in a particular historical epoch and culture (say, the last two or two and a half centuries in Europe and America).[3] The concept of literature in the West has been inextricably tied to Cartesian notions of selfhood, to the regime of print, to Western-style democracies and notions of the nation-state, and to the right to free speech within such democracies. "Literature" in that sense began fairly recently, in the late seventeenth or early eighteenth century, and in one place, Western Europe. It could come to an end, and that would not be the end of civilization. In fact, if Derrida is right, and I believe he is, the new regime of telecommunications is bringing literature to an end by transforming all those factors that were its preconditions or its concomitants.

One of Derrida's main points in *The Post Card* is that it is a feature of the new regime of telecommunications to break down the inside/outside dichotomies that presided over the old print culture. The new regime is ironically allegorized in *The Post Card* in somewhat obsolete forms, that is, not only in the many telephone conversations the protagonist (or protagonists) have with their beloveds but also in an old-fashioned remnant of the rapidly disappearing culture of handwriting, print, and the postal system: the post card. The post card stands as a proleptic anticipation of the publicity and openness of the new communications regimes. A postcard is open for anyone to read, just as e-mail today is by no means sealed or private. If an example of either happens to fall under my eye, as Derrida makes explicit for post cards and letters not only in *La carte postale* but also in the admirable essay called "Télépathie," I can make myself, or am magically made, into its recipient.[4] The post card message or the e-mail letter that happens to fall under my eye is meant for me, or I take it as meant for me, whoever its addressee. This certainly happens when I read the passage from *The Post Card* I have cited. The bad or even disgusting news the speaker conveyed to the graduate student—news of the end of literature, philosophy, psychoanalysis, and love letters—is also conveyed to me. I become the recipient of this bad news. The passions generated in the graduate student by what the protagonist said are also generated in me.

Perhaps the most disturbing thing Derrida says in the passage I have cited is that, in the power of the new regime of telecommuniations to bring an end to literature, psychoanalysis, philosophy, and love letters, "the political regime is secondary." More exactly, as Derrida says, "in this respect the political regime is secondary." "In this respect" means, I take it, that he does not deny (nor would I) the importance of political regimes, but that the power of the new regime of telecommunications is not limited or controlled, except in a "secondary" way, by the political regime of this or that nation. [The use of cell phones and uses of other such digital devices in the uprisings known as the Arab Spring, and in the current successes of ISIS and other dissident groups in Iraq, are examples of exploitation of digital gadgets in the Arab world.—JHM]

The second industrial revolution, as everyone knows, is the shift in the West, beginning in the mid-nineteenth century but accelerating ever since, from an economy organized around the production and distribution of commodities to an economy increasingly dominated by the creation, storage, retrieval, and distribution of information. Even money is now primarily information, exchanged and distributed all over the world at the speed of light by telecommunications networks that also transmit literature in digitized form. Several of Henry James's novels, for example, are now available on the Internet along with innumerable other literary works—works, that is, belonging to the now rapidly fading historical epoch dominated by the printing press.[5]

Photography, the telegraph, the typewriter, the telephone, the gramophone, cinematography, radio, tape recorders, television, and now CDs, VCRs, DVDs, cell phones, computers, communications satellites, and the World Wide Web—we all know what these new devices are and how their power and effects have accelerated over the last century and a half. The possession and the consequent effects of these devices, as Masao Miyoshi and others have frequently reminded us, are unevenly distributed among various countries and peoples of the world. Only about 50 percent, at most, of United States households at this point have personal computers, and of course the percentage is immensely smaller in many other countries. [That percentage is much larger now, especially if you include iPhones and iPads, those miniature computers.—JHM] Nevertheless, in one way or another and to one degree or another, these technological gadgets have already decisively changed almost everyone's life. The changes will accelerate as more and more people come to have access to the Internet, for example, just as so many people already have access to television. The changes occurring include a transformation of politics, of nationhood or citizenship, of culture, and of the individual's sense of selfhood, identity, and belonging, not to speak of a transformation of literature, psychoanalysis, philosophy, and love letters.

No doubt the effects of this endangering of various privacies and enclosures by prosthetic telecommunications devices (as the telephone is an extension of the ear) include the exacerbation, by reaction, of defensive nationalisms, often separatist nationalisms within once secure nation-states or unions, as is the case in Africa or in the Balkans today [In 2000.—JHM], and inspiration for the horrors of genocide and "ethnic cleansing." Fear of these new technologies also generates defensive moves like attempts by the United States Congress to control the Internet—for example, through the Communications Decency Act, which is clearly unconstitutional, a breach of the right to free speech guaranteed by the United States Constitution; the courts have judged it so.

What is perhaps most scandalous about the radical effects of new telecommunications is the way none of these gadgets' inventors, so far as I know, intended or foresaw any such thing as the effects their inventions have had. The inventors of the telephone or of the magnetic tape recorder were doing no more than exploiting technological possibilities, playing creatively with wires, electrical currents, vibrating diaphragms, plastic tapes, and so on. These scientists had no intention, so far as I know, of putting an end to literature, love letters, philosophy, or the nation-state. What is so scandalous is the incommensurability between cause and effect, in addition to the accidental aspect of the huge effect—no less than a radical disruption, interruption, break, or reorientation in human history.

The new telecommunications are having a powerful effect in creating local and transnational ideologies. It would be the rash intellectual who would dare to affirm that we have reached an "end of ideology."

Ideology does not vanish that easily, if ever or at all. Nor do I think that Marx's analysis of ideology in *The German Ideology* has by any means lost its pertinence today.[6] As I asserted at the end of chapter 1 of this volume, for both Marx and Louis Althusser, though in somewhat different ways, ideology is a phantasmal imaginary superstructural effect of human beings' actual material conditions of existence (that is, the mode of manufacture, distribution, and circulation of goods under which those human beings live). For both Marx and Althusser, ideology is not transformed through lecturing people, or through rational argument, but through changes in those material conditions of existence. Nor is ideology just an innocent subjective spectral insubstantial set of mistakes. It has power, often unfortunately, to intervene in history and make things happen—as, for example, in the effects in the state of California, where I live, of repressive immigration laws, and of the absurd law declaring English the official language of California. [I did not, in 2000, foresee the appearance of the Tea Party in the United States—a wacky ideology, if ever there was one, destructively detached from reality.—JHM] Though Paul de Man was not a Marxist (whatever, exactly, that means these days or has meant at any time), he was a good reader of Marx's *The German Ideology*. Both Marx and Althusser might have agreed with the definition of ideology that de Man gives in "The Resistance to Theory" when he says: "[T]his does not mean that fictional narratives are not part of the world and of reality; their impact upon the world may well be all too strong for comfort. What we call ideology is precisely the confusion of linguistic with natural reality, of reference with phenomenalism."[7]

I would add to what de Man says that it is not so much language as such that generates the delusions of ideologies but rather language as molded by one or another medium—voice, handwriting, print, television, or the computer connected to the Internet. All these reproductive technologies exploit the strange propensity to dwell in fictional or phantasmal spaces that each human being has. The bodies of readers, television viewers, users of the Internet—bodies in the sense of eyes, ears, nervous systems, brains, passions—are appropriated, by way of an extravagant propensity (especially peculiar, at least in its hyperbolic form, to human beings among living creatures) to become the theater of fictions, phantasmagoria, swarms of ghosts. We lend our bodies to the bodiless and then are prone to act in the material world on the strength of that fictitious embodiment. Cervantes's Don Quixote, Flaubert's Emma Bovary, and Conrad's Lord Jim acted in the social world on the basis of fantasies incarnated in them through reading books. This was a haunting that the reader of these novels repeats in reading about it, as he or she raises in turn the specters of Don Quixote, Emma Bovary, and Lord Jim. That is the work or working of ideology. How much more power even than books do these new communications technologies possess to do that work!

New communications technologies are making a quantum leap in the generation and imposition of ideologies. They do this through a kind of hallucinatory hypnotic conjuration. This is easy to see, though by no means easy, or perhaps even possible, to understand clearly. The means of understanding it are caught in the thing to be understood. It used to be the newspaper. Now it is television, cinema, and, increasingly, the Internet. These technologies and media, it might be argued, are in a sense ideologically neutral. They will transmit whatever they are told to say. Nevertheless, as Marshall McLuhan notoriously said, "the medium is the message." I take it that this means, as Derrida in his own way is saying, that a change in medium will change the message. To put this another way, "the medium is the ideology." Ideology, for de Man as for Marx and Althusser, in their somewhat different ways, is not an easily correctable error existing at the level of rational consciousness. It is a powerful unconscious error. In ideology, says Althusser, "men represent their real conditions of existence to themselves in imaginary form."[8] De Man's way of putting this, in the passage I cited in chapter 1 and have just cited again here, is to say that what we call ideology is a confusion between linguistic and natural reality. In ideology, something that is a purely linguistic phantasmal or spectral creation is taken to be an accurate representation of things as they are. This error is taken so much for granted as to be unconscious. Of course that is the way things are, we say to ourselves. Since an ideological aberration is so unconscious, so taken for granted, it is impossible to eradicate it simply by pointing out that it is an error, just as you cannot cure someone of being in love by pointing out the defects of the beloved.

I would add to these formulations, as I have already said, the claim that it is not only language as such that creates and enforces ideology but also language or other signs as generated, stored, retrieved, transmitted, and received by one or another technological prosthesis. This is as true of manuscript and then print culture as it is of digital culture today. In the essay by Althusser just cited, he lists the press, radio, and television as being among "the communications ISA" (that is, "ideological state apparatuses") along with education, the political system, and the juridical system.[9] The regime of print generated the possibility of literature, love letters, philosophy, psychoanalysis, and the modern concept of the nation-state. The new regime of telecommunications is now generating new forms replacing all these. These new media—cinema, television, the Internet—are not just passive matrices that transmit in unchanged form ideological or truth-telling content. They shape what is "sent" by their means, and they transform that "content," willy-nilly, into expressions of the messages that the medium itself powerfully imposes. That is what Derrida means by saying that "in this respect the political regime is secondary." You cannot write or send love letters or literature on the World Wide Web. When you try to do so, they turn into something else. Henry James's *The Golden Bowl* becomes a different thing when I download it from cyberspace. Nor are politics and the sense of citizenship the same to a user of the World Wide Web or to a television viewer as to an old-fashioned reader of newspapers. The transformation of political life by television has been strikingly evident in recent presidential elections in the United States. People vote on the basis of the way the candidates come across on television, not on the basis of an objective assessment of alternative programs, nor, any longer, on the basis of what they read in newspapers. Fewer people read newspapers at all.

It is easy enough to specify the most salient features of the new set of (no doubt ideological) presuppositions being transmitted now everywhere in the world by the new regime of telecommunications. It is easy because many authorities have already told us what they are, among them Jacques Derrida in the passages I have cited. The print age made possible the modern nation-state, the imperialist conquest of the world, colonialism, revolutions like the French and the American, psychoanalysis, love letters, and philosophy from Descartes through Locke and Hume to Kant, Hegel, Nietzsche, Husserl, and Heidegger (the latter three already, unwillingly and anxiously, belonging to the age of the typewriter and the gramophone).

I do not say that print was the single "cause" of these features of culture from the eighteenth to the early twentieth centuries. No doubt other factors contributed, other inventions like the steam engine, the postal system, the spinning jenny, gunpowder in its reinvented European form, more and more powerful and efficient guns, and so on, just as the internal combustion engine, the jet plane, the transistor, rocket engines, and so on, have been necessary for the second industrial revolution. What I do claim, however, is that all these features of the now fading culture depended on print, on newspapers, on clandestine printing presses turning out manifestos, on the printers who brought out, sometimes against censorship, the books of Descartes, Locke, Richardson, Thomas Paine, the Marquis de Sade, and so on, through Dickens, Balzac, Marx, and Dostoevsky, down to Proust and Joyce.

Print encouraged and reinforced the assumption of the separation of subject and object; the separate unity and autonomy of the self; the authority of the "author"; the difficulty or perhaps impossibility of knowing verifiably the mind and heart of the other person; the regime of representation or of a certain kind of mimesis ("*there* is reality," we used to say, "and *here* is its representation in the printed book, to be measured by its truth of correspondence to the extralinguistic reality that is out *there*"); the assumption of the nation-state's ethnic unity and autonomy, reinforced by all those ideological state apparatuses that Althusser lists, including "the communications ISA"; the enforcement of laws and regulations through printing them; the constant indoctrination of a certain national ideology through newspapers; and, finally, the development of the modern research university as the place where the ethos of a given nation state is inculcated in future citizens and servants of that state. Of course, these features were often contested in print media, but the media themselves, I am arguing, constantly reinforced what was being contested, even in the act of putting these features in question. "Give me control of the printing presses," it used to be said, "and I shall control the whole nation." Now such a person might say, "Give me control of all the televisions stations and all the radio talk shows, and I shall control the world."

All these features of print culture, the reader will note, depend on relatively rigid boundaries, frontiers, and walls: between one person and another; one class, race, or gender and another; one medium and another (print, picture, music); one nation-state and another; consciousness and the objects of which consciousness is conscious; extralinguistic things as they are and the representation of those things in language; one time and another (as reinforced, for example, by the tense structure of Western languages, as used in printed historical narratives or in novels).

When the printing press gradually gives way to cinema, television, and the Internet, as is now happening with increasing rapidity, all those frontiers, once more or less solid, are blurred. My self dissolves into a multiplicity of selves, each generated by whatever prosthetic device I happen to be using. That is one reason why love letters will no longer be possible. I become a different self on the telephone or on the Internet, no longer the same person as the one who wrote love letters and sent them through the postal system.

The subject/object dichotomy on which philosophy from Descartes to Husserl depended is also greatly weakened, since the television screen or cinematic screen or computer screen is neither objective nor subjective. It is, rather, an extension of a mobile subjectivity that is "wired" into it. That is one thing Derrida may mean by saying that the new regime of telecommunications will bring an end to philosophy.

The opposition between representation and reality is also shaken. All that swarm of television or cinematic or Internet images, so many ghosts invoked or conjured into existence by the machines, breaks down the distinction between fiction and reality, just as it breaks down the distinctions between present, past, and future. In television programs, it is often difficult to distinguish between news and advertising. A printed novel, at least in Western languages, tells the reader, by the system of verb tenses, whether something being described is to be thought of as taking place in an imaginary present or whether it belongs to something to be thought of as past for the present-tense narration. A television or cinematic image belongs to a strange ghostly species of nonpresent present. It is not always easy to tell whether something is "eyewitness news"—that is, something claimed to be happening at this moment—or a "simulation," as they say. Many people believed and perhaps still believe that the United States did not really land men on the moon, but that the images of the moon landing were created in some television studio. How would you be sure, since the only testimony is those dancing images on the screen?

The new communications media are also transforming the university, for better or for worse, making it less and less a self-enclosed ivory tower serving the interests of a single nation-state, and more and more penetrated by those transnational corporations that pay for its research. The new research university is also a place where new transnational communities and solidarities can be developed. The boundaries of the nation-state are also being broken down—for example, by the Internet, since more or less instantaneous access to sites from all over the world is possible for anyone with a computer, a modem, and a service provider. The Internet is a powerful force for globalization and for the weakening of the nation-state as well as for the assumption that universities serve a given nation-state.

The frontiers between the different media, finally, are also more and more erased. Visual images, auditory sequences (such as music), and words are all indifferently transformed by digitizing into streams of zeroes and ones. Like television and cinema, the computer monitor, with attached or incorporated audio speakers, mixes inextricably images that appeal to eye, ear, and the ability to decipher written language. The new regime of telecommunications is incorrigibly a multimedia affair. Reading as the private and exclusive activity of a man, woman, or child "curled up with a good book" gives way to "surround sight" and "surround sound." The latter inundate eye and ear with a swarm of ghosts that are neither present nor nonpresent, neither incarnate nor discarnate, neither here nor there, neither dead nor undead. These specters have enormous power to invade the mind, feelings, and imagination of the person who raises them by pressing the button on the remote control, and to bend mind and feelings to their shapes. Since many of these phantoms are figures of the utmost violence, as in so much of cinema and television today, it is as if the fears that, in the old print world, lurked in the depths of the unconscious are now brought out into the open, for better or for worse, where we can behold them face to face, see and hear them, not just read about them. The distinction between consciousness and unconsciousness, the basis of psychoanalysis, no longer holds. That, I suppose, is what Derrida may mean by saying the new regime of telecommunications is bringing an end to psychoanalysis, though he also specifies that psychoanalysis in Freud's day depended on letters, the postal system, handwritten or typed records, and the telephone.

Of course, all those books on my shelves are also powerful instruments, when I read them, for the conjuring of ghosts. They are, therefore, powerful tools for reinforcing the ideologies embodied in the medium of the printed book—the ghosts of Hegel's *Geist* or Heidegger's *Sein* when I read Hegel or Heidegger; the ghosts of the unconscious or of Freud's patients Irma, Anna, and Dora when I read Freud's writings; the swarming ghosts, when I read works of fiction, of all those characters in all those novels: Fielding's Tom Jones, Stendhal's Fabrizio, Flaubert's Emma Bovary, George Eliot's Dorothea, Henry James's Isabel, Joyce's Leopold Bloom. All books, as Friedrich Kittler says, "are books of the dead, like those from Egypt that stand at the beginning of [Western!—JHM] literature."[10] Books are so many powerful conjuring devices for raising all those phantoms, the phantoms inhabiting philosophy, psychoanalysis, love letters, and literature.

The ghosts on the television or cinema screen, however, seem much more objective, public, and shared, much less dependent on my own effort of conjuration than is the private act of reading a book. Moreover, as I have said, these new telecommunications technologies, so many new devices for raising ghosts in a new way, also generate new ideological matrices. They break down, for example, the barrier between subject and object, consciousness and the objects of consciousness, that is presupposed and sublated in Hegel's *Phenomenology*.

What should we do in this new and unprecedented situation? As I have suggested, with Derrida's help, the new telecommunications regime may have been created by capitalism, but it exceeds its creators and takes on a force and life of its own. This is what Derrida means by saying that "in this respect the political regime is secondary." This is also what gives us our chance. The openness of the new telecommunications can be appropriated for mobilization or for recuperation, for the creation of new alliances. How can this happen? One answer is to recognize that critique or diagnosis always has a performative as well as a constative dimension. Though these technologies have a powerful effect on the meaning of what is encoded in the new forms, they can nevertheless be appropriated for new forms of cooperative human praxis. We are not simply at their mercy. The appropriation of new communications technologies can take place in the name of new cyberspace communities of diversity. I call these, following Bill Readings, communities of dissensus, that is, communities of those who disagree, who cannot come to consensus. Giorgio Agamben calls this association of diversities "the coming community."[11]

The new communications technologies can also be used to facilitate performative acts of political responsibility. Those acts respond to a demand coming from the future anterior of that "democracy to come" as a sort of possible impossibility. If this perfect democracy were programmed as an inevitable future, if it were "possible" in the sense of being certainly foreseeable, it would not require our praxis. It is only as unforeseeable, as impossible without a break in the programmed continuity, that it invites or demands or obliges our performative praxis.

A model for this might be that sentence in the United States Declaration of Independence: "We hold these truths to be self-evident, that all men are created equal, that they are endowed by their Creator with certain inalienable rights, that among these are life, liberty and the pursuit of happiness." On the one hand, this sentence asserts that these truths are self-evident. They do not require political action in order to be made true. On the other hand, the sentence says: "*We hold* these truths to be self-evident." "We hold" is a performative speech act. It creates the truths it claims are self-evident and invites whoever reads these words to endorse them, to countersign them, to work for their fulfillment, just as an ancestor of mine, Stephen Hopkins of Rhode Island, signed the United States Declaration of Independence. The words invite us to work toward their fulfillment in further performative acts. The promise embodied in those words has by no means yet been entirely fulfilled in the United States. Though the words belong to the past, the past of the moment of the founding of our country, they invite from the future, as a future anterior, their more perfect fulfillment. The words call to us from the horizon of that democracy to come.

Well, what about literary study? Will it survive? Literary study's time is up. There is never time anymore to study literature "for itself," detached from theoretical or political reflection. It would be anachronistic to do so. I doubt very much if it will ever again be time, or if there will ever again be time. This gives yet another meaning, or perhaps the same one, to Hegel's famous dictum that art is a thing of the past:

> In allen diesen Beziehungen ist und bleibt die Kunst nach der Seite ihrer höchsten Bestimmung für uns ein Vergängenes.[12]

> In all these respects art, as far as its highest determination [or calling] is concerned, is and remains for us a thing of the past [*ein Vergängenes*]—a something past, a past thing.[13]

This means, too, though Hegel perhaps did not quite know it, that art, including literature as a form of art, is always also a thing of the future. It never quite successfully gets spirit into sensuous form so we can get on to the end of getting spirit into spiritual form. It is never time yet for art and literature. We dwell, as far as literature and literary study are concerned, in that perpetual in-between, always too late and always too early, untimely.

To shift—on Hegel's back, so to speak—to a slightly different register in conclusion, I assert that there never has been time for literary study. It was never the right time for it. Literary study always was, is now, and always will be untimely. Literature is a name for that component of sign systems, in whatever medium or mode, that is incapable of being rationalized in any form of collective, institutionalized, pragmatically valuable study in the university, whether in the old Cold War university or in the new global university with new departmental configurations now coming into being. This means that "literary study" is an oxymoron. What this oxymoron names will continue to take place, whenever it does (if it does) in odd moments stolen from such more practical concerns as making California competitive in the global economy. Literary study's time is always up. It will survive as it has always survived: as a ghostly revenant, a somewhat embarrassing or alarming spectral visitant at the feast of reason. Literature is potholes in the Information Superhighway, black holes in the Internet Galaxy. Nevertheless, though there's never time, though it is never the time, these holes, potholes or black holes—"literature" as survivor, as a feature of absolute singularity within any cultural forms, in whatever medium—will continue to demand urgently to be "studied," here and now, within whatever new institutional and departmental configurations we devise, and within whatever new regime of telecommunications we inhabit.

CHAPTER 5

Promises, Promises

Speech Act Theory, Literary Theory, and Politico-Economic Theory in Marx and de Man

The term "Marxist aesthetics" might mean Marx's own aesthetic theories. The term may most often be taken, however, to name an aesthetic theory derived from Marxism. This would be a secondary construction based on Marx's critique of political economy, that is, his ideas about labor, production, commodities, value, circulation, money, capital, surplus value, fetishism, class struggle, ideology, alienation, the superstructure, the coming dictatorship of the proletariat, and so on. Marx did not, except here and there—for example, in his celebrated references to Shakespeare's *Timon of Athens* and *Hamlet*, or in an important though elliptical passage at the beginning of the *Grundrisse*—have all that much to say about literature, art, music, or aesthetics.[1] Nevertheless, he often makes easy, and usually ironic, citations from Shakespeare and other writers to reinforce his own argument. It has been left, scholars tend to assume, to subsequent Marxists—Lukács, for example, or Adorno, or Benjamin, or Althusser, or Eagleton (to stick with European theorists), or many others around the world (for example, Fredric Jameson or Michael Sprinker in the United States)—to construct a Marxist aesthetics. What is striking about these theories is their somewhat dismaying diversity and heterogeneity. I am not a Marxist aestheticist, but when

Jacques Derrida, in *Specters of Marx,* makes a similar assertion, he is citing Marx:

> And we do not have to suppose that Marx was in agreement with himself. ("What is certain is that I am not a Marxist," he is supposed to have confided to Engels. Must we still cite Marx as authority to say likewise?)[2]

Marx's writings are not homogeneous, so even Marx was not a Marxist. So-called Marxists, in any case, do not hew closely to any single line of filiation with Marx. It might be better to return to Marx's own writings, as I propose to do here, to see if they might contain already Marx's own aesthetics or might even be, essentially and fundamentally, an aesthetic theory.

It may seem implausible to claim, as Jennifer Bajorek does in a brilliant and challenging dissertation prospectus, that *Capital* is itself, through and through, a work of literary theory—that is, exemplifies a subset of aesthetic theory.[3] It may seem even more implausible to claim, as Bajorek also does, that *Capital,* understood as a work of literary theory, is congruent with Paul de Man's literary theory, or that de Man's literary theory is also, like *Capital,* a critique of political economy. Marx, a literary theorist! De Man, a political theorist in resonance with Marx! Nevertheless, Bajorek's claim is in the right direction. Her claim builds on recent important readings of Marx by Jacques Derrida, Werner Hamacher, Andrzej Warminski, and others.[4]

Political economy is, for Marx, a sign system, a language. Marx at one point in *Das Kapital* (*Capital*) makes this explicit by calling the value system a "hieroglyphic" and making it parallel to human language.

> Es steht daher dem Werte nicht auf der Stirn geschrieben, was er ist. Der Wert verwandelt vielmehr jedes Arbeitsprodukt in eine gesellschaftliche Hieroglyphe. Später suchen die Menschen den Sinn der Hieroglyphe zu entziffern, hinter das Geheimnis ihres eignen gesellschaftlichen Produkts zu kommen, denn die Bestimmung der Gebrauchsgegenstände als Werte ist ihr gesellschaftliches Produkt so gut wie die Sprache.[5]

> Value, therefore, does not have its description branded on its forehead; it rather transforms every product of labor into a social hieroglyphic. Later on, men try to decipher the hiero-

> glyphic, to get behind the secret of their own social product: for the characteristic which objects of utility have of being values is as much men's social product as is their language.[6]

This hieroglyphic text works just as de Man says all "texts" do, among them literary texts: that is, as a "figure (or system of figures) and its deconstruction."[7] The relations of substitution, equivalence, and exchange among commodities within capitalism, as Marx describes them in the first volume of *Capital*, are, it is easy to see, a tropology, or "system of figures." So many yards of linen can be substituted for one coat, and so on, just as one word can be substituted for another in a metaphorical exchange or transfer.

The commodity system is of a specific kind, namely, that sort we call "logocentric." All the metaphorical exchanges, substitutions, and equivalents in this system are regulated by a "logos" that is outside the system while controlling and measuring it from within, immanently. Marx is as adept at understanding, manipulating, and deconstructing logocentrism, especially in its Christian, Hegelian, and capitalist forms, as is Derrida himself, though it is a moot question whether there are remnants of logocentrism in Marx's own thinking. This is the question of whether Marxism is or is not an ontology. That question is not all that easy to answer. Does the Marxist deconstruction of capitalism free itself entirely from the fantasies it so clearly recognizes in capitalism considered as a "text to be read"?

In the capitalist system, the "logos" is represented, according to Marx's analysis, by human labor and then by money. If *Capital* is a rhetorical treatise, or even a work of literary theory in the way it sees the commodity system as like a text dominated by metaphorical exchanges and figurative equivalences, and if Marx's theory is, moreover, one that is congruent with Paul de Man's literary theory in its deconstruction of metaphysics, the converse is also true, as Bajorek observes. When de Man says, "Literary theory can be said to come into being when the approach to literary texts is no longer based on non-linguistic, that is to say historical and aesthetic, considerations or, to put it somewhat less crudely, when the object of discussion is no longer the meaning or the value but the modalities of production and of reception of meaning and of value prior to their establishment—the implication being that this establishment is problematic enough to require an autonomous discipline of critical investigation to consider its possibility and its status," he is employing just the terminology Marx uses in his critique of political economy ("production," "value," "establishment," "meaning," "critical").[8] De Man, however, is using these terms to define literary theory's "coming into being." If *Capital* is a work of literary theory, de Man's work is a critique of political economy. De Man, interviewed by Stefano Rosso, responded to Rosso's question about the "frequent recurrence of the terms 'ideology' and 'politics' " in his recent work by saying, "I don't think I ever was away from these problems, they were always uppermost in my mind."[9] I believe we must take de Man at his word. That what he says is true can easily be demonstrated in his work, in detail.

Marx, however, is like de Man in another way. Marx is not just concerned to describe the capitalist sign system, any more than de Man just wants to show how tropological systems work in literary texts, political texts, or texts in general. Each wants to investigate how the sign systems in question got established, how they function, and how they might, therefore, be changed. Both want to "deconstruct" the systems they study, or to show how they deconstruct themselves. For both Marx and de Man, the goal of "theory," whether economic theory or literary theory, is to suspend the taking for granted of the sign system in question, and even to displace attention away from straightforward description of the way the system operates. Each wants to make an analysis of a given system's generation, of the way in which value and meaning are produced and established within it. The purpose of this, in both cases, is to make a "critique" that will allow or promise the possibility of a new start, perhaps a revolutionary one. Since "generation" and "establishment," in both cases, are speech acts, the impetus these systems have, once they have been generated and established by forms of positing, can be changed only by new forms of speech acts. Marx said, notoriously, in his Eleventh Thesis on Feuerbach, that his goal was not just to interpret the system but to change it: "The philosophers have only *interpreted* the world differently, the point is, to *change* it."[10] Any careful reader of de Man will see that his goal, too, is to liberate his readers from enchantment by erroneous readings, including readings of politics, in order to make way for new forms of politics and of life.

Without denying the big differences between Marx and de Man (one founded a worldwide political movement, the other participated in generating a new form of rhetorical analysis), it can nevertheless be said that a remarkable resonance, or *stimmung*, exists between them in their theoretical and practical procedures and conclusions. Several crucial congruences may be noted beyond the one already noted. The one already noted is the similarity of their deconstructive analyses of the sign systems they confront, so that Marx's *Capital* may indeed be seen as a work of "literary theory" while de Man's essays are works in the critique of political economy. One additional resonance between Marx and de Man is the stress, in both cases, on the way "critique" is not just constative, descriptive, truth telling but also performative, a speech act, a way of doing things with words. No reader of *Capital* can doubt that Marx's goal is not just neutral description. He wants to use his "critique of political economy" to promise strategies of action that will change the system or foresee its inevitable change. *Capital*, like *The Communist Manifesto*, is a work of messsianic promise. De Man's later work, in a similar way, was increasingly concerned with the way in which both literature and literary theory (like political theory, such as Rousseau's *Social Contract*) are speech acts, that is, ways of doing things with words. The problems of ideology and politics were never far from de Man's mind.

However unlike the two authors seem, both have liberation as their ultimate goal. Both recognize that this will be facilitated by emancipatory speech acts, not by mere analysis of a bad state of things. Jacques Derrida's way of formulating this is to define the act of interpretation itself, if it is done properly, as interventionist, performative, initiatory, a way of working toward the horizon of that "democracy to come" for which all men and women long, or ought to long. In *Specters of Marx,* Derrida speaks of "this dimension of performative interpretation, that is, of an interpretation that transforms the very thing it interprets."[11] He goes on to note that this formulation is unorthodox with regard both to traditional speech theory and to what Marx says in his Eleventh Thesis on Feuerbach.

De Man did not come for nothing from a family that had been socialist for generations. Both Marx and de Man wielded not physical action but language as their weapon of choice—in both cases, a powerful performative rhetoric of interpretation. Not the least puissant component of that language, in both cases, was rhetorical or linguistic analysis, the deconstruction of tropes or the demonstration that they deconstruct themselves.

To that may added the way both used irony. Both Marx and de Man are ironic writers through and through. Irony, however, as de Man correctly says in "The Concept of Irony," clearly has a "performative function" as well: "Irony consoles and it promises and it excuses."[12] It also functions as a tool for destroying what it ironizes.

A further congruence between Marx and de Man is the development, in both cases, of a theory of performative speech acts radically different from the standard theory derived from the work of J. L. Austin. In both cases, the sign systems they are analyzing—for Marx, the capitalist system; for de Man, literary works, or such works of political theory as Rousseau's *Social Contract*—operate performatively, on their own, without human intervention, certainly without the intervention of the self-conscious I or ego deliberately uttering a performative (for example, saying "I promise" in the proper circumstances). The latter features were essential requisites for a "felicitous" performative in J. L. Austin's theory in *How to Do Things with Words*.[13]

Every careful reader of *Capital* will have noticed in the early section, "Commodities," two remarkable passages, one where linen speaks, and the other where a table walks and stands on its head, in a spooky table-turning whereby the table speaks "metaphysical subtleties and theological niceties" ("metaphysischer Spitzfindigkeit und theologischer Mucken").[14] Within the capitalist system, men and women neither speak decisively nor make that messianic promise of the end of labor's alienation which is the central message of Marxism. It is the commodities, products of human labor—linen or a table—that speak and promise, that make decisions, on their own. Men and women are spoken to, interpellated, summoned, brought into existence as what they are within the stage of capitalism in which they live, by what that linen and that table think and say.

Let me look a little more closely at these two passages, to see just what they say and just how they work. I want to juxtapose them to de Man's assertions in order to demonstrate that the same sort of rhetorical analysis is employed in both cases. Both, moreover, ascribe an autonomous performative power to sign systems. Man in society may have created them, but they now act on their own, independently of any conscious human volition.

The first passage has to do with a species of revelation or uncovering that takes place through a strange form of speech. Marx constantly stresses the way the hidden abstract value generated by undifferentiated human labor shines forth in the coat or the linen when linen and coat are brought into relation with one another, even though "there is not an atom of matter" involved in this value. Similarly, in the following passage, speech is not fictitiously ascribed to cloth, but Marx asserts that it does literally speak. It speaks, moreover, in several different "dialects," each significantly different from all the others:

Man sieht, alles, was uns die Analyse des Warenwerts vorher sagte, sagt die Leinwand selbst, sobald sie in Umgang mit andrer Ware, dem Rock, tritt. Nur verrät sie ihre Gedanken in der allein geläufigen Sprache, der Warensprache. Um zu sagen, daß die Arbeit in der abstrakten Eigenschaft menschlicher Arbeit ihren eignen Wert bildet, sagt sie, daß der Rock, soweitt er ihr gleichgilt, also Wert ist, aus derselben Arbeit besteht wie die Leinwand. Um zu sagen, daß ihre geläuterte Wertgegenständlichkeit von ihrem steifleinenen Körper verschieden ist, sagt sie, daß Wert aussieht wie ein Rock und daher sie selbst als Wertding dem Rock gleicht wie ein Ei dem andern. Nebenbei bemerkt hat auch die Warensprache, außer dem Hebräischen, noch viele andre mehr oder minder korrekte Mundarten. Das deutsche "Wertsein" drückt z. B. minder schlagend aus als das romanische Zeitwort valere, valer, valoir, daß die Gleichsetzung der Ware B mit der Ware A der eigne Wertausdruck der Ware A ist. "Paris ist eine Messe wert."[15]

We see, then, that everything our analysis of the value of commodities previously told us is repeated by the linen itself, as soon as it enters into association with another commodity, the coat. Only it reveals its thoughts in a language with which it alone is familiar, the language of commodities [*der Warensprache*]. In order to tell us that labor creates its own value in its abstract quality of being human labor, it says that the coat, in so far as it counts as its equal, i.e. is value, consists of the same labor as it does itself. In order to inform us that its sublime [A better translation might be "purified."—JHM] objectivity [*ihre geläuterte Wertgegenständlichkeit*] as a value differs from its stiff and starchy existence as a body, it says that value has the appearance of a coat, and therefore that in so far as the linen itself is an object of value [*Wertding*], it and the coat are as alike as two peas. Let us note, incidentally, that the language of commodities also has, apart from Hebrew, plenty of other more or less correct dialects [*noch viele andre mehr oder minder korrekte Mundarten*]. The German word *Wertsein* (to be worth), for instance, brings out less strikingly than the Romance verb

> *valere*, *valer*, *valoir* that the equating [*Gleichsetzung*] of commodity B with commodity A is the expression of value proper to commodity A. *Paris vaut bien une messe!* [Paris is worth (deserves) a Mass.][16]

This is in many ways a remarkable passage, requiring much finesse to read and comprehend, even with all the help in doing this provided by Werner Hamacher's magisterial "*Lingua Amissa*: The Messianism of Commodity-Language and Derrida's *Specters of Marx*."[17] Hamacher's essay is centered on this passage. What in the world can it mean to say that the linen speaks—that it says, happily for Marx, just what Marx himself has been saying about commodities and value, and that it speaks in several different dialects, at least Hebrew, German, and French, not to mention English in the translation? The logic behind Marx's claim that linen speaks must be the following: Since the value that the linen embodies is entirely generated by social relations, and since language, as Marx argues in *The German Ideology* as well as in *Capital*, is inextricably entwined within social relations, inseparable from them, then it follows that because the linen manifests or reveals its value through its relation to the coat, it must do so in speech, since everything social is embodied in language. Since commodities are part of an intricate sign system, they can properly be said to speak, and of course they speak "the language of commodities." This is not a figurative invention or a "poetic" way of speaking on Marx's part. It is not a prosopopoeia ascribing speech to something inanimate. It is the literal truth. The linen speaks.

What the linen says reveals the strange way in which commodities have value. Value, it says, is not the same thing as the sensuous materiality of the linen, "its stiff and starchy existence as a body," but a "purified" or "refined" "objectivity as value" ("geläuterte Wertgegenständlichkeit"). A purified or clarified objectivity is something exceeding direct human comprehension and only visible in the signs of it, signs that are always incommensurate with what they signify—in this case, the coat as sign or "appearance" of the linen's value. These signs are, that is, what rhetoricians call "catachreses." The sublime objectivity of the linen's value "has the appearance of a coat" ("aussieht wie ein Rock"). Value cannot be seen directly. It can only appear in signs for it—in this case, in its appearance as a coat, the exchange equivalent of the linen.

From the point of view of their use value, the linen and the coat are quite different from one another. From the perspective of their exchange value, they "are as alike as two peas" (or two eggs, when the linen speaks German). This means that the relation of the coat and the linen is an odd sort of tautological metaphorical equivalence. The linen is like the coat. The coat is like the linen. This likeness, however, is not just a similarity but an identity, although (or rather therefore) one may be substituted for the other, as in metaphor. All this the linen says, speaking the language of commodities.

As Werner Hamacher demonstrates, however, and as Jacques Derrida implies in *Specters of Marx*, this saying is also a performative promise. The linen promises its possession of value and its exchangeability with the coat. This promise is embodied in the speaking appearance of the linen as value. It promises something that we would not otherwise have known, or it brings us good news not otherwise available—namely, that the commodity system will work, that there is value, *Wert*. Like all sublime revelations, it also makes a messianic promise: *I promise you I have value, and my value is manifested in the appearance of a coat, thereby guaranteeing my exchangeability with the coat*. A promise, to be a promise, must be capable of not being kept. In that sense, it may possibly not be a "felicitous" promise, in the Austinian sense of felicity. A promise is not really a promise until it is fulfilled. It binds the future. It is only completely itself in the future. That fulfillment, however, may not happen, in which case the promise would not really be a promise. This applies to the promise the linen makes; to the general promise global capitalism makes these days, a promise of peace and prosperity for all; to the promise Jesus makes in the Book of Revelation that He will come quickly; to the promise Marx finds within capitalism of its self-destruction through its internal contradictions; and to the promise Marx makes of the inevitable coming of the Communist millennium. All of these promises are subject to the general aporia of the promise as a form of speech act.

The justifiability of the religio-metaphysical language I have been using is indicated not only in Marx's attention to the word "value," in its various dialectics, but also in the curious phrase in French that ends the paragraph. "Value" is a Christian/metaphysical term, as, for example, in all the use of economic terminology in Christ's parables to express the ultimate value of the Kingdom of Heaven, something incommensurate with any earthly value, just as Marx's "abstract value" is a transcendental exceeding of any of its embodiments, manifestations, or *parousias* (in the appearance of a coat, for example). The Indo-European root for *valere*, *val-*, is the same as the toot of *Gewalt*, the key word in Walter Benjamin's "Zur Kritik der Gewalt" ("Towards a Critique of Violence").[18] "*Gewalt* is usually translated in English as "violence," as in the standard translation of Benjamin's title. To be of worth, to have value, *valere*, is to have executive or performative power, even violent power, *Gewalt*. The linen speaks Hebrew because that is the language of commerce [An ironic anti-Semitic feature is present in this nuance.—JHM], but also because Hebrew is a sacred language, the language of Scripture. The linen also, however, speaks German and French, uttering different ways of saying that commodity A is equal in value to commodity B, and that this equation is the expression of value proper to commodity A. Marx says that the Romance dialect is best apparently because it best expresses the nuance that moves from mundane commercial worth to sublime transcendent value. When Henry IV agreed in 1593 to convert to Catholicism, in order to gain the French throne, he is supposed to have said, "Paris vaut bein une messe!"—that is, in the English dialectic also spoken by linen, "Paris is certainly worth a Mass." In the Catholic Mass, bread and wine, of little worth in themselves, are transformed, transubstantiated, into the body and blood of Christ. Henry IV cynically turned this on its head by saying that it was worth converting to Catholicism and participating in a Catholic Mass in order to gain worldly sovereign power over Paris. He exchanged a Mass for Paris. Marx's point, made with allusive wit, is that this rich and complex double use of "to be worth" is possible only in French or in some other Romance language.

Marx's philological attention to nuances of implication in different languages is not unlike Paul de Man's attention to Kant's play on *Angemessenheit* and *Unangemessenheit*, for example, or to Kleist's exploitation of German words containing *fall* (*Beifall, Einfall, Zurückfall, Fälle*), or to Friedrich Schlegel's making much "of plays on *stehen* and *verstehen*, *stellen* and *verstellen*, of *verücken* [insanity], and so on"—verbal jokes that can work only in German.[19] Another similarity between Marx's philology and de Man's may be, in both cases, the use of philology for ironic polemical purposes. "Paris vaut bien une messe!" was already ironic when Henry IV said it, or was first said to have said it. It is even more ironic when Marx appropriates it to imply, indirectly, the consonance between the language of commodities, with its "metaphysical subtleties and theological niceties," and theological language proper, just as de Man's ironic distance from Heidegger is indicated when de Man changes Heidegger's pompous "Die Sprache spricht" to "Die Sprache verspricht (sich)," meaning that de Man changes Heidegger's "Language speaks" to "Language makes a slip of the tongue, or contradicts itself, or promises (itself)": oh, wonderful German language![20]

I am even now, however, not quite through with my passage from *Capital.* In the sentence just after the paragraph I have quoted, Marx uses another metaphor when he says "der Körper der Ware B [wird] zum Wertspiegel der Ware A" ("the physical body of commodity B becomes a mirror for the value of commodity A").[21] Marx's footnote to this sentence compares this mirroring to the way the concept "man" emerges when two men confront one another and each sees the other as his mirror image:

> [B]espiegelt sich der Mensch zuerst nur in einem andren Menschen. Erst durch die Beziehung auf den Menschen Paul als seinesgleichen, bezieht sich der Mensche Peter auf sich selbst als Mensch. Damit gilt ihn aber auch der Paul mit Haut und Haaren, in seiner paulinische Leiblichkeit, als Erscheinungsform der Gattung Mensch.[22]

> [A] man first sees and recognizes himself [*bespiegelt sich*] in another man. Peter only relates himself as a man through his relation to another man, Paul, in whom he recognizes his likeness [*als seinesgleichen*]. With this, however, Paul also becomes from head to toe, in his physical form as Paul, the form of appearance of the species man for Peter.[23]

The names "Peter" and "Paul" are not just any names. They recall their biblical counterparts and so bring "theological niceties" in once more. Moreover, the footnote about Peter and Paul echoes Rousseau's fable of a primitive man confronting another man and thinking he is a giant, thus inaugurating language in a lying metaphor. What Marx says also anticipates the analyses by Derrida and de Man, in their essays on Rousseau, of the way the concept "Man" emerges from the mirroring confrontation of one man with another and from an erroneous metaphor that is the origin of language. The names Marx chooses have yet another resonance, however—they may allude to the proverb about robbing Peter to pay Paul. This proverb presumably means, among other things, that since our obligations to both Saint Peter and Saint Paul are infinite, because both are intermediaries for our infinite and unfulfillable obligation to God, robbing one to pay the other is circular, robbing the same to pay the same. Such robbery leaves the one who does it just as much in debt as ever, but now a thief to boot. [The "mirror stage" in Lacan is also anticipated in this sequence, but I forbear to follow that similarity in dissimilarity here.—JHM]

The phrase "metaphysical subtleties and theological niceties" comes at the beginning of another remarkable paragraph in *Capital*, the one about the dancing table. Viewed from the perspective of its use value, there is nothing mysterious about a table:

> Es ist sinnenklar, daß der Mensch durch seine Tätigkeit die Formen der Naturstoffe in einer ihm nützlichen Weise verändert. Die Form des Holzes z. B. wird verändert, wenn man aus ihm einen Tisch macht. Nichtsdestoweniger bleibt der Tisch Holz, ein ordinäres sinnliches Ding.[24]
>
> It is absolutely clear [*sinnenklar*] that, by his activity [*Tätigkeit*], man changes the forms of the materials of nature in such a way as to make them useful to him. The form of wood, for instance, is altered if a table is made out of it. Nevertheless the table continues to be wood, an ordinary, sensuous thing.[25]

No problem. The mystery begins when the table becomes a commodity—that is, something with exchange value as representing a certain quantity of undifferentiated human labor:

> Aber sobald er als Ware auftritt, verwändelt er sich in ein sinnlich übersinnliches Ding. Er steht nicht nur mit seinem Füßen suf dem Boden, sondern er stellt sich allen anderen Waren gegenüber auf den Kopf, und entwickelt aus seinen Holzkopf Grillen, viel wunderlicher, als wenn er aus freien Stücken zu tanzen begänne.[26]
>
> But as soon as [the table] emerges as a commodity [*als Ware*], it changes into a thing which transcends sensuousness [*ein sinnlich übersinnliches Ding*]. It not only stands with its feet on the ground, but, in relation to all other commodities, it stands on its head, and evolves out of its wooden brain grotesque ideas [*Grillen*], far more wonderful than if it were to begin dancing of its own free will.[27]

Here the table becomes another example of immaterial materiality, a sensible supersensible thing ("ein sinnlich übersinnliches Ding"). Marx, the reader will remember, asserted in a famous formulation that Hegel had stood things on their heads, and that Marxist thinking had as its goal to set them right side up again. This passage is an example of that, since it shows the process whereby the table appears to be standing on its head and evolving out of its wooden brain all those "metaphysical subtleties and theological niceties" that Marx sees operative in bourgeois Christian ideology. The passage is permeated with Marx's characteristic ironic wit. It contains, once more, a disguised reference to religion—in this case, in the debased form of spiritualism and table-turning. In table-turning, it was believed, ghosts come back from the dead, make the table around which the adepts sit vibrate and dance, and prophesy the future (a form of messianic promise), just as my citations from de Man and Marx bring their speech back from the dead, for present purposes, to let them be heard making new promises for the future. Marx's footnote to the passage just quoted annotates the reference to spiritualism:

> Man erinnert sich, daß China und die Tische zu tanzen anfingen, als alle übrige Welt stillzustehn schien—um den andern Mut zu machen.[28]

> One may recall that China and the tables began to dance when the rest of the world appeared to be standing still—*pour encourager les autres* [to encourage the others].[29]

An editorial note in the English translation explains that this is "a reference to the simultaneous emergence in the 1850s of the Taiping revolt in China and the craze for spiritualism which swept over upper-class German society" while the rest of the world was "standing still" in the reactionary period after the failure of the 1848 revolutions.[30] The dancing tables encouraged the others to get moving again and to advance, through revolutionary activity, toward that promised democracy to come—that is, the dictatorship of the proletariat.

Three paragraphs later, in a powerfully argued comparison of what he calls the fetishism of commodities with religious fantasies, Marx makes what I would call a protodeconstructive analysis of "der mystische Charakter der Ware" ("the mystical character of the commodity"):[31]

> . . . hat die Warenform und das Wertverhältnis der Arbeitsprodukte, worin sie sich darsetellt, mit ihrer physischen Natur und den daraus entspringenden dinglichen Beziehungen gar nichts zu schaffen. Es ist nur das bestimmte gesellschaftliche Verhältnis der Menschen selbst, welches hier für sie gaukelspielerische Form eines Verhältnisses von Dingen annimmt. Um daher ein Gleichnis zu finden, müssen wir in die Nebelregion der religiösen Welt flüchten. Hier scheinen die Produkte des menschlichen Kopfes mit eignem Leben begabt, untereinander und mit den Menschen in Verhältnis stehende selbstständige Gestalten. So in der Warenwelt die Produkte der menschlichen Hand. Dies nenne ich den Fetischismus, der den Arbeitsprodukten anklebt, sobald sie als Waren produziert werden, und daher von der Warenproduktion unzertrennlich ist.[32]

> . . . the commodity-form, and the value-relation of the products of labor within which it appears, have absolutely no connection [*gar nichts zu schaffen*] with the physical nature of the commodity and the material [*dinglich*] relations arising out of this. It is nothing but the definite social relation between men themselves which assumes here, for them, the fantastic [*gaukelspielerische*] form of a relation between things. In order, therefore, to find an analogy we must take flight into the misty realm of religion [*in die Nebelregion der religiösen Welt*]. There the products of the human brain appear as autonomous figures [Marx means gods and goddesses.—JHM] endowed with a life of their own, which enter into relations both with each other and with the human race. So it is in the world of commodities with the products of men's hands. I call this the fetishism [*Dies nenne ich den Fetischismus*] which attaches itself to the products of labor as soon as they are produced as commodities, and is therefore inseparable from the production of commodities.[33]

What Marx here calls "fetishism" he elsewhere calls "ideology," defined by him in a way strictly consonant with Paul de Man's definition of ideology in *The Resistance to Theory*. I cite it once more: "What we call ideology is precisely the confusion of linguistic with natural reality, of reference with phenomenalism."[34] In Marx's case, it is the strange hieroglyphic language which linen speaks that is taken as a natural reality. For de Man, it is a feature of literary texts that they operate on their own, without the intervention of human will and consciousness, as when he says that Shelley's "The Triumph of Life" "warns" that though festishized relations are fantasy, they are inevitably "reintegrated in a historical and aesthetic system of recuperation that repeats itself regardless of the exposure of its fallacy."[35] The same irresistible fallacy is for Marx a determining feature of those sign systems that arise spontaneously as soon as men (and women, too, we ought to add) begin producing commodities and exchanging them.

This is what I mean by calling *Capital* a work of literary theory. I add to this the claim that it is not just any sort of literary theory but a deconstructive literary theory *avant la lettre*. Marx's analysis of festishism treats the social commodity system as a sign system and does with it just what literary theory does in de Man's formulation. It investigates "the modalities of production and of reception of meaning and of value prior to their establishment."[36] Another way to put this is to say that deconstruction, whether it acknowledges this or not, is the inheritor, faithful or not, of a form of analysis developed by Marx. If Marx is a deconstructionist, deconstruction is a form of Marxism.

I conclude with an observation about Marx's and de Man's relevance today. De Man wrote his essays in longhand, as did Marx. So far as I know, de Man never touched a computer. Both de Man and Marx still belonged to the age of handwriting and print. Nevertheless, I claim that de Man's politico-economico-literary theory applies just as well to digital "texts" as to printed ones. As for Marx, it is sometimes said that Marx's deconstructive analysis or "critique" of capitalist economy is no longer relevant, has become hopelessly old-fashioned and inapplicable, because he was describing an early stage of industrialism, of capitalism, and of Western imperialism. Our present information age, the age of the Internet and of what Derrida calls the new regime of telecommunications, is no longer governed to the same degree by the distribution and manufacture of physical commodities like linen and coats, Marx's examples. We are dominated, rather, by the generation, storage, retrieval, and circulation of information, including literature and money as well as music, oral and written speech, digitized images, and stocks and bonds, all dwelling on the same plane of digital existence. I answer that Marx, as I have shown, already saw commodities as disembodied, insofar as they embody exchange value. They are just so much socially generated "value"—that is, they are forms of information communicated by impersonal speech, as when the linen speaks, or when the table dances and expresses the metaphysical subtleties embodied in its wooden brain. As Werner Hamacher correctly says, and as I have already stressed, these are not projected personifications or prosopopoeias. They are literal descriptions. The cloth does literally speak, in the language of commodities, just as the computer speaks, in the language of zeroes and ones.

Marx's system of exchangeable commodities, which leads to the money system and then to advanced capitalism, does have, after all, a material embodiment or base, and so does our worldwide cyberspace information system. The linen, the coat, the paper on which money is printed, the computer's hard drive, the modulations of those electrical or optical currents necessary to transmit information—these are all material bases for the sign systems of value equivalence and exchange that they sustain. Marx's analysis of capitalism prepares prophetically for the information age and applies to it perfectly well. Whether he would have rejoiced in our information age as showing how right he was, or whether he would have seen it as an ultimate form of alienation that just puts off even further the happy day of the Marxist millennium, is another question, one not all that easy to answer.

CHAPTER 6

On the Authority of Literature

Poets are the unacknowledged legislators of the world.
—Percy Bysshe Shelley

What does it mean to believe, choose, or act "on the authority of literature"? Where does a text said to be "literature" get its authority? What is that authority's source, ground, or guarantee? Who or what validates it or authenticates it, "signs off" on it, takes responsibility for it? The author? The reader? Some divine or supernatural power? The circumambient society? The work's sources or influences? Some pre-existing reality that the work accurately copies, imitates, or represents? Can a work perhaps be self-authorizing? Just what would that mean—"self-authorizing"? All these ways of ascribing authority to literary works have had valence in the Western tradition, often at the same time, in incoherent profusion, down to the present day, as I shall show.

At the same time, it must be remembered and squarely faced, though it is difficult to do so for a lover of literature like me, that in spite of the lip service paid these days to literature's authority by politicians, the media, and educationists, fewer and fewer people, in Europe and America, at least, actually spend much time reading "literature" in the old-fashioned sense of canonical works in printed form—Chaucer, Shakespeare, Milton, Pope, Wordsworth, George Eliot, Virginia Woolf and the rest, for English literature. Literature has been granted enormous authority in our culture, but though that authority may still be tacitly or even explicitly acknowledged—for example, by the media—it is no longer so pragmatically operative, as no candid observer can doubt. If the books just stay there on the shelves, their authority is only potential. They must be read to be performatively effective.

If you are watching a film or television or playing a video game or surfing the Internet, you cannot at the same time be reading Shakespeare.

People spend, as all the statistical evidence suggests, more and more time doing the former. Poetry, it might be argued, does little legislating these days, unacknowledged or otherwise. Fewer and fewer people are decisively influenced even by such reading as they do. Radio, television, cinema, popular music, and now the Internet—these are more decisive in legislating citizens' ethos and values as well as in filling their minds and feelings with imaginary worlds. It is these virtual realities, rather than strictly literary ones, that have most performative efficacy these days to generate people's feelings, behavior, and value judgments. To speak of literature's authority is already to speak, to some degree, of a historical epoch that began in the late seventeenth or early eighteenth century in Europe with the rise of modern democracies and their concomitant print cultures. That epoch is now, perhaps, rapidly vanishing, whatever teachers of literature say, write, or do. Nevertheless, if someone happens for some reason to pick up *Hamlet* or *Middlemarch* or Yeats's poems or Tolstoi's *Anna Karenina*, these works may still exert their magic power. Literature still has great authority over me and, no doubt, over many others. Just what is that authority, and how does it work, or how has it worked, or how should it work?

When I was a child, I did not want to know that *The Swiss Family Robinson* had an author, much less that the book was originally written in German and that I was reading a translation. I did not want to know that the name on the title page designated the person who had made it all up. I did not think of it as a "fiction." Nor did I think the book copied some external historical reality. To me, the words printed on those pages seemed to be a magic formula allowing me access to a pre-existing virtual reality attainable only through just those English words. I did not have to wait for the New Criticism in the persons of William K. Wimsatt Jr. and Monroe Beardsley to discover or invent the "intentional fallacy" and so detach the author from the work, or for Michel Foucault's "What Is an Author?" or Roland Barthes's "The Death of the Author" to kill off the author. For me, he or she was never alive, or rather, even if I might have reluctantly admitted that the author existed, he or she did not seem to me the authorizing source and guarantee of the work, only a mediator or a transparent window to an already existing hidden world.

Though I am older and wiser now and know that Shakespeare wrote *Hamlet* and Johann David Wyss wrote *The Swiss Family Robinson*, I still feel more or less the same way about literary works. You can encounter Hamlet only by reading *Hamlet* or seeing a performance of it; Dorothea Brooke, only by reading *Middlemarch*; the Swiss family Robinson and their adventures, only by reading *The Swiss Family Robinson*. All the background information in the world—knowledge of the author's psychology and life, investigation of his or her "sources," knowledge of the author's society—will not predict, explain, or account retrospectively for Hamlet, for Dorothea Brooke, or for the Swiss Family Robinson and for the worlds those characters inhabit, nor for any of the thousands and millions of other virtual realities that literary works create or give access to when they are read. Moreover, I claim that each of those realities is *sui generis*, unique, individual, singular. You cannot get from one to another of them. An impenetrable barrier separates them from one another. This is true even for works by the same author except, perhaps, for serial works like Trollope's Barset novels, in which the same characters reappear. Even there, however, I am not so sure. The Dalloways are quite different in Virginia Woolf's *A Voyage Out* from what they are in *Mrs. Dalloway*.

Marcel Proust, I am happy to say, affirmed much the same thing about the "worlds" to which literature gives access. He ascribed the same power to lies, however, as to artworks, including literary ones. Moreover, he saw works by the same author as offering access to a single unique world, the world that belonged solely to that author. In that remaining mystification about the originating unity and authority of the author, he differed from my childish assumption that *The Swiss Family Robinson* had no author. Here is what Proust says about lies:

> The lie, the perfect lie [*Le mensonge, le mensonge parfait*], about people we know, about the relations we have had with them, about our motive [*notre mobile*] for some action, formulated by us in totally different terms, the lie as to what we are, whom we love, what we feel with regard to a being who loves us and believes that he has fashioned us in his own image [*nous avoir façonnés semblables à lui*] because he keeps on kissing us morning, noon, and night—that lie is one of the few things in the world that can open windows for us on to what is new and unknown, that can awaken in us sleeping senses for the contemplation of universes that otherwise we should never have known [*puisse nous ouvrir des perspectives sur du nouveau, sur de l'inconnu, puisse ouvrir en nous des sens endormis pour la contemplation d'univers que nous n'aurions jamais connus*].[1]

In a somewhat later passage, Proust's narrator says more or less the same thing about artworks:

> Each artist seems thus to be the native of an unknown country [*une patrie inconnue*], which he himself has forgotten, and which is different from that whence another great artist, setting sail for the earth [*appareillant pour la terre*], will eventually emerge.[2]

This general art doctrine is applied specifically to the music of Proust's fictive composer Vinteuil, whose music is the product of a prayer, call, or invocation that brings here musical forms that are in secret resonance with the composer's lost homeland:

> Composers do not actually remember this lost fatherland, but each of them remains all his life unconsciously attuned to it [*inconsciemment accordé en un certain unisson avec elle*]; he is delirious with joy when he sings in harmony with his native land.[3]

Artworks expand our lives by giving us access to all these incommensurate virtual universes. "The only true voyage of discovery," says Marcel,

> the only really rejuvenating experience [*le seul bain de Jouvence*], would be . . . to see the universe through the eyes of another, of a hundred others, to see the hundred universes that each of them sees, that each of them is; and this we can do with an Elstir [Proust's fictive Impressionist painter], with a Vinteuil.[4]

Our knowledge of these other worlds is owing to the artworks such creators have invented (that is, both made up and discovered) for us.

In a curious way, nevertheless, these unknown worlds are not dependent for their existence on the works that open them up, even though we can know them only through those works:

> Mlle Vinteuil's friend had disentangled, from papers more illegible than strips of papyrus dotted with a cuneiform script, the formula, eternally true and forever fertile, of this unknown joy, the mystic hope of the crimson Angel of the Dawn.[5]

"The mystic hope of the crimson Angel of the Dawn" refers to Marcel's metaphorical language describing the vision Vinteuil's septet opens up for him. If Vinteuil's septet had not been posthumously deciphered, his homeland would still have existed but would have remained unknown. Marcel draws a parallel between this contingency and what would have happened if Wagner or Hugo had died after they had written only their comparatively insignificant early works. What Marcel says of Hugo, if he had died without having written a line of the *Légende des Siècles* or the *Contemplations*, would apply also to Vinteuil's septet if Mademoiselle Vinteuil's friend had not done her laborious work of decipherment:

> What is to us his real achievement would have remained purely potential [*virtuel*], as unknown as those universes to which our perception does not reach, of which we shall never have any idea.[6]

For Proust, those incommensurable universes always already exist, one for each author, composer, or artist. These universes exist prior to the works that bring them down to this earth. They would continue to exist even if every copy of Vinteuil's septet, Wagner's *Tristan und Isolde*, Hugo's *Contemplations*, or Proust's *Recherche* were destroyed. A parallel may be drawn between what Marcel says here and two analogous assertions. Henry James, in the preface to *The Golden Bowl*, says that what he calls "the clear matter" of the novel exists independently of his notation of it in the actual words of the text. Jacques Derrida, in "Ponctuations: Le temps d'un thèse," says that the realm to which a literary work refers precedes that work and would go on existing even if all copies of the work were destroyed.[7]

A somewhat different version of this assumption had power in the long Christian tradition of the dream vision, still alive in secularized or heretical form in Shelley's "The Triumph of Life," in Blake's *The Marriage of Heaven and Hell*, or even in Dickens's *A Christmas Carol*. These writers were distantly following the example of the Hebrew prophets or of St. John, the presumed author of the Book of Revelation. In all these cases, the implication or even the overt assumption is that the realm to which the dream vision gives access has an existence prior to and independent of the account of it given by the poet or prophet. Dante's *Divine Comedy* is the most powerful and sublime of such dream visions. In all these cases, in quite diverse forms, the basic assumption is that the poem's authority derives not from the words of the poem and not from an inventive power in the poet but from the poem's accurate representation, in words, of a pre-existing supernal reality to which those words alone give other people access. The poet has "made up" nothing. He or she has only made an accurate description. The poet serves as a viewing glass for an otherwise unknown and unknowable world. That this world may be fictitious, factitious, perhaps the work of the devil (How would you know for sure about that?), explains the deep suspicion that church authorities had of dream visions. The canonized dream visions—for example, those represented by the prophetical books of the Old Testament or the Hebrew Bible—were the source of the church's authority. Trying to add new ones is another matter, perhaps a matter for burning.

William Blake transfers this religious notion of the prophet's authority to the poet's independent authority. He redefines prophets retrospectively as poets. In the visionary colloquy between the poet and the prophets Isaiah and Ezekiel in *The Marriage of Heaven and Hell*, Blake records the following assertion by Ezekiel:

> [W]e of Israel taught that the Poetic Genius (as you now call it) was the first principle and all the others merely derivative, which was the cause of our despising the Priests & Philosophers of other countries, and prophesying that all Gods would at last be proved to originate in ours & to be the tributaries of the Poetic Genius.[8]

My apparently mystified and childish notion of the independent existence of the world to which the words of *The Swiss Family Robinson* give access has, somewhat unexpectedly, support from authors as diverse and as sophisticated as Proust, James, and Derrida, not to speak of prophetical works and dream visions. Nevertheless, it must be confessed that this concept of literature's authority has relatively little general support these days, either from philosophers and theoreticians or from ordinary readers.

For Aristotle, the literary work, of which tragedy was for him paradigmatic, was embedded in the social reality it served and had a pragmatic, down-to-earth function within it. A tragedy, says Aristotle, is an imitation of an action, but that action most often is embodied in a story or myth that all the spectators of the tragedy already know—for example, the story of Oedipus. Those stories generally have to do with the enigmatic and inscrutable relations between gods and men (as, for example, in the unanswered question of why the god Apollo, in Sophocles's *Oedipus the King*, has decided to punish Oedipus so cruelly by making him unintentionally kill his father and marry his mother). Nevertheless, the social function of tragedy, for Aristotle, is this-worldly, even bodily. It purges from body and soul the bad emotions of pity and fear by arousing them and giving them an object. A tragedy functions thereby as a species of cathartic homeopathy. The authority of a tragedy, for Aristotle, does not derive from its author but from its inherence in society as a complex institution using myths known and owned by everyone for a specific collective social purpose.

Aristotle's assumptions about poetry's authority still have force in the widespread nineteenth- and twentieth-century assumption that literature is placed within its general circumambient culture as a public institution. Literature draws its authority from its social function and from the validity conferred on it by its users, and by those journalists and critics who ascribe value and use to it. The literary work's authority derives perhaps from the belief that the work is an accurate representation of social reality and reigning ideological assumptions, or perhaps from a belief that the work shapes those through effective deployment of what Kenneth Burke calls a strategy for encompassing a situation. The latter hypothesis recognizes a puissant performative function for literature. In all these cases, however, literature's authority is social. That authority is conferred from outside literature, not least by belief in its truth of correspondence to social things as they are.

Charles Dickens reaffirms the ideological assumption that good literature is validated by its truth of correspondence when he defends *Oliver Twist* by claiming that its representation of Nancy is "TRUE," or when he defends the spontaneous combustion of Krook in *Bleak House* in the same way. Dickens adduces a whole series of supposed historical cases of spontaneous combustion—in Verona, in Rheims, in Columbus, Ohio.[9] Recent evidence, quite surprisingly, has confirmed Dickens's belief, though such cases are not truly "spontaneous." They need some external source of combustion—a fire in a fireplace, for example—that ignites the victim. Does that modern scientific corroboration give the scene of Krook's spontaneous combustion in *Bleak House* greater authority in a present-day reader's eyes? It would be hard to deny that it does. In this tradition, in any case, literature has authority because it is seen to have representative validity. This assumption had tremendous force in nineteenth- and twentieth-century Europe and America. It is a basic presupposition of most of our pedagogy and critical writing even today.

Plato had a different idea from Aristotle's about poetry, as most people know. Or rather Plato had two ideas about poetry, though the first I shall discuss is undercut somewhat by Socrates's irony. In the *Ion*, the poet is seen as a somewhat dangerous rhapsode through whom the gods or some divine afflatus speaks. The inspired rhapsode is dangerous because he constitutes a decisive break or interruption in the status quo. The source of the rhapsode's authority is in one way or another supernatural. It is hard to gauge the degree of irony in Socrates's seeming praise of Ion for participating in the magnetic chain that transfers Homer's inspiration to Ion as reciter of Homer:

> . . . for a poet is a light and winged thing, and holy, and never able to compose until he has become inspired, and is beside himself, and reason is no longer in him. So long as he has this [reason] in his possession, no man is able to make poetry or to chant in prophecy.[10]

A long history of this assumption about the source of poetry's authority could be written, beginning with the Hebrew prophets and the Greek rhapsodes and going down through all those medieval Christian mystics who claimed direct access to visionary divine knowledge and were often burned as heretics when they were not canonized as saints. After that came multitudinous Protestant claims to the same sort of visionary authority—for example, John Bunyan's account of his inspiration, and then secularizations of that in the Romantic doctrine of supernatural inspiration, as when Shelley, in the "Defence of Poetry," claims that "the mind in creation is as a fading coal which some invisible influence, like an inconstant wind, awakens to transitory brightness."[11] For Shelley, "poets are the unacknowledged legislators of the World" because they are the avenue through which new knowledge and a new power to shape society come from divine sources, flow through the poet, and thence outward to change society.[12] W. B. Yeats, at the end of the nineteenth century, is still affirming more or less the same doctrine when he says:

> Solitary men in moments of contemplation receive, as I think, the creative impulse from the lowest of the Nine Hierarchies,

> and so make and unmake mankind, and even the world itself, for does not "the eye altering alter all"?[13]

Shelley's phrase "unacknowledged legislators of the World," however, is more complex than it may at first appear. Poets are lawgivers. They lay down the laws by which society operates and is governed. Poets play the role of Moses or Lycurgus, those aboriginal lawgivers who established the grounding laws originating two different cultures. Shelley's poets, however, are *unacknowledged* legislators, and they operate continuously, making and remaking mankind. I take it this means that poets work surreptitiously, stealthily, invisibly, as lawgivers. People do not know what is happening to them, whereas Moses's laws or Lycurgus's laws were publicly announced. In Moses's case, the Ten Commandments were inscribed on the stone tablets of the law for everyone to read when he brought them down from Mount Sinai. Poets, Shelley seems to be implying, are legislators in the sense that they establish in those who read their work the ideological and therefore unconscious or "unacknowledged" assumptions that govern behavior in a particular society.

Modern scholars in literary criticism, or the new historicism, or cultural studies often make different versions of the same assumption. For example, such scholars would assert, Anthony Trollope's novels strongly reinforce or even, to some degree, create the ideological assumption that such a thing as "being in love" exists. A young woman should always guide her decision about whether or not to accept a proposal of marriage by whether or not she is "in love with" the man who has proposed to her. Trollope often overtly asserts this idea. "[I]t must ever be wrong," he says in *An Autobiography*, speaking of Lady Glencora in *Can You Forgive Her?*, "to force a girl into a marriage with a man she does not love—and certainly the more so when there is another whom she does love."[14]

Plato's other concept of poetry, asserted in the *Republic*, is much more negative. It also has a long history, down to the present day. In the *Republic*, poetry is condemned, and the poets are exiled, just because poetry is a successful "imitation." All people should remain what they are. Moral probity depends on it. Poetry leads people astray because it exemplifies and encourages the knack that human beings have for pretending to be something or someone other than they are. Poetry makes all people actors and actresses, and everybody knows what immoral persons actors and actresses are. Plato's assumption is that the storytellers in the *Iliad* and the *Odyssey* are Homer himself, not a fictive "narrator." As long as Homer speaks in his own voice, his speech is moral. When he pretends to be Odysseus speaking and telling part of the story, however, radical immorality sets in. The trouble with pretending to be someone or something else is that there is no stopping it. It rapidly runs down through the sexist chain of being, from men to women to animals to inanimate objects, in a crescendo of degradation. Socrates's affirmation of this terrible danger in poetry is the classic condemnation of imitation in the Western tradition. Imitation is a species of dehumanizing or unmanning madness. Poetry, for Plato, has authority, all right, but it is the authority of radical evil, and so the poets must be banished from his ideal republic:

> We will not [says Socrates] then allow our charges, whom we expect to prove good men, being men, to play the parts of women and imitate a woman young or old wrangling with her husband, defying heaven, loudly boasting, fortunate in her own conceit, or involved in misfortune and possessed by grief and lamentation–still less a woman that is sick, in love, or in labor. . . . Nor may they imitate slaves, female and male, doing the offices of slaves. . . . Nor yet, as it seems, bad men who are cowards and who do the opposite of the things we just now spoke of [things done by men who are "brave, sober, pious, free"], reviling and lampooning one another, speaking foul words in their cups or when sober and in other ways sinning against themselves and others in word and deed after the fashion of such men. And I take it they must not form the habit of likening themselves to madmen either in words nor yet in deeds. For while knowledge they must have both of mad and bad men and women, they must do and imitate nothing of this kind. . . . Are they to imitate smiths and other craftsmen or the rowers of triremes and those who call the time to them or other things connected therewith?
>
> How could they, he [Adimantus] said, since it will be forbidden them even to pay any attention to such things?
>
> Well, then, neighing horses and lowing bulls, and the noise of rivers and the roar of the sea and the thunder and everything of that kind–will they imitate these?

> Nay, they have been forbidden, he said, to be mad or liken themselves to madmen.[15]

One aspect of James Joyce's work that is deliberately subversive or defiant of Plato is his imitation through words, in *Ulysses*, of the sound that a printing press makes, for example, or the sound of thunder in *Finnegans Wake*. The writer, Joyce claims, can and should imitate anything in words, in an exercise of his or her sovereign authority. The affirmation of that authority takes a hyperbolic form in Stephen Dedalus's Shelleyesque vocational commitment at the end of Joyce's *A Portrait of the Artist as a Young Man*: "Welcome, O life! I go to encounter for the millionth time the reality of experience and to forge in the smithy of my soul the uncreated conscience of my race."[16] Counter to such extravagant claims for the writer's authority, Plato's condemnation of the evils of imitation nevertheless echoes down through the centuries in the Western tradition—for example, in the Protestant condemnation of novel reading because it seduced young people, especially young women, to dwell in fictive worlds that led them astray from their real-world duties.

Novels themselves, in certain notorious cases, represent their own moral badness in an oblique affirmation of their dangerous authority and in an indirect warning to the reader to put down the book he or she is at that moment reading. Catherine Morland, the heroine of Jane Austen's *Northanger Abbey*, Flaubert's Emma Bovary, Conrad's Lord Jim, and many other fictional characters are morally corrupted and led to have absurd expectations about themselves and about the world by the reading of novels. Cervantes's Don Quixote is of course the archetype for this motif. Henry James follows this tradition when he has the gifted actress Miriam Rooth, heroine of *The Tragic Muse*, lack a fixed character of her own, just because she is so good an actress. She is nothing but whatever role she happens to be playing, even in "real life." Peter Sherringham, the rising young diplomat who falls in love with Miriam and has played Pygmalion to her Galatea, reflects, at one crucial moment in the novel, on Miriam's strange and distressing lack of character. You never know where to have her:

> It came over him suddenly that so far from there being any question of her having the histrionic nature she simply had it in such perfection that she was always acting; that her existence was a series of parts assumed for the moment, each

> changed for the next, before the perpetual mirror of some curiosity or admiration or wonder—some spectatorship that she perceived or imagined in the people about her. . . . [Her] identity resided in the continuity of her personations, so that she had no moral privacy, as he phrased it to himself, but lived in a high wind of exhibition, of figuration—such a woman was a kind of monster in whom of necessity there would be nothing to "be fond" of, because there would be nothing to take hold of. . . . The girl's face made it vivid to him now—the discovery that she positively had no countenance of her own, but only the countenance of the occasion, a sequence, a variety—capable possibly of becoming immense—of representative movements.[17]

A plausible case could be made for seeing my childhood submission to the "virtual reality" to which *The Swiss Family Robinson* gave me access as pernicious escapism. It was the beginning of a bad habit that has kept me in lifelong subservience to fantasies and fictions rather than soberly engaged in the "real world" and in fulfilling my responsibilities there. I can, as a matter of fact, still remember my mother's voice when she exhorted me to stop reading and go outside to play. Proust's Marcel, an inveterate reader as a child, received similar admonitions. Children nowadays who spend all the time they can playing video games are not all that different from the habitual reader in the now fading heyday of print culture. A video game is another kind of virtual reality, as is a network news program. These are no doubt less valuable fictive worlds, we inveterate readers of "canonical" texts would assert, though perhaps the difference is not so great as we might wish.

Some supernatural grounding authority, the solid reality of the extraverbal social world as ground, the sheer bad or good power of "fictions" to generate behavior-changing credence in those who submit themselves to them—all these concepts of the source of literature's authority have had force throughout our whole tradition. They have had force, often in the same societies or in the same writers and readers at once, in living contradictions that never seem to have bothered people much. The role of literature in nineteenth- and twentieth-century European and American culture has been no more than a special case of this incoherent mix. A fourth ground of literature's authority will complete my repertoire.

Roland Barthes had to exert some effort to kill off the author because it is so strong a part of our tradition to believe that what gives the literary work its authority is the author who stands behind it and validates it, gives it a solid ground. An immense amount of research, especially in English literature and continental Renaissance literature as well as in current continental theory, has persuaded many people that selfhood is "constructed," a matter of "self-fashioning," not innate or inborn or God-given. Selfhood is a product of surrounding ideological and cultural forces, including, of course, those embodied in what we would now call "literary works." Montaigne's essays are, among other things, a reflection on the variability and diversity from time to time of subjectivity and the self. The self, the "moi," is "ondoyant et divers." A good many people from Shakespeare's day to the present have nevertheless continued to believe that selfhood is God-given, fixed, unitary, and permanent from birth. Confidence in that is an important part of our religious and legal traditions, whether Christian, Judaic, or Moslem. How could you hold someone morally or legally responsible for an act if he or she is not the same person from moment to moment? The belief that the self is wavering and diverse provides a marvelous cop-out from moral responsibility. It allows you to say, "That was a different me who promised to do that. You can't blame me for *not* doing it."

In both cases, however, whether selfhood is seen as constructed or as innate and fixed, the notion of the author as the authorizing source and guarantee of the work that he or she writes has had, in different ways, wide allegiance. This notion might be defined by saying that the author tends to be held responsible for what he or she has written—held responsible, that is, by censoring authorities, for example, and by the reading public, and by scholars and teachers who write about or give courses on "Shakespeare" or "Dickens" or "Emily Dickinson" (meaning the works that these writers are presumed, on good authority, to have written). An enormous industry of biographical scholarship and popular writing, from Samuel Johnson's *Lives of the Poets* down to the latest "authoritative biography" of some canonical or noncanonical writer, reinforces the assumption that you can blame the author for what he or she has written, and that you can understand the work by way of knowledge about the author.

Popular media outlets like the *New York Times Book Review* tend today to review all biographies, good or bad, of famous or not so famous authors while ignoring serious critical works about those same authors. The genre of the interview is another example of that. The interview is a feature of the media worldwide. I myself have been interviewed repeatedly in the People's Republic of China. I imagine that far more people in China have read interviews with me in newspapers and magazines than have read my work, even though a good bit of that has been translated into Chinese. Derrida has been interviewed so often, and is so eloquent in response even to banal questions, that he has published a distinguished book made up exclusively of interviews, *Points de Suspension*.[18]

"An Explorer of Human Terrain," by Mel Gussow, an interview with the US black author Alice Walker in "The Arts," a section of the *New York Times*, represents all the complex intertwined ideology that lies behind the interview as a genre.[19] To call Walker "an explorer of human terrain" presumes that the human terrain is there to be explored. The writer is like a scientist or ethnographer writing a description of what he or she has found during a voyage of exploration. Gussow's story is accompanied by a charming photograph of Alice Walker herself in her Berkeley, California, house. She has a big smile and looks like a nice person. The assumption of this interview is that readers will be more interested in the author than in her writings and will see the latter as flowing directly from her psychology. Though the ostensible occasion of Gussow's interview is the publication of a new book of stories by Walker, *The Way Forward Is with a Broken Heart*, practically nothing is said about the stories apart from their directly autobiographical content. According to Gussow, the stories represent or reflect Walker's love for Melvyn Leventhal, a white civil rights lawyer, and the eventual breakup of her marriage to him. The authority of Walker's stories is their direct expression or representation of her life. This means that their accuracy of representation of the "real world," as she has experienced it, is the guarantee of their worth. Implicit in Gussow's concentration on Walker's life in this interview is the idea that if you know all about her life, you will hardly need to read her work.

Along with that assumption, an idea of inspiration that at least distantly echoes Plato's *Ion* surfaces momentarily and incongruously, though it can be justified as just something Walker happens to believe. Walker, the reader is told, thinks of her work as giving a life beyond the grave to the previous generations of her family:

> "It was heartbreaking to think that somehow they wouldn't survive in a form that was faithful to them—who they were and the way they sounded," she said. Through her writing she has been able to lend a certain fulfillment to lives that had been limited.[20]

That granting of survival through words in Walker's most famous work, *The Color Purple*, occurred through an act of creation in which Walker was "beside herself" and wrote almost like a spiritualist medium through whom her characters spoke:

> After her divorce she wrote *The Color Purple*, and it was a bolt of inspiration. She wrote it so fast, in longhand in a little spiral notebook, that it was "almost like dictation." As an artist, she says, she is a conduit for her mother and their relatives. . . . In a postscript to *The Color Purple*, she called herself an "author and medium."[21]

The ideological complex assumed in "An Explorer of Human Terrain" has been and is so ubiquitous in our culture that an author is unlikely to avoid being held responsible for what he or she has written by saying, "Don't blame me. I am just an insubstantial and baseless construction of the ideology of my gender, class, and race. I cannot help writing the way I do." Nor can the author escape responsibility by saying, as Jacques Derrida says an author can do in a democracy with the right to free speech, "Don't blame me. That is not me speaking, but an imagined, created, fictive narrator. I am exercising my right to say anything and to put anything in question. Don't make the naive mistake of confusing the narrative voice with the author. I am not an axe-murderer. I am just imagining what it would be like to be one (Dostoevsky's *Crime and Punishment*)."[22] The almost unanimous response would be to say, "Never mind that. You wrote it, and by way of whatever cunningly devised relays and cover-ups, those words came from your subjectivity and are authorized by you, as writing subject. We hold you responsible for what you have written and for all its effects, good and bad."

If the author has been granted enormous authority in our culture as the authorizing source of what he or she has written and published, this authority has taken two distinct forms. The author has had attributed to him or her a constative power, the power to tell the truth, to represent accurately his or her circumambient society. The author has also been assumed to have what might be called a performative authority—that is, the power to manipulate words in such a way that they will operate as speech acts, as ways of doing things with words that will have effects on readers.

What Anthony Trollope says, in *An Autobiography*, about the novelist's responsibility to tell the truth may be taken as an example of the first form of authorial authority. Trollope firmly believes that it is the duty of novelists to teach virtue in their novels, but he believes that the chief means of doing this is to tell the truth, the whole truth, and nothing but the truth about human life:

> By either [poetry or novels], false sentiment may be fostered, false notions of humanity may be engendered, false honour, false love, false worship may be created; by either, vice instead of virtue may be taught. But by each, equally, may true honour, true love, true worship, and true humanity be inculcated; and that will be the greatest teacher who will spread such truth the widest.[23]

The reader will note that Trollope here mixes constative and performative language. The novelist's primary responsibility is the constative one—to tell the truth—but this truth telling is performatively effective. It "engenders," "creates," or "inculcates" either virtue or vice in the novelist's readers.

Henry James's preface to volume 15 of the New York edition of his works makes explicit just how this magic charm may work to make a literary text a felicitous speech act. The volume contains a set of short stories about writers—"The Lesson of the Master," "The Death of the Lion," and "The Figure in the Carpet"—as well as others, several of which were first published in *The Yellow Book*, Henry Harland's somewhat notorious *fin de siècle* journal. James responds as follows to a friend's charge that the writer-protagonists of these stories are "unrealistic" because no writer with a selfless dedication to high art, no "artist enamoured of perfection, ridden by his idea or paying for his sincerity," exists these days in England:

> If the life about us for the last thirty years refuses warrant for these examples, then so much the worse for that life. The *constatation* would be so deplorable that instead of making it we must dodge it: there are decencies that in the name of the general self-respect we must take for granted, there's a kind of rudimentary intellectual honour to which we must, in the interest of civilisation, at least pretend.[24]

There are, it seems, times when it is "indecent" to tell the truth in an accurate *constatation*.

If such representations as Neil Paraday, Henry St. George, and Hugh Vereker (heroes of James's stories in this volume) do not have the authority of being accurate copies of social and historical truth, where, then, do they get their validity? James gives two answers to this question.

One is to confess that these characters are drawn from the depths of his own mind and intimate experience:

> . . . the material for any picture of personal states so specifically complicated as those of my hapless friends in the present volume will have been drawn preponderantly from the depths of the designer's own mind. . . . [T]he states represented, the embarrassments and predicaments studied, the tragedies and comedies recorded, can be intelligibly fathered but on his own intimate experience.[25]

That's all well and good, but how does such a designer generate a reader's belief in such fictions and so give the fictions at least a spurious authority? The answer is that the writer cunningly and deliberately manipulates words so as to make them performatively efficacious charms inducing trust and belief in the reader. This might be paralleled by Albertine's "charming art of lying with simplicity" ("l'art charmant qu'elle avait de mentir avec simplicité"),[26] which beguiles Marcel, in Proust's *À la recherche du temps perdu*, into believing that Bergotte is still alive and able to carry on a conversation with Albertine, when Bergotte is already dead; or which persuades Marcel that he has seen Albertine having a conversation in the street with a woman who he knows for certain has been absent from Paris for months. Suppose, says Marcel, I had happened to be in the street at that time and had seen with my own eyes that Albertine did not encounter the woman:

> I should then have known that Albertine was lying. But is this absolutely certain even then? . . . A strange darkness [*Une obscurité sacrée*, a sacred darkness: the reference is to Homer, where goddesses either are sometimes invisible or appear as ordinary mortals.—JHM] would have clouded my mind, I should have begun to doubt whether I had seen her alone, I should hardly even have sought to understand by what optical illusion I had failed to perceive the lady, and I should not have been greatly surprised to find myself mistaken [*trompé*], for the stellar universe is not so difficult of

> comprehension as the real actions of other people, especially of the people we love, fortified as they are against our doubts by fables devised for their protection [*fortifiés qu'ils sont contre notre doute par des fables destinées à les protéger*].[27]

Here is Henry James's description of a similar conjuring force on the writer's part—in this case, a dangerous performative power to engender trust in the reader in what is not really true to life:

> And then, I'm not ashamed to allow, it was *amusing* to make these people "great," so far as one could do so without making them intrinsically false. . . . It was amusing because it was more difficult—from the moment, of course I mean, that one worked out at all their greatness; from the moment one didn't simply give it to be taken on trust. Working out economically almost anything is the very life of the art of representation; just as the request to take on trust, tinged with the least extravagance, is the very death of the same. (There may be such a state of mind brought about on the reader's part, I think, as a positive desire to take on trust; but that is only the final fruit of insidious proceedings, operative to a sublime end, on the author's side; and it is at any rate a different matter.)[28]

The writer is a species of confidence man. The last thing a confidence man should do is to make a direct appeal to be taken on trust. That would give the game away. The writer as confidence man must take a different tack. By various "insidious proceedings" of word manipulation, the author must put together a text that will induce the reader to take on trust a fiction that has no provable correspondence to reality. James is describing here, strictly speaking, a form of speech act, or of what speech act theorists call performative language, a way of doing something with words. Commenting on the "all-ingenious 'Figure in the Carpet,'" James says, "Here exactly is a good example for you of the virtue of your taking on trust—when I have artfully begotten in you a disposition."[29]

My exploration of the various ways in which authority has been claimed for literature has culminated, with James's help, in a recognition that this authority derives from a performative use of language artfully begetting in the reader a disposition to take on trust the virtual reality the reader enters when he or she reads a given work. That certainly happens; it happened to me, for example, when I read *The Swiss Family Robinson* as a child. The problem with this view of literature is that—somewhat paradoxically, given what James says—it cuts the literary work off from its author. If Jacques Derrida, Paul de Man, and I are right, the performative and cognitive functions of language are incompatible.[30] As de Man puts this, speaking of "the disjunction of the performative from the cognitive":

> [A]ny speech act produces an excess of cognition, but it can never hope to know the process of its own production (the only thing worth knowing). . . . Performative rhetoric and cognitive rhetoric, the rhetoric of tropes, fail to converge.[31]

Reading James's "The Death of the Lion" or "The Figure in the Carpet" gives knowledge of the virtual reality that the story generates, but the reader can never know whether this is just what James intended. The work has such effect as it does happen to have on a given reader. If each work is, as I claim, unique, its performative effect will be unique, not authorized by prior conventions. It will be a form of speech act not condoned in standard speech act theory. The performative effect of the work is, moreover, dissociated from authorial intent or knowledge. This disjunction is already anticipated by the father of speech act theory, J. L. Austin, when he tries, at least momentarily, to separate the "felicity" of a speech act from the subjective intention of the one who enunciates it. If I can always say, "I did not mean what I said," and thereby get out of a promise or a commitment, then the way is open for bigamists, welshers on bets, and other such low people to get away with it. It is better, Austin affirms, to say, "My word is my bond." It does not matter what I was thinking when I uttered such and such words or wrote them. The effect they have must be honored.[32]

If this assumption is applied to literature considered as a speech act—particularly if we think, as I believe we should think, of each work as singular, *sui generis*—then this returns me to where I was at the beginning, when I was enchanted by *The Swiss Family Robinson*, which acted on me in the way it did act without my having any knowledge whatsoever about the author or what he thought he was doing in the work. It worked to open up a virtual reality reachable in no other way, and impossible to account for fully by its author's designs or by any other feature of the reading act's context. The literary work is self-authorizing.

Insofar as a literary work is seen as performative rather than constative, it must be subject to the general law of noncognizability that governs speech acts. Something will happen when a work is read, but just what will happen cannot be foreseen, known, or controlled. Every teacher of literature knows, often to his or her dismay, that strange and unpredictable things happen when students read an assigned work. Each literary work creates or reveals a world—a world furnished with characters possessed of bodies, speeches, feelings, thoughts, and dwelling within buildings, streets, a landscape, weather, and so on—in short, a virtual reality. It seems as if that reality has been waiting somewhere to be uncovered, exposed, transmitted, or "beamed" to the reader by the words on the page, just as more modern technologies create virtual realities on the screen or in the perception of the one who wears a virtual reality apparatus.

What are the characteristics of the virtual reality to which a literary work gives access? The first important feature is that it cannot be decided whether the virtual reality we enter when we read a novel by Trollope or James, or a poem by Yeats, pre-existed and is revealed by the author in an act of response to it, or whether that virtual reality is factitiously created by the words the author has chosen or has happened to write. No evidence exists to adjudicate certainly between these two alternatives. The undeniable and irresistible authority of literature remains poised between these two possibilities. It is impossible to decide between them, though nothing could be more important than to know decisively, once and for all. The second important feature of literary works, considered as magic formulas giving access to virtual realities, is that we can know of each such virtuality only what the words reveal. What the characters in a novel are saying and thinking when the narrator turns his or her back on them can never be known. Each literary work hides secrets, as Derrida has affirmed.[33] What song the Sirens sang to Odysseus; the contents of Milly's letter to Densher in James's *The Wings of the Dove*; everything about all those novels Dostoevsky is said to have had in his head but never wrote down; what Charlotte and the Prince said and did that day in Gloucester, in James's *The Golden Bowl*; whether the narrator's friend gave or did not give a counterfeit coin to the beggar in Baudelaire's "La fausse monnaie";[34] whether Albertine, in Proust's *À la recherche du temps perdu*, was or was not a lesbian—these are forever unknown and unknowable. I conclude that it is an essential feature of literature's authority to hide secrets that can never be revealed.

CHAPTER 7

The (Language) Crisis of Comparative Literature

Two current "crises in comparative literature" may be identified. One has to do with language. The other, about which I shall say little in this lecture, has to do with the rise of new media. Literature, in the old-fashioned sense of printed books containing novels, poems, or plays, is less and less central to the intellectual work of the young scholars who are moving into tenured positions. This has happened partly through "theory" as developed and institutionalized, in all its incoherence, especially within comparative literature departments. Students and faculty now do cultural studies, postcolonial studies, film studies, media studies, minority discourse studies, and women's studies. They watch films, videos, or television, or they surf the Net, rather than reading Dickens or Tolstoi or Flaubert. They have more and more a sense that people in general, even the educated public, do not read Dickens or Tolstoi or Flaubert, much less Celan or Rimbaud or Keats, with a feeling that it really counts for their lives. Literature in the old-fashioned sense has a smaller and smaller place as just one little patch in the immense heterogeneous hybrid patchwork quilt that makes up culture. As Alan Liu put this in an e-mail to me, the most compelling task facing literary studies today is "the future of literature in an age of 'new media.' " I shall take this "crisis" for granted as the context of what I have to say about the language crisis of comparative literature.

More than forty years ago [Now fifty years.—JHM], René Wellek published "The Crisis of Comparative Literature." He thought the crisis lay in unnecessary disagreements about the methodological foundations of the discipline, and in difficulties about establishing an object of study: "The most serious sign of the precarious state of our study," he said, "is the fact that it has not been able to establish a distinct subject matter and a specific methodology. I believe that the programmatic pronouncements of Baldensperger, Van Tieghem, Carré, and Guyard have failed in this essential task."[1] One hears little these days, one way or the other, about these patriarchal worthies, or even about Wellek himself. In Wellek's view, the missing foundations had already been solidly laid, by himself, in his combination of "intrinsic" and "extrinsic" comparisons against the background of an assumption that "[c]omparative literature has the immense merit of combating the false isolation of national literary histories: it is obviously right (and has brought a mass of evidence to support this) in its conception of a coherent Western tradition of literature woven together in a network of innumerable interrelations."[2] Wellek's essay ends with a noble and inspiring, even visionary, peroration:

> Once we grasp the nature of art and poetry, its victory over human mortality and destiny, its creation of a new world of the imagination, national vanities will disappear. Man, universal man, man [*sic*] everywhere and at any time, in all his variety, emerges and literary scholarship ceases to be an antiquarian pastime, a calculus of national credits and debts and even a mapping of networks of relationships. Literary scholarship becomes an act of the imagination, like art itself, and thus a preserver and creator of the highest values of mankind.[3]

Those are amazing sentences, in more ways than one! "Man, universal man"! "Victory over human mortality and destiny"! Literary scholarship an act of the imagination, "like art itself"! Now that the way out of the crisis in comparative literature had been clearly indicated, Wellek thought, it ought to be just a matter of getting on with it—getting on, that is, with "comparing the literatures." My last phrase is an allusion to a cartoon published around that time in the *Harvard Advocate*. The cartoon shows Harry Levin and Renato Poggioli, the patriarchs of comparative literature at Harvard, dressed in plumber's clothes and carrying plumber's tools, knocking at the door of someone's house. "We have come to compare the literatures," the caption says. This is extremely witty and unexpectedly subtle. It assumes that something is broken in "the literatures," and that comparing them is a way to fix that. "Comparing the literatures" is like "fixing the faucet" so the water can flow once more. A couple of decades after publishing "The Crisis of Comparative Literature," Wellek brought out, in 1983, in a conservative journal, *The New Criterion*, an essay titled "Destroying Literary Studies."[4] The discipline of literary studies, he averred, was being destroyed by new developments in theory—more specifically, by his Yale colleagues, the so-called Yale mafia. He did me the honor of including me in the lot and sent me an offprint with an inscription ("Your faithful colleague, René," or something of the sort). Paul de Man had a similarly inscribed copy on his bedside table as he lay dying. Given what had happened at Yale after Wellek's retirement, one can see why he was dismayed. Talk about "crisis"!

One problem with Wellek's title is that it is an oxymoron. The word "crisis" names a turning point of some kind, a critical dividing line, as when, in the crisis of a disease, the patient either gets better or dies. Comparative literature, however, is always in crisis. As a discipline it is especially designed to embody, in an acute form, a perpetual crisis in literary studies. What is that crisis? It is sometimes said that comparative literature is perpetually in crisis because, unlike the national language disciplines, each of which has a canon and a finite literary history, comparative literature has no defined literary canon to study. Its implied mission is to "compare," whatever *that* means, all the literatures, primarily by men, in any language (though of course, in the old days, primarily in European languages). When comparative literature was founded, its model was such older disciplines as comparative mythology and comparative linguistics; like them, it aspired to scientific or positivistic objectivity. This lack of a definite canon, it is often said, means that comparative literature is held together only by method or theory, and one knows (Wellek learned!) how impossible it is to get people in comparative literature to agree about theory and method.

Another way to put this is to say that comparative literature has been especially the place where theory and the teaching of theory have perforce been institutionalized. Comparatists have, at bottom, nothing else to teach, though they exemplify the theory by way of examples set side by side and drawn from different national literatures, whereas those safely ensconced in a national-literature department can go on elucidating individual canonical works with a clear conscience, and without doing any explicit theorizing at all. That does not mean, of course, that they do not have a tacit theory and methodology. The crisis in comparative literature arises from the cacophony of competing theories, not all of which can be simultaneously valid if intellectual coherence is the goal.

I suggest that the perpetual crisis of comparative literature arises not from methodological or theoretical disagreements but rather from the question of translation, in the widest sense of that term. The center of comparative literature as a discipline is not "theory" but the vexed and more or less insoluble problem of translation—from language to language, from culture to culture, or from one subculture to another within a larger regional culture. Let me try to explain how that is the case, and what particular form of the perpetual crisis in comparative literature is most acute today. The fundamental problem is one of language competence. The world swarms with languages, thousands of them—dozens in Europe, over two thousand, I am told, in Africa. The United States is now definitely a multilingual country. How can I learn any language other than my own mother tongue with enough intimacy or inwardness to be really "inside" that language and able to understand the culture it expresses? Even British English and American English are different enough to lead to all sorts of misunderstandings on the part of American students and American teachers of British literature. The apparent identity of the languages hides the degree to which British literature remains alien to us Americans, as American English remains opaque to those in European countries who, in increasing numbers, do "American studies." At a conference in France, I heard a young French scholar of American literature claim that, among our idiomatic oaths, we often say, "I swear by the tomb of George Washington." Maybe there are people in the United States who say that, but I have never heard it in my life. How often do I get Dickens or Trollope wrong in the same kind of way? To give a trivial example, what we in the United States call a "vest" is called a "waistcoat" in England, while "vest" there means "undershirt." An American I know caused great confusion in London shops by trying to buy a knitting pattern and wool for a "vest." The shopkeepers imagined she might be knitting a hair shirt for her husband. Saying "et" for "ate" is bad grammar in the United States, but in England it is, or was, a sign of aristocratic breeding. I heard it recently used unselfconsciously by a professor of English in Sweden. Henry James, in *The Wings of the Dove*, spends a whole paragraph presenting, in indirect discourse, the nonaristocrat Densher's analysis of the nuances of meaning in an "Oh!"

uttered by Lord Mark when he was introduced to Densher: "It wasn't, that is, he knew, the 'Oh!' of the idiot, however great the superficial resemblance: it was that of the clever, the accomplished man; it was the very speciality of the speaker, and a deal of expensive training and experience had gone to producing it," and so on.[5] One wonders, even so, how completely James ever came to understand the linguistic nuances of social intercourse in England, however many years he had lived there.

With languages that are more markedly different, the difficulty is even more obvious. For example, even if I am able to read French well, just how likely am I to notice—as Jacques Derrida *did* notice, in a seminar—that Proust, in *À la recherche du temps perdu*, in the episode of Bergotte's death and Albertine's lies about it, uses a string of words with the root *prendre* (*comprendre*, *apprendre*, meaning "to take," "to take in," "to grasp"), and that grasping the nuances of the passage depends on seeing this? The words all designate the act of taking in, by the senses or by the intelligence, but they also express the power we have to take in what a lie tells us is there, even if we have not actually seen (since it does not exist) whatever this is with our own eyes. I alluded to this passage of the *Recherche* in the previous chapter, but now I must cite it in both French and English, to make the point that *la conviction crée l'évidence* (conviction creates the facts):

> J'appris [says Marcel], ai-je dit, que ce jour-là Bergotte était mort . . . et je n'appris que bien plus tard l'art charmant qu'elle [Albertine] avait de mentir avec simplicité. . . . Le témoignage de mes sens, si j'avais été dehors à ce moment, m'aurait peut-être appris que la dame n'avait pas fait quelque pas avec Albertine. . . . Est-ce bien sûr encore? . . . Une obscurité sacrée se fût emparée de mon esprit, j'aurais mis en doute que je l'avais vue seule, à peine aurais-je cherché à comprendre par quelle illusion optique je n'avais pas aperçu la dame.[6]

> I learned [says Marcel], as I have said, that Bergotte had died that day . . . it was not until much later that I discovered her [Albertine's] charming skill in lying naturally. . . . The evidence of my senses, if I had been in the street at that moment, would perhaps have informed me that the lady had not been with Albertine. . . . But is this absolutely certain even then? A strange darkness would have clouded my mind,

> I should have begun to doubt whether I had seen her alone,
> I should hardly have sought to understand by what optical
> illusion I had failed to perceive the lady.[7]

The translation says "learned," "discovered," "informed," and "understand" for all these words with the root *prendre*. These are perfectly correct translations, but they totally obscure Proust's play on the root, thereby exemplifying once more the Italian adage *traduttori traditori*, "translators are traitors."

Comparative literature as a discipline has tended to deal with the problem of translation by tacitly assuming (whatever lip service is paid to learning other languages, particularly other European languages) that everything can be translated, without essential loss, into one dominant language. How could comparative literature get on with its work of fixing the plumbing if some one language—namely, the language used by a particular scholar in his or her particular essay or book—were not taken as a solid, unproblematic platform or Archimedean lever on the basis of which other languages can be compared or exchanged? This view from without would include even the dominant language now seen as an object of study, not as the presupposed ground for disciplinary discourse. That dominant language (American English, for us in the United States) becomes the relay station into which all other languages are translated, and within which they are "compared." Étiemble, the once reigning French comparatist, imagines, in one of his programmatic statements, French comparative literature (that is, Étiemble himself) presiding over a great organ console that translates all the languages comparatively into one another, via French: Outer Mongolian into Bulgarian, Basque into Norwegian, and so on. René Wellek knew many European languages, but his magisterial *A History of Modern Criticism: 1750–1950* is written completely in English, though it has been translated into many languages, including some non-European languages (for example, Chinese and Persian).[8] In the primary English version, the citations from Novalis, Bahktin, Sainte-Beuve, and the rest are given in the original languages in small print in appendices, where those who wish to do so may read them. The implied claim is: "Trust me. I know all these languages. You can be confident that I have put all my citations from foreign critics into accurate English translations. Check it out if you wish."

The current crisis in comparative literature arises not only from recognizing that comparative literature as a discipline has always been in cahoots with the cultural imperialism of one or another dominant language, even when it has been unconscious of being so, but also from recognizing that there is something fishy about calling a multivolume study *A History of Modern Criticism* when it is really a history of modern criticism in the West, leaving out China, Japan, India, all of Africa, minority languages, most women, and so on. In an age of globalization, it is easy to see, the Eurocentrism and sexism of traditional Western comparative literature is profoundly suspect. How can that be rectified?

The answer commonly given today involves some kind of return to comparative World Literature. Courses and textbooks in World Literature are springing up everywhere, like mushrooms that appear magically overnight. A large market for such textbooks apparently exists, and not just in the United States. In an age of globalization, is it not right that comparative literature should globalize itself, and that we should teach our students about literature from all over the world, not just from Europe and the United States? I agree with that, and I even agree that it is better to have read Proust and the Chinese *Classic of Poetry* in translation than not to have read them at all. Nevertheless, it is easy to see what is drastically wrong with this strategy.

Most textbooks and courses in World Literature still use English as the base language. What else can they do, since so many of our students are monolingual English speakers, though an increasing number have English only as a second language? But even if some of our students know Spanish or Chinese, it is unlikely that they will also know Hindi or Gikuyu. Such textbooks simply expand to global dimensions the hegemony of English that was present, not all that covertly, in Eurocentric comparative literature in the United States. In such textbooks, all the selections, from whatever languages from around the world, are perforce given in English. The ideological implication is that anything can be translated into English without essential loss.

The second problem with such textbooks and such courses is that their scope is so vast that the selections are necessarily selective, with a vengeance. Anthologies of a single national literature, such as the *Norton Anthology of English Literature*, are bad enough. They never seem to have all the particular texts you happen to want to teach. Anthologies of World Literature must represent a complex literary tradition like the Chinese one (if Chinese poetry may even be called "literature" in the Western sense) by a few poems from the Chinese *Classic of Poetry* and a chapter from *The Dream of the Red Chamber*. This would be like representing English literature by a scene from *Hamlet* and a few lyrics by

Wordsworth. The synecdochic ratio of part to whole is too large to be genuinely representative. At that scale, any selection is invidious. Moreover, if I am right about the difficulties of translating even a neighboring language like French or German into English, how much more likely is it that to translate is to traduce in the case of a non-European language?

Let me give a few specific examples of these problems before presenting my solution—my project for a responsible global comparative literature. I have already given an example from Proust. Two more I give now are from European languages. Three are from non-European languages.

I am told on good authority that the translations of the great novels of Latin American magic realism are good enough, but that an immense amount of nuanced meaning is lost in translation. The original Spanish or Portuguese is full of idioms, allusions, and covert references that, for the most part, do not carry over into English. This means, I conclude, that even if these novels are taught in English, they should be taught by someone who knows Spanish or Portuguese and who knows the culture, other literature, and other artworks that are the context of these works. Only such a person can explain to the students, by means of specific textual examples, the way the work is embedded in its context, or rather has its context embedded in transformed shape within it. Teachers who cannot do this are not really competent to teach these works. This is a good example of the way the perpetual crisis of comparative literature arises from the problem of translation in the broadest sense of the term.

My second European example is Thomas Wyatt's wonderfully sweet and powerful sonnet "Whoso List to Hunt," an adaptation of Petrarch's 190th *Rime* and one of the greatest poems in English about unsatisfied male sexual desire:

> Whoso list to hunt? I know where is an hind!
> But as for me, alas! I may no more,
> The vain travail hath wearied me so sore;
> I am of them that furthest come behind.
> Yet may I by no means my wearied mind
> Draw from the deer; but as she fleeth afore
> Fainting I follow; I leave off therefore,
> Since in a net I seek to hold the wind.
> Who list her hunt, I put him out of doubt
> As well as I, may spend his time in vain!
> And graven with diamonds in letters plain,

There is written her fair neck round about,
"*Noli me tangere*; for Cæsar's I am,
And wild for to hold, though I seem tame."[9]

The meaning of Wyatt's poem derives in part, of course, from its relation to its source. The teacher would need to know Italian in order to set the two poems side by side. Petrarch's poem is extremely beautiful. One can see why Wyatt admired it enough to make a "translation," in the sense of a transmogrification. Petrarch's poem exemplifies what Chaucer, in *The Canterbury Tales*, called Petrarch's "rethorike sweete," which "Enlumyned al Ytaille of poetrie." Here is the poem by Petrarch, followed by Anna Maria Armi's English translation:

Una candida cerva sopra l'erba
Verde m'apparve, con duo corna d'oro.
Fra due riviere, all'ombra d'un alloro,
Levando 'l sole, a la stagione acerba.

Era sua vista sí dolce superba,
Ch'i' lasciai per seguirla ogni lavoro;
Come l'avaro, che 'n cercar tesoro,
Con diletto l'affanno disacerba.

"Nessun mi tócchi—al bel collo d'intorno
Scritto avea di diamanti e di topazî—
Libera farmi al mio Cesare parve."

Et era 'l sol giá vòlto al mezzo giorno;
Gli occhi miei stanchi di mirar non sazî,
Quand'io caddi ne l'acqua, et ella sparve.

A pure-white doe in an emerald glade
Appeared to me, with two antlers of gold,
Between two streams, under a laurel's shade,
At sunrise, in the season's bitter cold.

Her sight was so suavely merciless
That I left work to follow her at leisure,
Like the miser who looking for his treasure
Sweetens with that delight his bitterness.

Around her lovely neck "Do not touch me"
Was written with topaz and diamond stone,
"My Caesar's will has been to make me free."

Already toward noon had climbed the sun,
My weary eyes were not sated to see,
When I fell in the stream and she was gone.[10]

To grasp Wyatt's poem, to see the differences and similarities, the reader needs more even than the placement of Wyatt's poem side by side with Petrarch's. The conceit of "Whoso List to Hunt" is to figure the speaker's vain courtship of an unnamed woman (said to be perhaps Anne Boleyn) as like a deer hunt: others can continue the hunt for her, but he gives up the chase (the latter motif is absent in Petrarch, whose speaker, in line 14, falls in the stream in the midst of unsated admiration of the beautiful deer):

The vain travail hath wearied me so sore;
I am of them that furthest come behind.
Yet may I by no means my wearied mind
Draw from the deer; but as she fleeth afore
Fainting I follow; I leave off therefore,
Since in a net I seek to hold the wind.
Who list her hunt, I put him out of doubt
As well as I, may spend his time in vain![11]

The real reason Wyatt's speaker gives up the chase, however, is that the deer is marked as belonging to another of sovereign power: King Henry VIII himself. This is figured in the way Caesar's hinds (that is, deer) wore a collar that said, in Latin of course, "Touch me not, for I am Caesar's." If you killed one of Caesar's deer, you got into big trouble. Wyatt expresses this in the last four lines of the sonnet, culminating in the magical final couplet:

And graven with diamonds in letters plain,
There is written her fair neck round about,
"*Noli me tangere*; for Caesar's I am,
And wild for to hold, though I seem tame."[12]

I say nothing about the way the encompassing of the lady's "fair neck" is expressed by the lingering extra syllable, "round," in line 12: "There is written her fair neck round about." Nor will I say anything about the contradiction between the lady's possession by the king and the assertion that she remains wild, untamed, unable to be possessed by anyone: "And wild for to hold, though I seem tame." Nor will I say anything about the irony that lies in the figure of the collar around the lady's neck, a figure proleptic of the fatal line inscribed by the executioner's axe, if the lady is indeed Anne Boleyn. Many readers who have grown up inside the English-speaking tradition will remember this variation on a popular ballad: "Oh, Anne Boleyn was once King Henry's wife, / Until the axman ended quite her life."

The phrases "*Noli me tangere*, for Caesar's I am," with their complex echoes of the Bible, are most relevant to my topic, however. In Matthew 22:21, Jesus answers the followers of the Pharisees and the Herodians, who have come to "entangle him in his talk," by saying, "Render therefore unto Caesar the things which are Caesar's: and unto God the things which are God's." The king's hind, Anne Boleyn, is Caesar's and must be rendered unto Caesar, just as Jesus says tribute money must be paid to the Roman occupiers in coin that bears Caesar's image. One of the most moving scenes in the New Testament comes in John 20, when Mary Magdalene recognizes that she confronts the risen Christ and, not, as she had thought, the gardener. The recognition that turns her around, converts her, in more ways than one, happens when he calls her by name, "Mary," and she answers him: "Rabboni, which is to say, Master" (John 20:16). This is one of the few places where the original language that Jesus and his followers spoke, Aramaic, is carried over into the King James Bible. It seems as though what Mary actually said must be cited, as a kind of magic password or Shibboleth. Jesus then says to Mary, "Touch me not: for I am not yet ascended to my father" (John 20:17). "Touch me not" would be "Noli me tangere" in the Latin Vulgate Bible. This "touch me not" clashes strangely with the later scene in which Jesus invites Thomas Didymus, "Doubting Thomas," to touch his, Jesus's, hands with the nail holes in them, and to thrust his hand into the wound in Jesus's side. It is not clear that Thomas actually does this, but he looks, and seeing is believing the promise that a touch would be possible (John 20:27–29):

> Then saith he to Thomas, "Reach hither thy finger, and behold my hands; and reach hither thy hand, and thrust it into my side: and be not faithless, but believing." And Thomas answered and said unto him, "My Lord and my God." Jesus saith unto him, "Thomas, because thou hast seen me, thou

> hast believed; blessed are they that have not seen, and yet have believed."

Wyatt's "*Noli me tangere*, for Caesar's I am" echoes in complex, ironic, and almost blasphemous ways this already complex and ironically clashing set of biblical texts. Those texts involve the question of how a subversive religious organization can best survive under persecution and occupation, just as the speaker in Wyatt's poem needs to keep his hands off the king's property and render unto Henry the things that are Henry's. The texts involve also the opposition between touching and not touching, touching and seeing, believing because you have seen as against the much superior believing in things unseen. If you do not happen to know Petrarch, the Bible, and Caesar's way of marking his deer as his own, then much of the meaning of Wyatt's poem will be lost on you. Reading it is an act of comparative literature, which the field of English Renaissance literary studies has always been.

Now I turn to my three non-European examples, where my ignorance means that I tread on shaky ground. My basic presumption, however, is that non-European literary texts are just as complex in their relation to their traditions as Western texts are, and that just as much intertextual, interlinguistic knowledge is necessary for their understanding as is the case with my European examples.

First case in point: suppose I want to teach with authority, or responsibly write about, *A Grain of Wheat*, a 1967 work by the Kenyan novelist Ngugi wa Thiong'o. This novel was published in English. It is therefore part of world anglophone literature. No problem. Critics have detected strong influences from Conrad in *A Grain of Wheat*. Echoes of Conrad further assimilate *A Grain of Wheat* to the English tradition. (By the way, I don't really see these all that pervasively myself.) The title, after all, comes from the Christian Bible. The epigraph for the whole novel is a citation about a grain of wheat from I Corinthians 15:36. The disclaimer statement, a very Western gesture ("All the characters in this book are fictitious"), is dated from Leeds in November 1966. All the superficial signs, and many more that are integral to the tone of the novel's storytelling, embed it in the English tradition. Without needing to know all that much about Ngugi or about Kenya, I can, with a clear conscience, include *A Grain of Wheat* in a syllabus for one of my courses, lecture about it, or write about it in an essay.

Even the preliminary note, prior to the title page in the Heinemann revised edition of 1986, might give one a little pause, however.

Heinemann, a "division of Reed Publishing (USA) Inc.," in spite of its Teutonic-sounding name, is very much part of the global proliferation of English-language books. Heinemann has, or had, offices in Florence; Prague; Melbourne; Auckland; Singapore; Tokyo; Paris; Madrid; Athens; Johannesburg; Chicago; São Paulo; Ibadan, Nigeria; and Gaborone, Botswana. That is an imperial list if ever there was one! In this prefatory note, the reader learns that Ngugi's novel of 1980, *Devil on the Cross*, was written in Ngugi's native language of Gikuyu "during the author's one-year detention in prison, where he was held without trial after the performance by peasants and workers of his play *Ngaahika Ndeenda* [I will marry when I want]. *Devil on the Cross* was then translated into English and many other languages." Thereafter, Ngugi's work has often been written and published first in Gikuyu and then translated into English, including the big novel on which he is currently working. [That work in progress was published in 2006 as *Wizard of the Crow* (New York: Pantheon, 2006).—JHM] The prefatory note says, "Ngugi is an active campaigner for the African language [Which one? There are some 2,400!—JHM] and form." One example of this process was a witty and forceful polemical essay published in the 1980s in the *Yale Journal of Criticism* on facing pages, if I remember correctly, with the text in Gikuyu and English. The essay argues eloquently that the worldwide domination of English has bad political implications, and it proposes Gikuyu as a substitute. Gikuyu, Ngugi says, is a language capable of Shakespearean eloquence, and it is spoken by millions of people. Happily, he observes, it lacks the political implications of submission to worldwide universal English, the chief language of imperialism.

When I turn to the novel itself, *A Grain of Wheat*, I find many Gikuyu words left untranslated—for example, words denoting everyday utensils, but also more important words like *uhuru*, which apparently means "independence" in Gikuyu. A satellite launched in 1970 to search the sky for X-ray-emitting sources was called *Uhuru*, no doubt in celebration of Kenyan independence. On the novel's second page, the reader is told that Mugo "took a jembe and a panga" and walked through the dusty village streets "to reach his new strip of shamba."[13] What is a *jembe*, or a *panga*, or a *shamba*? The context indicates that the first two objects are agricultural tools like a shovel or a hoe, and that the third term denotes a strip of garden land, but the effect of giving these words in Gikuyu is strategically to remind the reader that the English she is reading translates a culture that takes place in another language. Occasionally, but only occasionally, whole sentences are given in Gikuyu and left untranslated, as when something that the dead freedom fighter Kihika used to say is given in Gikuyu: "Kikulacho kiko nguoni mwako," which, the context suggests, has something to do with "a friend not a friend," the one who betrayed Kihika to the white man. When it is suggested that the traitor was Karanja, Mumbi says "Ngai!" What does that mean? Probably it means "No!"—but that is a guess.[14] To some degree, it might be said that Ngugi taunts his readers with their ignorance of Gikuyu. A little earlier than the quotation of what Kihika used to say, Mumbi reports herself as resisting Karanja's advances by saying, "Don't you call me Mumbi, Mumbi."[15] That's really strange! This and some other passages, however, indicate that "Mumbi" both has a conceptual meaning in Gikuyu and is the name of one of the chief female characters in *A Grain of Wheat*. The clergyman, the Reverend Morris Kingori, begins his prayer in the Uhuru celebration by saying, "God of Isaac and Jacob and Abraham, who also created Gikuyu and Mumbi, and gave us, your children, this land of Kenya . . . ."[16] If I were to try to teach *A Grain of Wheat*, my ignorance of Gikuyu would make me the blind leading the blind, or like that young French scholar of oaths in American literature and common speech who thinks that we frequently swear by the tomb of George Washington.

Just what does all this mean for a responsible reading or teaching of *A Grain of Wheat*? It means that what may matter most in it is not echoes of Conrad (though the episode of Kihika's entry into Mugo's hut, just after he has murdered a murderous white official, does recall the opening of Conrad's *Under Western Eyes*) but formal features, ways of storytelling, idioms, proverbs, rhythms, modes of feeling that are, so to speak, translated from Gikuyu (no doubt imperfectly) into English in this English-language version of a Gikuyu book. In an oral communication, Ngugi wa Thiong'o has confirmed to me that this is the case.

Ngugi's shift to Gikuyu as his primary language is not, the evidence suggests, just a political move. He has found that he can best say what he wants to say only in his native language. The comparison with Conrad is of course ironic, since Conrad's native language was Polish. Conrad almost decided to write in French. The great power of his writing in English may derive, to some degree, from the way it always remained an alien language for him—English as a second, or rather third, language. Some rudimentary knowledge of the Gikuyu language, its narrative traditions, its idioms, I conclude, is a necessity for a just reading of *A Grain of Wheat*, along with some knowledge, of course, of modern Kenyan history and culture. The novel cannot, with justice, be assimilated into some hypothetical homogeneous world anglophone literature. I also conclude that teaching or writing about *A Grain of Wheat* is properly the business of comparative literature programs, not of English departments as traditionally conceived. Departments of national languages should be, or in any case *are*, being translated into comparative literature departments. (I mean this in the same sense in which Bottom, in Shakespeare's *A Midsummer Night's Dream*, is "translated" when his head becomes an ass's head: "Bless thee, Bottom. Thou art translated!") Departments of national languages are being exploded from within to become versions of comparative literature or comparative studies departments. I am aware that it will take a long and bitter struggle to gain *uhuru* from the hegemony of English. Too many people conscientiously believe, in their heart of hearts, that Newt Gingrich was right when he said, in a speech in Iowa, that the future of civilization depends on the dominance of the English (or rather the American) language.

My second case in point is from Chinese literature. The tradition of Chinese literature is thousands of years long. It is extremely rich and complex. It takes Stephen Owen 1,212 pages in his magisterial *An Anthology of Chinese Literature: Beginnings to 1911* to present a representative selection in English.[17] That is why Chinese is so good an example of what is problematic about representing Chinese literature by a few snippets in an anthology of World Literature. Even Owen's anthology remains controversial, both in its choices and in his translations. It is not even certain that it is right to call it "Chinese literature" or "poetry," since anything like an exact equivalent of those words does not exist, so I am told, in Chinese. The protocols for writing Chinese "poetry," and its uses over the centuries within Chinese culture, are different, to a considerable degree, from poetry and its uses in Euro-American culture. Our poetry is allusive and full of echoes of earlier poetry, echoes that an adept reader needs to recognize (of Milton, for example, in Wordsworth's *The Prelude*), but nothing in our traditions quite matches the subtlety of echo in Chinese so-called poetry, at least so I am told. For an adept reader, so I am told, the use of a single strategically placed Chinese character or cluster of characters will make a poem that seems to be about peach blossoms and a beautiful woman into a reference to a political situation that was the context of another poem written centuries before. The echo implicitly claims a parallel between the political situation then and the political situation now. To understand Chinese so-called poetry, you must learn how to read Chinese—a lengthy task.

I want to exemplify my main point, however, with an anecdote. A couple of years ago, I wrote an essay on Henry James's *The Portrait of a Lady*. My interpretation centers on a reading of the climactic episode in which Caspar Goodwood's forcible kiss of Isabel leads her to turn away from him and take the straight path back to Rome and back to her awful husband, Gilbert Osmond. Unlike his models, the bad husbands in George Eliot's *Middlemarch* and her *Daniel Deronda*, Osmond does not seem likely to die conveniently. I got interested in kisses and found some admirable kisses in English literature—for example, Adam's touching kiss of Eve's tears in *Paradise Lost* (5:134). Hardly a major narrative work in English literature is without at least one kiss. I also found some wonderful material about kisses in philosophical texts—for example, Novalis's claim, in the *Blutenstaub*, that "the first kiss is the beginning of philosophy"; or Thomas de Quincey's report, in "The Last Days of Immanuel Kant," that Kant, speechless on his deathbed, signaled to his last faithful disciple to kiss him on the lips;[18] or Derrida's kiss of Jean-Luc Nancy's lips in a dream, after Nancy's heart transplant (that kiss is recorded in Derrida's *Le toucher, Jean-Luc Nancy*).[19] Derrida also makes reference to Novalis's theory of the kiss and comments on it.[20] To what Derrida says I add, speculatively, that for Novalis the first kiss is the beginning of philosophy because, as the exit from narcissistic isolation, it initiates dialectical thinking: from self to other, thesis to antithesis. This happens by way of what Derrida calls "auto-hétéro-affection."

When I decided to use my essay on the kiss in *The Portrait of a Lady* as the basis of one of my talks during a visit to the People's Republic of China, my wife asked me if I knew whether or not it is decent to talk about kisses in China. That began to worry me. I e-mailed a friend in the People's Republic, who assured me that it was all right, that Chinese people see lots of kissing in Western films. Then, out of curiosity, I checked through Stephen Owen's big anthology of Chinese literature.[21] I did not find a single kiss there, though a few of Owen's selections are quite erotic. Why is this? Why is kissing routine in English literature but apparently taboo in Chinese so-called literature, at least until after 1911, when the big influence from the West began? Could it be that Owen, for some inscrutable reason (I can think of some), has left out all the Chinese poems with kisses? Though I have asked a number of experts about this, both Western and Chinese, their answers are somewhat evasive and inconclusive. I concluded that if I wanted to understand this phenomenon and its meaning for Chinese so-called literature, I would need to learn Chinese, in more than one sense of that phrase. I would need to learn the language but would also need to learn the whole cultural complex made up of distinct ways to see, feel, and behave, as that cultural complex has changed through the centuries. I would need to read Chinese literature for myself to find out if it contains any kisses.

My third and final case in point is from India. At Irvine, a gifted PhD student of mine, Simona Sawhney, did excellent work of a more or less traditional kind up through her qualifying examinations, which she passed with flying colors. After that came a hiatus, during which she was not getting on with a dissertation. Finally she resurfaced with a quite different orientation from her previous work. She had decided she wanted to study the political and cultural role that classical Indian literature (if you can call it "literature") has played in contemporary India, during the struggle for liberation from British rule and afterward. She had undergone something approaching a conversion experience, or at any rate the experience of finding a true vocation. This experience has recently been duplicated in thousands of cases of young literary scholars who have swerved away from the methods and materials they learned in graduate school. Such people are remaking the discipline of literary studies—globalizing it, among other changes. Simona Sawhney enjoyed the advantage, to start with, of having fluent Hindi and Punjabi, but she did not know Sanskrit. Irvine does not teach Sanskrit, but Berkeley does. Sawhney transferred herself to Berkeley while remaining a University of California at Irvine student (happily, you can do that in the University of California system). She studied Sanskrit at Berkeley, and she taught in Berkeley's Department of South and Southeast Asian Studies. She then wrote a brilliant dissertation on fundamentalist movements in modern India and on the relation between sacred and secular in modern Indian culture. One of her teachers at Berkeley agreed to join her dissertation committee. The dissertation had chapters on Gandhi, on the reception of Rushdie's *The Satanic Verses*, and on some hymns from the *Rig-Veda*. "Focusing on Indian literature," Sawhney wrote, "I propose that even the most canonical works of the Hindu tradition are too heterogeneous and complex to sanction the construction of a monolithic past, such as the one imagined by fundamentalists. While fundamentalism may be understood as a reaction to colonialism and neocolonialism, a postcolonial modernity can only emerge from a critical reading of both our 'own' *and* the colonizers' histories." [22]

Professor Sawhney is now at work on what promises to be a fascinating book on Sanskrit literature in twentieth-century India. [Dr. Simona Sawhney went on to become a professor of South Asian literature and critical theory at the University of Minnesota. She has recently moved back home (a big loss for US teaching and scholarship) to New Delhi, where she teaches in the Department of Humanities and Social Sciences at the Indian Institute of Technology.—JHM] I have seen two essays drawn from this manuscript. Both essays, using different examples, show the complex way in which allusions to classical Sanskrit literature function in modern Indian literature written in Hindi. They are remarkable essays, models of the new globalized comparative literature in their linguistic knowledge, in their subtle appropriation of modern literary theory, and in their penetrating comments (for example, on the different attitudes toward war and violence in the Sanskrit tradition and in the Greek epic tradition—in order to write with authority about the latter comparison, and for the sake of the teaching that she wants to do, Professor Sawhney has studied classical Greek).[23]

I take the story of Simona Sawhney, a story still in the making, as paradigmatic, even parabolic. Her work, I claim, shows that the new globalized comparative literature must be done not in English but on the basis of knowledge of whatever languages are necessary. Sawhney's work shows that it is entirely possible, if you have enough enterprise, to get— in one way or another, by hook or by crook—whatever languages you need. Her work also shows that it is irresponsible to do otherwise.

I conclude with three modest proposals for a new globalized, non-Eurocentric comparative literature.

First, I applaud the globalization of comparative literature, its moves away from Euro-centrism. That, I propose, is the way to go.

Second, a responsible global comparative literature, I propose, will involve the presumption that such languages as are necessary for serious work will have to be learned, even if a given university does not teach them. The model here is anthropology, which assumes as one of its protocols the possibility and the necessity of learning the language of whatever culture is being studied. In any case, much work in comparative literature these days is a form of social science and has much to learn from the protocols of social science (for example, the necessity to get signed consent forms when studying living people). I am aware, and most cultural anthropologists have long been aware, of the historical complicity of anthropology in Western imperialism. That is certainly an acute danger for a globalized comparative literature (for example, in the importation of Western theory into the study of non-European literatures). This process is both productive and profoundly problematic. Thoughtful awareness of the danger of inadvertent imperialism will help, as it has in cultural anthropology. I do not see that it is necessarily an imperialist gesture to require knowledge of the languages used in the literatures studied, though it can be plausibly argued that learning the language of another culture is an act of aggression against that culture, especially if the learner is European and the language learned is non-European. This does not mean, however, that we Euro-Americans should study other cultures only in English translation. It is better to take the risk of learning the other language than to assume that everything can be turned, without essential loss, into English.

Third, this change in attitude toward language study is already taking place in those many young scholars of whom Simona Sawhney is a synecdochic example. These young scholars are learning non-European languages on their own initiative, without much help from their Eurocentric teachers. Nevertheless, I propose that the new globalized comparative literature institutionalize in its curricula and requirements, as anthropology has done, the requirement to learn non-European in addition to European languages. This will be necessary in order to "compare the literatures" responsibly—in order, that is, to respond to the call made on us by other cultures to read their literatures and understand their societies.

CHAPTER 8

The Indigene and the Cybersurfer

L'inavouable de la communauté, c'est aussi une souveraineté qui ne peut que se poser et s'imposer en silence, dans le non-dit.
—Jacques Derrida, *Voyous*[1]

In a call for papers for *Globalization and Indigenous Cultures*, a special issue of *ARIEL*, the editors, Fengzhen Wang and Shaobo Xie, define our present worldwide situation in apocalyptic terms. We are, they say, experiencing the rapid destruction of indigenous cultures by three corrosive forces working together. These are global capitalism, Western (primarily American) popular culture, and new communications technologies. Widely used new forms of telecommunications fuel the irresistible hegemony of capitalism and American popular culture. Technology, capitalism, and American popular culture cooperate to uproot and destroy every autochthonous culture around the whole world. "The processes of globalization," say Wang and Xie, "are irresistibly sucking every nation and community into their hegemonic orbit. . . . The desire of global capitalism challenges and undermines all traditional forms of human interaction and representation. Multinational capital with its hegemonic ideology and technology seems to be globally erasing difference, imposing sameness and standardization on consciousness, feeling, imagination, motivation, desire, and taste. In exchange for multinational capital investment and for access to American lifestyles, fashions, values, and conveniences glorified and romanticized by Hollywood films, the underdeveloped and pre-modernized of the earth are unabashedly and unhesitantly surrendering their landscapes, resources, traditions, and cultural heritages to cultural capitalism."[2]

The image of the "hegemonic orbit" into which indigenous cultures are being "sucked" is particularly forceful. Western cultural capitalism is a kind of black hole into which everything around it swirls and then disappears, never again to be seen.

Since I want to challenge, to some degree, the paradigm so cogently expressed by Wang and Xie, let me begin by saying that I agree, for the most part, with the dismal picture they present of the destructive effects of global capitalism and Western popular culture. I would add to their picture the present terrifying mutation, in the American government, of global capitalism and the ideologies of Western popular culture into a straightforward push toward global military conquest. This means a transformation of US civil society into a permanent "state of emergency," a permanent "state of exception," a permanent "state of war." This goes along with a state of unrelieved and unrelievable terror that justifies the suspension of civil liberties and of constitutional rights. If the goal of the so-called terrorists is to strike terror into the hearts of American citizens, they have certainly succeeded in that, with the eager cooperation of the American government and the American mass media. Examples of the mediatic generation of terror are the endlessly repeated television shots of the Twin Towers falling down on 9/11 and the endless repetitions of the phrase "the war on terror" and "weapons of mass destruction." The threat to national security posed by the "terrorists" is used to justify repression at home, in the name of "homeland security." It also justifies aggression abroad, again in the name of "homeland security."

The slogan of imperialism used to be "Trade follows the flag." Often, in nineteenth-century Western imperialism, the missionaries were there first, attempting to convert the "heathen savages" to Christianity. When the missionaries got in trouble, an occupying army had to be sent in to protect them. "Trade"—that is, economic exploitation—followed soon after. Conrad's *Heart of Darkness* is the classic representation in a fictional work of this historical process. Nowadays a better slogan would be "The flag follows trade," with the supposed justification of "making the world a safer place for democracy"— that is, US capitalism. Global capitalism invades first. Military invasion follows to secure it. Total domination by capital can be secured, in the end, only by actual military occupation. An example is the invasion and occupation of Iraq, which "liberates" Iraqi oil for Western exploitation. The new and unprecedented American foreign policy of "pre-emptive strikes" can justify the bombing and invasion of more or less any country that President Bush and his advisers define as "evildoers." Who will be next? Iran? Saudi Arabia? Syria? North Korea? Libya? Defiance of the United Nations and the refusal to sign any international agreements or treaties—for example, the Kyoto Protocol on global warming, or the agreement to set up an international court authorized to try perpetrators of war crimes—means that the United States has become the chief rogue state. We operate in defiance of international law and global opinion. That is precisely the definition of a rogue state.[3] We are armed to the teeth with the "weapons of mass destruction" that we deny other countries the right to have. The Bush administration, so we are told, is quietly increasing its nuclear arsenal.

History shows, however, that empire building eventually overreaches itself and self-destructs, as happened with the Roman Empire and with the British Empire, on which it used to be said that the sun never sets. Gigantic budget deficits in the United States are perhaps a presage of that ultimate collapse. Or perhaps the destruction of our environment and the inundation of our coastal cities by global warming will bring the end of the US empire. Or perhaps it will be massive deaths from an inadequately funded health care system. Or perhaps the center of global capitalism will shift to other countries, to the European Union or to the People's Republic of China. The latter, so I understand, will soon have the world's largest economy. The largest number of websites by the year 2008 will probably be in Chinese, not in English. [I don't think that has happened, but perhaps it has happened or will happen.—JHM] The end of empire will take a while, however. Meanwhile, we United States citizens, and people around the world, must endure much grief.

As you can see, I think things are even worse than Wang and Xie say. In this truly frightening situation, it is hard to keep one's head or to think clearly. Nevertheless, I want to meditate a little further about the paradigm of global conquest by "cultural capitalism" that Wang and Xie describe, especially as it postulates the ongoing destruction of indigenous communities.

The first thing to note is that the discourse of the Wang/Xie statement is a Western cultural product through and through, as is the present essay. Both, by an apparently implacable necessity, perform the thing they deplore—that is, the diffusion and hegemony of American cultural creations. "Hegemony" is part of the jargon of Western Marxist cultural studies, as in the work of Ernesto Laclau. The term "postmodernism" is associated with the work of Frederic Jameson. "Globalization," as Jacques Derrida has cogently argued in recent seminars, is a thoroughly Western Christian concept (for example, in the notion of "World Literature"). The concept of "world" is dependent on the theological notion of "the world," as used in the Bible or in St. Augustine, or even when we speak today about "worldly concerns." That connection explains why Derrida prefers the French word *mondialisation*, "worldifying," to the English "globalization." *Mondialisation* more saliently brings out the theological roots of "globalization" as a concept.

Wang and Xie's paradigm, moreover, depends as well on a problematic binary opposition between the indigene and what I am calling the cybersurfer. Wang and Xie more or less take for granted that either sort of person coincides with his or her social and cultural placement, with little or nothing left over or left out. We are what our surrounding culture makes us. When global culture invades any region, everybody there gradually becomes a cybersurfer, no longer an indigene. This assumption that the individual is saturated by his or her cultural milieu is an important issue, to which I shall return.

The cybersurfer is the quintessential victim of American values and technology. He or she is the "computer nerd" who will soon be found in every country all over "the world," playing computer games that graphically display scenes of the utmost violence, in which the player actively participates, listening to pirated MP3 songs by the hundreds that express the complexities of American popular culture, and communicating by way of e-mail, chat rooms, or cell phone with other computer freaks all over the world. [No Facebook or Twitter in 2003!—JHM] A cybersurfer is homeless, rootless, without privacy, exposed in all directions to invasions of his or her home enclosure by various technotelecommunications devices (as I call them). Global cultural capitalism promises that everyone can soon become a computer nerd.

The indigene, however, is as much a Western concept as the cybersurfer is a product of Western cultural capitalism. The notion of the indigene is implicitly associated with the idea of the "noble savage," and with the enthnographical search for what Maurice Blanchot, discussing Claude Lévi-Strauss's *Tristes Tropiques*, calls "man at point zero."[4] The indigene lives unselfconsciously where he or she was born, as the etymology of the word avers. It means "born within." On the island off the Maine coast where I live most of the year, an important distinction is made between those "from here" and those "from away." It takes three or four generations, at least, of one family born on the island, its members living out their lives there, for the latest generation to become included among those "from here."

The indigene is rooted permanently in "one dear perpetual place," to cite W. B. Yeats's phrase in "A Prayer for My Daughter."[5] He or she remains in the state celebrated so nostalgically and so beautifully by Wallace Stevens in "The Auroras of Autumn": the indigene was in what is now a lost state of oneness with the others in the community, the "we"; Stevens calls it "a time of innocence":

> . . . That we partake thereof,
> Lie down like children, in this holiness,
> As if, awake, we lay in the quiet of sleep,
>
> As if the innocent mother sang in the dark
> Of the room and on an accordion, half-heard,
> Created the time and place in which we breathed . . .
>
> IX
>
> And of each other thought—in the idiom
> Of the work, in the idiom of the innocent earth,
> Not of the enigma of the guilty dream.
>
> We were as Danes in Denmark all day long
> And knew each other well, hale-hearted landsmen,
> For whom the outlandish was another day
>
> Of the week, queerer than Sunday. We thought alike
> And that made brothers of us in a home
> In which we fed on being brothers, fed
>
> And fattened as on a decorous honeycomb.
> This drama that we live—We lay sticky with sleep.[6]

All the salient features of the Western concept of the indigene, or of what it is like to live in an undisturbed indigenous culture or community, are movingly chanted in this passage. Stevens is an American poet who has expressed as well as any of our great poets our sense of homeland places, whether it is Hartford, Connecticut, where Stevens lived, or Pennsylvania Dutch country, where Stevens was born, or Florida, where he vacationed, or even Tennessee, as in "Anecdote of the Jar": "I placed a jar in Tennessee . . ."[7] One thinks of all the American place names in Stevens's poetry—for example, of the magical line "The wood-doves are singing along the Perkiomen" in "Thinking of a Relation Between the

Images of Metaphors," or of "The Idea of Order at Key West," or of a mention of "the thin men of Haddam" in "Thirteen Ways of Looking at a Blackbird," or of the line "Damariscotta da da doo" in "Variations on a Summer Day."[8] Perkiomen is the name of a small river in Stevens's native Pennsylvania; Haddam is the name of a small town in Connecticut. Damariscotta is the name of a coastal village in Maine; it is a Native American name meaning "river of little fish."[9] The list of American place names in Stevens's poetry could be extended. Stevens's early poem "Sunday Morning" celebrates the particularities of the US landscape as determining the life that is lived there.[10] Many other Stevens poems assert the same presupposition, as in the line in "The Comedian as the Letter C": "The natives of the rain are rainy men."[11]

Just what are those "salient features" of an indigenous community, according to Stevens? I say "indigenous community" because Stevens stresses that it's an experience shared by a "we": "We were as Danes in Denmark all day long." This assumption that the indigene lives in a community of other indigenes like himself or herself is one main feature of Stevens's indigene ideology. To be an indigene is to be part of a collectivity and to have collective experience. An indigenous community, moreover, is located in a place, a milieu, an environment, that is cut off from the outside world, the "outlandish," the "queer." One might almost call the outside world uncanny, in the sense implied by the German word *unheimlich*, literally "unhomelike." Indigenes are "hale-hearted landsmen." They belong to the land, to its rocks, rivers, trees, soil, and ways of living on the land. They would feel uprooted if they moved elsewhere. The indigene feels at home in his place, as Danes feel at home in Denmark, or as bees are at home in their honeycomb.

To be an indigene is to be innocent, childlike. The indigene's innocence is like that of Adam and Eve before the fall. The indigenes know not good and evil. They do not suffer the "enigma of the guilty dream" that torments fallen men and women—for example, the terrifying Oedipal male dream of having killed one's father and slept with one's mother. Indigenes lack self-consciousness, as though they were sleepwalkers, or asleep while awake. They are "sticky with sleep." "Sticky" here is associated with the decorous honeycomb on which the indigenes feed. Their at-home-ness makes their milieu a kind of sleep-inducing narcotic, as eating the honey they have collected puts bees to sleep, makes them "sticky with sleep."

Not only are the indigenes not aware of themselves, lacking the painful self-awareness and habit of guilty introspection that are supposed to characterize Western man. The indigenes are also not aware of their environment, in the sense of holding it at arm's length and analyzing it. They take their milieu for granted as something that has always been there and always will be, eternally, as Denmark is for the Danes, according to Stevens. The widespread resistance to the evidence of global warming may be generated in part by this mythical assumption that our environment is unchangeable, endlessly renewable. Surely our home on Mother Earth will not change enough to make it uninhabitable! Why does Stevens choose Danes as exemplary of an indigenous community? I suppose because they live in a small country, have a homogeneous culture, and speak a "minority" language that cuts them off from others. That fits most people's idea of an indigenous community, including the one presupposed in the Wang/Xie call for papers.

To mention language leads me to note that language plays a crucial role in Stevens's description. An indigenous community is created not just through shared ways of living, building, and farming on a particular homeland soil. It is also created out of language, by way of language—a particular language, moreover, that belongs to that place. One radical effect of the global hegemony of Western cultural capital is to endanger if not extinguish so-called minority languages everywhere. The indigenous peoples who inhabited the state of Maine, where I live in the United States, had dwelled here for as much as twelve thousand years before the white man came. By "here" I mean right here, within a mile of where I am writing this. On a nearby shore there is a large shell midden going back at least seven thousand years. We eradicated most of the indigenes and their culture in a couple of centuries. Only a few still speak the "native languages" of the Penobscots or the Micmacs. The goal of some of them now is to run gambling casinos, hardly consonant with maintaining their "native culture." A dozen indigenous languages can disappear forever in California in a single year as the last "native speaker" of each one of them dies.

Thinking of the vanishing of indigenous languages makes the language theme in Stevens's lines all the more poignant. He sees an indigenous community as generated by language, in an act of maternal and artistic creation that mimes the creation of the world, as described in Genesis, out of the primordial darkness: "As if the innocent mother sang in the dark / Of the room and on an accordion, half-heard, / Created the time and place in which we breathed . . . / And of each other thought." Why "on an accordion"? I suppose because it is a "folk instrument." An accordion is suitable for creating the togetherness of a folk. Perhaps it is also because overtones of consonant togetherness in the word "accord" are buried in the word "accordion." The members of an indigenous community are in accord. They are "of one accord." In an assertion that recalls Heidegger's argument in "Bauen Wohnen Denken" ("Building Dwelling Thinking"), and in his essays on Hölderlin's poems, Stevens asserts that the time and the place of an indigenous community are not there to begin with and then occupied by the people.[12] A native language creates the homeland that gives a people breathing room, a place to breathe and therefore also to speak to one another.

Stevens's sentence just cited ends with the phrase "And of each other thought." The language that creates the time and the place of an indigenous community is also the medium in which the "natives" or "autochthons" think of one another. Each indigene can penetrate the minds of his or her fellows because they all speak the same language, the same "idiom" (that is, a dialect peculiar to a specific group). It is the "idiom of the work"—an idiom, I take it, special to the work—that the innocent mother plays on the accordion, though there may also be an overtone of "work" as the collective creation of an indigenous community through language, and through the physical transformation of the environment. This would be akin to the Marxist notion of work or Heidegger's notion of *Bauen*, building. The mother's accordion work is also in "the idiom of the innocent earth." The earth is innocent because it, too, has not yet fallen with Adam and Eve's fall. The language spoken by indigenes is, as *they* are, born of the earth and remains rooted in it. Language, for Stevens here, is the embodiment of thought. Each native knows what his or her fellows are thinking because, as we say, they all "speak the same language." The result is that "we knew each other well" because, in Stevens's sexist formulation, "we thought alike / And that made brothers of us in a home / In which we fed on being brothers." I shall return to this exclusion of women in the invocation of "brotherhood," blood brotherhood.

This at-home-ness, finally, means that the place and the community dwelling within it are sacred. These happy autochthons "lie down like children, in this holiness." The creation of a community, through an idiomatic language and a collective living together, speaking together, and thinking together, creates a sacred place, makes the whole place sacred.

Wonderful! Hooray! Or, as Stevens puts this exuberance a few lines later in "The Auroras of Autumn," "A happy people in a happy world— / Buffo! A ball, an opera, a bar."[13] Only two problems shadow this celebration. One is that the indigenous community is a myth, or, in Stevens's terminology, an "idea." One could say that all Stevens's work goes to demonstrate that this is the case. The homogeneous community of indigenes is always a matter of something that hypothetically once existed and no longer exists. "We *were* as Danes in Denmark," but that is no longer so. As Stevens puts this:

> There may always be a time of innocence.
> There is never a place. Or if there is no time,
> If it is not a thing of time, nor of place,
>
> Existing in the idea of it, alone,
> In the sense against calamity, it is not
> Less real.[14]

An indigenous community is real enough, but it has the reality of something that exists only in the idea of it, before or after time, and outside of all place.

The other menace that shadows this idea is that even this mythical innocent community was always darkened by the terror of invasion. It exists as "the sense against calamity," but that calamity is always imminent. That calamity appears suddenly as a stark fear or terror just a few lines beyond the long passage I have been discussing:

> Shall we be found hanging in the trees next spring?
> Of what disaster is this the imminence?
>
> Bare limbs, bare trees and a wind as sharp as salt?[15]

The poem, after all, is called "The Auroras of Autumn." Its chief figure is terrifying autumnal displays of aurora borealis, or northern lights, as they presage winter. Simply to name all the features of an indigenous community, even in a lyric poem so celebratory of the idea of it as is Stevens's, is to destroy it by bringing it self-consciously into the light. To name it is to call up its specular mirror image: the terror of its destruction. This obverse is generated out of its very security, as a sense of disaster's imminence. "A happy people in a happy world" sounds, and is, too good to be true. To imagine having it is to be terrified of losing it. The imagination of being at home, in a homeland or *Heimat*, instantly raises the fearful ghost of the *unheimlich*, the uncanny, the terrorist at the door, threshold, or frontier, or most likely already secretly resident somewhere inside the homeland.

Jennifer Bajorek, in a brilliant essay titled "The Offices of Homeland Security, or, Hölderlin's Terrorism," has shown how the rhetoric of the Bush administration, in a sinister way, has echoed the mystified appeal of Fascist states (for example, the Nazi state) to the notion of a "homeland" mingling *Blut und Erd*, that is, racial purity and rootedness in one dear particular place.[16] Our newly created Office of Homeland Security, now renamed the Department of Homeland Security and elevated to Cabinet rank, presupposes that we are a homogeneous homeland, an indigenous people whose security is endangered by terrorists from the outside, racially and ethnically strangers, who are probably also already inside, *unheimlich* presences within the homeland. As Bajorek recalls, Bush said in a speech of 20 September 2001, "Either you are with us or you are with the terrorists."[17] [Such ethnocentrism or chauvinism is no doubt one reason for the fierce opposition now by conservatives to immigration reform that would give illegal immigrants a chance to become United States citizens.—JHM]

It is easy to see what is fraudulent about this use of "homeland" and "security." I do not deny the "terrorist threat." Lots of people hate the United States. Nevertheless, the United States is not and never was a "homeland" in the sense that this word implies. Relatively few US citizens stay in the places where they were born. We are nomads, even if we were born here. I was born in the state of Virginia, but my family left when I was a few months old, and I have never been resident there since. I have lived all over the place in the United States, as most of our citizens have. Large numbers of our citizens, moreover, are immigrants, many quite recent immigrants. Almost all of us are descended from immigrants who occupied an alien land. In my case, some of my male ancestors were late-eighteenth-century German unwilling immigrants, remnants of mercenary soldiers in the British army who were captured by the Americans, allowed to settle, and joined what were known as the "Pennsylvania Dutch" ("Dutch" for *Deutsch*, German). Only the tiny number of Native Americans can truly call themselves indigenes. Of course their ancestors, too, were once newcomers, invaders from Asia who crossed by the Bering land bridge just after the last ice age. The United States is made up of an enormous diversity of different races and ethnic groups speaking many different languages.

The Department of Homeland Security in its surveillance activities has made many citizens or residents of the United States markedly less secure, certainly far less able to maintain the privacy of their homes or of their e-mail or of information about the books they read, just as the invasion of Iraq in the name of national security has arguably made our "homeland" far less secure. [When I wrote this essay, in 2003, I had no knowledge of the almost universal spying on digital and phone materials by the National Security Agency, now ongoing.—JHM] We have multiplied many times over the terrorist threat and have led a country like North Korea to conclude that its only possible safety lies in developing deterrent nuclear weapons as fast as possible. To be "secure," as Bajorek observes, means to be "without care," and, as I have shown in Stevens's poem, the myth of the indigenous community generates the terror of losing it. It generates the insecurity it would protect us against.

Bajorek's paper, in a subtle, balanced, and careful analysis, shows that the notions of homeland security, and of an indigenous German community ascribed by Heidegger to Hölderlin, are a mystified misreading. Rather, in his poems about rivers and valleys and mountains—for example, "Heimkunft/An die Verwandten" (Homecoming/To the related ones), read in admirable detail by Bajorek—Hölderlin presents the homeland as the place lacking ground, an *Abgrund*. It is a place of unhealed fissures and unfathomable abysses rather than the place where an indigenous community (in the sense in which I have identified it, with Wallace Stevens's help) could dwell. "[I]f for Hölderlin 'home,'" says Bajorek, "if and insofar as it is a place, can only be a place to which one returns, and more precisely to which one is *always* returning, this is not only because the home that man makes on this earth is not a dwelling place ('Wohnen ist nicht das Innehaben eine Wohnung'). It is because, for Hölderlin, 'being-there' is always a 'being-elsewhere' and first 'takes place' by way of a departure."[18]

I conclude at this point in my argument that the concept of indigenous communities, as invoked by Wang and Xie, is perhaps somewhat suspect. It depends on a Rousseauistic and, perhaps to some degree, Marxist myth of "man at point zero." It would be prudent to doubt that such a thing ever existed in reality or exists in reality anywhere in the world today. I say "Marxist myth" because, as Blanchot shows in "Man at Point Zero," Lévi-Strauss's disappointed search for an ideal innocent indigenous community among the Nambikwara of South America was motivated in part by dubious Marxist notions of postcapitalist communities of happy proletarians enjoying their dictatorship, in a repetition of the happy savage communities at the beginning of human history.

Another Western notion of community, of much more recent origin, has been developed by twentieth-century theorists. Wang and Xie's concept of community corresponds more or less closely to the well-known theory of community developed by Benedict Anderson.[19] Without denying the cogency of Wang and Xie's assertions of the truly deplorable effects of global cultural capitalism, I want now to identify that alternative notion of community, and to think what it might mean for a possible resistance to the hegemony of global cultural capitalism. This notion of an "unworked" or "unavowable" or "secret" community, the "community of those who have nothing in common," is developed in the work of Georges Bataille, Maurice Blanchot, Giorgio Agamben, Alphonso Lingis, Jacques Derrida, and Jean-Luc Nancy.[20]

Blanchot's *La communauté inavouable* focuses on the investigation of community as it appears throughout Bataille's work. Nancy makes references to Bataille that are essential to his argument. These six writers are by no means singing the same tune or preaching the same doctrine, however. They do not make a community of the Same, as of Danes in Denmark, any more than American popular culture is a monolithic, monolingual, univocal ideology. The writers I have listed propose one form or another of an alternative notion of community. This is the "community," as Bataille puts it, in a sentence used by Blanchot as the epigraph for *The Unavowable Community*, "of those who do not have a community" ("la communauté de ceux qui n'ont pas de communauté").[21] The thinking of these theorists is, however, heterogeneous. They contest one another, if implicitly. Each of these six writers, moreover, is to some degree heterogeneous in what he says about community, as Blanchot makes a point of affirming about Bataille. An immense trajectory would be necessary to track the thought about community of all six. Oversimplifying radically, I shall focus most on Nancy's *La communauté désoeuvree* (*The Inoperative Community*), and on just one paragraph of that (the title of the published English translation uses the word "inoperative," but I prefer "unworked," in spite of its being a neologism, because of its economic or Marxist overtones). Nancy's thought about community is subtle, complex, and not all that easy to grasp. I have space, however, to look closely at only one passage.

First, though, I ask once more: What is a community? How would you know when you encountered one or lived in one? The word "community" is part of a family of words in "commun . . ." or "common . . . ," or "con . . ." : "communion," "communism," "communication," "commune," "commonality," "common" itself, as in the phrase "in common," "condominium," and so on. The paradox of community can be indicated by the Greek word for "common" or "shared by the community": *koine*. Koine is the name of the Hellenistic dialectic of Greek, derived largely from Attic. It became "common," in the centuries just before and after Christ's birth, to the whole Hellenistic world, replacing local dialects. The New Testament was written in Koine. That makes it exoteric, accessible to the whole world, the initial means of the global spread of Christianity and its development into a "world religion." At the same time, the New Testament expresses an esoteric doctrine defining the in-group of those who understand and believe. As Jesus explains in the parable of the sower, if you don't get it, you won't get it. He answers the disciples who ask why he speaks in parables by saying the following (I give his words in what is now our worldwide Koine, English, and in the King James version, so closely associated with the birth of British imperialism): "Because it is given to you to know the mysteries of the kingdom of heaven, but to them it is not given. For whosoever hath, to him shall be given, and he shall have more abundance: but whosoever hath not, from him shall be taken away even that he hath. Therefore speak I to them in parables: because they seeing see not; and hearing they hear not, neither do they understand" (Matthew 13:11–13). Christianity is at once a worldwide community and the most exclusive in-group that can be imagined.

The word "community" must be distinguished from such related words as "culture," "ethnicity," "group," "nation," "collectivity," "in-group" (defined by the *American Heritage Dictionary* as "a group united by common beliefs, attitudes, and interests characteristically excluding outsiders"), "troupe," "set," "society," "association," "religion," "collection," "gang," "organization," "amalgamation," and so on. We use the word "community" all the time in everyday discourse, without thinking much about it. We speak of a "close-knit community," of a "community of believers," of the "local community," of a "community center" (meaning a building where community activities take place), of the "European community," of the "Islamic community," of a "community of readers," or even of "cybercommunities," and so on. Scientists speak of "communities of microbes." The meanings of these phrases seem clear enough.

The word "community," however, as is usually the case with such conceptual terms, becomes problematic as soon as you detach it from such everyday uses and ask, "What is a community?" The word, as I have already suggested, implies beliefs and assumptions shared, held in common, taken for granted, by a group. We normally assume an upper and a lower limit in size for a community. A community or "amalgamation" of two does not quite seem right, though Jean-Luc Nancy proposes to call the duo of two people in love a form of community, as does Blanchot. A community nevertheless needs at least a third as witness, *terstis*, someone who gives testimony to the transactions between any two. In practice, three persons are hardly enough; nor is a single family, even an "extended" one, ordinarily thought of as making up a community. We commonly think of a community as made up of a fairly large number of people, not all related by birth or marriage, who share assumptions and dwell together in the same place. My "we" in the previous sentences, however, appeals to a hypothetical community of those who think of community as I do. They hardly need to dwell in the same place. They are the community of my readers who agree with me (if there are any), wherever they may be living.

Even so, an ideal community (if there is such a thing) is, in most people's idea of it, made up of men and women dwelling together in Yeats's "dear perpetual place." They live together under the aegis of shared beliefs, institutions, laws, and assumptions. Examples would be monks in a monastery, or people living together in the same rural village or city neighborhood. At its upper limit of size, a community frays off into being something else—a nation, for example. The "American people" hardly form a community, whatever appeals politicians may make to some imagined unity, as when they say, "The American people do not want universal health care," when what they mean is that the for-profit health maintenance organizations (HMOs) and pharmaceutical companies do not want universal health care. The "Arab community" is not really a community in the sense in which I am using the word. It is too big, too diverse. The "American people" is also too big, too diverse, too heterogeneous to be a community. We speak too many different languages, are too much divided between rich and poor, haves and have-nots, and have too many different religious faiths and ethnic allegiances to be called a "community." The "European community" is more a metaphor for an assemblage of nations than the name for a community in the strict sense of people living together and sharing the same values and assumptions. The term nevertheless may appeal to that, as a horizon to be reached when all of Europe comes to have the same laws, currency, and economic system. Economic unity, however, hardly makes a community in the usual sense of the word.

The ideal community I have in mind is made up of a relatively small group of people living in the same place who speak the same language and have the same religious beliefs and the same institutions. Stevens, as I have shown, eloquently celebrates this ideal. Each individual member of such a community has, as Louis Althusser would put it, been interpellated to be what he or she is by the various circumambient local ideological apparatuses—school, church, laws, the media—that impinge on him or her. This assemblage makes felicitous speech acts possible: marriages that keep the community going; promises made and kept; the making of contracts to buy, sell, or exchange; the making of efficacious wills transmitting money and property to the next generation; the rule of law and custom; the just incarceration of lawbreakers; and so on.

For J. L. Austin, and for standard speech act theory generally, the felicity of speech acts depends on the existence of a viable community. A viable community is one with fixed laws, institutions, and customs accepted and acted on by all members of the community. For a performative to work, says Austin in *How to Do Things with Words*, "there must exist an accepted conventional procedure having a certain conventional effect, that procedure to include the uttering of certain words by certain persons in certain circumstances."[22] Later on, speaking of legal decisions, Austin says, "The whole point of having such a procedure [a preordained, ritualized assembly of performative words and rules along with infallible ways to identify who is authorized to use them] is precisely to make certain subsequent conduct in order and other conduct out of order: and of course for many purposes, with, for example, legal formulas, this goal is more and more nearly approached."[23] Who "accepts" the "accepted conventional procedure"? Though Austin does not say so, he must mean "accepted by some working community."

Just how are the people living together in such a community related to one another? Here one may oppose two models of community. The first is the ordinary commonsensical one that most people have in mind, explicitly or implicitly, when they speak of community. The other is a less intuitive model of community that is inextricably entwined with the first. One resists taking the second one seriously, since it is hard to think and has disastrous consequences for the first model. The second model of community "unworks" the first. I made up the neologism "unworked" on the basis of the literal meaning of Jean-Luc Nancy's *La communauté désoeuvrée*. The English version, again, translates *désoeuvrée* as "inoperative." "Inoperative" has the advantage of being a real English word, but it is hardly an accurate carrying over of the nuances of the French word *désoeuvrée*. The latter carries an implicit reference to the Marxist notions of production and of products that are the "works" of the workers' work, just as a common notion of human communities sees them as the work of a group living and working together. They have constructed the community over time. It is the product of their combined and cooperative work, the result of a social contract they have explicitly or implicitly signed. Their collective work has constituted it, sometimes on the basis of an explicit "constitution," just as the community of my university department, if it is a community, is governed by a departmental "constitution."

This commonly accepted model of community sees the individuals within it as pre-existing subjectivities. These subjectivities have bound themselves together with other subjectivities for the common good. Their mode of communication with one another can be called "intersubjectivity." This communication is an interchange between subjectivities. Such an interchange presupposes that the other is like me. Our common language makes it possible for me, in spite of my individuality, to communicate to my neighbor what I am thinking and feeling, what I am, or to understand through language and other signs what the other person is thinking and feeling. We "knew each other well, hale-hearted landsmen." These cohabiting subjectivities have made together a language, houses, roads, farms, industries, laws, institutions, religious beliefs, customs, mythical or religious stories about their origin and destiny that are told communally or written down in some sacred book to be recited to the group. For example, Christian church services include each week readings from the Old and New Testaments that are synecdoches for a recital of the whole Bible. The whole Bible is spoken aloud in the church over the course of several years. The Bible is the sacred Book that binds the community together.

Literature within such a community is the imitation, or reflection, or representation of community, the construction of cunningly verisimilar miniature models of community. *Bleak House* allows you to carry the whole of Dickens's London in your pocket. Literature is to be valued for its truth of correspondence to a community already there, for its constative value, not for any performative function it may have in constituting communities. Valid language—for example, the language of literature—is primarily and fundamentally literal, not (except as embellishment) figurative, just as the conceptual terms describing this model of community are to be taken literally, *à la lettre*. The primary figure employed is the figure of synecdoche. This figure allows a few examples to stand for the whole, as Gridley, the Man from Shropshire in *Bleak House*, stands for the whole class of those whose lives have been destroyed by the Court of Chancery.

The individuals living together in such a community no doubt think of themselves as finite, as mortal, and one of their community places is the cemetery; nevertheless, mortality does not essentially define community life. The community's constant renewal from generation to generation gives it a kind of collective immortality, just as the living together of individuals in a community tends to project a hypothetical sempiternal "community consciousness" or "collective consciousness." Each separate individuality participates in, is bathed or encompassed in, this collective consciousness, as a fish swims in water, or as Danes all know Danish. Death tends to be covered over, suppressed, quickly forgotten, as is notoriously the case within many American communities, if they can be called that, today.

It is possible (though it would be an error) to see Victorian novels—for example, George Eliot's novels, or Dickens's, or Anthony Trollope's—as straightforwardly based on such a conception of community and as reflecting or imitating such actually existing communities. An example of such fictive communities is the Barsetshire community in Trollope's Barset novels. The omniscient narrators in such novels are the expression of that collective consciousness of the community I mentioned earlier. Victorian multiplotted novels are, according to this view, "models of community." They are cunning miniature replicas of communities that actually existed historically. Their object of representation is not one individual life story but a whole community. The existence of such communities, in reality and in fictive simulacra, so this (false or only partially true) story about Victorian novels goes, ensures the execution of felicitous performatives. In Trollope's novels, as in Victorian fiction generally, the most important speech acts or writing acts are the marriages of marriageable young women and the passing on from generation to generation, by gifts, wills, and marriage settlements, of money, property, and rank. Most often in Victorian novels, these two themes are combined. The heroine's marriage redistributes property, money, and rank and carries it on to the next generation.

Another model of community has been articulated in recent years. This has been done in different but more or less consonant ways by the theorists already listed. The widely influential book by Benedict Anderson, *Imagined Communities*, is, on the whole, no more than a subtle, postmodern version of the first model of community, the one whose features I have already sketched out. I shall describe an alternative to this, primarily in Nancy's terms, in what I have called the "unworked" community.

Nancy sees persons not as individualities but as "singularities." Persons are agents, and each is fundamentally different from all the others. Each harbors a secret alterity that can by no means be communicated to any other singularity. These singularities are essentially marked by their finitude or mortality. Each is from moment to moment, from the beginning, defined by the fact that it will die. Here is Nancy's expression of this (Blanchot cites this passage in part in *La communauté inavouable*; he says it is the essential affirmation in Nancy's *La communauté désoeuvrée*):

> That which is not a subject opens up onto a community whose conception, in turn, exceeds the resources of a metaphysics of the subject. Community does not weave a superior, immortal, or transmortal life between subjects (no more than it is itself woven of the inferior bonds of a consubstantiality of blood or of an association of needs), but it is constitutively, to the extent that it is a matter of a "constitution" here, calibrated on [*ordonnée à*] the death of those whom we call, perhaps wrongly, its "members" (inasmuch as it is not a question of an organism). But it does not make a work of this calibration. Community no more makes a work out of death than it is itself a work. The death upon which community is calibrated [*s'ordonne*] does not *operate* the dead being's passage into some communal intimacy, nor does community, for its part, *operate* the transfiguration of its dead into some substance or subject—be these homeland [*patrie*], native soil or blood, nation, a delivered or fulfilled humanity, absolute phalanstery [*phalanstère absolu*: the word "phalanstery" refers to a community of the followers of Charles Fourier, from *phalanx* (any close-knit or compact body of people) plus *monastère* (monastery)], family, or mystical body. Community is calibrated on death as on that of which it is precisely impossible to *make a work* (other than a work of death, as soon as one tries to make a work of it). Community occurs in order to acknowledge this impossibility, or more exactly—for there is neither function nor finality here—the impossibility of making a work out of death is inscribed and acknowledged as "community."
>
> Community is revealed in the death of others; hence it is always revealed to others [*La communauté est révélée dans la mort d'autrui: elle est ainsi toujours révélée à autrui*]. Community is what takes place always through others and for others. It is not the space of the *egos* [*des* moi]—subjects

> and substances that are at bottom immortal—but of the *I*'s [*des* je], who are always *others* [*des* autrui] (or else are nothing). If community is revealed in the death of others, it is because death itself is the true community of *I*'s that are not *egos*. It is not a communion that fuses the *egos* into an *Ego* or a higher *We*. It is the community of *others* [*C'est la communauté des* autrui]. The genuine community of mortal beings, or death as community, establishes their impossible communion. Community therefore occupies a singular place: it assumes the impossibility of its own immanence [*l'impossibilité de sa propre immanence*], the impossibility of a communitarian being in the form of a subject. In a certain sense community acknowledges and inscribes—this is its peculiar gesture—the impossibility of community [*La communauté assume et inscrit—c'est son geste et son tracé propres—en quelque sorte l'impossibilité de la communauté*].[24]

The reader will see that Nancy's model of community puts in question, point by point, all the features of Stevens's indigenous community, the happy state of Danes in Denmark. Each person is a "singularity," that is, wholly other to all the others. Each singularity, in Nancy's model of community, is not a self-enclosed subjectivity such as the first model assumes. Each singularity is exposed, at its limit, to a limitless or abyssal outside that it shares with the other singularities from the beginning, by way of their common mortality. Their community is defined by the immanence of death. This death we experience not in our own death, since that cannot be "experienced," but in the death of another, the death of a friend, a neighbor, a relative.

The language defining this other model of community is necessarily figurative, catachrestic, since no literal language exists for it. Even conceptual words are used "anasemically," that is, against the grain of their dictionary or normal semantic meanings. They are also used with an implicit or explicit play on their metaphorical roots. Examples of such words in Nancy's book are *singularité* itself, or *désoeuvrée*, or *partagé*, or *com-parution*, or *limite*, or *exposition*, or *interruption*, or *littérature* as in his phrase "literary communism." Blanchot's complex use of the word *désastre* in *L'écriture du désastre* is another, analogous example, with its play on the word *astre* (star) buried in the word *désastre*.[25] I give the words in the original French because their nuances are not easily translated.

The first model of community is easy to understand because it is the one most of "us" take for granted. Nancy's model is more difficult to understand or to think. One resists thinking it or taking it seriously because it is devastating, a disaster, for the other model. Nancy's systematic dismantling of that other model's assumptions confirms this. No subjectivities, no intersubjective communication, no social "bonds," no collective consciousness, exist in Nancy's "unworked community."

Nancy thinks by way of the permutation of certain key terms that recur, that are incorporated again and again in new formulations. These attempt once more to say what cannot be said. They keep trying to say what is, strictly speaking, unsayable. The last sentence of *The Inoperative Community*, in the original French form, avers just this (the original version has just the first three chapters of the five chapters in the English version): "Here I must interrupt myself: it is up to you to allow to be said what no one, no subject, can say, and what exposes us in common."[26]

This essential "impossibility of saying" determines several features of Nancy's style.

First, the key words he uses are twisted away from their normal or idiomatic use. They are suspended from everyday discourse. They are, as it were, held out in the open, dangling, unattached. This happens because they tend to detach themselves through their iteration in different syntactic combinations with other key words.

A second stylistic feature is outright contradiction, unsaying in the same sentence what has just been said, as in "allow to be said what no one, no subject, can say." Well, if no subject can say it, who or what can be imagined to say it?

A third feature is an odd sort of implicit spatialization of the story Nancy tells. The figures of limit, sharing/shearing, articulation, suspension, exposition, and so on, are all implicitly spatial. These words invite the reader to think again what Nancy is thinking in terms of a certain weird space in which the topographical terms are withdrawn as soon as they are proffered. The limit, for example, is not an edge, border, or frontier, since there is nothing that can be confronted beyond it. It is like the cosmologists' finite but unbounded universe. You confront a limit, a boundary, but you cannot get out of your enclosure because no beyond exists, no transcendent outside. *Partagé*, to give another example, is a double antithetical word meaning both "shared" and "sheared," divided. It is a spatial or topographical word, but you cannot easily map something that is both shared and sheared, *partagé*. Nancy has written a whole book, *Le partage des voix*, exploiting the contradictory nuances of the French word *partage*.[27]

A final feature of Nancy's style (which is to say, of his "thought") is that the model of community he proposes is explicitly the negation (though that is not quite the right word) of the community model that most people have in mind when one asks, "What is a community?" The two models are neither antithetical nor the negations of each other, in the Hegelian sense of a determinate negation allowing for dialectical sublation. Each presupposes the other, is entangled with the other, is generated by the other as soon as you try to express it alone, for example, in a novel or in a theoretical treatise, such as Nancy's books, or such as these paragraphs you are now reading, or such as the lines from Stevens I read earlier. The commonsense model presupposes preexisting self-enclosed "individuals," "subjectivities," "selves," "persons." These egos are finite, no doubt, mortal, no doubt, but totalizing, oriented toward totality, and in that sense immortal. These individuals then encounter other individuals and subsequently establish, by intersubjective communication leading to a compact or contract, a society, a community made up of shared stories (myths of origin and end), a language, institutions, laws, customs, family structures with rules for marriage and inheritance, gender roles, and so on, all organically gathered together, and all the combined work of individuals living in the same place. A group of people living and working together establishes an immanent close-knit community—geographically located, closed in on itself, autochthonous, indigenous. Language is a tool that "works," or makes—that is, produces—the interchanges of community.

Nancy says we now know no such community ever existed, though the first sentence of *The Inoperative Community* reaffirms this familiar historical myth. The myth, or ideologeme, presumes that such communities once existed, and that modernity is characterized by their dissolution. "The gravest and most painful testimony of the modern world," says Nancy, "involves all other testimonies to which this epoch must answer (by virtue of some unknown decree or necessity, for we bear witness also to the exhaustion of thinking through History), is the testimony of the dissolution, the dislocation, or the conflagration of community."[28] The commonly presumed model is always already unworked, *désoeuvré*, by the alternative model. The alternative model is a negation, if not in the dialectical sense allowing some synthetic *aufhebung*, then at least in the sense that it says no to the other one. It defines itself point by point as opposed to the "first" model. In place of individuals with self-enclosed subjectivities, Nancy puts singularities that have always been *partagés*, shared, sheared, open to an abyssal outside. Singularities are extroverted, exposed to other singularities at the limit point where everything vanishes. Language in such a community becomes literature, writing (*écriture*) in the Blanchotian or Derridean sense, not sacred myth. Literature is the expression of the unworking of community.

Here is a key example of Nancy's mode of expressing what the "unworked" or "inoperative" community is like. I give the passage in its English translation, though with French words or phrases along the way where the nuance of the French is important:

> Communication consists before all else in this sharing and in this compearance [*com-parution*] of finitude: that is, in the dislocation and in the interpellation that reveal themselves to be constitutive of being-in-common—precisely inasmuch as being-in-common is not a common being. The finite-being exists first of all according to a division of sites, according to an extension—*partes extra partes*—such that each singularity is extended (in the sense that Freud says: "The psyche is extended"). It is not enclosed in a form—although its whole being touches against its singular limit—but it is what it is, singular being (singularity of being), only through its extension, through the areality that above all extroverts it in its very being—whatever the degree or the desire of its "egoism"—and that makes it exist only by *exposing it to an outside*. This outside is in its turn nothing other than the exposition of another areality, of another singularity—the same other. This exposure, or this exposition-sharing, gives rise, from the outset, to a mutual interpellation of singularities prior to any address in language (though it gives to this latter its first condition of possibility). Finitude compears, that is to say it is exposed: such is the essence of community.
>
> Under these conditions, communication is not a bond. The metaphor of the "social bond" unhappily superimposes upon "subjects" (that is to say, objects) a hypothetical reality (that of the "bond") upon which some have attempted to confer a dubious "intersubjective" nature that would have the virtue of attaching these objects to one another. This would be the economic link or the bond of recognition. But compearance is of a more originary order than that of the

> bond. It does not set itself up, it does not establish itself, it does not emerge among already given subjects (objects). It consists of the appearance of the between as such: you *and* I (between us)—a formula in which the *and* does not imply juxtaposition, but exposition. What is expressed in compearance is the following, and we must learn to read it in all its possible combinations: "you (are/and/is) (entirely other than) I [*toi (e[s]t) (tout autre que) moi*]." Or again, more simply, *you shares me* [*toi partage moi*] [or "You shears me"].
>
> Only in this communication are singular beings given—without a bond *and* without communion, equally distant from any notion of connection or joining from the outside and from any notion of a common or fusional interiority. Communication is the constitutive fact of an exposition to the outside that defines singularity. In its being, in its very being, singularity is exposed to the outside. By virtue of this position or this primordial structure, it is at once detached, distinguished, and communitarian. Community is the presentation of the detachment (or retrenchment) of this distinction that is not individuation, but finitude compearing.[29]

Well, there is Nancy for you, at his most dense. You must read and reread to make sense of it. If "myth," for Nancy, is the linguistic expression of those living together according to the first model of community, "literature" names the contestation of that by one expression or another, however implicit, of the second model of community. This gives literature (which includes, for Nancy, philosophy, theory, and criticism as well as literature proper in the sense of novels, poems, and plays) an explicitly political function, as he asserts at the end of "Le communisme littéraire," the third and final part of *La communauté désoeuvrée* in its original French version:

> It is because there is community—unworked always, and resisting at the heart of every collectivity and in the heart of every individual—and because myth is interrupted—suspended always, and divided by its own enunciation—that there exists the exigency of "literary communism." And this means: thinking, the practice of a sharing of voices and of an articulation according to which there is no singularity

> but that exposed in common, and no community but that offered to the limit of singularities.
>
> This does not determine any particular mode of sociality, and it does not found a politics—if a politics can ever be "founded." But it defines at least a limit, at which all politics stop and begin. The communication that takes place on this limit, and that, in truth, constitutes it, demands that way of destining ourselves in common that we call a politics, that way of opening community to itself, rather than to a destiny or to a future. "Literary communism" indicates at least the following: that community, in its infinite resistance to everything that would bring it to completion (in every sense of the word *achever*—which can also mean "finish off"), signifies an irrepressible political exigency, and that this exigency in its turn demands something of "literature," the inscription of our infinite resistance.
>
> It defines neither *a* politics, nor *a* writing, for it refers, on the contrary, to that which resists any definition or program, be these political, aesthetic, or philosophical. But it cannot be accommodated within every "politics" or within every "writing." It signals a bias in favor of the "literary communist" resistance that precedes us rather than our inventing it—that precedes us from the depths of community. A politics that does not want to know anything about this is a mythology, or an economy. A literature that does not say anything about it is a mere diversion, or a lie.[30]

One more question must be asked and an answer posited. If the first kind of community ensures the felicitous uttering of performatives—promises, marriage oaths, contracts, wills, and the like—what about speech acts in the second kind of community? No solid ground for doing things with words is offered by the community joining a "set, a group of 'exposed' singularities that are wholly other to one another," by way of the impossibility of community. None of the conditions for felicitous speech acts laid out by Austin in *How to Do Things with Words* is met within an "unworked community." The members are not enclosed selves or egos capable of taking responsibility for what they say and enduring through time so that promises made yesterday may be kept today. No social contract or constitution making possible the establishment of functioning laws and institutions exists. No transparent "intersubjective" communication can be counted on to certify for me the sincerity of speech acts uttered by another person. Such a community is *inavouable*, unavowable, in the double sense that Blanchot means the word to have in *La communauté inavouable*. An unworked community remains secret, unable to be publicly avowed. Blanchot's example is the secret community that Georges Bataille and his associates established, a community committed to the clandestine sacrifice of one or another of its members by beheading (hence the name "Acéphale" in Bataille's *L'Apprenti Sorcier du cercle communiste démocratique à Acéphale*). Such a community is certainly something one would want to keep secret, though one might note that the early secret communities of Christians performed a ritual sacrifice, commemorating Christ's crucifixion, in the communion service. This ritual was modeled on the sacrifices, sometimes actually bloody, in ancient Near Eastern mystery cults. United States solidarity is held together, it might be argued, by the enactment, over and over again, of the "death penalty": those on death row will die so that our community may remain intact.

Such an unworked community is "unavowable" in another way, however. It does not provide solid ground for any avowals or speech acts. This does not mean that speech acts do not occur within unworked communities, nor does it mean that speech acts may not be efficacious. What it does mean, however, is that such speech acts are not endorsed by any public laws and institutions. They work by a resolution to go on being true to them, a resolution continuously self-generated and self-sustained. Such speech acts are a kind of lifting oneself by one's bootstraps over that abyss to which Nancy and Blanchot give the name "death."

Matthew Arnold expresses something like this form of unavowable vow in the contradictory last stanza of "Dover Beach." Arnold's formulation is Blanchotian in its positing of a love between singularities that is without grounds in love as a universal, Love with a capital L. Nor does it have grounds in any of the other universals—certitude, peace, joy, light, and so on—that would seem necessary prerequisites for felicitous vows of fidelity exchanged between lovers. Arnold's speaker exhorts his beloved to join him in what Blanchot might have called an *amour sans amour*. This would be the only love possible in an unworked community:

> Ah, love, let us be true
> To one another! For the world, which seems
> To lie before us like a land of dreams,
> So various, so beautiful, so new,
> Hath really neither joy, nor love, nor light,
> Nor certitude, nor peace, nor help for pain . . . .[31]

One word cognate with "community," "communion," leads to Christian communion and to Freud's theories of the primal horde. Here a challenge to Nancy by Jacques Derrida will help me to refine further the two notions of community. Derrida's target is not Nancy's *La communauté désoeuvré* but his *L'expérience de la liberté* (*The Experience of Freedom*).[32] In fairness to Nancy, it must be said that what Derrida objects to in *L'expérience de la liberté*—that is, the emphasis on "brotherhood"—is lacking in *La communauté désoeuvrée*. The members of a community of the first kind, says Nancy in *The Experience of Freedom*, are in communion with one another by way of what they share. What they share is that they have killed the father and have shared, sheared out ("partagé") his body and eaten it. This makes them "brothers," "semblables." ("Hypocrite lecteur—mon frère—mon semblable," says Baudelaire in the apostrophe to the reader at the beginning of *Les fleurs du mal*.[33]) They are the same. They share a guilt. They are all like one another. Hence they are transparent to one another, like the brothers in Stevens's poem. The French revolutionary motto, "Liberty, equality, fraternity," links freedom to fraternity. That freedom needed to be asserted in a violent act against monarchal sovereignty. The French revolutionaries shared the guilt of killing the king. Modern English democracy has the beheading of King Charles I on its conscience. (The Alhambra in Granada, Spain, was the scene of the killing of the primal father in reverse: the sultan had thirty-six princes beheaded; the Fountain of the Lions ran with their blood.)

A fraternal community is united in its opposition to those who are not semblables, who are different, who do not take communion, who do not act in the name of Christ's words to his disciples at the Last Supper, a brotherhood if ever there was one: "This do in remembrance of me." Such a community is a community of intolerance, often of unspeakable cruelty to those outside the community, as the Christians expelled Arabs and Jews from Spain, the Arabs ultimately from the Alhambra. Such a community depends for its solidarity on exclusion. You are either with us or against us, and if you are against us you are "evildoers," as George W. Bush called Iraq, North Korea, Somalia, and so on—in the end, every other nation but the United States, and then only a small group there, the rest being sympathizers, "focus groups," peaceniks, communists, subversives, hidden terrorists, friends of terrorists: in short, evildoers. This happens by an implacable and frightening suicidal logic that is built into democracy, defined as a brotherhood of semblables. Ultimately only Bush and his cronies are left among the good people, and then they will begin bumping one another off, as one or another of them falls on his (or her) sword. The latter phrase has been used recently to describe the way the head of the CIA, George Tenet, has taken responsibility for the lie in George W. Bush's State of the Union address of 2003 about Iraq seeking uranium from Niger.

Where, by the way, are the women in this paradigm—sisters, mothers, wives, lovers? Are they not non-semblables, unlike the men? Maurice Blanchot thinks so, as did Marguerite Duras. In "The Community of Lovers," a chapter in *The Unavowable Community*, Blanchot—on the basis of a reading of Duras's *récit* titled *The Malady of Death*—proposes, with reference to Levinas and to the story of Tristan and Isolde, another version of the "unavowable community" that he has delineated in the first part of his book. This one is the impossible "community of two" made up of two lovers:

> And let us also remember that even the reciprocity of the love relationship, as Tristan and Isolde's story represents it, the paradigm of shared love, excludes simple mutuality as well as a unity where the Other would blend with the same. And this brings us back to the foreboding that passion eludes possibility, eluding, for those caught by it, their own powers, their own decision and even their "desire," in that it is strangeness itself, having consideration neither for what they can do nor for what they want, but luring them into a strangeness where they become estranged from themselves, into an intimacy which also estranges them from each other. And thus, eternally separated, as if death was in them, between them? Not separated, not divided: inaccessible and, in the inaccessible, in an infinite relationship.[34]

Derrida, in *Voyous*, is closer to Blanchot than to Nancy's notion of a brotherhood of free men. Against Nancy (and also against Levinas), he poses a community of dissimilars, non-semblables. This community is made up of neighbors who are defined by their absolute difference from on another:

> . . . pure ethics, if there is any, begins with the respectable dignity of the other as the absolute *unlike*, recognized as nonrecognizable, indeed as unrecognizable, beyond all knowledge, all cognition and all recognition: far from being the

> beginning of pure ethics, the neighbor as like or as resembling, as looking like, spells the ruin of such an ethics, if there is any.[35]
>
> . . . l'éthique pure, s'il y en a, commence à la dignité respectable de l'autre comme absolu dissemblable, reconnu comme nom reconaissable, voire comme méconnaissable, au-delà de tout savoir, de toute connaissance et de toute reconnaissance: loin d'être son commencement, le prochain comme semblable ou resssemblant nomme la fin ou la ruine de l'éthique pure, s'il y en a.[36]

I end by asking: Suppose one were to take seriously Nancy's notion of a community of singularities—or, in Lingis's phrase, a community of those who have nothing in common?[37] How would this lead one to think differently from Wang and Xie the effects of globalization?

The first thing to say is that Nancy's conception of community and the tradition to which it belongs are as much Western inventions as is any other product of cultural capitalism. Nancy's community of singularities is Western through and through. This is evidence that "Western ideology" is not some monolithic thing. Nevertheless, Nancy's concept of community is, like other such products, asserted with apodictic universality. It is not just Western men and women who are singularities in Nancy's formulations but all men and women everywhere, at all times. Nevertheless, Nancy's ideas are a Western product, perhaps even a product of the resources of the French language. I do not see any way out of this aporia. Any idea of community will be idiomatic, the product of a given language. It will, however, tend to express itself as universal. Nevertheless, it would be plausible to argue that each community should have its own singular idea of community, appropriate only for that community alone. That would raise questions about my own essay, not to speak of Nancy's universalizing affirmations. How can I speak except from within my own tradition? The whole issue of *ARIEL* devoted to thinking in English about globalization and the destruction of indigenous cultures may be a form of the thing it would resist.

The second thing to say, if we take Nancy's model of community seriously, is that it disqualifies—to some degree, at least—Wang and Xie's oppositon between the happy indigene and the cybersurfer, the former at home in his or her particular culture, the latter completely penetrated by global capitalism, corrupted by it, deprived of his or her specificity and made the same as everyone else. You will remember how Wang and Xie put this: "Multinational capital with its hegemonic ideology and technology seems to be globally erasing difference, imposing sameness and standardization on consciousness, feeling, imagination, motivation, desire, and taste."[38] According to Nancy's model of community, the singularity of neither indigene nor cybersurfer is touched by (for the former) the interpellations of indigeneous culture or (for the latter) the leveling American popular culture. Beneath their superficial cultural garments, both indigene and cybersurfer remain singular, wholly other to one another, even though they may be living together as indigenes or, on the contrary, communicating via e-mail or AOL Instant Messenger as cybersurfers. [Today I would put Facebook and Twitter in place of Instant Messenger. The social media in wide use have changed rapidly.—JHM] To put this in Heideggerian terms, the loneliness of *Dasein*, fundamentally characterized by its *Sein zum Tode*, "being towards death," remains intact beneath the alienating superficialities of *Das Man*, the "they." This happens in spite of the way Heidegger characterizes *Dasein* as primordially a *Mitsein*, a "being together."[39] It is as true as ever now that each man or woman dies his or her own death.

Nevertheless, it is plausible to argue that dwelling within the uniqueness of a so-called indigenous culture—that is, a local way of living untouched by globalization, if such a thing remains—is a better way to live the otherness of singularities to one another than is dwelling within the global homogenizing culture that is rapidly becoming the most widely experienced way to be human today. Diversity of cultures, languages, idioms, I agree, is a good in itself, just as is a diversity of plant and animal species. Moreover, certain local cultures, it may be, are closer to recognizing the immanence of death in their religious and cultural expressions than is Western popular culture's bland avoidance of death through the banal spectacular presentation of death in cinema and television. [Today I would add "video games."—JHM] Each local culture has to resist global capitalism as best it can. One way, as Nancy suggests, is through what he calls "literary communism"—that is, literature, including philosophy and critical theory, as well as poems, novels, cinema, and television shows, that confronts our solidarity in singularity, even though that cannot ever, he argues, be "confronted." Blanchot's *récits* might be models of such literature. Alas, precious little of that is being written or produced for the new media today.

Finally, I do not think much is gained by vilifying telecommunications technology as such. For one thing, these technologies are here to stay.

Hand-wringing will not make them go away. Moreover, cinema, television, cell phones, and computers are relatively neutral, in spite of the way their importation transforms any "indigenous" culture. The cultural force of these prosthetic devices, however, depends on the uses that are made of them. They can be used to reinforce and preserve local languages and local ways of life, however difficult it may be to do that. An essay in *Scientific American* by Mark Warschauer, "Demystifying the Digital Divide," distinguishes sharply between projects that simply set up computers in "underdeveloped countries," in which case they are likely to be used primarily to play computer games, and those projects that use computer installations to help support and maintain a local culture.[40] Warschauer's prime example is the Gyandoot ("purveyor of knowledge") project in Madhya Pradesh, an impoverished region of India. This project circulates, through an intranet, information about crop prices, medical treatment, and so on, that is intended to help maintain and improve the "indigenous culture," not destroy it, though one might still argue that the presence of computers is in itself the beginning of the end for that local culture.

The leveling effects of global cultural capitalism are enormously powerful, but small-scale local ways can be found to resist those forces in the name of the idiomatic and the singular. Though Western critical theory and literature are concomitants of global cultural capitalism, they can be used to support resistance to globalization, just as the telecommunications products of capitalism can be mobilized against capitalism. It is a matter of deliberate choice, not necessarily passive submission to an inevitable juggernaut. Or rather the resistance to global capitalism is a matter of certain anomalous forms of speech acts performed within "indigenous communities," now seen as gatherings of singularities. These speech acts perform local transformations of the global situation that just possibly might help maintain the local community of singularities. Somewhat paradoxically, another product of the West—its literature—may offer models for this. Examples are Wallace Stevens's poems and those Victorian novels that often in the end, almost in spite of themselves, assert the unknowable singularity and solitude of their characters in the crucial decisions that they make. Demonstrating that persuasively, however, would be another story.

CHAPTER 9

"Material Interests"

Modernist English Literature as Critique of Global Capitalism

Joseph Conrad's *Nostromo* is extremely complicated in its narrative organization. It offers narratologists great opportunities to demonstrate in detail the various kinds of narrative complexity employed by modernist authors such as Faulkner, Woolf, James, and Conrad himself. Just about every narrative device identified by specialists in narrative form is employed in one way or another: time shifts; analepsis; prolepsis; breaks in the narration; shifts in "focalization" from one character's mind to another by way of the "omniscient" (or, as I should prefer to say, following Nicholas Royle, "telepathic"[1]) narrator's use of free indirect discourse, or by way of interpolated first-person narration or spoken discourse; shifts by the narrator from distant, panoramic vision to extreme close-ups; retellings of the same event from different subjective perspectives; citations of documents; and so on.[2]

The chronological trajectory of the history of Sulaco, a province of the imaginary Central American country Costaguana, can be pieced together from these indirections. The story begins in the middle and then shifts backwards and forward in a way that the reader may find bewildering as he or she wonders just where on the time scale a given episode is in relation to some other episode. It is as though all these episodes were going on happening over and over, continually, in the capacious and atemporal mind of the narrator, like the endless succession of similar days and nights over the Golfo Placido in the setting of *Nostromo*. The story is presented in an almost cubist rendering, rather than by way of the impressionist technique Conrad is often said to have employed. If the goal of *Nostromo* is to reconstruct the history of Sulaco, the formal complexity of the novel does more than implicitly claim that form is meaning (that is, that the complexity was necessary if Conrad was to tell the story he wanted to tell). *Nostromo*'s narrative complications also oppose what it suggests is false linear historical narration to another, much more complex way to recover through narration "things as they really were." I shall return at the end of this essay to the question of the social, political, and ethical "usefulness" of modernist narration of this sort.

Fredric Jameson's slogan "Always historicize" means that we should read modernist English literature, or any other literary work of any time, in its immediate historical context. He is no doubt right about that. Nevertheless, certain works of English literature from the beginning of the twentieth century have an uncanny resonance with the global situation today. Examples would be the exploitation of Africa by the Wilcox family in E. M. Forster's *Howards End*, or the presentation of the effects of combat on Septimus Smith in Virginia Woolf's *Mrs Dalloway*. Charles Gould and the American financier Holroyd in Joseph Conrad's *Nostromo* are additional salient examples. Their collaboration is remarkably prophetic of the current course of American global economic aspirations as well as of the effects of these on local cultures and peoples around the world. I shall indicate some of those disquieting consonances later.

If *Nostromo* is a novel not so much about history as about alternative ways to narrate history, this means its goal is not to recover a single life story (as, say, *Lord Jim* does) but to recover the story of the ways a whole group of individuals were related, each in a different way, to the surrounding community as it evolved through time. *Nostromo* is a novel about an imagined community, a fictitious one based on Conrad's reading about South American history.

A spectrum or continuum can be identified of different ways in which the individual may be related to others, going from smaller to larger groups. At the small end is my face-to-face encounter with my neighbor, with my beloved, or with a stranger, in love, friendship, hospitality, or hostility. A family, especially an extended family or a clan, is a larger group, bound in this case by ties of blood or marriage. A community is somewhat larger. A community is a group of people, living in the same place, who all know one another and who share the same cultural assumptions. They are not necessarily related by blood or marriage, however. A nation is larger still. Most commonly, a nation is made up of a large number of overlapping but, to some degree, dissonant communities. Largest of all is the worldwide conglomeration of all human beings, living on the same planet and all more and more subject to the same global economic and cultural hegemony. At each of these levels, the individual has a relation to others, different in each case and subject to different constraints and conventions. In a given case, of course, it is often difficult if not impossible to maintain a sharp boundary between the different-sized groups.

Each form of living together, or of what Heidegger called *Mitsein*, has been the object of vigorous theoretical investigation in recent years—for example, Levinas's focus on the face-to-face encounter of two persons; or Jacques Derrida's similar focus, but with a radically different notion of *Mitsein*, in *The Politics of Friendship*; or work on the concept of community by Bataille, Blanchot, Nancy, Lingis, and others.[3] In what I shall say about Conrad's *Nostromo*, I shall interrogate primarily the relation of the individual to the community (or lack of it) in this novel, in the context of an intervention by global capitalism.

It can certainly be said that the citizens of Sulaco form a community, at least in one sense of the word "community." The inhabitants all live together in the same place. All share, more or less, the same moral and religious assumptions. Whether rich or poor, white, black, or Native American, they have been subjected to the same ideological interpellations, the same propaganda, the same political speeches, proclamations, and arbitrary laws. Most of all, they share the same history—what Don José Avellanos calls "Fifty Years of Misrule," the title of his never-to-be-published manuscript (though the narrator, magically and quite improbably, has read it and can cite from it).[4] Sulaco is a community of suffering, but as one revolution after another brings only more injustice and senseless bloodshed, it could nevertheless be argued that it is a true community. It is small enough so that most people know one another. Don Pépé, who runs the mine, knows all of the workers by name. Almost all belong to a single religious faith, Catholic Christianity.

If the reader reconstructs the story from a distance, putting the broken pieces of narration back in chronological order, *Nostromo* appears to be a tale of nation building, of the creation of one of those "imagined communities" that Benedict Anderson describes in his book of that name.[5] Through a series of seriocomic events and accidents, the province of Sulaco—after fifty years of misrule in Santa Marta, capital of the Costaguanan central government—becomes a prosperous, modern, peaceful, independent state, the Occidental Republic of Sulaco. An example of the fortuitous "causes" of this historical change is the cynical plan for secession devised by the skeptic Martin Decoud shortly before his death. His plan is not motivated by political zeal or belief but by his love for Antonia Avellanos. Nevertheless, Captain Joseph "Fussy Joe" Mitchell, in his fatuous incomprehension, recounts the creation of the Republic of Sulaco as a connected story whose destined endpoint is the present-day prosperous nation. Captain Mitchell, the English superintendent of the offices of the Oceanic Steam Navigation Company in Sulaco, recounts the sequence, in tedious detail, "in the more or less stereotyped relation of the 'historical events' which for the next few years was at the service of distinguished strangers visiting Sulaco."[6]

The pages that follow the immediately preceding citation give an example of Captain Mitchell's version of Sulaco history. Captain Mitchell is the spokesperson for an exemplary "official history," with its naive conception of "historical events" as following one another in a comprehensible linear and causal succession. Conrad quite evidently disdains such history writing. That false kind of history is represented, to one degree or another, in those sourcebooks on South American history by Masterman, Eastlake, Cunninghame Graham, et al., that Conrad had read.[7] Though *Nostromo* is about the nation building of an imaginary South American republic, not a real one, it is nevertheless, among other things, a paradigmatic example of an alternative mode of history writing, much more difficult to bring off. Conrad implicitly claims that this counterhistory is much nearer to the truth of human history and much more able to convey to readers the way history "really happens."

If the reader looks a little more closely, however, at what the narrator says about Sulaco society, it begins to look less and less like a community of the traditional kind—that is, less and less like a community of those who have a lot in common, like those egalitarian rural English villages on the Welsh border that Raymond Williams, in *The Country and the City*, so much admires, even though he resists idealizing them.[8] For one thing, Sulaco "society" is made up of an extraordinary racial and ethnic mixture, a product of its sanguinary history, as the narrator emphasizes from the beginning. The Spanish conquistadores enslaved the indigenes, the Native Americans. Wars of liberation from Spain led to wave after wave of military revolutions, one tyranny after another, with incredible bloodshed, cruelty, and injustice. Nevertheless, a large class of aristocratic, hacienda-owning, cattle-ranching, pure-blooded Spanish people, "creoles," remains. They are the core of the Blanco party. Black slaves were imported. Then a series of migrations from Europe—people coming either as workmen, political exiles, or imperialist exploiters—brought Englishmen, Frenchmen, Italians, even a few Germans and Jews. To add to the mix, sailors deserted from merchant ships, sailors like Nostromo, an Italian seaman, who settled in Sulaco and went to work at the Oceanic Steam Navigation Company, reporting to Captain Mitchell. Much intermarriage has occurred, or course. Bits of three languages other than English exist in the novel: Spanish, French, and Italian. The narrator often uses Spanish names for occupations and ethnic identifications as well as for place names, such as Cordillera, the name of the overshadowing mountain range. A good bit of the conversation in the novel must be imagined to be carried on not in the English the narrator gives but in Spanish. Decoud and Antonia are native-born Costaguanans, but they have been educated in France. They talk to one another in French. Giorgio Viola, the old Garibaldino, and his family are Italian, as is Nostromo. They speak Italian to one another. This is signaled even in this English-language book by the way Nostromo addresses Viola as "Vecchio," Italian for "old man." Conrad does not specify what language the descendants of black slaves and the indigenes speak, but presumably some original African or Native American languages persist beneath their Spanish. Charles Gould and all his family are English, though Gould was born in Costaguana and educated in England, as is the custom in that family. His wife is English, though her aunt has married an Italian aristocrat, and Charles Gould meets his future wife in Italy. The railroad workers are partly locals (Indios), but engineers from England run the operation, and some workmen are European.

Sulaco, I conclude, is a complex mixture of races, languages, and ethnic allegiances. In this, by the way, Sulaco is not all that different from the United States, though so far we have had only one successful "democratic revolution," ushering in government of the people, by the people, and for the people, with liberty and justice for all. I say these words with only a mild trace of irony, though in 1776 the liberty, justice, and equality did not extend to black slaves, of course, or to Native Americans, or to women. My houses in Maine are on land taken from the Native Americans who lived in the Penobscot Bay region for at least seven thousand years before the white man came and destroyed their culture in a few generations. The phrase "liberty and justice for all" still has a hollow ring for many Americans, such as the African American men and women who populate our prisons in such disproportionate numbers, or who swell the ranks of the unemployed.

The Sulaco (non)community exists, moreover, like the United States one, as a complex layering of differing degrees of power, privilege, and wealth, with the African Americans and Indios at the bottom, extending up through European working-class people to the Creoles and to the dominating quasi-foreigners like Charles Gould. Though the Gould family has been in Sulaco for generations, they are still considered Anglos, *Inglesi*. They are English in appearance, sensibility, mores, and language. The chief form of social mobility in Sulaco is through bribery, chicanery, or outright thievery (such as Nostromo's theft of the silver) or by way of becoming the leader of a military coup and ruling the country through force, as the indigene Montero momentarily does in *Nostromo*. It isn't much of a community!

Martin Decoud, at one point, sums up succinctly the nature of the Sulaco (non)community in a bitter speech to his idealistic patriotic beloved, Antonia Avellanos. He quotes the great "liberator" of South America, Simon Bolívar—something for which the "author's note" at the beginning of the text apologizes, oddly enough. I suppose that is because the citation is a parabasis suspending momentarily the dramatization of a purely imaginary Central American state with an intrusion from actual history. In the "author's note," Conrad has been defending, ironically, the "accuracy" of his report of Sulaco history, based as it is on his reading of Avellanos's "History of Fifty Years of Misrule." The joke (almost a "postmodern" rather than "modernist" joke) is that Avellanos's "History" is fictitious, along with the whole country of which it tells the story. No way exists to check the accuracy of Conrad's account against any external referent, nor is there any way to check what the narrator says against what Avellanos says. This reminds Conrad that some actual historical references do exist in the novel, and that these are a discordance:

> I have mastered them [the pages of Avellanos's "History"] in not a few hours of earnest meditation, and I hope that my accuracy will be trusted. In justice to myself, and to allay the fears of prospective readers, I beg to point out that the few historical allusions are never dragged in for the sake of parading my unique erudition, but that each of them is closely related to actuality—either throwing a light on the nature of

> current events or affecting directly the fortunes of the people of whom I speak.[9]

"Actuality"? "Current events?" The words must refer here to the pseudoactuality of Costaguana history. One such parabasis-like intrusion is Decoud's citation of Bolívar:

> "After one Montero there would be another," the narrator reports, in free indirect discourse, Decoud as having said, "the lawlessness of a populace of all colors and races, barbarism, irremediable tyranny. As the great Liberator Bolivar [*sic*] had said in the bitterness of his spirit, 'America is ungovernable. Those who worked for her independence have ploughed the sea.'" He did not care, he declared boldly; he seized every opportunity to tell her [Antonia] that though she had managed to make a Blanco journalist of him, he was no patriot. First of all, the word had no sense for cultured minds, to whom the narrowness of every belief is odious; and secondly, in connection with the everlasting troubles of this unhappy country it was hopelessly besmirched; it had been the cry of dark barbarism, the cloak of lawlessness, of crimes, of rapacity, of simple thieving."[10]

Though what the narrative voice reports Decoud as having said agrees, more or less, with what the narrative voice itself says, speaking on its own, it should nevertheless be remembered that Decoud is explicitly presented as an "idle boulevardier." He only thinks he is truly Frenchified. His corrosive skepticism leads ultimately to his suicide. One might say that Decoud is a side of Conrad that he wants to condemn and separate off from himself. That would leave someone who is earnestly committed to the endless hard work of the professional writer, someone who earns his daily bread by putting words on paper. Conrad's letters to Cunninghame Graham often express, it must be said, a skeptical pessimism that is close to Decoud's, as in one famous passage about the universe as a self-generated, self-generating machine: "It knits us in and it knits us out. It has knitted time, space, pain, death, corruption, despair, and all the illusions—and nothing matters."[11] Moreover, what Decoud says matches closely what the narrator says about Sulaco's deplorable history.

How did Sulaco come to be such a (non)community, or—to give Jean-Luc Nancy's term a somewhat different meaning from his own—how did Sulaco come to be an "unworked" or "inoperative" community, a "communauté désoeuvrée"? Nancy's book begins with the unqualified statement that "[t]he gravest and most painful testimony of the modern world, the one that possibly involves all other testimonies to which this epoch must answer (by virtue of some unknown decree or necessity, for we bear witness also to the exhaustion of thinking through History), is the testimony of the dissolution, the dislocation, or the conflagration of community."[12] *Nostromo* is a parabolic fable or allegory, a paradigmatic fiction, of the dissolution, dislocation, or conflagration of community. Just how does this disaster come about, according to Conrad? Who are the villains in this sad event? It is an event that can no longer even be understood historically. Nancy's view of "thinking through history," the reader will note, is quite different from Jameson's when the latter says, "Always historicize!" The dislocation of community must be borne witness to as something that we, or rather I, have experienced even if we (I) cannot explain it: "I have witnessed the conflagration of community. I testify that this is what has happened. I give you my personal word for it." The magically telepathic narrative voice in *Nostromo* is such a witness.

No doubt Conrad, quite plausibly, ascribes a lot of stupidity and knavery as well as limitless greed, thievery, and wanton cruelty to his Costaguanans. Someone had to obey orders and torture Dr. Monygham or Don José Avellanos. Someone had to do as he was told and string Señor Hirsch up to a rafter by his hands tied behind his back, just as someone has had to commit Saddam Hussein's tortures in Iraq, and someone had to push the buttons and pull the triggers to kill all those Iraqi soldiers and civilians when we took over Iraq, and some particular people did that torturing of the detainees in the Iraqi jail, Abu Ghraib, even if they acted on orders from higher up. Someone has pulled the triggers or devised the bombs to kill all the teachers, physicians, government officials, and other "intellectuals" in Iraq who have been assassinated since "the end of hostilities," not to speak of all the Iraqi civilians and police who have been killed. Someone had to wield all those machetes that butchered men, women, and children, whole villages of them, in Rwanda just a few years ago. A human decision and a human act were necessary to drop all those bombs on Kosovo, or to murder all those Chechnyans, or to retaliate against that with human suicide bombs in Moscow. Human beings are boundlessly capable of lethal cruelty to one another. It will not do to blame the "authorities" for this or to say, "I was just carrying out orders." We have seen a lot of examples of this human propensity for murder, rape, and sadistic cruelty all over the world in recent years. *Nostromo* provides a parabolic representation of this aspect of human history. These traits of human nature, organized in civil wars and revolutions, have certainly stood in the way of the imaginary Sulaco's becoming a community, to put it mildly.

Nevertheless, one needs to ask just what has made these deplorable aspects of "human nature"—aspects that always stand in the way of law, order, democracy, and civil society—especially active in Sulaco. The answer is twofold.

First there was the murderous invasion of South America by the Spanish, which killed many of the indigenous population and enslaved the rest, driving them into forced labor and destroying their culture. Mrs. Gould has a sharp eye for the present condition of the indigenous population. She sees them during her travels all over the country with her husband to get support for the new opening of the mine and to persuade the Indios to come as workmen for the mine:

> Having acquired in southern Europe a knowledge of true peasantry, she was able to appreciate the great worth of the people. She saw the man under the silent, sad-eyed beast of burden. She saw them on the road carrying loads, lonely figures upon the plain, toiling under great straw hats, with their white clothing flapping about their limbs in the wind; she remembered the villages by some group of Indian women at the fountain impressed upon her memory, by the face of some young Indian girl with a melancholy and sensual profile, raising an earthenware vessel of cool water at the door of a dark hut with a wooden porch cumbered with great brown jars.[13]

This passage is a good example of that shift from a panoramic view to the specificities of an extreme close-up—in this case, in a report of Mrs. Gould's memory as it diminishes from her general knowledge of "the great worth of the people" to that "earthenware vessel of cool water at the door of a dark hut with a wooden porch cumbered with great brown jars." Conrad's narrator observes that many bridges and roads remain in Sulaco as evidence of what slave labor by the Indios accomplished.[14] Whole tribes, the narrator says, died in the effort to establish and work the silver mine. At several places, the narrator describes the Native American remnant in their sullen reserve.

"For whatsoever a man soweth, that shall he also reap" (Galileans 6:7). The consequences of the Spanish conquest remain as the inaugural events in that whole region. The effects of these events cannot be healed or atoned for even after hundreds of years. They still stand in the way of the formation of any genuine community, Christian or secular, in the usual sense of the word "community." This "origin" was not a unified and unifying originating event, like the big bang that initiated our cosmos, from which Costaguanan history followed in linear and teleological fashion toward some "far-off divine event" of peace and justice for all. It was rather a moment of what Jean-Luc Nancy calls, in a play on the word, "exposition."[15] The indigenous community, whatever it was like (and it will not do to idealize it too much; pre-Columbian history in South America was extremely bloody, too), was disposed of by being displaced, posed or placed beside itself, unseated, ex-posed. This happened through the violent occupying presence of an alien culture bent on converting the "savage heathens" to Christianity and on enslaving them as workers in the Europeanizing of Sulaco.

This divisive violence at the origin, or origin as polemos, division, exposition, also helps account for the way South American history, in what Conrad in *A Personal Record* calls this "imaginary (but true)" version of it, is a long story of civil wars, tyrannies, and revolutions.[16] Nor has this history come to an end. Twentieth-century events in Brazil, Argentina, Panama, Uruguay, Chile, and Haiti bear witness to this. (A bloody rebellion against the Haitian government of Aristide, led by armed paramilitary forces and parts of the army, was taking place at the moment I first drafted this essay, on 10 February 2004. The Bush government, in typical US interventionist fashion, put its support behind Aristide's ouster. Never mind that he was the democratically elected president.) These sad, historically "true" events are the background, or the assumed subsoil, of the "imaginary" story Conrad tells.

The next phase of Sulacan society that the narrator records is the subsequent invasion of Europeans, in a second wave, after South American republics achieved independence. This was the invasion of global capitalism. It was already in full swing in Conrad's day. Of course that invasion is still going on today. It is more often now transnational corporations, often but not always centered in the United States rather than in Europe, that are doing the exploiting. *Nostromo*'s main action is a fable-like exemplum of the effects of Western imperialist economic exploitation. The novel can be read with benefit even today as an analysis of capitalist globalization. The novel circles around one signal event in such a history: the moment when foreign capital, what Conrad calls "material interests," makes it possible to resist a threatened new local tyranny. This happens by way of a successful counterrevolution, and the establishment of a new regime. The Occidental Republic of Sulaco will allow foreign exploitation—in this case, the working of the San Tomé silver mine—to continue operating peacefully in a stable situation, a nation with law and order. The silver will flow steadily north to San Francisco to make rich investors constantly richer. This prosperity leaves the men who work the mine still earning peasants' wages, though they now have a hospital, schools, better housing, relative security, and all the benefits that Christian churches can confer. Nevertheless, references to labor unrest, strikes and the like, are made toward the end of the novel. Conrad's narrator gives a haunting picture of the mine workers at a moment of the changing of shifts:

> The heads of gangs, distinguished by brass medals hanging on their bare breasts, marshaled their squads; and at last the mountain would swallow one-half of the silent crowd, while the other half would move off in long files down the zigzag paths leading to the bottom of the gorge. It was deep; and, far below a thread of vegetation winding between the blazing rock faces, resembled a slender green cord, in which three lumpy knots of banana patches, palm-leaf roofs, and shady trees marked the Village One, Village Two, Village Three, housing the miners of the Gould Concession.[17]

What is most terrifying about this process of exploitation is Conrad's suggestion of its inevitability, at least in the eyes of the capitalist exploiters. It does not matter what are the motives of the agents of global capitalism, how idealistic, honest, or high-minded they are. They are coopted in spite of themselves by a force larger than themselves. Charles Gould has inherited the Gould Concession from his father. The father was destroyed by the mine, since, though he was not working it, constant levies were made on him by the central government in Santa Marta until he was ruined financially and spiritually. "It has killed him," says Charles Gould, when the news of his father's death reaches him in England. He resolves to atone for that death by returning to Sulaco, raising capital on the way, and working the mine—just as, it might be argued, George W. Bush is making up for the failed assassination attempt against his father (or, as he said in a press conference several years ago, he thinks he has a divine calling to invade Iraq and bring democracy to the world). What goes on in the mind of George W. Bush is inscrutable, and probably extremely strange, frighteningly strange, an imminent threat. Nevertheless, one may guess that one of Bush's motives for the invasion of Iraq was a desire to make up for his father's failure to "take out Saddam Hussein" and secure Iraqi oil for Western use. [Remember that this was written in 2004. I still think my assessment was right.—JHM]

Charles Gould was, as I have said, born in Sulaco. His sentimental and idealistic belief is that what he calls "material interests" will eventually bring law and order to his unhappy homeland, since these will be necessary to the working of the mine. "What is wanted here," he tells his wife, "is law, good faith, order, security. Anyone may declaim about these things, but I pin my faith to material interests. Only let the material interests once get a firm footing, and they are bound to impose the conditions on which alone they can continue to exist. That's how your money-making is justified here in the face of lawlessness and disorder. It is justified because the security which it demands must be shared with an oppressed people. A better justice will come afterwards. That's your ray of hope."[18] That noble but naive confidence finds its echoes in today's neoconservative arguments for bringing democracy to Iraq by way of securing the smooth working of the oil industry there, our present-day form of "material interests." The latter (oil exploitation) is bound to bring the former (Western-style capitalist democracy), in good time, since oil exploitation requires law and order. This is the "trickle-down theory," or, in George W. Bush's words, "it's our calling to bring democracy to the world," "to change the world."

Actually, Gould is, in spite of his English sentimental idealism and practical efficiency, no more than a tool of global capitalism. The latter is represented, as every reader of the novel will remember, by Holroyd, the sinister American businessman and entrepreneur from San Francisco. Holroyd funds the reopening of the San Tomé mine as a kind of personal hobby. It is one small feature of his global enterprise. That enterprise includes, as a significant detail, a commitment to building Protestant churches everywhere the influence of his company reaches. Or rather Holroyd funds not the mine but Charles Gould. It is Gould he has bought, not the mine. He has done so out of his confidence in Gould's integrity, courage, practicality, mine-engineering know-how, and fanatical devotion to making the mine successful at all costs. Holroyd's recompense is the steady flow north to San Francisco, by steamer, of large amounts of silver from the port of Sulaco.

Holroyd has a canny sense of the precariousness of the San Tomé enterprise. He is ready at a moment's notice to withdraw funding if things go badly—for example, through a new revolution installing another tyrannical dictator who will take over the mine for his own enrichment. Nevertheless, Holroyd sees global capitalism as destined to conquer the world. He states this certainty in a chilling speech to Charles Gould. Gould does not care what Holroyd believes as long as he, Gould, gets the money necessary to get the mine working. Holroyd's speech is chilling because it is so prescient. A CEO of ADM (Archer Daniels Midland, "Supermarket to the World"), or Enron, or Bechtel, or Fluor, or Monsanto, or Texaco, or Halliburton might have endorsed Holroyd's grandiose beliefs. Dick Cheney, for example, in an earlier role, was CEO of Halliburton before he became vice president. He might have made such a speech, at least in private, to confidantes or confederates. It is not insignificant that Holroyd's big office building of steel and glass is in San Francisco, since so many transnational corporations even today are situated in California, if not in Texas. Conrad foresaw the movement of global capitalism's center westward from Paris and London, first to New York and then to Texas and California. What Conrad did not foresee is that it would be oil and gas rather than silver or other metals that would be the center of global capitalism. Nor did he foresee that the development and use of oil and gas would cause environmental destruction and global warming that would sooner or later bring the whole process of economic imperialism to a halt, if nuclear war does not finish us all off before that.

Western-style industrialized and, now, digitized civilization, as it spreads over all the world, requires oil and gas not just for automobiles and heating but for military might and explosives; for the airplanes that span the globe; for plastics, metal, and paper manufacture; and for the production of fertilizers and pesticides that grow the corn and soybeans that feed the cattle that make the beef that feeds people. Corn is also the source of the ethanol that contributes greatly to global warming. Oil is essential to the manufacture of personal computers, television sets, satellites, fiber-optic cables, and all the rest of the paraphernalia of global telecommunications and mass media. Surprisingly, it takes two-thirds as much energy to produce a personal computer as to produce an automobile, a large amount in both cases. When the oil and gas are gone, in fifty years or less, we are going to be in big trouble, up the proverbial creek without a paddle, unless we turn soon, in a big way, to renewable energy—solar panels and wind farms.

Holroyd, by the way, is a perfect United Statesian, that is, a mixture of many races. He is also a splendid example of religion's connection to the rise of capitalism, this "millionaire endower of churches on a scale befitting the greatness of his native land."[19] "His hair was iron gray," says the narrator, "his eyebrows were still black, and his massive profile was the profile of a Caesar's head on an old Roman coin. But his parentage was German and Scotch and English, with remote strains of Danish and French blood, giving him the temperament of a Puritan and an insatiable imagination of conquest."[20] Here is this insatiable capitalist's prophetic account of the way US-based global capitalism is bound to take over the world:

> Now what is Costaguana? It is the bottomless pit of ten per cent loans and other fool investments. [The reader will remember the huge losses that the Bank of America and other banks incurred some years ago from bad South American loans. These American banks, in their boundless greed, seem to have forgotten the lesson that Conrad's Holroyd already knew.—JHM] European capital had been flung into it with both hands for years. Not ours, though. We in this country know just about enough to keep in-doors when it rains. We can sit and watch. Of course, some day we shall step in. We are bound to. But there's no hurry. Time itself has got to wait on the greatest country in the whole of God's universe. We shall be giving the word for everything—industry, trade, law, journalism, art, politics, and religion, from Cape Horn clear over to Smith's Sound, and beyond too, if anything worth taking hold of turns up at the North Pole. And then we shall have the leisure to take in hand the outlying islands and continents of the earth. We shall run the world's business whether the world likes it or not. The world can't help it—and neither can we, I guess.[21]

Holroyd makes this remarkable statement to Charles Gould, during the latter's visit to Holroyd's office in San Francisco to raise venture capital for the mine. The "great Holroyd building" is described as "an enormous pile of iron, glass, and blocks of stone at the corner of two streets, cobwebbed aloft by the radiation of telegraph wires."[22] That sounds pretty familiar except that today such a building—for example, the Enron building in Houston—has more glass and less visible iron and stone.[23] The cobweb of telegraph wires would be replaced by invisible underground fiber-optic cables or by discrete satellite dishes. Nevertheless, Conrad's circumstantial account of the determining role of the telegraph and of transoceanic cables in Sulaco's affairs anticipates the role of new forms of global telecommunications today.

Gould's reaction to Holroyd's speech about the way the United States will take over the world is a slight disagreeable uneasiness caused by a sudden insight into the smallness, in a global perspective, of the silver mine that fills his whole life. Holroyd's "intelligence was nourished on facts," says the narrator, and, oddly, he says Holroyd's words were "meant to express his faith in destiny in words suitable to his intelligence, which was unskilled in the presentation of general ideas."[24] This observation is odd because Holroyd's speech, it seems to me, expresses with great eloquence the "general idea" or ideological presuppositions of US "exceptionalism," its presumption that it is our destiny to achieve imperialist economic conquest of the world, with military help when necessary. Holroyd's megalomaniac conceptions are not all that solidly nourished on fact. Charles Gould, on the other hand, "whose imagination had been permanently affected by the one great fact of a silver-mine, had no objection to [Holroyd's] theory of the world's future. If it had seemed distasteful for a moment it was because the sudden statement of such vast eventualities dwarfed almost to nothingness the actual matter in hand. He and his plans and all the mineral wealth of the Occidental province appeared suddenly robbed of every vestige of magnitude."[25]

My own reaction to Holroyd's speech is that chill or frisson I mentioned as a reaction to Conrad's prescience. It is also the reflection that US global economic imperialism may already be coming to an end, like all imperialisms, as China is about to become the world's largest economy, as Indian software displaces Silicon Valley, as US jobs flee by the hundreds of thousands to worldwide "outsourcing" and offshore manufacturing (a million jobs lost to China alone in the last few years), and as non-Americans like the Australian Rupert Murdoch are coming to dominate the global cable and satellite media, not to speak of newspapers. The triumph of global capitalism means the eventual end of nation-state imperialist hegemony. That includes the United States. We should make no mistake about that. Dick Cheney, it might be argued, had more power when he was CEO of Halliburton than he has as vice president of the United States, in spite of all the mischief he has done and is doing in the latter capacity. [Remember that this lecture was given in 2004.—JHM] The American people could have refused to re-elect him if they had chosen to do so, whereas he was not subject to such inconvenient restraint when he was CEO of a multinational corporation.

Somewhat paradoxically, one of the best ways to understand what is happening now in our time of globalization is to read this old novel by Conrad, written just a hundred years ago. That is one answer to the question of literature's "usefulness" that I posed at the beginning of this essay. The way military intervention by the United States is necessary to secure and support its worldwide economic imperialism is indicated in one small detail in *Nostromo*. The narrator notes that at the climax of the successful secession and establishment of the new Occidental Republic of Sulaco, a US warship, the *Powhattan* (a real US Navy ship, by the way, ironically named for a Native American chief), stands by in the offing, to make sure that the founding of the new republic does not go amiss. This parallels the historical fact that when Panama, through the United States' conniving, split off from Colombia after Colombia refused to approve the building of the Panama Canal, American naval vessels stood by to make sure that the split really happened and that the Colombians did not try to take Panama back.

The whole tale of US military and economic intervention (not to speak of covert action) in South America would be too long to tell here. Conrad's *Nostromo* gives an admirable emblematic fictional example of it. Whether Conrad himself agreed unequivocally with Holroyd's economic determinism is another question, just as it is questionable whether Conrad expresses without qualification his own radical skepticism through the Parisian dandy Decoud, "the man with no faith in anything except the truth of his own sensations," as though he were a perfect "impressionist."[26] I think the answer is no in both cases.

The biographical evidence—for example, that provided succinctly by Cedric Watts—indicates that though Conrad learned a lot about South American history and topography from Eastlake, Masterman, et al., it was especially through his friendship and conversations with the Scottish socialist aristocrat R. B. Cunninghame Graham (descendant of Robert the Bruce) and through reading Graham's writings that Conrad achieved his understanding of and attitude toward the bad things that Western imperialism had done over the centuries in South America.[27]

I conclude that, as many distinguished previous critics have noted (Edward Said and Fredric Jameson, for example), *Nostromo* is, among other things, an eloquent and persuasive indictment of the evils of military and economic imperialism exercised by so-called First World countries, especially the United States, against so-called Third World countries everywhere. The reader needs to be on guard, however, against confusing analogy with identity. I have used words like "allegory" and "parable" and "fable" and "consonance" and "uncanny resonance" to indicate that *Nostromo* is a commodious emblem of historical events—economic imperialism, in this case. Such historical events have recurred from time to time in post-Renaissance world history. They take place, however, in significantly different ways at different moments in history, as, for example, oil and gas have replaced silver as the preferred loot from Third World countries, or as new telecommunications, e-mail, cell phones, and the Internet have replaced the telegraph lines and undersea cables of Conrad's day. The differences, we must always remember, are as important as the similarities. A parable is not a work of history. It is a realistic story that stands for something else by way of an indirect mode of reference. One might call each such a literary work a "reading" of history. Literature, to express this in Conrad's own terms, is a way of using language in a mode that is "imaginary (but true)."

The claim I am making is complex and problematic. I am sticking my neck out in making it. It is impossible, in a short essay, to do justice to the complexity in question here. A parable is not the same mode of discourse as an allegory, nor is either of them the same as an emblem or a paradigm or a reading. Careful discriminations would need to be made to decide which is the best term for Conrad's writing procedure, in *Nostromo*, of making an imaginary story "stand for" history. That little word "for" in "stand for" is crucial here, as is the word "of" in the phrases "parable of" and "emblem of" and "allegory of" and "paradigmatic expression of" and "reading of." What displacement is involved in that "for"? What is the force of "of" in these different locutions? What different ligature or separation is affirmed in each case? The differences among these instances of "of" might generate a virtually endless analysis of *Nostromo* in their light.

I have used a series of traditional words for Conrad's displacement of "realist" narration in order to say something else. The multiplicity is meant to indicate the inadequacy of all of them. *Nostromo* is, strictly speaking, neither a parable nor an emblem nor an allegory nor a paradigm nor a reading. Each of these words is, in one way or another, inadequate or inappropriate. A parable, for example, as mentioned earlier, is a short realistic story of everyday life that stands for some otherwise inexpressible spiritual truth. An example is Jesus's parable of the sower, in Matthew 13:3–9. *Nostromo* is hardly like that. All the other words I have used can be disqualified in similar ways. Nevertheless, it is of the utmost importance not to read *Nostromo* as a straightforward piece of "historical fiction." Historical realities as Conrad knew them—not from direct experience but rather primarily from reading, as well as through conversations with Cunninghame Graham—are used as the "raw material" for the creation of a fictive "world" that is "imaginary (but true)."

Conrad's own phrase is perhaps, after all, the best way to express the use of realist narrative techniques to create a place swarming with people and events that never existed anywhere on land or sea except within the covers of copies of *Nostromo* (and in Conrad's imagination). The magnificent opening description of the sequestered province of Sulaco, cut off from the outside world by the Golfo Placido and by the surrounding mountains, is one way this isolation of Sulaco's imagined (non)community is expressed in the novel. The second part of Conrad's phrase, "but true," argues that the fictive events that take place in *Nostromo* correspond to the way things really happened in Central America at that stage of its history—that is, the moment of US imperialist and global-capitalist intervention. The words "but true" suggest a claim by Conrad that this transformation of historical fact into a complex modernist narrative form is better than any history book at indicating the way history actually happens. History happens, that is, in ways that are distressingly contingent. History is "caused" by such peripheral factors as Decoud's love for Antonia Avellanos, or Nostromo's vanity. Conrad's phrase "imaginary (but true)" is, after all, echoing, with his own modernist twist, what Aristotle said in the *Poetics* about the way poetry is more philosophical than history is because history "relates what has happened" whereas poetry relates "what may happen."[28] The "modernist twist" is the implicit claim that the narrative complexities and indirections I have been identifying get closer to "what has happened" than "official" histories do. Aristotle would probably not have approved of those complexities, any more than Plato, in *The Republic*, approved of Homer's "double diegesis" in pretending to narrate as Odysseus.

In spite of these complexities, the bottom line of what I am saying is that *Nostromo*'s indirect way of "standing for" the real South American history that Conrad knew from books and hearsay also means that, *mutatis mutandis*, it is an indirect way of helping its readers understand what is going on in the United States and in the rest of the world today, in 2004.[29] That understanding would then make possible, it might be, responsible action (for example, by voting) as a way of responding to what is going on. This, I am aware, is an extravagant claim for the social, ethical, and political usefulness of literature. I develop this claim at greater length in later chapters of this book.

I conclude also, finally, that *Nostromo* demonstrates—to my satisfaction, at least—that all its notorious narrative complexities of fractured sequence, reversed temporality, and multiple viewpoints are not goods in themselves. Not telling a story by way of a single point of view and in straightforward chronological order can be justified only if, as is the case with *Nostromo*, such extravagant displacements or "ex-positions" are necessary to get the meaning across more successfully to the reader's comprehensive understanding.

CHAPTER 10

Who's Afraid of Globalization?

My question might be rephrased as "Who *ought* to be afraid of globalization?" The answer to my title question is that a lot of people all over the world *are* afraid of globalization. This group includes a heterogeneous collection of environmentalists, isolationists, trade unionists, conservatives, and anxious liberals. These people protest at meetings of the World Bank and the World Trade Organization, and against the North American Free Trade Agreement. The group includes those in non-Western countries who fear that globalization means nothing more or less than worldwide Americanization and the consequent destruction of indigenous cultures everywhere. This will accompany, they fear, the total hegemony of US economic and cultural imperialism. Our neoconservatives who hope this will happen call this Americanization, in their jubilatory naiveté, the "new world order." The group that fears globalization also includes, however, those in the United States who want to make illegal immigrants guilty of a felony, to deport them all back to Mexico, and to erect a seven-hundred-mile wall on the Texas-Mexico border. It includes also those in the United States who wring their hands over the loss of jobs in the United States to outsourcing, a million or more jobs lost to China alone in the last few years, along with a consequent large annual trade deficit with China, as we buy more and more goods and services from China. These goods are in general extremely well made, just as Chinese services are extremely well performed in places like call centers in Dalian. The Chinese, like the Indians, do this for a fraction of the cost of the same goods and services in the United States. In the long run, this will probably lower the standard of living in the United States and Europe while gradually raising it everywhere else, as more and more highly skilled and highly paid US workers are laid off because what they do can be done more cheaply and just as well or better in places like China or India or Malaysia. That is what Thomas Friedman, in a helpful and highly detailed book about the effects of the new global technologies, calls the flattening of the world.[1]

Ought this strange mixture of people be so afraid of globalization? That is a different question. One answer is that being afraid of it is not going to stop it. Fear, moreover, is a bad state of mind in which to deal with a planetary change of unprecedented scope and rapidity. Better is to understand it and to try to take advantage of it, to deflect it in constructive ways—no easy task. Globalization, in any case, is not going to stop or go away.

Marx and Engels, in a famous and quite remarkable paragraph in the *Communist Manifesto*, foresaw what today we call globalization, both as an economic *mondialisation*, to give it its French name, and as a cultural "worldwide-ification." I am thinking of the section in the *Manifesto* that begins with the claim that

> [a]ll fixed, fast-frozen relations, with their train of ancient and venerable prejudices and opinions, are swept away, all new-formed ones become antiquated before they can ossify. All that is solid melts into air, all that is holy is profaned, and man is at last compelled to face with sober senses his real conditions of life, and his relations with his kind.
>
> The need of a constantly expanding market for its products chases the bourgeoisie over the entire surface of the globe. It must nestle everywhere, settle everywhere, establish connections everywhere.
>
> The bourgeoisie has through its exploitation of the world market given a cosmopolitan character to production and consumption in every country. To the great chagrin of Reactionists, it has drawn from under the feet of industry the national ground on which it stood. All old-established national industries have been destroyed or are daily being destroyed. They are dislodged by new industries, whose introduction becomes a life and death question for all civilized nations, by

> industries that no longer work up indigenous raw material, but raw material drawn from the remotest zones; industries whose products are consumed, not only at home, but in every quarter of the globe.[2]

This paragraph of the *Manifesto* ends with these prophetic sentences:

> In place of old local and national seclusion and self-sufficiency, we have intercourse in every direction, universal interdependence of nations. And as in material, so also in intellectual production. The intellectual creations of individual nations become common property. National one-sidedness and narrow-mindedness become more and more impossible, and from numerous national and local literatures there arises a world literature.[3]

"World literature," *Weltliteratur*—the word and the idea are Goethe's. Though Marx did not foresee the iPod, he did see what changes technological innovation makes. Today he would be speaking not of world literature but of a homogeneous worldwide culture of the new media: television, films, popular music, the Internet, e-mail, podcasts, videos, digital photos sent by e-mail, and so on.

Marx and Engels saw the globalization of capitalism as both a catastrophe and an opportunity. It would be a catastrophe for the old European nation-states because it would weaken their hegemony. That weakening Marx and Engels more or less welcomed. Globalization would also mean, they foresaw, the victory of capitalism as a worldwide single economic system of exploitation, commodification, and commodity festishism. They also saw global capitalism, however, as the chance for communism, through the death of capitalism when it inevitably overreaches itself through a process of autoimmune self-destruction. The workers, they confidently prophesied, will rebel to usher in the dictatorship of the proletariat. Marx and Engels, you will remember, do not appeal to the workers of this or that nation to organize within that country and resist. They say, "Workingmen [*sic*] of all countries, unite!" If Marx and Engels predicted the globalization of capitalism, communism, as defined in the *Manifesto*, was itself explicitly a form of globalization. Marx and Engels saw also that both forms of globalization, economic and cultural, involve the weakening of nation-state hegemonies and national cultures, for better or for worse.

Just what is our present-day form of globalization? It is a strange mixture of overlapping features. Moreover, what we call "globalization" is occurring at different rates, to different degrees, and in different ways in different parts of the world. Large numbers of people everywhere are not globalized at all or only lightly globalized. My wife, for example, has so far not learned to use a computer. I have to do her Googling for her, and type out on my keyboard the e-mails she has written in longhand, with a pencil, to our children and grandchildren. Moreover, one should remember that globalization has been accompanied by unparalleled economic exploitation, ethnic wars, suffering, and death. Jacques Derrida speaks eloquently about this aspect of globalization in *Specters of Marx*:

> For it must be cried out, at a time when some [such as Francis Fukuyama] have the audacity to neo-evangelize in the name of the ideal of a liberal democracy that has finally realized itself as the ideal of human history: never have violence, inequality, exclusion, famine, and thus economic oppression affected as many human beings in the history of earth and of humanity.[4]

What was true in 1993, when Derrida wrote these words, is even more true and more glaringly obvious now, thirteen years later. [Now twenty-two years later.—JHM]

I have said that globalization is a heterogeneous process. Economic globalization is not the same thing as the global diffusion of teletechnological devices and applications like computers, cell phones, and e-mail, though the former absolutely depends on the latter. Neither of these is the same thing as the environmental degradation, caused primarily by "developed" countries, that is causing global warming. None of those three is the same as the globalization of media, though that, too, depends on the new technology. The globalization of media means, among other things, the worldwide, more or less instantaneous diffusion of news and advertising as well as the concentration of media in the hands of people like Ted Turner and Rupert Murdoch. The globalization of mass media is not the same thing, however, as the global diffusion of cultural forces like film, television, computer games, and popular music, even though they use the same teletechnological/prestidigitizing devices and equipment: iPods, wireless networks, fiber-optic cables, communications satellites, computers, and increasingly complex cell phones with e-mail, digital cameras, videoconferencing, game playing, podcasting, and basic computing built in.

The crucial element in all these features of globalization, the common denominator, is the new communications technologies. Without those, globalization in any of its current forms would be impossible—no globalization (at least in its current hyperbolic form) without the cell phone, the computer, and the iPod. These have swept the world in a remarkably short time. I can remember the time, not so many years ago, when the first browser, Mosaic, gave the user magical access to a handful of websites. If Thomas Friedman shows how the new technologies and a worldwide economy are penetrating more or less everywhere, he also shows how, in the long run, and indeed already, a "flat" world, or level playing field, is likely to reduce US power and give countries like China and India enormous economic and cultural power.[5] Let us hope they use it wisely, for the benefit of mankind, more wisely than the United States is using its own power these days. We are using our economic, technoscientific, and military power in self-destructive as well as outwardly destructive ways—for example, by causing enormous environmental damage that is hastening global warming, or by running up gigantic deficits that will sooner or later bankrupt our economy. [That was a mistake. Deficits are not our problem. Tax breaks for the rich and for corporations are rather the problem.—JHM]

Globalization of the new teletechnologies is making epochal changes in the way we live now. I have hinted at the transformation of scholarship and of the university. Anyone anywhere now with a computer can have access to an enormous distributed database of scholarly information and online texts allowing authoritative research into almost anything. It is becoming less and less necessary to own that traditional basis of research and teaching in the humanities: printed books. It is not necessary, for example, to own hard copies, as they are called, of Henry James's novels. They are almost all available online for free. I have cited the *Communist Manifesto* from an online version I obtained in a few seconds by way of Google. Collaborative scholarship can be carried on by teams that are made up of individuals spread all over the world, not just located in a single university. I am this year, in 2006, involved in an ambitious collaborative research project on narratology ostensibly located at the Center for Advanced Study in Oslo, though I will have spent a total of only three weeks there during the year. Research essays are written on a computer and sent anywhere in the world instantaneously as e-mail attachments. I write all my letters of recommendation on the computer and send most of them by e-mail. Dissertation chapters are sent to me by e-mail. I am learning to read, annotate, and comment on them on the computer screen. The whole minute-to-minute process of my professional life has been utterly changed by the computer, in a few short years.

These new teletechnological devices have also made radical changes in ethical and political life, at least in my country, and probably also wherever globalization has reached. The model of ethical interaction used to be the face-to-face encounter with my family member or neighbor, who stood there before me in flesh and blood, as in Levinas's ethical theory of the *visage*, and even in Derrida's model of ethical life in *The Politics of Friendship*, *The Gift of Death*, and elsewhere.[6] Most nineteenth- and twentieth-century Western novels focus on the face-to-face encounter as the situation in which ethical confrontation and decision are carried on, though sometimes letters are important. Anthony Trollope's novels and those of Henry James consist primarily of a succession of scenes in which two characters confront one another in the give-and-take of dialogue. One example is the moving scene in Trollope's *The Last Chronicle of Barset* in which Archdeacon Grantley's hatred of Grace Crawley as an unsuitable potential wife for his son (since her impoverished clergyman father has been—falsely, it turns out—accused of theft) melts into love and admiration in a moment, when he actually meets her: "As he looked down upon her face two tears formed themselves in his eyes, and gradually trickled down his old nose. 'My dear,' he said, 'if this cloud passes away from you, you shall come to us and be my daughter.' "[7]

Ethical life is radically different now from Trollope's representation of it. The most important ethical relations in an individual's life may be mediated by one or many of the new teletechnologies—by e-mail, chat rooms, podcasts, computer games collectively played, and so on. A member of my own family is now happily married to a woman he first met online because they shared an interest in the same rather arcane website. She lived thousands of miles away.

If ethics have been fundamentally changed by globalization, the change in political life is even more dramatic. A forceful paragraph in Derrida's *Specters of Marx* describes the way parliamentary democracy of the old-fashioned Western sort has been disabled by television:

> . . . politicians become more and more, or even solely, characters in the media's representation at the very moment when the transformation of the public space, precisely by the media,

> causes them to lose the essential part of the power and even of the competence they were granted before by the structures of parliamentary representation, by the party apparatuses that were linked to it, and so forth. However competent they may personally be, professional politicians who conform to the old model tend today to become *structurally* incompetent. . . . They were thought to be actors of politics, they now often risk, as everyone knows, being no more than TV actors.[8]

I add that since 1993, in my country, at least, other teletechnological devices have intervened, for better or for worse, to disable parliamentary democracy: electronic voting machines that may be easily altered; political blogs that affect the way people vote; radio talk shows that have an enormous political effect; gerrymandering of congressional districts on the basis of electronically gathered voting statistics; the instantaneous diffusion of public opinion polls gathered electronically; the obscene alliance of companies large and small with government (for example, through lobbying) so that the federal drug coverage called Medicare Part D was written by and for the pharmaceutical companies, not for the good of the American people; the ownership and conduct of the media by politicians (for example, the running of Fox News by an ex-head of the Republican National Committee); the hiring of a telemarketing firm, apparently under directions from the White House, to jam the telephone lines of Democratic get-out-the vote offices during the last presidential election;[9] the apparent cooperation of the telephone company AT&T in the illegal electronic surveillance of United States citizens, "allowing the government to listen in on its customers' phone calls, read their e-mail and monitor their Web activity without the requisite legal showing";[10] and so on and on. All these changes in ethics and politics depend absolutely on the new teletechnologies. It is even possible to call this new situation, as Tom Cohen has done, "post-democracy."[11]

Globalized cultural studies seems at first to be a specifiable corner of globalization, but "cultural studies" is a distressingly (or delightfully) vague term, depending on how you feel about it, or them. Nothing human is alien to cultural studies, to appropriate Terence's famous remark: *Homo sum: humani nil a me alienum puto*.

I found that citation in a few seconds on Google, by the way. This is a good example of the effects of the new globalizing technologies on my own work. Google is amazing, as is *Wikipedia*, the online, collectively written, constantly updated encyclopedia. As with any encyclopedia, users need to remain suspicious of *Wikipedia*. Nevertheless, Google and *Wikipedia* level the playing field. You do not need to be next door to a great library if you have a computer. Mossback professors tend to say this is too easy. Students no longer learn how to use the library, or to discriminate good information from bad. Any library, however, contains a lot of bad or inaccurate information, whereas mistakes in *Wikipedia* are almost instantly corrected by a volunteer army of specialists. I can see no particular virtue in slogging around the library, as in the days when "scholarship was mostly legwork," as my doctor-father at Harvard, Douglas Bush, put it. He meant scholarship involved walking up and down miles of stacks in a research library looking for the books you wanted. Better ways exist to get exercise.

You can, as I suggested, make cultural studies mean more or less anything you like. The history of science, for example, including the story of how these new communications devices came to be invented, is a form of cultural studies, as is study of culinary and dress customs, advertising, the way people "play" the stock market, the "culture" of global corporations—as in Alan Liu's wonderful book, *The Laws of Cool*[12]—and so on. Cultural studies is actually closer to social sciences like anthropology and sociology than to what used to go on in traditional language and literature departments in the humanities. My university has just set up the new Center for Ethnography in our School of Social Sciences. According to the press release, "The center will explore social and cultural life from the perspective of those experiencing it. One of the center's first projects, funded by Intel Corp., will look at how technology changes people's definitions of 'public' and 'private.'" That sounds like cultural studies to me. I have no objection to the way humanities departments are remaking themselves as forms of social science, though I do think courses training humanists who want to do cultural studies in the protocols of ethnography and sociology would be a good thing. It would perhaps even be a necessary thing, if cultural studies is to be carried on in a responsible way. I see no particular point in training people to read Shakespeare who are actually going to do a comparative study of dress customs in London, New York, New Delhi, and Beijing. Such scholars need a different kind of professional training.

In practice, aspects of modern popular culture like film, television, computer games, dress fashion, popular magazines, and popular music often hold center stage when cultural studies is carried on in the humanities, even though many practitioners of cultural studies were trained in more traditional humanities disciplines. It is only reasonable that young humanists should want to study such topics. These cultural forms have far more power to determine ideologies and everyday life than does the once dominant cultural form, literature. These new cultural forms are where the action is. The computer game industry has larger revenue than all of Hollywood. The computer game that my granddaughter, a graduate student in neuroscience, habitually plays—*World of Warcraft*, by Blizzard Entertainment—had 1.5 million subscribers in the People's Republic of China the first month it came out in Chinese, in 2005.[13]

The new prestidigitizing machines magically create widely shared virtual realities, as in television news. In any country in the world, television news is carefully crafted to look like immediate reality. Television news is in fact, in complex ways, cunningly constructed as what Jacques Derrida calls an "artifactuality." We are surrounded by such ghostly virtual realities. We live our lives in terms of them. What is most amazing is the rapidity with which these gadgets—for example, cell phones and computers—have swept the world, just as iPods have done and as movies did earlier in the twentieth century. They seem to be irresistible. You might argue that if they Americanize everybody, this is only because nobody seems to be able to resist using them. No one is forcing people to use e-mail, cell phones, or iPods. People everywhere have eagerly embraced their "Americanization."

Why is this? I answer that human beings apparently need virtual realities. They will therefore embrace whatever technology offers such artifactualities, from the printed book to the iPod. People take to spectral virtual realities as a duck takes to water. That is a truly amazing human propensity. These devices respond to that need, but so did literature in its heyday. Reading a mystery story, or a novel (my habitual way of entering a virtual reality), is in this like playing a computer game or watching the evening news on television or watching a film, in spite of the big differences among these various forms of entering an artifactuality. At bottom, however, they are just different forms of technological magic. Today this magic takes the form of what I call "prestidigitalization." All these magics require some material means: the words on the page; the images on the screen, and the voices that accompany them; the sounds that reach my ear from the cell phone, sounds that I identify as my friend's voice. The study of ideology is a spectrology, that is, the study of virtual realities. Ideology, as Marx and Engels argued in *The German Ideology*, and as Jacques Derrida shows in detail in *Specters of Marx*, is fundamentally religious in nature.[14] Virtual reality machines at any time are a way of transmitting ideological ghosts, specters, spooks, like those images on a television screen or in a film, or like those ghosts that are raised when I read a novel: Trollope's *The Last Chronicle of Barset*, or Toni Morrison's *Beloved*, or Ha Jin's *Waiting*.

On the one hand, the new teletechnologies are in a sense indifferent. They are just dumb machines. They do not dictate what use is made of them, though they certainly shape those uses. You can say anything you like in any language into a cell phone. A Chinese person on the street speaking Chinese into his or her cell phone is using the device more or less in the same way as an American person does: to talk to someone wirelessly at a distance. A lot of different ways exist, however, to do that. These devices make radical changes in the way people live their daily lives, but different changes in different local cultures.

Another way to put this is to say that some theories of the bad effects of globalization assume too easily that human beings are one single coherent thing. Ordinary people are, I claim, capable of being many different people at once, of having multiple identities. For example, they can use computers or cell phones while retaining many or most features of their traditional culture: ways of dressing and eating, forms of courtship and marriage. Most important, perhaps, are the specificities of a particular native language. An example of this would be those Chinese who work in call centers. They are trained to speak idiomatic English in several versions or accents: American, Canadian, Australian, or British. They work long hours at what seems to an American like an incredibly low pay scale. They then go home to eat Chinese food, to think and speak in Chinese, to be related to their families and friends in Chinese ways. They are hybrid creatures. But then each human being is, and always has been, a congeries of different heterogeneous persons. The present human condition is just an extreme example of the human propensity for each person to be a swarm of different incompatible people, all at once.

I have elsewhere said a lot about the virtues of keeping literary study alive in these days of cultural studies, about the fundamental differences between literary study and cultural study, and about the need to read philosophy and theory in order to understand literature. Literary study, I have argued, is or should be always specific—that is, an attempt to read this or that literary work in all its uniqueness and singularity—whereas cultural studies tends, like anthropology and sociology, to be more interested in the typical, the average.

I want to end this brief essay, however, by saying something apparently quite different. I think one of the most urgent tasks of a globalized cultural studies today is to make local and then comparative, highly empirical, studies of just what effects on people's daily lives these essential requisites of globalization, the new communications devices, are actually having. It is not so much popular music per se that should be studied but popular music as transmitted from all over the world to anywhere in the world and then listened to on an iPod by specific people in specific cultural situations. It is not so much assuming that films have a universal content, the same for all viewers, as studying the ways films are seen and reacted to in perhaps quite different ways in different local cultures. It is not so much assuming that cell phones have a universal effect, the same everywhere, as studying specific local uses of cell phones. It is not so much assuming that computers or search engines like Google have a universal effect, the same everywhere, as studying the different ways people in different cultures actually use these devices. What is the actual effect on people's personalities, in different specific situations, when people play computer games, or use e-mail, or create their own podcasts? That, in my view, is the frontier of a globalized comparative cultural studies today. If I had my life to live over, I would make such study my life's work in teaching and writing. Such work would not just be objective description and analysis. It would take as its mission teaching people how best to use these new teletechnologies, how to be more than passive recipients of all those ghostly artifactualities, just as, in the old days when literature was the chief molder of citizens' ethical orientations, disciplines like the New Criticism had as their goal to teach people how to read and how to avoid being bamboozled by literature.

What skills will be necessary for these new disciplines? These disciplines hardly yet exist in coherent and institutionalized form. These skills will be quite different from the skills I was taught in college and graduate school to prepare me to teach and do research in literary history, literary criticism, and literary theory. Just what this new discipline will be like must be left to those who will invent it. I claim, however, that it should marry, in an unlikely alliance, the research procedures and protocols of ethnography with the analytical acumen and resistance to old-fashioned hermeneutics of so-called deconstruction. Tom Cohen's admirable *Hitchcock's Cryptonymies* offers, in film studies, a model for this new discipline.[15]

CHAPTER 11

A Comparison of Literary Studies in the United States and China

New telecommunications devices are a major factor influencing literary studies worldwide these days. That includes literary studies in the People's Republic of China. By mid-2007, 500 million cell phone subscriptions existed in China, and 3 billion people worldwide, half the world's population, are estimated to have cell phones by now. Not all of these users send text messages, but one has only to take a stroll on the downtown streets of any Chinese city to see how many people use cell phones on the street, as is the case in the United States. They are walking and talking at the same time. A group of Chinese writers some colleagues and I from a conference in the People's Republic of China met with a couple of years ago were conspicuously concerned with getting their work adapted for Chinese television. They were more interested, it almost seemed, in having their work on television than in getting their novels published in printed books.

The effect of the new telecommunications devices is to diminish, for better or for worse, the cultural role of printed-book literature in China, as in other countries around the world. Young people in China more and more watch television or go to the cinema, or talk on cell phones, or instant message, or read online fiction, or play computer games, or surf the Net. While they are doing any of these things, Chinese young people are not reading the Chinese *Classic of Poetry*, or *The Dream of the Red Chamber*, or the works of Lu Xun, any more than American young people spend as much time reading Shakespeare, Jane Austen, or Toni Morrison as they might be doing if the new telecommunications devices did not occupy so much of their time. Attempting to come to terms with this massive and epochal shift in media is surely a basic reason for the shift from literary studies to cultural studies in China, in the United States, and around the world. Printed-book literature no longer counts for as much in most people's lives as a way of learning how to behave—for example, in courtship and marriage. We learn about courtship and marriage from cinema, television sitcoms, and the like, not from Jane Austen.

Institutionalized literary study is reacting differently in different countries to this change in dominant media. China is different from the United States in this area, as in so many others, but similarities exist, too. Moreover, literary study in Chinese universities is by no means uniform from one institution to another, just as the situation in the United States is highly reticulated, different from one university and college to another. In both cases, it may be hypothesized, this is because changes in curricula are happening so rapidly, at least in the United States, that no standard new curriculum or configuration of departments has yet been established. Therefore, sweeping generalizations taking the form "Literary and cultural studies conducted in China are this or that, and different from those studies in the United States" should be viewed with skepticism.

Here are some of my impressions of literary and cultural studies in China, including my thoughts on how such studies can be compared and contrasted with those in the United States.

To begin with, the conferences and the classes I have lectured for in China have been remarkably like American ones. Same format for the conferences: groups of papers followed by discussion after each group, with breaks for coffee and community meals. I have seen practically no evidence of thought control, and the last thing these professors and students seem to be is Marxist in a serious sense. Only once, in a roundtable free-for-all discussion at the end of a conference, did I find myself, to my great surprise, listening to a sharp give-and-take among Chinese colleagues about whether freedom of speech exists in China. The older scholars said, "Yes, of course." Several younger ones said, "No!" It was an odd moment because it was so uncharacteristic.

The hotels where I have stayed are remarkably like American ones. University classes in China are, like American ones, lectures followed by a question-and-discussion period. The classrooms and the students are also remarkably like American ones. I have encountered practically nothing of the mysterious or exotic East, though one does eat with chopsticks, and the food is a bit different and often very good, to say the least. The various forms of Chinese cuisine are among the greatest in the world. The papers published by Chinese scholars in journals like *Foreign Literature Studies*, from Central China Normal University in Wuhan, seem remarkably like papers published in similar journals or collections of essays in the United States and Europe. For example, the issue of *Foreign Literature Studies* from December 2006 (volume 28, number 6) has essays with titles like "The Interpretation of Dreams in Shakespeare's Plays," "Tradition and Innovation: A Comparative Study of Proust and Balzac," and "Flaubert's Game: The Narrative Strategy of *Madame Bovary*" along with some more overtly theoretical essays, like "Was Ezra Pound a New Historicist? Poetry and Poetics in the Age of Globalization." It all sounds pretty familiar.

I have been impressed, from my first visit to China up through my most recent ones, by the intelligence and intellectual verve of professors as well as students. Chinese academics and students are quite amazing. Professors and students alike exude a quiet confidence that they are doing something important, and that they are capable of doing it well. Somewhere in the background is the assumption that the Chinese are best. China is one of the few places in the world in which I have felt vaguely like a "minority," in spite of everyone's kindness and respectful politeness. On my first visit, in 1988, I was, along with others from different disciplines (history, business, philosophy, sociology), sent by the American Academy of Arts and Sciences to discuss the future of our disciplines with matching colleagues in the prestigious Beijing branch of the Chinese Academy of Social Sciences (CASS). I was supposed to represent Western literary theory. Most of those from the Institute of Foreign Literature who attended my seminar were quite old, apparently knew no Western language but Russian, and were leftovers from the old days of Soviet presence in China. All these are long gone now. They have been replaced by brilliant younger scholars, often trained in places like Harvard. The transformation of that branch of CASS matches similar amazing transformations in political and academic institutions throughout China that have occurred since Tiananmen Square. That event happened a year after my first visit.

I have mentioned some similarities between higher education in China and in the United States, in addition to the ways in which I feel at home, *chez moi*, in Chinese universities and conferences. Let me now suggest some differences between literary study in China and in the United States.

Although universities in both countries are embedded in the politics, economy, and culture of the surrounding nation-state, universities in the United States are at this moment in a somewhat problematic condition. The US economy is in recession. This has necessarily also affected universities. American universities have in the past two decades become more and more dependent on corporations for support. Less and less money is coming from government agencies like the National Science Foundation, the National Institutes of Health, and the National Endowment for the Humanities. More and more research money is coming to American universities from big pharmaceutical companies, big oil companies, telecommunications companies, and the like. American universities are themselves run more and more like corporations, with astronomically high pay for the presidents and rules of accountability for professors, departments, and programs (that is, records of money made through grants and research). Part-time employees who are paid less than a living wage do more and more of the teaching. Such "adjuncts" have no chance at tenure, and few or no benefits. Tuition costs have risen astronomically so that many students graduate from undergraduate schools or professional schools owing literally hundreds of thousands of dollars to the banks from which they have borrowed. Since disciplines are changing so rapidly, the curricula in literature departments are in some disarray, with little uniformity from university to university, and little consensus about just what ought to be taught and how the various courses ought to hang together in a coherent way. I used to imagine a state legislator in California paying a visit to the University of California at Irvine's English department or to Irvine's Department of Comparative Literature, having a look at the courses being offered, and asking us to explain the rationale for just that conglomeration of courses. I do not think we could do that. Freedom to teach what you like is an immense privilege, from which I have greatly benefited over the years, but it works better if you have at least some colleagues who are teaching courses related to your own and who agree on the general goals of teaching in a given discipline. That consensus has markedly weakened in recent years.

The situation in Chinese universities is quite different. For one thing, the Chinese economy, as everyone knows, is on a roll, with high increases in gross domestic product from year to year. This means that lots of state money is apparently available for supporting and enlarging old universities and for creating new ones. Though getting into the best universities is highly competitive in China, as it is in the United States, I gather that the costs, once you are accepted, are relatively low, even though the life of a Chinese student is rather austere, from what I have seen. Almost all the faculty is tenured.

Though "monitors," I am told, are assigned to each class, I am assured by a young Chinese university literature teacher whom I asked for information that considerable freedom is allowed in teaching, within the set curriculum, and that teachers encourage innovation from their students. Here is what he says:

> For the convenience of teaching, teachers usually follow a certain literary history book, but the goal is not "collective agreement." Teachers encourage and value innovation and originality in interpretation, as far as the student can justify his interpretation. In my literature class I tell students, "For the interpretation of literary texts, we come to disagree, not to agree, with each other. It's disagreement that actually helps to enrich the literary texts. Academic journals only accept articles expressing new ideas."

A more or less universal curriculum for, say, English literature is set by a state committee, the Steering Committee of Foreign Languages of the Ministry of Education. Professors are expected to teach books on that list, while the department generally is expected to cover what looks to me like a more or less coherent, though conspicuously conservative, canon and set of topics, with emphasis in compulsory courses, as might be expected, on such topics as basic English, advanced English, phonetics, listening, reading, English writing, English grammar, interpretation, and translation, but also including compulsory courses in English linguistics, English literature, American literature, academic writing, and optional courses in English essays, English drama, English poetry, English novels, teaching methodology, and "rhetorics" (whatever that is, in this case).

Though not all that many Chinese universities offer courses in Australian and/or Canadian literature, some do nevertheless offer courses like Australian literary history, studies in contemporary Australian fiction, the study of Patrick White, and so on. My informant says not all of these are covered in a given university department, and that university departments of English differ from one to another in which of these many authors they teach. My informant says:

> Foreign literature courses usually cover the masterpieces by representative writers of important literary schools/periods. I don't think there is strict uniformity in the works chosen from university to university. Teachers may also cover contemporary writers like John Barth, Doris Lessing, etc. Chapters from a novel, rather than the whole book, are read and discussed in class. Students are expected to know the outline of the novel before they start reading the chosen chapters closely.[1]

I shall conclude now with further evidence about literary scholarship and teaching in China that to some degree marks differences from what my informant tells me. This evidence has to do with my analysis of a group of essays by distinguished Chinese scholars, primarily but not exclusively still teaching in the People's Republic, on the outlines of modern Chinese literature (that is, literature written after May 1919, the date widely accepted as a turning point in the development of Chinese literature). These essays were commissioned by Professor Wang Ning of Tsinghua University for a special issue of the US journal *Modern Language Quarterly* (*MLQ*).[2] The goal of these essays was somewhat special: namely, to introduce modern and postmodern Chinese literature to American academics in other fields, and to argue for the inclusion of modern and postmodern Chinese literature as an important part of "World Literature" in this age of globalization. Certain features of these essays may be explained by this specific goal. They may in other ways not be "typical" or "characteristic."

The essays in this issue of *MLQ* have a double orientation. They want to show how Chinese literature assimilated and transformed Western literature after the opening up of China to the outside world in 1919. At the same time, they want to show that modern Chinese literature is still continuous with Chinese classical literature and has its own history and periodization, one that differs from the literary history and periodization of the West. Moreover, quite a difference exists, as might be expected, between the essays of scholars who have been trained in China and have remained there and the work of scholars who have been trained in the United States and Europe and have either returned to teach in China or have remained in exile. A whole genre of the modern Chinese novel is devoted to narratives about Chinese young people who come to study in the United States, Canada, or Europe.

I have identified six ways in which the essays in the *MLQ* issue just cited differ somewhat from similar work on Western literature by Western scholars. I take these differences as a handy way to characterize literary and cultural studies in the United States, as opposed to such study in present-day China:

First, the Chinese scholars have relatively little overt interest in saying something new. They have in general more concern for establishing a consensus, or for speaking for one that already exists. We in the West, on the contrary, are taught to assume that we must always say something new, something never said before, in order to justify publishing an essay or book. Douwe Fokkema, the only Western scholar whose work appears in this issue of *MLQ* discussed here, begins his long circumstantial essay on Chinese postmodernist fiction with the assertion that his essay claims to show that "there is a Chinese postmodernism that differs from European and American postmodernism"; his opening sentences imply that no one before him has got the relation of modern and postmodern quite right for China.[3] Ming Dong Gu, who teaches now in the United States and may be assumed to have appropriated some of our assumptions, claims to be saying something about Lu Xun that differs from previous criticism. Westerners tend to assume that in literary study, if something has been said before, no reason exists to say it again. The Chinese, at least those in this issue of *MLQ*, tend to believe that if it is true, it ought to be said again and again, passed on from generation to generation of students and scholars. Like all of my contrasts, these are tendencies, not absolute differences, and I'll be greatly interested in what you [I meant my audience in Nanjing.—JHM] have to say about this issue. Is my informant right about the value in China of novelty in teaching and scholarship? If so, are the *MLQ* essays therefore somewhat atypical?

Second, the Chinese scholars whose work is featured in this collection of essays have much concern for getting the sequence of "periods" or "phases" right—in getting them correctly named and correctly characterized. That may have been an important part of Wang Ning's charge to them. We all, both Chinese and Westerners, take comfort in being able to say, with confidence, "I am now reading a postmodern work," or a "modernist work," or whatever. Periodization, however problematic, gives readers a sense of security. It may, however, be so satisfying to pigeonhole that doing so serves as a substitute for actually reading the work. Saying, "Aha! That is a postmodern feature" may keep the reader from trying to see just what a given passage means in its context, just what is singular about it, just how it may not be amenable to easy categorizing. Periodization is a big part of literary study both in the West and in China. It is nevertheless relatively less important for us in the West these days. Periodization for us Westerners tends to be taken for granted, or even held in suspicion as an overgeneralizing or a smoothing out of important differences among writers of a given time and place. We, or at least *I*, tend to be more interested in the specificity of work by a given author, the way he or she does *not* fit period designations. It is easy to show, for example, as I tried to do for Cervantes in another essay, that all the features of postmodern style, as itemized by the most influential theorists (Fredric Jameson, for example), including all those features identified by Douwe Fokkema in the *MLQ* issue, can be shown to be already present in works at the beginning of Western (and, I gather from these essays, Chinese) fiction—for example, in Cervantes's early-seventeenth-century "The Dog's Colloquy," or in Cao Xueqin's mid-eighteenth-century *A Dream of Red Mansions* (*Hongloumeng*).

Ming Dong Gu argues, in his chapter on *A Dream of Red Mansions* (formerly translated as *The Dream of the Red Chamber*) in his admirable *Chinese Theories of Fiction*, that this great work already has many "postmodern" features.[4] Ming Dong Gu's authoritative essay in the *MLQ* collection, "Lu Xun and Modernism/Postmodernism," shows that writing by Lu Xun (1881–1936) combines modernist and postmodernist themes and stylistic features, even though Lu Xun did not yet, at the time he wrote his stories, prose poems, and essays, have access to Western modernist works, much less to Western postmodernist works (since they did not yet exist). He concludes that Lu Xun partly picked up features of traditional Chinese literature that are "postmodernist" and partly made up new forms of experimental style on his own hook.[5]

Though Ming Dong Gu's essay accepts now established periodizations and has as its goal to periodize Lu Xun's work, the perhaps inadvertent result of his essay is to put a lot of strain on periodization. If postmodernist stylistic features can be found in literary works over the centuries, both in the West and in China, it would seem to follow that period categorizing is an extremely suspect enterprise, and that stylistic, conceptual, and narratological features that we gives names to like "postmodernist" are really ahistorical possibilities of language use in what we call literature.

Douwe Fokkema's concern in his essay in MLQ is to discriminate among the three culturally distinct forms of postmodernism while holding to a claim that "postmodernism," in any of the three kinds he discusses, is always characterized by the assumption that "the conventional relation between signifier and signified does no longer apply."[6] Maybe so, but surely that disconnect is a feature of many earlier literary works, too—for example, of Sterne's *Tristram Shandy*, not to speak of Cervantes's *Don Quixote*. Fokkema's use of periodization nevertheless differs somewhat from its use by some of the Chinese scholars in the *MLQ* issue in that he sees period styles as rather more complex or reticulated than they do, and in that he goes on to exemplify what he says by more abundant citation of examples.

Third, the Chinese scholars tend to assume that historical context more or less completely determines a given author's writings. That may be a vestigial Marxist concept, but much of American and European cultural studies makes the same assumption. Here is an example from Chen Yongguo. His model of historical determinism is relatively complex and subtle but nevertheless firmly presupposed. Though Chen invokes a shadowy organic or naturalist metaphor—"The modernist poetry as a form of New Poetry does not *rise* out of nothing" (my italics)—he defines modernist poetry as having two different causes, one the social and historical conditions in China, the other the influx of intellectual influences from the West. The effect of these causes, moreover, is complex and therefore not easily predictable. Nevertheless, the two causes, Chen asserts, are determinative, in whatever special mix they operate with respect to a given case.[7]

Fokkema has a quite different and, to me, somewhat surprising view of the relation of postmodern writers to their historical and social context. I say "surprising" because most people in Western cultural studies these days, for example, would take a quite different view, one closer to Chen Yongguo's position. Fokkema distinguishes quite sharply—much more sharply than, say, Fredric Jameson or Jean-François Lyotard would be likely to do—between postmodernism as a literary style and postmodernity as an economic, social, and historical condition. "I will consider," says Fokkema, "postmodernism as a current in literature, as a literary sociolect used by writers, critics and general readers, and as distinct from 'postmodernity,' which is a concept referring to contemporary social and political conditions that have been analyzed by Lyotard, Harvey, Bertens and, on the basis of extensive empirical research, by Ronald Inglehart." Fokkema admits that historical conditions play a role. "We must," he says, "take geographical, cultural, and historical differences into account." Nevertheless, he claims that the shift from modernism to postmodernism (like, he implies, any other such shift in styles) comes about just because writers get tired of one style and want to shift to another: "The effect of any style or literary sociolect, including modernism and postmodernism, will in due course be exhausted, so that people will want to hear something different. . . . [T]he new generation feels that the established views of social life and economic conditions are inadequate and out of date, and should be replaced by new interpretations of society."[8] As W. B. Yeats says ("Two Songs from a Play") in a somewhat different tonal register:

Everything that man esteems
Endures a moment or a day.
Love's pleasure drives his love away,
The painter's brush consumes his dreams.

Though Fokkema relates his concept of stylistic change to a physiological explanation, "the hypothesis that continuous repetition of the same neuronal impulses yields diminishing results," his formulations somewhat resemble those in Harold Bloom's *The Anxiety of Influence*.[9] Changes in stylistic conventions, according to Fokkema, are governed by an internal logic that has relatively little to do with history. A new generation just wants and needs to be different. A given sociolect exhausts itself by neuronal repetition. In a sense it would be fair, though somewhat hyperbolic, to say that for Fokkema a new literary sociolect does "rise out of nothing." Even Fokkema's more moderate formulations (more moderate than the formulation I have just cited) constitute a striking claim. "People will want to hear something different," he says.[10] His formulations have, in any case, made me think again about the issue.

Fourth, another characteristic of the essays by scholars writing from China in this special issue of *MLQ* is what appears to a United Statesian, or at least to one like me, a high level of abstraction in descriptive formulations about a given author or "school" (such as the Chinese Nine Leaves school of modernist poets). Of course Fokkema uses abstractions, too, as when he characterizes Chinese postmodernism as manifesting "exuberant fabulation," "metalinguistic criticism," and the coexistence of modernism and postmodernism. As is characteristic of most Western literary scholars, however, Fokkema feels obliged to exemplify these abstractions, to prove that they are correct. He does this by somewhat detailed discussion of specific works, with abundant citations, as, for example, in the pages devoted to Wang Shuo's 1989 work *Qianwan bie ba wo dang ren (Please Don't Call Me Human)*, or in similar analyses of several other works.[11] Chen Yongguo's essay, by contrast, though it discusses the whole of twentieth-century Chinese poetry, includes only two short citations from that poetry.[12]

The discourse of the Chinese scholars in this special issue of *MLQ* often relies on a triple process of abstraction. First abstraction: individual works, when they are specified at all except by title, are, as in the occasional discussion in other essays of Chinese novels, represented by what is most easily translated—plot summary and character description. Second abstraction: the specificity of individual works tends to receive little emphasis; all the works in a given group or school (such as those of the Nine Leaves school) tend to be discussed as if they were all the same, or at least as if what is most important about them is the features they share with one another and with their "period." Third abstraction: those common features are defined in conceptual formulations, as when Chen Yongguo says of the Obscure poets:

> Squeezed between the intensity of desire and the barrenness of reality, these young poets have to struggle hard to express themselves on the one hand and to conceal themselves on the other, and therefore, the artistic strategy of intended obscurity achieved in unconventional images is mingled with direct statements and instinctive expression of intensified emotions. Besides the fragmentary, unconventional and incomprehensible images, such binary oppositions as self and society, history and present, reality and illusion, reason and absurdity, fleetingness and eternity, etc., achieve their unity in the unbridled dissemination of the poetic passion.[13]

I have no doubt that what Chen Yongguo says is true. His essay gives me a great hunger to see some of those poems he names, even in English translation, so I can see just how they exemplify his formulations about "reality and illusion, reason and absurdity, fleetingness and eternity, etc.," or just how they are actually "obscure" in their use of "unconventional images." Generating such a hunger to read for oneself is one of the great virtues of all the essays in this issue of *MLQ*. I have happily discovered that a good bit of modern Chinese literature exists in English translation on the Internet—for example, a long list of works by Lu Xun at the Marxists Internet Archive.[14]

Fifth, a concomitant of infrequent citation in the essays by these scholars from China is that little stylistic or formal analysis is made.

Little attention is given to what we Westerners would call "rhetorical" or "narratological" features. Such lack of attention is, however, also more and more the case with United States cultural studies these days. Fokkema, however, does a bit of rhetorical analysis. He speaks, for example, of the way

> [t]here are few stylistic devices that Wang Shuo does not resort to [in *Please Don't Call Me Human*]. He tries repetition, long sentences without punctuation, nonsensical reasoning, blowing up political jargon into absurd proportions, thus producing such a hilarious story that his references to the Cultural Revolution or the "fat man" have been considered a joke and politically harmless, at least in more tolerant times.[15]

It would have been nice to have been given some examples of these stylistic devices. Nevertheless, Fokkema tacitly recognizes that "stylistic devices" are crucial to meaning, whereas, in spite of knowledge of Barthes, Derrida, et al., and admiration for them, among Chinese literary scholars, little stylistic analysis occurs in their own work, at least in the essays in this collection. Other Chinese scholars whose work I know—for example, Shen Dan, a professor at Peking University—do perform stylistic analysis (in her case, of a "narratological" kind). For us, the New Criticism and the ensuing "deconstruction" have been decisive, even for those scholars (for example, some cultural critics) who are quite hostile to them. The "death of deconstruction" keeps being announced, but somehow deconstruction refuses to die. It may be dead, but it walks like a ghost in broad daylight to haunt our cultural criticism. Ming Dong Gu (who, as mentioned, is working in the United States) does pay attention to the role of small linguistic details—as, for example, in the fascinating things he has to say about the metaphorical meaning of characters' names in the two great traditional Chinese novels he discusses at length, the *Jin Ping Mei* and the *Hongloumeng*, in his *Chinese Theories of Fiction*.

Sixth, and finally, the Chinese scholars in the special issue of *MLQ* pay much attention to the translation of Western works into Chinese as a decisive feature in the development of modern Chinese literature. They pay little attention, however, to the way linguistic differences between Chinese and Western languages may decisively affect what can be said in a given language and may therefore limit translation. The assumption almost seems to be that Chinese literature can be translated into English, and Western literature into Chinese, without important losses. I doubt that this is really the case, and they would no doubt agree, since Chinese language and culture are so different from Western language and culture. As someone ignorant of Chinese, I long to be told something about the effect on literary form and meaning of writing in Chinese as opposed to writing in English, German, or French. This would require setting versions of "the same text" side by side in Chinese and in some Western language, with a detailed discussion of semantic, grammatical, syntactical, and rhetorical differences, as well as differences in generic assumptions. Something of this sort occurs in Ming Dong Gu's admirable *Chinese Theories of Fiction*.[16] Ignoramus that I am, I get a glimpse from his work of what may be lost in translation in either direction. American scholars of Chinese literature (for example, Haun Saussy) tend, as might be expected, to be much more interested than Chinese scholars in the specificities of Chinese spoken and written language and in the effects these have on meaning.

As I began by stressing, it is important to see the similarities as well as the differences between Chinese teaching and scholarship in literature, and the differences I have identified are not universals. Nevertheless, I think we still have much to learn from each other. As I have more than once said publicly, if I had my life to live over again I would learn Chinese, and I mean *really* learn it, so I could read Chinese literature, classical and modern, for myself.

APPENDIX: "EXTRACURRICULAR" AND SELECTED ADDITIONAL READINGS FOR ENGLISH MAJORS

I. Extracurricular Reading Booklist for English Majors

1. British Literature

Kingsley Amis, *Lucky Jim*
Jane Austen, *Pride and Prejudice*
Arnold Bennett, *The Old Wives' Tale*
Elizabeth Bowen, *The Death of the Heart*
Charlotte Brontë, *Jane Eyre*
Emily Brontë, *Wuthering Heights*
Anthony Burgess, *A Clockwork Orange*
Samuel Butler, *The Way of All Flesh*

A. S. Byatt, *Possession*
Lewis Carroll, *Alice's Adventures in Wonderland*
Angela Carter, *The Company of Wolves*
Agatha Christie, *Murder on the Orient Express*
Ivy Compton-Burnett, *A Family and a Fortune*
Joseph Conrad, *Heart of Darkness*; *Lord Jim*
Daniel Defoe, *Robinson Crusoe*
Charles Dickens, *David Copperfield*
Sir Arthur Conan Doyle, *Adventures of Sherlock Holmes*
Margaret Drabble, *The Waterfall*
Daphne Du Maurier, *Rebecca*
George Eliot, *Middlemarch*
E. M. Forster, *Howards End*; *A Passage to India*
John Fowles, *The French Lieutenant's Woman*
John Galsworthy, *The Man of Property*
William Golding, *Lord of the Flies*
Graham Greene, *The Human Factor*
Thomas Hardy, *Tess of the D'Urbervilles*; *Jude the Obscure*
Aldous Huxley, *After Many a Summer*
Henry James, *Daisy Miller*
James Joyce, *A Portrait of the Artist as a Young Man*
Rudyard Kipling, *Kim*
Charles Lamb, *Tales from Shakespeare*
D. H. Lawrence, *Sons and Lovers*
John Le Carré, *The Spy Who Came in from the Cold*
Doris Lessing, *The Grass Is Singing*
David Lodge, *Nice Work*
W. Somerset Maugham, *The Moon and Sixpence*; *Of Human Bondage*
Iris Murdoch, *The Black Prince*
George Orwell, *1984*
Salman Rushdie, *Midnight's Children*
Sir Walter Scott, *Ivanhoe*
C. P. Snow, *The Affair*
Muriel Spark, *The Prime of Miss Jean Brodie*
Robert Louis Stevenson, *Treasure Island*
Johathan Swift, *Gulliver's Travels*
William Makepeace Thackeray, *Vanity Fair*
Evelyn Waugh, *A Handful of Dust*
H. G. Wells, *The Invisible Man*

Oscar Wilde, *The Picture of Dorian Gray*
Virginia Woolf, *Mrs Dalloway*; *To the Lighthouse*

2. American Literature

Sherwood Anderson, *Winesburg, Ohio*
James Baldwin, *Go Tell It on the Mountain*
Saul Bellow, *Seize the Day*; *Henderson the Rain King*
William S. Burroughs, *Naked Lunch*
Willa Cather, *My Ántonia*
Kate Chopin, *The Awakening*
Stephen Crane, *The Red Badge of Courage*
Theodore Dreiser, *Sister Carrie*; *An American Tragedy*
Ralph Ellison, *Invisible Man*
William Faulkner, *Go Down, Moses*; *The Sound and the Fury*
F. Scott Fitzgerald, *The Great Gatsby*
Alex Haley, *Roots*
Nathaniel Hawthorne, *The Scarlet Letter*
Joseph Heller, *Catch-22*
Ernest Hemingway, *The Sun Also Rises*; *The Old Man and the Sea*
James Jones, *From Here to Eternity*
Maxine Hong Kingston, *The Woman Warrior*
Harper Lee, *To Kill a Mockingbird*
Sinclair Lewis, *Main Street*
Jack London, *The Call of the Wild*; *Martin Eden*
Norman Mailer, *The Naked and the Dead*
Carson McCullers, *The Heart Is a Lonely Hunter*
James A. Michener, *Centennial*
Margaret Mitchell, *Gone with the Wind*
Toni Morrison, *The Bluest Eye*
Vladimir Nabokov, *Lolita*
Frank Norris, *The Octopus*
J. D. Salinger, *The Catcher in the Rye*
Erich Segal, *Man, Woman and Child*
Upton Sinclair, *The Jungle*
John Steinbeck, *The Grapes of Wrath*
Harriet Beecher Stowe, *Uncle Tom's Cabin*
William Styron, *Sophie's Choice*
Mark Twain, *The Adventures of Huckleberry Finn*
Alice Walker, *The Color Purple*

Robert Penn Warren, *All the King's Men*
Edith Wharton, *The Age of Innocence*
Thornton Wilder, *The Bridge of San Luis Rey*
Thomas Wolfe, *Look Homeward, Angel*
Herman Wouk, *The Winds of War*
Richard Wright, *Native Son*

3. Canadian Literature

Morley Callaghan, *That Summer in Paris*
Northrop Frye, *The Great Code*
Margaret Laurence, *The Stone Angel*
Stephen Leacock, *Sunshine Sketches of a Little Town*
Malcolm Lowry, *Under the Volcano*
Hugh MacLennan, *The Watch That Ends the Night*
L. M. Montgomery, *Anne of Green Gables*

4. Australian Literature

Martin Boyd, *Lucinda Brayford*
Peter Carey, *Oscar and Lucinda*
Miles Franklin, *My Brilliant Career*
Thomas Keneally, *Schindler's List*
Alex Miller, *The Ancestor Game*
Henry Handel Richardson, *The Fortunes of Richard Mahony*
Christina Stead, *The Man Who Loved Children*
Randolph Stow, *To the Islands*
Patrick White Voss, *The Tree of Man*

5. Chinese Culture

Yung Ming, *My Life in China and America*
Chiang Monlin, *Tides from the West*
Tcheng Ki Tong, *The Chinese Painted by Themselves*
Ku Hung Ming, *The Spirit of the Chinese People*
Fei Hsiao Tung, *Peasant Life in China*
Lin Yu Tang, *My Country and My People*
A Retrospective of Chinese Literature: Classical Poetry
A Retrospective of Chinese Literature: Classical Prose
A Retrospective of Chinese Literature: Classical Fiction
A Retrospective of Chinese Literature: Modern Poetry
A Retrospective of Chinese Literature: Modern Prose
A Retrospective of Chinese Literature: Modern Fiction

II. Selected Readings in British Literature

Geoffrey Chaucer, *The Canterbury Tales*; *Popular Ballads*; "Robin Hood and Allin a Dale"; "The Babes in the Wood"
William Shakespeare, *The Merchant of Venice*; *Hamlet*; "Sonnet 18"; "Sonnet 29"
Francis Bacon, *Of Wisdom for a Man's Self*
John Milton, *Paradise Lost*; "On His Blindness"
John Bunyan, *The Pilgrim's Progress*
Joseph Addison, "Adventures of a Shilling"
Richard Steele, "The Spectator Club"
Daniel Defoe, *Robinson Crusoe*
Jonathan Swift, *Gulliver's Travels*
Alexander Pope, "An Essay on Criticism"
Henry Fielding, *The History of Tom Jones, a Foundling*
Samuel Johnson, "Letter to Chesterfield"
Oliver Goldsmith, *The Vicar of Wakefield*
Richard Brinsley Sheridan, *The School for Scandal*
William Blake, "London"; "The Tyger"
Robert Burns, "A Man's A Man For A' That"; "Robert Bruce's March to Bannockburn"; "A Red, Red Rose"
William Wordsworth, "She Dwelt among the Untrodden Ways"; "To the Cuckoo"; "I Wandered Lonely as a Cloud"; "The Solitary Reaper"
Samuel Taylor Coleridge, "Kubla Khan"
Sir Walter Scott, *Ivanhoe*
Jane Austen, *Pride and Prejudice*
Charles Lamb, "Dream Children: A Reverie"
William Hazlitt, "On Familiar Style"
George Gordon, Lord Byron, "The Isles of Greece"; "She Walks in Beauty"
Percy Bysshe Shelley, "Ode to the West Wind"; "To a Skylark"
John Keats, "On First Looking into Chapman's Homer"; "Ode to a Nightingale"
Thomas Hood, "The Song of the Shirt"; "Ernest Jones"; "The Song of the Lower Classes"; "The Song of the Future"
Alfred, Lord Tennyson, "The Eagle"; "Ulysses"; "Break, Break, Break"
Robert Browning, "Home Thoughts from Abroad"; "Prospice"
Charles Dickens, *Oliver Twist*; *David Copperfield*

William Makepeace Thackeray, *Vanity Fair*
Elizabeth Cleghorn Gaskell, *Mary Barton*
Charlotte Brontë, *Jane Eyre*
Emily Brontë, *Wuthering Heights*
George Eliot, *Silas Marner*
Thomas Carlyle, *Heroes and Hero Worship*
John Ruskin, selected books
George Meredith, *The Egoist*
William Morris, *News from Nowhere*
Samuel Butler, *Erewhon*
Thomas Hardy, *Tess of the D'Urbervilles*
Robert Louis Stevenson, *Treasure Island*
Isabella Augusta Gregory, *The Rising of the Moon*
Oscar Wilde, *An Ideal Husband*
George Bernard Shaw, *Widower's Houses*
George Gissing, *The Private Papers of Henry Ryecroft*
Joseph Conrad, "An Outpost of Progress"
Rudyard Kipling, "The Lost Legion"
William Butler Yeats, "A Deep-Sworn Vow"; "Easter 1916"
H. G. Wells, *Ann Veronica*
(Enoch) Arnold Bennett, *The Old Wives' Tale*
John Galsworthy, *The Forsyte Saga*
Saki, "Dusk"
E. M. Forster, *A Passage to India*
John Millington Synge, *Riders to the Sea*
Bertrand Russell, "A Free Man's Worship"
W. Somerset Maugham, *Of Human Bondage*
John Masefield, *The Locked Chest*
Giles Lytton Strachey, *Queen Victoria*

III. Selected Readings in American Literature

1. Literature of the Colonial American Revolution

   Benjamin Franklin

2. American Romanticism

   Edgar Allan Poe
   Henry David Thoreau
   Walt Whitman

Herman Melville
Emily Dickinson

3. The Age of Realism and Naturalism

Mark Twain
Henry James
Theodore Dreiser

4. Twentieth-Century American Literature before World War II

Robert Frost
Ezra Pound
T. S. Eliot
F. Scott Fitzgerald
William Faulkner
Ernest Hemingway
John Steinbeck

5. African American Literature

W. E. B. Du Bois
Langston Hughes
Ralph Ellison
James Baldwin
Toni Morrison

6. The Triumph of American Drama

Eugene O'Neill
Tennessee Williams
Arthur Miller

7. Post–World War II American Literature

Saul Bellow
J. D. Salinger

CHAPTER 12

Globalization and World Literature

And fast by hanging in a golden Chain
This pendant world, in bigness as a Starr
Of smallest magnitude close by the Moon.
Thither full fraught with mischievous revenge,
Accurst, and in a cursed hour he hies.
. . .
. . . [Satan] toward the coast of Earth beneath,
Down from th'Ecliptic, sped with hop'd success,
Throws his steep flight in many an Aerie wheele,
Nor staid, till on *Niphates* top he lights.
—John Milton, *Paradise Lost*, II:1051–55, III:739–42

World Literature in its recently resurrected form is indubitably a concomitant of economic and financial globalization as well as of new worldwide telecommunications. Marx and Engels long ago, in the famous passage of the *Communist Manifesto* that I cited in chapter 10 of this book, prophetically said just that: "And as in material, so also in intellectual production. The intellectual creations of individual nations become common property. National one-sidedness and narrow-mindedness become more and more impossible, and from the numerous national and local literatures there arises a world literature" ("Und wie in der materiellen, so auch in der geistigen Produktion. Die geistigen Erzeugnisse der einzelnen Nationen werden Gemeingut. Die nationale Einseitigkeit und Beschränktheit wird mehr und mehr unmöglich, und aus den vielen nationalen und lokalen Literaturen bildet sich eine Weltliteratur").[1]

We are on all sides asked by the media to think globally and given information about globalization in its current form. We have also been granted for the first time in human history an ability to look at the earth from outer space, that is, from outside what is happening here. Millions of people all over the world have seen one or another of the unsettling spaceship or satellite photographs. They provide a distant and detached perspective on the earth.

To be, or to pretend to be, wholly detached and objective is, nevertheless, perhaps diabolical. John Milton imagined Satan as one of the first space travelers in literature, as in the passages from early in *Paradise Lost* I have begun by citing.[2] Satan was not exactly detached, since his goal was to bring about the fall of man, but he certainly could see the whole earth from a distance, hanging in space, as all the sons and daughters of Eve can do nowadays. We are not exactly detached and indifferent, either.

World Literature's time has come (again). The new World Literature is a concomitant of current globalization. I strongly support the project of World Literature. The present context for developing a rigorous discipline of World Literature is, however, quite different from, for example, the context in which Goethe two centuries ago proposed the reading of *Weltliteratur*. Our present context includes the many facets of globalization today: worldwide economic and cultural interaction; unprecedented travel and migration; a worldwide financial crisis made possible by the global interconnection of banks and other financial institutions; humanly caused climate change that is altering life both human and nonhuman worldwide, and that may even lead to the extinction of the species *homo sapiens*; the development of new teletechnologies like the computer, cell phones, e-mail, the Internet, Facebook, and Twitter. These communications devices and platforms connect people all over the world in unprecedented ways.

The recent impressive development of a new discipline called "World Literature" seems pretty far from climate change, the World Wide Web, and the financial meltdown, but I think it can be shown to be a somewhat different version of a pattern of inadvertent reversal evident in those forms of globalization. The renewed emphasis on the teaching and study of world literature has without doubt been a response to manifold forms of technological and economic globalization. Another quite different response is the widespread takeover of literature departments by those kinds of social studies called "cultural studies," "postcolonial studies," "ethnic studies," "women's studies," "film studies," and so on. These developments also seem to me a good thing. It is harder and harder to justify the separate study of a supposedly homogeneous national literature, or to justify the isolated study of literature separately from other cultural forms. Widespread migration from all over the world to all over the world has meant that more and more people worldwide live in ethnically diverse communities where many languages are spoken, if you can any longer call them communities. In one section of Montreal in Canada, I am told, an astonishing fifty-six different languages are spoken. It seems natural and inevitable these days to look at literature globally.

Doing that, however, differs radically from the shift to cultural studies and its ilk. The latter tends to take for granted that print literature is playing a smaller and smaller role in most people's lives as newer media and platforms like film, television, Facebook, and computer games replace printed novels, plays, and poems.

The ethos of fewer and fewer people worldwide is determined to any large extent by reading "literature," in the traditional Western sense of printed novels, poems, and plays. This transformation is no doubt occurring unevenly around the globe, but it is happening to some degree everywhere. I wish this were not so, but the evidence shows that it is the case. Statistical evidence shows the astounding number of hours a day many people spend surfing the Web or using a cell phone. People these days use the Net, talk or text on their iPhones, send e-mail, play computer games, listen to MP3s, go to the movies, or watch television or online films—all worthy activities. They do everything, however, but read Shakespeare or Jane Austen. Literature in the old-fashioned sense, such of it as is left, is migrating to e-readers like Amazon's Kindle or Apple's iPad. Amazon now sells more e-books than hardcover printed books.

Literature in the traditional sense tends to be marginalized in cultural studies, as it is in the lives of the mostly younger scholar-teachers who "do cultural studies." The new discipline of World Literature, on the contrary, might be seen as a last-ditch effort to rescue the study of literature. It does this by implicitly claiming that studying literature from around the world is a way to understand globalization. This understanding allows one to become a citizen of the world, a cosmopolitan, not just a citizen of this or that local monolingual community. In the course of developing the new World Literature, however—through the planning of courses, the publication of textbooks, and the training of competent teachers—some problems arise. Here are three important challenges to the new World Literature:

One: the challenge of translation. No single student, teacher, or ordinary reader can master all the hundreds of languages in which world literature is written. Any literary work can be translated into any language, but difficulties of translation always exist. Will World Literature have a single master language, such as Chinese or English, into which a given textbook will translate all the selections? That would appear to be a form of cultural imperialism. How can World Literature avoid being dominated by some single national academic culture?

Two: the challenge of representation. A scholar can spend his or her whole life studying a single national literature and still not master it. World Literature will of necessity—for example, in textbooks or courses—work by way of relatively brief selections from the literatures of many countries or regions. Such selections will always be to some degree biased or controversial. How can this bias be avoided as much as possible? Who will have the authority to decide which works in a given language or in a given national literature belong to world literature? What will be the criteria for the decisions to include or exclude? Does Franz Kafka, for example, belong to world literature? The book on Kafka by Gilles Deleuze and Félix Guattari is subtitled *Toward a Minor Literature*.[3] Is that a true description? Does being "minor" mean Kafka's works do not belong to "world" literature? How would you know for sure one way or the other?

David Damrosch, in the brilliant introductory essay of his *What Is World Literature?*, touches with wisdom and impressive learning on all the issues I am raising. He sidesteps the problem of setting a canon of world literature by saying that "world literature is not an infinite, ungraspable canon of works but rather a mode of circulation and of reading."[4] Teachers of World Literature and editors of textbooks on World Literature still need to decide, however, which works to help circulate and get read. Such experts also need to decide what to tell students about a work from a culture that is different from their own. Damrosch identifies succinctly the challenges to doing this. "A specialist in classical Chinese poetry," he says, "can gradually, over years of labor, develop a close familiarity with the vast substratum beneath each brief T'ang Dynasty poem, but most of this context is lost to foreign readers when the poem travels abroad. Lacking specialized knowledge, the foreign reader is likely to impose domestic literary values on the foreign work, and even careful scholarly attempts to read a foreign work in light of a Western critical theory are deeply problematic."[5]

Three: the challenge of defining what is meant by "literature." Goethe, in one of those famous conversations with Eckermann about world literature, serenely affirms his belief that "literature" is a universal, something possessed by every human culture everywhere at all times. When Eckermann, Goethe's fall guy or straight man, resisted reading Chinese novels by asking whether the one they have been discussing is "perhaps one of their most superior ones," Goethe responded firmly:

> "By no means," said Goethe; "the Chinese have thousands of them, and had when our forefathers were still living in the woods.
>
> "I am more and more convinced," he continued, "that poetry is the universal possession of mankind. . . . the epoch of world literature is at hand, and everyone must strive to hasten its approach."[6]

Even within a relatively homogeneous, though multilingual, culture, such as that of Western Europe and America, "literature" is not quite so easy to define or to take for granted as Goethe makes it sound. Nonetheless, one might say of literature what a US Supreme Court justice famously said about pornography: "I can't define it, but I know it when I see it." Literature in its modern Western form is not even three centuries old. Is it legitimate to globalize that parochial notion of what is meant by "literature"? The modern Western idea of literature is parochial in the sense of being limited to Western culture during one historical time—the time of the rise of the middle class, of increasing literacy, and of the printed book. It seems unlikely that what we Westerners have meant by "literature" for the last couple of centuries would hold true worldwide. How can a discipline of World Literature respect the many different conceptions of "literature" in different times and places throughout the world? Damrosch recognizes that "literature" means something different in each culture, but he says we can define literature as whatever people in diverse times and places take as literature. All of us, in all our diversity of cultures and conceptions of literature, know a piece of literature when we see one.

The effort to globalize literary study, admirable as it is, encounters through its deployment intrinsic features in so-called literature that unglobalize the project. These features of diversity tend, or ought to tend, to return literary study not so much to the dispersed and self-enclosed investigations of national literatures in a given language in a given time and place as to the one-by-one reading of individual works that we have decided are examples of literature. The narrowness and parochialism of segregated national-literature study is just what the redevelopment of World Literature is trying to escape. Comprehensive study of even a single national literature, however, is a Herculean, perhaps impossible, task. In the end, no literary work, it may be, fits the periodizing or generic generalizations that can be made about it. To speak of "the Victorian novel" is a mystified projection of unity where immense variation actually exists.

The new discipline of World Literature, I conclude, problematizes itself, or ought to problematize itself, through rigorous investigation of the presuppositions that made the development of World Literature as an academic discipline possible and desirable in the first place. Does that mean it is not worthwhile to read a few pages of Chinese, Kenyan, or Czech literature in English translation, with succinct expert commentary? Would it be better not to read bits of those literatures at all? By no means. The challenges to the discipline of World Literature I have identified do mean, however, that one should not exaggerate the degree to which courses in World Literature are any more than a valuable first step toward giving students global knowledge of literatures and cultures from all corners of the earth.

I have stressed the challenges and difficulties faced by World Literature as a discipline concomitant with the new forms of globalization. That does not mean World Literature should not flourish. Shakespeare, in the various plots of *As You Like It*, shows pretty conclusively that love in the sense of sexual desire and love in the sense of spiritual affection may not by any means be reconciled. They form an aporia, an impasse. No bringing together of lust and love. The play ends triumphantly, however, with four marriages. These break through the impasse. Let World Literature thrive, say I, just as Shakespeare's mad King Lear says, "Let copulation thrive."[7]

Coda added after the conference:

As I expected, I learned much from all the papers at the Fifth Sino-American Symposium on Comparative Literature in Shanghai, whose topic was "Comparative Literature in the Phase of World Literature." By meeting and hearing so many of the leaders worldwide in the revived discipline of World Literature, I learned that World Literature is thriving globally and that a consensus is beginning to emerge about what World Literature is and what it does, what its conventions and protocols are.

I found Thomas Beebee's paper especially relevant to my own reflections about World Literature. That paper asks, "What in the World does Friedrich Nietzsche have against *Weltliteratur*?" I found Professor Beebee's paper extremely provocative, not least by way of the citations from Nietzsche's *The Birth of Tragedy* and *Beyond Good and Evil*, the exegesis of which generated his essay. I had so much to say about both Beebee's paper and the citations on his handout that I refrained from commenting at the time he presented his paper, from fear of impolitely taking up too much time in the discussion. The following remarks are no more than an extended footnote to Thomas Beebee's admirable paper.

Just what does Nietzsche have against *Weltliteratur*? In order to be brief, and to avoid an interminable exegesis, I limit myself almost completely to the citations in Beebee's handout. Readers of the major essays on *The Birth of Tragedy* by Paul de Man, Andrzej Warminski, Carol Jacobs, and Thomas Albrecht will know how complex, contradictory, and controversial *The Birth of Tragedy* is.[8] Warminski, in "Reading for Example," for example, gives an example of the problems of translation I have mentioned. He shows that Walter Kaufmann, in the standard translation of *The Birth of Tragedy*, misleadingly translates the German word *Gleichnis* as "symbol," thereby importing the whole Romantic ideology of symbol into Nietzsche's text, whereas *Gleichnis* actually means "parable," or "figure," or "image."[9]

What Nietzsche says in the striking passage from *The Birth of Tragedy* that Beebee began by citing adds one more challenge to the enterprise of World Literature to the three I have already identified and discussed. Readers of Nietzsche's "Vom Nutzen und Nachtheil der Historie für das Leben" ("On the Advantage and Disadvantage of History for Life") will remember that Nietzsche argues, paradoxically and even scandalously, that it is healthy to forget history so we can get on with living productively in the present.[10] We need to start afresh without the great weight of history on our shoulders. The title has been translated in many different ways, in exemplification of what I said earlier about translation and World Literature, but my German dictionary gives "advantage" and "disadvantage" as the primary meanings of *Nutz* and *Nachtheil*. This essay is Nietzsche's version of James Joyce's definition of history as "the nightmare from which I am trying to awake." Nietzsche's and Joyce's view of history seems paradoxical and scandalous, I mean, to us humanities professors who have given our lives to studying the history of literature, including for many now World Literature. Nietzsche himself was charged with an obligation to study literary history as a professor ordinarius of classical philology at the University of Basel. Appointed at twenty-four, he was one of the youngest ever called to such a post. The Nietzschean view is the opposite of the by no means implausible counterassertion that those who forget history are condemned to repeat it.

Nietzsche's basic assumption, in the extracts from *The Birth of Tragedy* and *Beyond Good and Evil* that Beebee discusses, is that we now live trapped in the meshes of an Alexandrian culture: "Our whole modern world is entangled in the net of Alexandrian culture" ("in dem Netz der alexandrinischen Cultur befangen"). It proposes as its ideal the theoretical man equipped with the greatest forces of knowledge ("Erkenntnisskräften"), and laboring in the service of science ("Wissenschaft"), whose archetype and progenitor is Socrates."[11] Just what do these two sentences mean? They mean that, like the citizens of Alexandria in the twilight of the ancient Greek world, we in the modern world know everything and have accumulated all knowledge, such as was gathered in the famous Library of Alexandria, or as was collected in the great European university libraries of Nietzsche's time, or as is encompassed by the Internet today. In these days of global telecommunications, you can get information about almost anything by Googling it from almost anywhere in the world. Moreover, even our art, as Nietzsche repeatedly emphasizes, has been enfeebled by becoming imitative, by being cut off from fresh sources of inspiration. Our poets and artists know too much about the histories of poetry and art. This is Nietzsche's version of what Harold Bloom, in the mid-twentieth century, was to call "the anxiety of influence."[12]

Nietzsche takes a dim view of this. Why? Why does Nietzsche define the power of knowing everything as similar to being entangled in a net? It might seem a wonderful asset to have knowledge of everything under the sun at one's fingertips. On the contrary, Nietzsche holds that just as a wild animal, a fish, or a bird caught in a net is deprived of the ability to live its life freely, so Alexandrian people are paralyzed, prevented from living a normal human life, by knowing too much. Nietzsche's concept of a proper human life is to live and act in the present, in a particular situation and oriented toward the future, forgetting the past. One of Beebee's citations shows Nietzsche quoting Goethe praising Napoleon to Eckermann as the type of the nontheoretical man, who embodies "a productiveness of deeds" ("eine Productivität der Thaten").[13] Normal human beings dwell within a local culture. This culture includes indigenous literature and other art forms. Such a culture is sequestered from other cultures and takes its assumptions, as well as its native language, as universals. The Greeks saw all those who did not speak Greek as "barbarians." It sounded as if they were stammering "bar . . . bar . . . bar," not speaking anything intelligible. Learning another language seemed pointless or dangerous to the Greeks. It would lead to dissonance, to the multiplication and dissolution of the self.

The word "dissonance" appears in the second of Beebee's citations. It is taken from the last section of *The Birth of Tragedy*, section 25. The word "dissonance" appears with increasing frequency toward the end of *The Birth of Tragedy*:

> If we could imagine dissonance become man [*eine Menschwerdung der Dissonanz*]—and what else is man?—this dissonance, to be able to live, would need a splendid illusion [*eine herrliche Illusion*] that would cover dissonance with a veil of beauty [*einen Schönheitsschleier über ihr eignes Wesen*].[14]

A more literal translation would say "spread a veil of beauty over its own being." The word *ihr* ("its") could refer either to dissonance or to man, but Nietzsche's argument, after all, is that man is essentially dissonance. They are the same. Man is dissonance in living human form. (Present-day readers are likely to note, by the way, the imperturbable sexism of Nietzsche's formulations. He speaks of dissonance become man, not man and woman. *Mensch* apparently includes everyone, both men and women. Sexual difference does not matter to Nietzsche, at least not in these citations. "Birth," *Geburt*, is used in the title without apparent reference to the fact that only women can give birth.)

Just what is Nietzsche's "dissonance"? Thomas Beebee was perhaps too reticent or too intellectually chaste to say anything, so far as I can remember his oral presentation, about that dissonant can of worms, the vexed opposition between the Dionysian and the Apollonian that ambiguously organizes the whole of *The Birth of Tragedy*. That opposition is especially salient as the leitmotif of section 25. In incautiously opening that can of worms, I say the opposition "ambiguously" organizes *The Birth of Tragedy* because though at first it seems that the Dionysian and the Apollonian are in clear opposition, it turns out that matters are not quite so simple. The Dionysian, it appears, refers to the underlying cacophony of the universal Will, "the Dionysian basic ground of the world" ("dionysischen Untergrund der Welt").[15] Music and Greek tragedy (Sophocles and Aeschylus, but not Euripides) are direct expressions of this Dionysian "basic ground of all existence" ("Fundamente aller Existenz"):[16]

> Music and tragic myth are equally expressions of the Dionysian capacity of a people [*der dionysischen Befähigung eines Volkes*], and they are inseparable [*untrennbar*].[17]

The full title of Nietzsche's book is, after all, *The Birth of Tragedy out of the Spirit of Music* (*Die Geburt der Tragödie aus dem Geiste der Musik*). Just why Nietzsche says "spirit of music" rather than just "music" is a difficult question to answer. Apparently the spirit of music precedes actual musical compositions, such as those operas by Wagner that are Nietzsche's prime example of the modern Dionysian. The spirit of music and music, it is implied, are two different things. In any case, the Apollonian seems clearly opposed to the Dionysian. "Man" cannot face the Dionysian directly and go on living. It has to be covered over with a veil of beautiful illusion: "this dissonance [that is, dissonance become man in a *Menschwerdung*], in order to be able to live, would need a splendid illusion that would spread a veil of beauty over its own being." As T. S. Eliot puts this, "human kind / Cannot bear very much reality."[18]

This opposition seems clear enough. It has an Apollonian reasonable clarity. The more one reads carefully, however, everything Nietzsche wrote about the Dionysian and the Apollonian, including the abundant notes written prior to *The Birth of Tragedy*, Nietzsche's letters of the time, the recanting "Attempt at a Self-Criticism" written for the third edition of the book (1886), and the comments on *The Birth of Tragedy* in *Ecce Homo* (written in 1888, published in 1908), the more complicated matters become. The edition of 1886 even had a different title: *Die Geburt der Tragödie. Oder: Griechenthum und Pessimismus* (*The Birth of Tragedy, or Hellenism and Pessimism*). More and more the careful reader comes to recognize that the Dionysian and the Apollonian, even at the time of the first edition of *The Birth of Tragedy* (1872), are not opposites. They are, to borrow Carol Jacobs's word, "stammering" permutations of one another as slightly different "transfigurations" or figurative displacements of an original dissonance that, *pace* Schopenhauer, can never be expressed directly, only figured by one or another catachresis.[19] "Dissonance," after all, is not music but the absence of music in clashing sound, just as stammering is language that is not language but the product of a speech impediment that produces repetitive dissonant sounds. Even in section 25, the same word, "transfiguration" (*Verklärung*), is used to define what music, tragic myth, and Apollonian illusion all do in different ways: "Music and tragic myth are equally expression of the Dionysian capacity of a people, and they are inseparable. Both derive from a sphere of art that lies beyond the Apollonian; both transfigure a region in whose joyous chords dissonance as well as the terrible image of the world fade away charmingly" ("beide verklären eine Region, in deren Lustaccorden die Dissonanz eben so wie das schrecklicke Weltbild reizvoll verklingt"):[20]

> Of this foundation of all existence—the Dionysian basic ground of the world—not one whit more may enter the consciousness of the human individual than can be overcome again by this Apollonian power of transfiguration [*apollinischen Verklärungskraft*].[21]

The reader is left, in the end, with an opposition not between the Dionysian and the Apollonian but between the primordial, underlying dissonance, on the one hand, and, on the other, both the Dionysian and the Apollonian in all their various permutations as forms of the same transfiguration (in the sense of turning into figures) of what mankind cannot face directly and still go on living. These apparently clear figures, however, betray their origin in their own stammering dissonance. Jacobs, in her brilliant essay, has conclusively demonstrated this in her admirable reading of the notebooks (especially notebook 9) preliminary to *The Birth of Tragedy*; her essay culminates in an exegesis of Nietzsche's use of the word *stammeln* ("stammer"), both in the notebooks and, once, in *The Birth of Tragedy* itself, and her difficult insight might be summarized by an extrapolation of her epigraph from *The Birth of Tragedy*: "Thus the intricate relation of the Apollonian and the Dionysian may really be symbolized by a fraternal union of the two deities: Dionysus speaks the language of Apollo; and Apollo, finally, the language of Dionysus" ("So ware wirklich das schwierige Verhältniss des Apollinischen und des Dionysischen in der Tragödie durch einen Brunderbund beider Gottgeiten zu symbolisiren: Dionysus redet die Sprache des Apollo, Apollo aber schliesslich die Sprache des Dionysus").[22]

In truth, Nietzsche—as Albrecht argues along with Jacobs, de Man, and Warminski—saw both the Dionysian and the Apollonian as generating out of their own stammering dissonance the illusion of primordial dissonance, rather than just being figurative transfigurations of it. My word "catachresis," the tropological name for a "forced or abusive transfer," hints at this possibility.[23] I refrain from pursuing this rabbit any further down its rabbit hole. It is a good example of the way an innocent-looking word—"dissonance," in this case, like "quicken" in Yeats's "The Cold Heaven"—can lead to a virtually interminable reading that ultimately includes everything the author wrote and its dissonant (and therefore untotalizable) intellectual, cultural, and linguistic context.

Nietzsche's harsh judgment of Goethean *Weltliteratur* is a concomitant of this larger set of contextual assumptions. Devotees of World Literature know many languages, many cultures, many literatures. They set these all next to one another in simultaneity, as exemplary of a universal or global literature that began thousands of years ago and that still flourishes everywhere in the inhabited world. The new efflorescence of World Literature today is clearly a form of globalization, as I began by asserting. What Nietzsche in *Beyond Good and Evil* saw, ironically, as "civilization," "humanizing," "progress," or "the *democratic* movement in Europe" ("Civilisation, Vermenschlichung, Fortschritt, die demokratische Bewegun Europa's")—that is, as "an immense *physiological* process . . . the slow emergence of an essentially *super-national* and nomadic species of man" ("einer wesentlich übernationalen und nomadischen Art Mensch") "who possesses, physiologically speaking, a maximum of the art and power of adaptation as his typical distinction," has now reached a hyperbolic level.[24]

The new nomadic species of man takes many forms today, but it might be personified in the scholar who travels all over the world by jet plane, as I do, to attend conferences and to give papers that are heard by participants who come from all over the world, the globe compacted to the size of a lecture hall.

In light of this brief establishment of a wider context for world literature as Nietzsche saw its "disadvantage" ("Nachtheil") for life, I now turn back to the first citation Thomas Beebee made from *The Birth of Tragedy*. The narrower context of Nietzsche's putdown of world literature is Goethe's celebration of it in that famous interchange with Eckermann about Chinese novels as a manifestation of world literature, already cited. The Chinese, Goethe told Eckermann, had novels when we Europeans were still living in the woods. "The epoch of world literature is at hand, and everyone must strive to hasten its approach," said Goethe with his usual somewhat ironic cheerfulness. It is coming anyway, so why not hasten its coming—or rather, we *should* therefore hasten its coming. Goethe, as opposed to Nietzsche, saw no danger in world literature. In his serene and sovereign imperturbability, he welcomed its coming, perhaps because he was sure he would be part of it.

Nevertheless, the effects on Goethe's Faust of total knowledge should give the reader pause. Beebee's citations include one reference in *The*

Birth of Tragedy to Goethe's Faust as the type of modern man's omniscience turning against itself in a perpetual dissatisfaction:

> How unintelligible [*unverständlich*] must *Faust*, the modern cultured man, who is in himself intelligible, have appeared to a true Greek. . . . Faust, whom we have but to place beside Socrates for the purpose of comparison, in order to see that modern man is beginning to divine the limits of this Socratic love of knowledge [*Erkenntnislust*] and yearns for a coast in the wide waste of the ocean of knowledge [*aus dem weiten wüsten Wissenmeere*].[25]

Well, just what does Nietzsche have against *Weltliteratur*? Here is the crucial passage Beebee cites; it must be scrutinized closely:

> Our art reveals this universal distress [*diese allgemeine Noth*]: in vain [*umsonst*] does one [*dass mann*] depend imitatively [*imitatorisch*] on all the great productive periods and natures; in vain does one accumulate the entire "world-literature" around modern man for his comfort; in vain does one place oneself in the midst of the art styles and artists of all ages, so that one may give names to them as Adam did to the beasts: one still remains eternally hungry, the "critic" without joy or energy [*ohne Lust und Kraft*], the Alexandrian man, who is at bottom a librarian and corrector of proofs, and wretchedly goes blind from the dust of books [*Bücherstaub*] and from printers' errors [*Druckfehlern*].[26]

(I am myself at this moment an Alexandrian going blind from book dust and from the attempt to get all my German words spelled correctly and all the commas and numbers in my text and in my notes right.) Just what is the "universal distress," the unassuaged need for "comfort," the eternal hunger, which modern man suffers? The passage just cited from *The Birth of Tragedy*, like other passages from Nietzsche's writings, indicates that it is the distress of a successful Socratic, Faustian, or even Kantian or Hegelian search for total knowledge, empirically verified and epistemologically sound. This search has turned against itself through its very success. This reversal has left modern man in a state of universal distress, typified by Faust's eternal dissatisfaction. The immediate context of the passage just cited from section 18 of *The Birth of Tragedy* states this clearly, though the whole section is complex and would demand a lengthy exposition. To put what Nietzsche says in an oversimplifying nutshell, the search by "theoretical," scientific, or scholarly man for the power and equanimity granted by a comprehensive knowledge has reversed itself by reaching the irrational and illogical, from which theoretical man recoils in fear:

> It is certainly a sign of the "breach" ["*Bruches*"] of which everyone speaks as the fundamental malady [*Urleiden*] of modern culture, that the theoretical man, alarmed and dissatisfied at his own consequences, no longer dares entrust himself to the terrible icy current of existence [*dem furchtbaren Eisstrome des Daseins*]: he runs timidly up and down the bank. So thoroughly has he been pampered by his optimistic views that he no longer wants to have anything whole [*ganz haben*], with all of nature's cruelty attaching to it. Besides, he feels that a culture based on the principles of science [*auf dem Princip der Wissenschaft*] must be destroyed when it begins to grow *illogical*, that is, to retreat [*zurück zu fliehen*] before its own consequences.[27]

This is the "distress" ("Noth") of which Nietzsche speaks in the following sentence, the first in the first citation Beebee discussed: "Our art reveals this universal distress" ("Unsere Kunst offenbart diese allgemeine Noth").

Just how does this revelation through the art of the present moment—that is, the moment of the late nineteenth century in Europe—occur? It happens, says Nietzsche, through the Alexandrian derivative and imitative quality of today's art. Present-day artists and poets know too much literary history and too much art history to produce other than feeble imitations of the great productive artists and poets of the past. Nietzsche's formulations take place through a cascade of phrases beginning with "in vain." It is as a member of this sequence that the failure of world literature to give modern man comfort in his distress is asserted (my italics in English):

> . . . *in vain* [*umsonst*] does one depend imitatively on all the great productive periods and natures; *in vain* does one accumulate the entire "world-literature" around modern man for his comfort [*zum Troste*]; *in vain* does one place oneself in

> the midst of the art styles and artists of all ages, so that one may give names to them as Adam did to the beasts: one still remains eternally hungry [*der ewig Hungernde*]. . . .[28]

Categorizing art styles and periods in the literature of all ages and countries (for example, "Baroque," "Romantic," or "Victorian"), work all we literary historians perform, is as arbitrary and ungrounded as those names Adam gave to all the beasts.

The bottom line is that for Nietzsche, world literature, far from giving modern man comfort in his distress, fails completely to do that. In fact, turning to world literature is one of the signal ways that distress manifests itself and is exacerbated. As far as Nietzsche is concerned, it would be better not to know, better to forget all those alien literatures that swarm around the globe. It would be better to live as Nietzsche implies Athenian Greeks did—that is, in joyful possession of a narrow local culture that ignored all other cultures and literatures and saw them as barbarous.

Nietzsche's view of Greek culture is not quite so simple, however. *The Birth of Tragedy* ends with paragraphs asserting that Athenian Apollonian beauty was a compensation for Dionysian madness:

> . . . in view of this continual influx of beauty [*diesem fortwährenden Einströmen der Schönheit*], would he [someone today imagining himself a curious stranger in ancient Athens] not have to exclaim, raising his hand to Apollo: "Blessed people of Hellas! How great must Dionysus be among you if the god of Delos [Apollo] considers such magic necessary to heal your dithyrambic madness."[29]

Nietzsche imagines an old Athenian responding:

> "But say this, too, curious stranger: how much did this people have to suffer [*leiden*] to be able to become so beautiful [*so schön*]!"[30]

Nietzsche's forceful rejection of world literature already manifests, in hyperbolic form, the reversal that was the climax of the lecture I gave at the Shanghai symposium. The new discipline of World Literature, I said, "problematizes itself, or ought to problematize itself, through rigorous investigation of the presuppositions that made the development of World Literature as an academic discipline possible and desirable in the first place." One of the bad effects of the discipline of World Literature, according to Nietzsche, is that it transforms scholars into something like what Nietzsche became or feared to become as a professor of classical philology. Nietzsche's description is memorably sardonic. It recalls George Eliot's description, in *Middlemarch*, of Edward Casaubon and his futile pursuit of the Key to All Mythologies. Here again is Nietzsche's description: "the 'critic' without joy or energy, the Alexandrian man, who is at bottom a librarian and corrector of proofs, and wretchedly goes blind from the dust of books and from printers' errors." It may have been in part fear of becoming like this "critic" that led Nietzsche to resign his professorship. His main overt reason was trouble with his eyesight. Here is Eliot's description of Causabon: "Poor Mr. Casaubon himself was lost among small closets and winding stairs, and in an agitated dimness about the Cabeiri, or in an exposure of other mythologists' ill-considered parallels, easily lost sight of any purpose which had prompted him to these labors."[31] What circulates in Casaubon's veins is neither blood nor passion but marks of punctuation, just as Nietzsche's dry-as-dust scholar spends his time with misprints. As one of Casaubon's sharp-tongued neighbors, Mrs. Cadwallader, says, "Somebody put a drop [of his blood] under a magnifying-glass, and it was all semicolons and parentheses."[32] In both cases, culture as enshrined in texts is reduced to the materiality of the letter or of punctuation marks, such as have preoccupied me in revising and creating notes for this essay. Friedrich Nietzsche, the precociously brilliant young professor of classical philology, may have written an outrageously unorthodox first book as a way to avoid becoming just another classical philologist.

I end with one final observation. I intended to make a few brief comments about Thomas Beebee's admirable paper and about the citations from Nietzsche on which he focused. As I might have foreseen, my comments have got longer and longer and might be yet longer. They parallel the comments I made in another lecture in China, indicating what students might need to be told in order to be able to read W. B. Yeats's "The Cold Heaven." [See chapter 13 of this volume—JHM] In both cases, the commentaries extend themselves indefinitely. What Thomas Beebee and then I, following in his footsteps, have said about Friedrich Nietzsche's theory of *Weltliteratur* indicates that theoretical statements about the revived discipline of World Literature require as much contextualizing exposition as do works of world literature themselves. Such statements must be *read*, and they must be *contextualized*.

I do not think we can ever go back to a world of isolated societies, each with its own indigenous culture. To wish we could all be like the happy ancient Athenians, as Nietzsche sometimes seems to do, is, in my view, a form of unproductive nostalgia. We must make do with what we have, which is a worldwide Alexandrian culture. The new efflorescence of World Literature as an academic discipline is a natural concomitant of this. Its great value is that even if it does not give "comfort," it does help us to understand and to live productively in the new uncomfortable world of global intercommunication and global wandering that Nietzsche calls "nomadism."

CHAPTER 13

Cold Heaven, Cold Comfort

Should We Read or Teach Literature Now?

. . . an entire epoch of so-called literature, if not all of it, cannot survive a certain technological regime of telecommunications (in this respect the political regime is secondary). Neither can philosophy, or psychoanalysis. Or love letters.
—Jacques Derrida, "Envois," *The Post Card*

By "we" in my title I mean we students, teachers, and the ordinary citizens of our "global village." It is by no means certain that calling the global amalgamation of cultures a village is still at all appropriate. By "read" I mean careful attention to the text at hand, that is, "close reading." By "literature" I mean printed novels, poems, and plays. By "now" I mean the hot September of 2010, the culmination of the hottest six months on record. This is clear evidence, for those who have bodies to feel, of global warming. I mean also the time of a barely receding global financial crisis and worldwide deep recession. I mean the time of desktop computers, the Internet, iPhones, iPads, DVDs, MP3s, Facebook, Twitter, Google, computer games by the thousand, television, and a global film industry. I mean the time when colleges and universities are, in the United States at least, losing funding and shifting more and more to a corporate model. As one result of these changes, 70 percent of university teaching is now done by adjuncts, that is, people who not only do not have tenure but who also have no possibility of getting it. They are not "tenure-track." By "now" I mean a time when calls on all sides, from President Obama on down in the government, and by the media left and right, are being made for more and better teaching of math, science, and engineering while hardly anyone calls for more and better teaching in the humanities. The humanities, as a high administrator at Harvard—perhaps its then president, Lawrence Summers—is reported to have said, "are a lost cause."

Should or ought we to read or teach literature in such a "now"? Is it an ethical obligation to do so? If so, which works? How should these be read, and who should teach them?

During the nineteen years I taught at The Johns Hopkins University, from 1953 to 1972, I would have had ready answers to these questions. These answers would have represented our unquestioned consensus at Hopkins about the nature and mission of the humanities. A (somewhat absurd) ideological defense of literary study, especially study of British literature, was pretty firmly in place at Hopkins during those years. We in the English Department had easy consciences because we thought we were doing two things that were good for the country: (1) teaching young citizens the basic American ethos (primarily by way of the literature of a foreign country, England, that we had defeated in a revolutionary war of independence—the absurdity of that project only recently got through to me); and (2) doing research that was like that of our scientific colleagues in that it was finding out the "truth" about the fields covered by our disciplines (languages, literatures, art, history, philosophy). *Veritas vos liberabit*, the truth shall make you free, is the motto of Hopkins—a quotation from the Bible, by the way, something said by Jesus (John 8:32), in which "truth" hardly means scientific truth. *Lux et veritas*, light and truth, is the motto of Yale. Just plain *Veritas* is Harvard's slogan. Truth, we at Hopkins believed (having forgotten the source of our motto), included objective truth of every sort—for example, the truth about the early poetry of Alfred, Lord Tennyson, or about the poetry of Barnaby Googe. Such truth was a good in itself, like knowledge of black holes or of genetics.

Hopkins, as is well known, was the first exclusively "research" university in the United States. It was founded on the model of the great German research universities of the nineteenth century. In literary study that meant inheritance of the German tradition of Romance philology, Germanic philology (which included English literature), and classical philology, all of which flourished at Hopkins. Such research needed no justification beyond the intrinsic value accorded to the search for truth, and the not entirely persuasive assumption that humanities scholars who were doing that kind of research would be better teachers of literature as the precious repository of our national values. The word "research" was our collective leitmotif. Every professor at Hopkins was supposed to spend 50 percent of his time (we were almost all men) doing research in his field of specialty. That included humanities professors.

Hopkins was to an amazing degree run by the professors, or at least it seemed so to us. Professors made decisions about hiring, promotion, and the establishment of new programs. These decisions were made through a group of professors called the Academic Council. The faculty elected them. Though there was no established quota, the council always included humanists and social scientists as well as scientists. This means that the scientists, who could have outvoted the humanists, were cheerfully electing humanists. Outside support for research at Hopkins came not from industry but primarily through government agencies like the National Science Foundation, the National Institutes of Health, and the National Endowment for the Humanities and federal legislation like the National Defense Education Act. We benefited greatly from the Cold War mentality that thought the United States should be best in everything, even the humanities. None of the teaching was done by adjuncts, though graduate students taught composition and also discussion sections of large lecture courses. Most students who received the PhD obtained good tenure-track appointments. Misleading statistics even indicated that a shortage of PhDs in the humanities was about to happen, so the English Department at Hopkins briefly instituted a three-year PhD in that field. Two of my own students finished such a PhD and went on to hold professorships at important universities. This shows that a PhD in English need not take twelve years or more, the average time today.

Hopkins was in my time there a kind of paradise for professors who happened to be interested in research as well as in teaching. Hopkins then was the closest thing I know to Jacques Derrida's nobly idealistic 2001 vision of a "university without condition," a university centered on the humanities and devoted to a disinterested search for truth in all areas.[1] It is a great irony that Derrida's little book was delivered as a President's Lecture at Stanford University, since Stanford is one of the great US elite private universities, one that is and always has been deeply intertwined with corporate America and—by way of the Hoover Institution, located at Stanford—with the most conservative side of American politics.

Well, what was wrong with Hopkins in those halcyon days? Quite a lot. Practically no women were on the faculty, not even in nontenured positions—not a single one in the English Department during all my nineteen years at Hopkins. The education of graduate students in English was brutally competitive, with a high rate of attrition, often by way of withdrawal by the English faculty of fellowship funds initially granted to students who were later judged not to be performing well. Some students whom we "encouraged to leave" took PhDs elsewhere and had brilliant careers as professors of English. Hopkins, finally, was up to its ears in military research at the Applied Physics Laboratory. The Johns Hopkins School of Advanced International Studies was not then, and still is not today, what one would call a model of liberal thinking. In spite of all this, Hopkins was a wonderful place (for us men!) to be a professor of the humanities in the fifties and sixties.

Now, over fifty years later, everything is different in US universities and colleges from what it was at Hopkins when I taught there, as almost everyone involved knows quite well. Even in the fifties and sixties Hopkins was the exception, not the rule. Nowadays, over 70 percent of the teaching, as I have said, is done by adjuncts without prospects of tenure. Often they are deliberately kept at appointments just below half-time so they do not have medical benefits, pension contributions, or other benefits. All three of my children hold doctorates, as does one grandchild, and none of the four has ever held a tenure-track position, much less achieved tenure. Tenure-track positions in the humanities are few and far between, with hundreds of applicants for each one and an ever-accumulating reservoir of unemployed humanities PhDs. Funding for the humanities has shrunk both at public and private colleges and universities, as has financial support for universities and colleges generally. Books by Marc Bousquet, Christopher Newfield, Frank Donoghue, and Jeffrey J. Williams, among others, have told in detail the story of the way US universities have come to be run more and more like business corporations governed by the financial bottom line, or, as Peggy Kamuf puts it, the "bang for the buck."[2] The humanities cannot be shown to produce much bang of that sort at all.

Universities have consequently become more and more trade schools offering vocational training for positions in business, engineering, biology, law, medicine, and computer science. The weakening of American public universities has been accompanied by a spectacular rise in for-profit and partly online universities like the University of Phoenix. These are openly committed to training that will get you a job. John Sperling, the head of the Apollo Group that developed the University of Phoenix, says that Phoenix "is a corporation. . . . Coming here is not a rite of passage. We are not trying to develop [students'] value systems or go in for that 'expand their minds' bullshit."[3] The president of Yale University, Richard Levin, an economist, in a lecture given before the Royal Society in London, "The Rise of Asia's Universities,"[4] enthusiastically praises China for more than doubling its institutions of higher education (from 1,022 to 2,263), for increasing the number of higher education students from 1 million in 1997 to more than 5.5 million in 2007, and for setting out deliberately to create a number of world-class research universities that will rank with Harvard, MIT, Oxford, and Cambridge. The numbers Levin cites are no doubt far higher now. Levin's emphasis, however, is all on the way China's increased teaching of math, science, and engineering will make it more highly competitive in the global economy than it already is. Levin, in spite of Yale's notorious strength in the humanities, says nothing whatsoever about humanities teaching or its utility either in China or in the United States. Clearly, the humanities are of no account in the story he is telling.

It is extremely difficult to demonstrate that humanities departments bring any financial return at all, or that majoring in English is preparation for anything but a low-level service job or a low-paying job teaching English. Many a student at an elite place like Yale can safely major in the humanities because she will take over her father's business when she graduates, or because he will go on to law school or business school and get his vocational training there. Lifelong friendships with others who would come to be important in business, government, or the military have been in any case more important in such elite places than any vocational training. The presidential race between George W. Bush and John Kerry in 2004 was, somewhat absurdly, between two men who did not do all that well academically at Yale but who were members of Yale's most elite secret society, Skull and Bones. Whoever won, Yale and the political power of the Skull and Bones network would also win.

Enrollments in humanities courses and numbers of majors have, not surprisingly, especially at less elite places, shrunk to a tiny percentage of the undergraduate and graduate population.[5] Only composition and beginning language courses, plus required distribution courses, are doing well in the humanities. Legislators, boards of trustees, and university administrators have taken advantage of the recent catastrophic recession to take more control over universities, to downsize and to manage what is taught. The state of California, for example, is broke. That has meant frozen positions, reduced adjunct funding, and salary reductions for faculty and staff in the great University of California system of between 5 and 10 percent, depending on rank. Teaching loads are being increased for above-scale professors—that is, for those who have done the most distinguished research and who have been rewarded by being given more time to do that. The humanities have especially suffered. [This was written in 2010.—JHM]

This is the not entirely cheerful situation in which my question—"Should we read or teach literature now? Do we have an ethical obligation to do so?"—must be asked and an attempt to answer it must be made. How did this disappearance of the justification for literary study happen? I suggest three reasons:

1. The conviction that everybody ought to read literature because it embodies the ethos of our citizens has almost completely vanished. Few people any longer really believe, in their heart of hearts, that it is necessary to read *Beowulf*, Shakespeare, Milton, Samuel Johnson, Wordsworth, Emerson, Dickinson, Whitman, Dickens, Woolf, Stevens, and Conrad in order to become a good citizen of the United States.
2. A massive shift in the dominant media, away from printed books to all forms of digital media—what I call "prestidigitalization"—has meant that literature in the old-fashioned sense of printed novels, poems, and dramas plays a smaller and smaller role in determining the ethos of our citizens. Middle-class readers in Victorian England learned how to behave in courtship and marriage by entering into the fictive worlds of novels by Charles Dickens, George Eliot, Anthony Trollope, Elizabeth Gaskell, and many others. Now people satisfy their need for imaginary or virtual realities by watching films, television, and DVDs as well as by playing computer games and listening to popular music. Amazon announced in July 2010 that for the first time the company was selling more e-books (to be read on iPads or Kindles) than hardcover printed books. A high point of the summer of 2010 for a colleague and friend of mine in Norway, a distinguished humanities professor, was his trip to Rotterdam to hear a Stevie Wonder concert at the North Sea Jazz Festival, followed by a repeat performance of the same concert in his home town of Bergen. He e-mailed me with great excitement and enthusiasm about these

concerts. Stevie Wonder is obviously of great importance in shaping this humanist's "ethos." Whenever I give a lecture on some literary work in any place in the world, members of my audience, especially the younger ones, always want to ask me questions about the film of that work (if a film has been made), not about the printed text.

3. The rise of new media has meant more and more the substitution of cultural studies for old-fashioned literary studies. It is natural for young people to want to teach and write about things that interest them—for example, film, popular culture, women's studies, African American studies, and so on. Many, if not most, US departments of English these days are actually departments of cultural studies, whatever they may go on calling themselves. Little literature is taught these days in US departments of English. Soon Chinese students of English literature, American literature, and worldwide literature in English will know more about these than our indigenous students do. A recent list of new books published at the University of Minnesota Press in literature and cultural studies did not include one single book on literature proper.

Just to give three examples out of hundreds of career-orientation shifts: First, Edward Said began as a specialist on the novels and short stories of Joseph Conrad. He went on to write a book that is theory-oriented, *Beginnings*, but his great fame and influence rest on political books like *Orientalism, The Question of Palestine*, and *Culture and Imperialism*. As a second, quite different, example, Joan DeJean is a distinguished professor of Romance languages at the University of Pennsylvania, but she does not write about French literature in the old-fashioned sense of plays by Racine, novels by Marivaux or Flaubert, poems by Baudelaire, or novels by Duras (all men but Duras, please note). Her influential books include, among others, *The Essence of Style: How the French Invented High Fashion, Fine Food, Chic Cafes, Style, Sophistication*; and *The Age of Comfort: When Paris Discovered Casual—and the Modern Home Began*. In short, Professor DeJean does cultural studies, with a feminist slant. The third example is Frank Donoghue, who began his career as a specialist in eighteenth-century English literature. He published in 1996 a fine book, *The Fame Machine: Book Reviewing and Eighteenth-Century Literary Careers*. Around 2000, Donoghue shifted to an interest in the current state of the humanities in American universities. In 2008 he published *The Last Professors: The Corporate University and the Fate of the Humanities*. Now he lectures frequently all over the United States as an expert on the corporatizing of the American university.

I have briefly sketched the present-day situation in the United States within which the question "Should we read or teach literature now?" must be asked: the smaller and smaller actual influence of literature on common culture; fewer and fewer professors who teach literature as opposed to cultural studies; fewer and fewer tenured professors of literature in any case; fewer and fewer books of literary criticism published, and tiny sales for those that are published; radically reduced enrollment in literature courses in our colleges and universities; rapid reduction of literature departments to service departments teaching composition and, in fewer and fewer universities, the rudiments of foreign languages and foreign cultures. The attitude seems to be more and more "What, me worry? Everybody everywhere speaks English anyhow, or ought to."

The usual response by embattled humanists is to wring their hands, become defensive, and say that literature ought to be taught because we need to know our cultural past, or need to "expand our minds," or need the ethical teaching we can get from literary works. Presidents of the Modern Language Association of America (MLA) have in their presidential addresses over the decades echoed what Matthew Arnold said about the need to know, as he puts it in an iterated phrase in *Culture and Anarchy*, "the best that has been thought and said in the world." Robert Scholes, for example, in his 2004 MLA presidential address, asserted: "We need to show that our learning is worth something by . . . broadening the minds of our students and helping our fellow citizens to more thoughtful interpretations of the crucial texts that shape our culture. . . . We have nothing to offer but the sweetness of reason and the light of learning."[6] "Sweetness and light" is of course Arnold's repeated phrase, in *Culture and Anarchy*, for what culture gives. That book was required reading in the freshman English course all students took at Oberlin College when I became a student there, in 1944.

I think the noble Arnoldian view of the benefits of literary study is pretty well dead and gone these days. For one thing, we now recognize more clearly how problematic and heterogeneous the literary tradition of the West actually is. It by no means teaches some unified ethos, and many of its greatest works are hardly uplifting, including, for example, Shakespeare's *King Lear*. About reading *King Lear*, the poet John Keats said in a sonnet, "On Sitting Down to Read King Lear Once Again":

For once again the fierce dispute,
Betwixt damnation and impassion'd clay
Must I burn through.[7]

As for Keats himself, Matthew Arnold wrote to his friend Clough: "What a brute you were to tell me to read Keats' letters. However, it is over now: and reflexion resumes her power over agitation."[8] Neither work seemed to its readers all that edifying. Nor is American literature much better. Of one of our great classics, *Moby Dick*, its author, Herman Melville, said, "I have written a wicked book." Furthermore, it is not at all clear to me how reading Shakespeare, Keats, Dickens, Whitman, Yeats, or Wallace Stevens is any use in helping our students to deal with the urgent problems that confront all of us these days in the United States: climate change that may soon make the species *Homo sapiens* extinct; a deep global recession and catastrophic unemployment (30 million out of work) brought on by the folly and greed of our politicians and financiers; news media like Fox News that are more or less lying propaganda arms of our right-wing party but are believed in as truth by many innocent citizens; an endless and unwinnable war in Afghanistan; catastrophically rising heath care costs that will soon consume 25 percent of our gross domestic product—we all know these problems, whatever our attitude toward them is. [This was written before the Affordable Health Care Act made it possible for 16 million additional people to get health care insurance.—JHM] Young people in the United States need to get training that will help them get a job and avoid starving to death. They might nevertheless, as I argue at the end of this lecture, benefit from courses in "rhetorical reading" that would teach them how to tell truth from falsehood in Internet postings.[9]

Well, why in the world should we read and teach literature now, in these dire circumstances? I now return to this question. In order to make the question less abstract, I shall confront it by way of a short poem by W. B. Yeats. I greatly admire this poem. It moves me greatly. It moves me so much that I want not only to read it but also to teach it and talk about it to anyone who will listen. The poem is called "The Cold Heaven." It is from Yeats's volume of poems from 1916, *Responsibilities*. Here is the poem:

The Cold Heaven

Suddenly I saw the cold and rook-delighting heaven
That seemed as though ice burned and was but the more ice,
And thereupon imagination and heart were driven
So wild that every casual thought of that and this
Vanished, and left but memories, that should be out of season
With the hot blood of youth, of love crossed long ago;
And I took all the blame out of all sense and reason,
Until I cried and trembled and rocked to and fro,
Riddled with light. Ah! when the ghost begins to quicken,
Confusion of the death-bed over, is it sent
Out naked on the roads, as the books say, and stricken
By the injustice of the skies for punishment?[10]

I long ago wrote a full essay on this poem.[11] More recently, I discussed it briefly again at a conference on World Literature at Shanghai Jiao Tong University. At Jiao Tong I used Yeats's poem as an example of how difficult it is to transfer a poem from one culture to a different one. Now I want to consider the poem as a paradigmatic exemplification of the difficulties of deciding whether we should read or teach literature now. Should I read or teach this poem now? My answer is that there is no "should" about it, no compelling obligation or responsibility. I can read or teach it if I like, but that decision cannot be justified by anything beyond the call the poem itself makes on me to read it and teach it. Least of all do I think I can, with a straight face, tell students or administrators that reading the poem or hearing me teach it is going to help them find a job, or help them mitigate climate change, or help them resist the lies told by the media, though I suppose being a good reader might conceivably aid resistance to lies. Reading the poem or teaching it is, however, a good in itself, an end in itself, as Kant said all art is.

The mystical poet Angelus Silesius (1624–1677) affirmed, in *The Cherubinic Wanderer*, "The rose is without why; it blooms because it blooms."[12] Like that rose, "The Cold Heaven" is "without why." The poem, like a rose, has no reason for being beyond itself. You can read it or not read it, as you like. It is its own end. Young people these days who watch films or play computer games or listen to popular music do not, for the most part, attempt to justify what they do. They do it because they like to do it and because it gives them pleasure. My academic friend from Bergen did not try to justify his great pleasure and excitement in hearing, at great expense, the same Stevie Wonder concert twice, once in Rotterdam and again in Bergen. He just e-mailed me his great enthusiasm about the experience. It was a big deal for him, just as reading, talking, or writing about Yeats's "The Cold Heaven" is a big deal for me. That importance, however, is something I should not even try to justify by its practical utility. If I do make that attempt, I am bound to fail.

A natural response when I see a film I like or hear a concert that moves me is to want to tell other people about it, as my correspondent in Bergen wanted to tell everybody about those Stevie Wonder concerts. These tellings most often take the form "Wow! I saw a wonderful movie last night. Let me tell you about it." I suggest that my desire to teach Yeats's "The Cold Heaven" takes much the same form: "Wow! I have just read a wonderful poem by Yeats. Let me read it to you and tell you about it." That telling, naturally enough, takes the form of wanting to pass on what I think other readers might find helpful, to lead them to respond to the poem as enthusiastically as I do.

I list, in an order following that of the poem, some of the things that might need to be explained not only to a Chinese reader but also, no doubt, to a computer-games-playing Western young person ignorant of European poetry. David Damrosch recognizes with equanimity, as do I, that when a given piece of literature circulates into a different culture from that of its origin (for example, by translation), it will be read differently.[13]

I am not talking here, however, about a high-level culturally embedded reading, but just about making sense of Yeats's poem. This need to make sense might arise, for example, in trying to decide how to translate this or that phrase into Chinese. Here are some things it might be good to know in trying to understand "The Cold Heaven":

1. Something about Yeats's life and works.
2. The verse form used. (Three iambic hexameter quatrains rhyming *abab*—is it an odd sort of sonnet in hexameters rather than pentameters, and missing the last couplet?)
3. That Yeats recurrently uses "sudden" or "suddenly" in his lyrics, as in the opening of "Leda and the Swan": "A sudden blow . . . ."
4. What sort of bird a rook is, and why it is delighted by cold weather.
5. The double meaning of "heaven," as "skies" and as the supernatural realm beyond the skies, as in the opening of the Lord's Prayer, said daily by millions of Christians: "Our Father who art

in heaven." (Compare "skies" at the end: "the injustice of the skies for punishment.")

6. What an oxymoron (burning ice) is, and the history in Western poetry of this particular one.
7. The semantic difference between "imagination" and "heart" as well as the nuances of each word.
8. What the word "crossed" means in "memories . . . of love crossed long ago," both as the word alludes to Shakespeare's Romeo and Juliet as "star-crossed lovers" (that is, as fated by the stars to disaster in love) and as it refers to the biographical fact of Yeats's disastrous love for Maud Gonne (she turned him down repeatedly, so it is to some degree absurd for him to take responsibility for the failure of their love; he did his best to woo her).
9. The difference between "sense" and "reason" in "I took the blame out of all sense and reason." (Or is this just tautological? A. Norman Jeffares cites T. R. Henn's explanation that "'out of all sense' is an Irish (and ambiguous) expression meaning both 'to an extent far beyond what common sense could justify' and 'beyond the reach of sensation.'"[14])
10. The double meaning of the past participle "riddled" in the marvelous phrase "riddled with light" ("riddled" as punctured with holes, like a sieve, and "riddled" as having a perhaps unanswered riddle or conundrum posed to one; being "riddled with light" is paradoxical because light is supposed to be illuminating, not obscuring).
11. How to unsnarl the lines centering on "quicken" in "when the ghost [meaning disembodied soul] begins to quicken, / Confusion of the death bed over" ("quicken" usually refers to the coming to life of the fertilized egg in the womb, so an erotic love-bed scene is superimposed on the death-bed scene).
12. Which books are meant in the phrase "as the books say." (Which books? Those books in esoteric philosophy and folklore that Yeats read.)
13. How to relate "injustice of the skies for punishment" to the usual assumption that heaven punishes only justly, gives us our just deserts after death. (Why and how can the skies be unjust? By blaming the poet for something that was not his fault? Relate this to Greek and later tragedy: it is not Oedipus's fault that he has killed his father and fathered children on his mother—or is it?)

14. Why the last sentence is a question, and whether it is a real question or a merely rhetorical one. (Would the answer find its place if the blank that follows the twelve lines of this defective sonnet were filled? The poem seems both too much in line lengths and too little in number of lines.)
15. That Yeats, like other European poets of his generation, was influenced in this poem and elsewhere by what he knew, through translations, of Chinese poetry and Chinese ways of thinking. (Chinese readers especially might like to know this, or might even observe it on their own. The volume *Responsibilities*, which contains "The Cold Heaven," has an epigraph from someone Yeats calls, somewhat pretentiously, "Khoung-Fou-Tseu," presumably Confucius: "How am I fallen from myself, for a long time now / I have not seen the Prince of Chang in my dreams."[15] Chinese readers might have a lot to say about this Chinese connection and about how it makes "The Cold Heaven" a work of world literature.)

All this information would be given to my hearers or readers, however, not to "expand their minds" but in the hope that it might help them admire the poem as much as I do and be moved by it as much as I am. Yeats's poem can hardly be described as "uplifting," since its thematic climax is a claim that the skies are unjust and punish people for things of which they are not guilty. That is a terrifying wisdom. Telling others about this poem is not something I *should* do but something I cannot help doing, something the poem urgently calls on me to do.

Do I think much future exists in US colleges and universities or in our journals and university presses for such readings? No, I do not. I think this dimming of the future for literary studies has been brought about partly by the turning of our colleges and universities into trade schools, preparation for getting a job, institutions that have less and less place for the humanities, but perhaps even more by the amazingly rapid development of new teletechnologies that are fast making literature obsolete, a thing of the past. Even many of those who could teach literature, who were hired to do so, choose rather to teach fashion design, or the history of Western imperialism, or film, or some one or another among those myriad other interests that have replaced literature.

I add in conclusion, however, somewhat timidly and tentatively, one possible use that studying literature and literary theory might have, or ought to have, in these bad days. Students in any field might benefit from courses in "rhetorical reading" that would teach them how to tell truth from falsehood in Internet postings.[16] Citizens, in the United States at least, are these days inundated with a torrent of distortions and outright lies from politicians, the news media, and advertising on television and radio. Even my local public television station, supposedly objective, runs, daily and repeatedly, an advertisement in which the giant oil company Chevron promotes itself under the slogan "The Power of Human Energy." A moment's thought reveals that Chevron's interest is in energy from oil, not human energy. Chevron is devoted to getting as much money as it can (billions and billions of dollars a year) from extracting fossil fuels out of the earth, and thereby contributing big-time to global warming. The advertisement is a lie.

Learning how to read literature "rhetorically" is primary training in how to spot such lies and distortions. This is so partly because so much literature deals thematically with imaginary characters who are wrong in their readings of others—for example, Elizabeth Bennett in her misreading of Darcy in Jane Austen's *Pride and Prejudice,* or Dorothea Brooke's misreading of Edward Casaubon in George Eliot's *Middlemarch*, or Isabel Archer's misreading of Gilbert Osmond in Henry James's *The Portrait of a Lady*. (My choice of these heroines does not mean that it is only women who make such mistakes in Victorian novels. Think of Pip in *Great Expectations,* or of Lydgate in *Middlemarch,* or of Conrad's Lord Jim!)

Literature is also training in resisting lies and distortions in the skill it gives in understanding the way the rhetoric of tropes and the rhetoric of persuasion work. Such expertise as literary study gives might be translated to a savvy resistance to the lies and ideological distortions politicians and talk show hosts promulgate—for example, the lies of those who deny climate change, or the lying claims, believed in by high percentages of Americans, that Barack Obama is a Muslim and a socialist, and is not a legitimate president because he was supposedly not born in the United States. The motto for this defense of literary study might be the challenging and provocative claim made by Paul de Man in "The Resistance to Theory." "What we call ideology," says de Man, "is precisely the confusion of linguistic with natural reality, of reference with phenomenalism. It follows that, more than any other mode of inquiry, including economics, the linguistics of literariness is a powerful and indispensable tool in the unmasking of ideological aberrations, as well as a determining factor in accounting for their occurrence."[17]

The chances that literary study would have this benign effect on many people are slim. One can only have the audacity of hope and believe that some people who read and study literature and literary theory might be led to the habit of unmasking ideological aberrations such as those that surround us on all sides in the United States today. The chances are slim because of the difficulty of transferring what you might learn from, say, a careful reading of *The Portrait of a Lady* to the unmasking of dominant ideologies whose meaning is that thoughtful people are those who only vote Republican because their income happens to place them in the top 2 percent of all Americans and because maximizing their wealth in the short term is their only goal. Another great difficulty is the actual situation in American universities today, as I have described it. Derrida's "The University without Condition" was not exactly greeted with shouts of joyful assent when Derrida presented it as a lecture at Stanford. In spite of their lip service to teaching so-called critical thinking, the politicians and corporate executives who have so much power over public as well as private American colleges and universities are unlikely to support something that would put in question the assumptions on the basis of which they make decisions about who teaches what. They need colleges and universities these days, if at all, primarily to teach math and science, technology, engineering, computer science, basic English composition, and other skills necessary for working in a technologized capitalist economy. The ability to do a rhetorical reading of *Pride and Prejudice* and transfer that skill to decoding politicians' and advertisers' lies is not one of those necessities. I have never yet heard President Barack Obama so much as mention literary study in his eloquent speeches about the urgent need to improve education in the United States.

CHAPTER 14

Mixed Media Forever

The Internet as Spectacle; or, The Digital Transformation of Literary Studies

Literature involves voiding, rather than the affirmation, of aesthetic categories. One of the consequences of this is that, whereas we have traditionally been accustomed to reading literature by analogy with the plastic arts and with music, we now have to recognize the necessity of a non-perceptual, linguistic moment in painting and music, and learn to *read* pictures rather than to *imagine* meaning.
—Paul de Man, *The Resistance to Theory*

The word "spectacle," as in the title of the conference in Las Vegas ("Modernism and Spectacle") where this lecture was first presented, calls up from my mental data bank three names: Guy Debord, Jean Baudrillard, and Maurice Blanchot—Debord, of course, for *The Society of the Spectacle*, Baudrillard for *Simulacra and Simulation*, Blanchot for his theory of the "image" in "Two Versions of the Imaginary" ("Les deux versions de l'imaginaire") and "The Song of the Sirens" ("Le chant des Sirènes").[1] The ideas of these three writers can hardly be reconciled, but they are to some degree in resonance. All are in different ways influenced by Marx. Both Debord and Baudrillard were in one way or another sociologists who deplored what they saw as a bad new society dominated by advanced capitalism and the images created through mass media, advertising, and so on. Both Debord and Baudrillard were deeply influenced by the semiotics of the time. Both were photographers, Debord as a more or less professional filmmaker. He made a film of *The Society of the Spectacle*.[2] For Debord, "spectacle" is "a social relation among people that is mediated by images consisting of mass media, advertising, and popular culture."[3] For Baudrillard, present-day society has reached what he calls the "fourth stage" in the development of simulacra—that is, imitations that hollow out their originals. The fourth stage is "pure simulation," an interplay of simulacra without any relation to "reality" whatsoever. It is a complete transformation of society by television, film, print, and the Internet into depthless spectacle.[4] Today we would add Netflix, Facebook, Twitter, and video games to this list. Debord's "society of the spectacle" and Baudrillard's society of pure simulation are strongly analogous, in spite of important differences in terminology and modes of argumentation that need to be kept in mind. Baudrillard was a professional philosopher, while Debord was a filmmaker influenced by surrealism.

Visiting Las Vegas is a help in understanding what Debord meant by a society of spectacle and what Baudrillard meant by a display of simulacra. Las Vegas is perhaps the most spectacular confirmation anywhere in the world that Debord and Baudrillard were right about the way we live now, in the midst of extraordinary simulations surrounded by desert. A half-scale model of the Eiffel tower complete to the last rivet, a Venetian lagoon complete with gondolas, a cunning replica of a French bistro, and so on and on![5] I say nothing of the way the casinos are simulacra, simulations of our global financial system. That system in turn is itself a hyperbolic version of our society of spectacle, multiplying worthless credit default swaps into huge fortunes in an immense hall of mirrors. All these endless substitutions depend, by the way, on the Internet and on software algorithms that can make stock trades automatically in a fraction of a second or rig the slot machines in a casino so the house will surely make whatever "take" is legally allowed.

Blanchot's idea of the "image" is quite different from Debord's spectacle or from Baudrillard's simulacra. I adduce Blanchot to indicate that all twentieth-century theorists of the image were not singing the same tune. Blanchot presents a subtle theory of "the image" as the essence of the imaginary embodied in literary language. Speaking, for example, in a characteristic torrent of paradoxes, of Proust's breakthrough when two sensations coincided in a time out of time that made it possible for him to become a writer at last, Blanchot says: "Yes, at this time, everything becomes image, and the essence of the image is to be entirely outside, without intimacy, and yet more inaccessible and more mysterious than the innermost thought; without signification, but summoning the profundity of every possible meaning; unrevealed and yet manifest, having that presence-absence that constitutes the attraction and the fascination of the Sirens."[6] You can see that this formulation, in spite of important distinctions, is not entirely different from Debord's spectacle or Baudrillard's simulacra. Blanchot's imaginary is a dangerous vanishing point within which one might be swallowed up and disappear. This danger is figured in the threat to Ulysses of the Sirens' song. Blanchot tends to identify the imaginary with death or with an endless process of dying. The imaginary also exists as narrative (*récit*), as opposed to the evasions of the novel (*roman*). Blanchot's examples in the essays I have cited are Ulysses in his approach toward (or refusal to approach) the real song behind the Sirens' infinitely luring song, Proust's Marcel in his search for (*recherche de)* lost time, and Ahab's pursuit of the white whale in *Moby Dick*.[7]

Recent critical thinking has sometimes made a stark contrast between verbal media and visual ones. The contrast has often been couched in historical terms. What Debord and Baudrillard say is posited on a theory of history as a series of distinct epochs determined in a Marxist way by modes of production and distribution, and by the media dominant at a given time. During the epoch when print literature dominated—that is, during the eighteenth, nineteenth, and part of the twentieth centuries—the primary cultural media (books, magazines, and so on) were linguistic: printed words on paper pages. More and more as the twentieth century progressed, however, new and primarily visual media gradually came into cultural dominance: photography, film, television, video, and now the Internet with all its concomitants, such as video games. Even popular music online is often accompanied by videos, as though we can no longer listen without having something to look at. Before, we needed to be expert in reading printed words. Now we must be expert in deciphering the implications of visual images, such as those in films or video games, and the need to be good readers of printed literature has lessened.

Few people would hold to quite so stark a contrast, but most of us have some idea, however vaguely held, that verbal and visual media are quite different and require different academic disciplines ("film studies," say, as against "literary studies") and quite different methodologies of interpretation. These seem to be quite plausible assumptions until you begin to think a little about the actual history of the two media.

Verbal and visual media have been from the beginning mixed in various ways at various times. That is my primary thesis in this essay. Whatever there may have been originally of the ideographic in Western alphabetic languages has long since mostly disappeared, as opposed to an ideographic language like Chinese in which the character for "exit" still looks, to me at least, like an open mouth or a doorway. Mastery of a distinctive calligraphic style used to be a requirement in China for officials, from the emperor down to the lowliest bureaucrat. Nevertheless, recent scholars have studied the way the visual aspect of purely verbal texts in Western languages changes to some degree the meaning we assign: type font and type size, roman as against italics or bold, capitals as against use of colored type, amount of space between lines and in the margins, binding, marks of punctuation like dashes and exclamation points that are not voiced, and so on. My computer has a long list of fonts that I can choose from in different point sizes. The creation of fonts is work for highly skilled visual artists. My composition of this essay on my computer involves, at least implicitly, a whole set of choices designed to make what I compose look right to me on the page. A newspaper headline is in large type so it looks as if it is shouting and is really important: ROMNEY CHOOSES RYAN AS RUNNING MATE. On the other side, even the most purely visual set of signs invites being read as if it were a kind of writing, as my epigraph from Paul de Man asserts ("we now have to recognize the necessity of a non-perceptual, linguistic moment in painting and music, and learn to *read* pictures rather than to *imagine* meaning").

By imagining meaning, I imagine, de Man meant the transformation of the words on the page into mental visual images, as when we vividly imagine the faces, bodies, and surrounding scenes of characters in novels on the basis of verbal clues the novel gives. Examples are the reader's internal image of what those waves crashing on the shore in the interludes of Virginia Woolf's *The Waves* looked like, or what Wallace Stevens's jar in Tennessee looked like in "Anecdote of the Jar": "And round it was, upon a hill. . . ."; "[It was] tall and of a port in air."[8] In spite of de Man's denigration of imagining meaning, I think what might be called a spontaneous internal cinema accompanies, for most people, the reading of a verbal text. But reading pictures also happens for those adept in purely visual sign systems, what de Man calls "the necessity of a non-perceptual, linguistic moment in painting and music," "learning to *read* pictures." What de Man meant by reading, alert readers of de Man's essay "The Resistance to Theory" will know. He meant attention to "the linguistics of literariness," that is, the aberrational implications of figurative language.[9] A familiar example of using the linguistics of literariness to read pictures is the way we read montage, the juxtaposition of distinct scenes, according to tropological rhetoric, as a metaphor, metonymy, or synecdoche. Eisenstein's crowd scene in his *Battleship Potemkin*, set side by side with a shot of swarming maggots, is a famous case of this, but such *readable* tropes are a staple of the purely visual side of films and other visual media, even when they are not accompanied by printed or spoken words.

Here I want to discuss two concrete examples of this *readable* visual imagery, one from the cover of the *New Yorker* for 23 July 2012, one from an advertisement in the August 2012 issue of *Wired* magazine.[10] Both these pictures exemplify in complex ways Debord's society of spectacle and Baudrillard's final stage of the world as interacting simulacra, a world with no reality behind it or referred to by it.

The brilliant *New Yorker* cover I will "read" shows a nuclear family (father, mother, and two teenage children, a boy and a girl) standing side by side in tropical clothes on a beach at the edge of the ocean, with a backdrop of palm trees. In the foreground is the shadow of someone taking a digital photograph of the group. He stands just where you are, dear viewer, which makes you the one taking the snapshot that makes up the cover. All four of the family members are holding iPhones or some similar gadget. All are texting or tweeting or using Facebook. They are paying no attention whatsoever to the beautiful scene they have come to visit, nor to one another. So much for the salutary togetherness of the nuclear family! Their facial expressions, especially those of the father and mother, are tense, even anguished. They are grimacing or clenching their teeth with concentration. They are plugged in. They are mere attachments to their digital machines. That is the way we live now. Such people are perhaps what all human beings will be like in the twilight of the Anthropocene.

The readable meaning of this cover is attained without the use of a single word. "A picture is worth a thousand words." In this case, the meaning is generated by the ironic and discordant juxtaposition of the beautiful tropical scene and the family all isolated from one another and all wholly absorbed in their smartphones. The viewer is put in complicity by way of the shadow in the foreground that shows that viewer taking a photo with another smartphone. Ironic incongruous juxtaposition is a readable/unreadable trope that can also be expressed purely in words, or in a mixture of words and images.

In my second example, from *Wired*, the meaning is generated by metonymies that turn from side-by-sideness to the similarity of metaphor. In this ad for a beverage that Coca-Cola, the parent company, has branded *glacéau smartwater*®, visual images and words combine to produce a complex meaning. A beautiful and provocatively dressed young woman with parted lips sits in an expensive leather-upholstered convertible holding a big bottle of this water erect in her left hand. (The model is Jennifer Aniston.) The traditional association in ads of sex with fast, expensive cars is shamelessly exploited once more. The young woman's right hand calls attention to her open, unbuttoned blouse, her almost exposed left breast, and to what is hidden lower down, where her dangling fingers point. She is looking just over the viewer's left shoulder, as if about to turn to look you straight in the eye. She has a tastefully elegant bracelet on her right wrist and a matching necklace. The caption at the bottom reads, with tasteful alliterative terseness, "Good taste travels well." The message is clear. You would be smart to drink this water because it will give you good taste in two senses: the taste of the water (which has electrolytes, and does taste good); and the social good taste that will earn you a ride with the young woman, also in two senses. A promise that drinking this "smart" water will enhance your manliness may also be read in that proffered bottle. It must work sort of like Cialis. I speak from the perspective of a heterosexual male, as you will notice. I suppose a good percentage of *Wired*'s readers are in that category. Many names on the masthead are female, however, and stories about women software entrepreneurs are included in the magazine.

Most people are so used to seeing and "reading" such ads in magazines, on television, and on the Internet that they take their interpretation for granted or just let them work their magic "unconsciously," which is what the ad makers probably intend. As Marshall McLuhan long ago recognized in *The Gutenberg Galaxy*, *Understanding Media*, and other books, however, "The medium is the message" (or "mass age" or "mess age" or "massage," according to his puns).[11] McLuhan had little to learn from Debord or Baudrillard. He "got it" already, with brilliant completeness, including the recognition that "spectacular" juxtapositions of visual images work like verbal tropes. All these double meanings are achieved by means of visual puns and metonymies that become metaphors: the taste of the bottled water is like the promised taste of the young woman, sex is like a fast car, and so on. To carry this interpretation even a step further, there is a snap-buttoned leather box in the foreground of the ad that might be read as an invitation to a further act of unbuttoning. In this ad, everything is turned into image and becomes a siren song promising, in Blanchot's words, "movement toward a point—one that is not only unknown, ignored, and foreign, but such that it seems, before and outside of this movement, to have no kind of reality."[12] I know that drinking this water will not really lead to possession of the sexy young woman in her expensive car, but the ad nevertheless generates a movement in me toward the unfulfillable promise these images make. I know I am just looking at a photograph of Jennifer Aniston, who probably survives on carrot juice and who takes whatever pose the photographer requests. The whole thing is a sham, a simulacrum, a spectacle, a "model," as in "fashion model," "late-model car," "model train," and "model pupil," a paradigm for others. The ad is made more powerful and persuasive by being placed side by side in *Wired* with a great many other such ads for high-end commodities of all kinds. The allure of each rubs off on the others.

When *Wired* first appeared, not all that many years ago (January 1993), it was a geeky pamphlet running interesting (to me) stories about the latest developments in the high-tech world—computers, software, interactive games, and the Web.[13] *Wired*'s avowed "patron saint" was McLuhan. *Wired* rapidly, to my amazement, became a multitudinous 124-page advertising spectacle (in the Debordian sense) interspersed with short entries and a few slick essays with titles like (in the issue that contains the Glacéau Smartwater ad) "Spycraft for Nerds," "Undead," and "Do you really want to be like Steve Jobs?" (The latter words are in white on the cover, inscribed over the forehead of a photo of Steve Jobs, with the word "really" in yellow.) *Wired* is nothing if not extremely sophisticated in its graphic design and its mixing of typefaces. It has won many awards for design as well as for content. "Undead" is a longish piece about a new treatment for rabies. The cover alludes, in a teasing come-on, to "curing the disease behind zombies and werewolves." It is difficult to tell the short essays from the full-page ads, and hard to find something listed in the table of contents, since none of the ad pages are numbered. This, I suppose, is to entice you into looking at a lot of ads while you are trying to find that essay about zombies and werewolves. (*Wired* apparently makes so much money from ads that a year's subscription to this sumptuous spectacle cost only $14.99 at the time when this essay was given as a lecture.)

The transformation of *Wired* has been truly amazing. It began as a McLuhan-like interpretation of media, featuring authors like Nicholas Negroponte of the MIT Media Lab. It now describes itself as providing in-depth coverage of current and future trends in technology.[14] A subscription to *Wired* gives you free access to all of *Wired*, digitized on an e-reader app but without the advertising. No more talk about Creative Commons, open source, and sidestepping copyright limitations. *Wired* has become a spectacle, a panorama of simulacra itself in need of demystification, a capitalist tool. That transformation corresponds to the rapid expansion and commodification of the Internet as it has turned into a full-blown Debordian spectacle or collection of Baudrillardian simulacra. This spectacular transformation of the Internet is especially evident in the use of Facebook, Twitter, and so on, in political campaigns, like the presidential race that was going on when I first wrote this lecture in August 2012. The terms "truth" and "lie," as Debord and Baudrillard in different ways argued and demonstrated, have ceased to have relevance to this complex tissue of mixed-media assertions. If you say often enough that Barack Obama is a Kenyan socialist Muslim bent on destroying capitalism, or that he is the Antichrist, a lot of people will believe it (10 percent of Americans go for the Antichrist lie), just as many will associate Mitt Romney primarily with that vacation drive to Canada with his dog strapped to the roof of his car. The latter event apparently did happen in reality, but it becomes a mediatic simulacrum when used over and over in campaign rhetoric.

I return now to my claim that multimedia in different forms and mixes has characterized verbal texts from the beginning. That means it is a mistake to think of a radical change in the twentieth century from print media to graphic media—from printed novels, say, to films—with each requiring different disciplines and methodologies of interpretation. What is needed, rather, is a flexible procedure of "reading" appropriate to each given mixture of media at a given time. Paul de Man, in "The Resistance to Reading," called this procedure a use of "the linguistics of literariness," that is, the rhetoric of tropes, to read all sorts of cultural phenomena. In a still challenging formulation, quoted in earlier chapters of the present volume, he said that "more than any other mode of inquiry, including economics, the linguistics of literariness is a powerful and indispensable tool in the unmasking of ideological aberrations, as well as a determining factor in accounting for their occurrence."[15] The changes in media have been all along, rather, a matter of complex changes in balance through the centuries among forms of expression that always have been, and always will be, mixed.

Most scholars will agree with this if they think a little about it, but the recent supposed shift from print to graphic modes has been a powerful ideological presupposition, wrong though it demonstrably is. The permutations in the mixture of media can be followed from the combination of verbal and graphic modes in carvings on Greek and Roman tombstones and funerary monuments, to medieval illustrated manuscripts, to the sumptuous graphic title pages and other illustrations in early printed books (modern title pages still commonly have graphic elements), to seventeenth-century emblem books, to Hogarth's great eighteenth-century mixed-media etchings, to printed novels that from the beginning have so frequently had illustrations (for example, the admirable illustrations for Dickens's novels by Cruikshank and Phiz), to Dante Gabriel Rossetti's mixed-media compositions juxtaposing poems and pictures (such as his *Aspecta Medusa*), to the sinister illustrations by Aubrey Beardsley for Pope's "The Rape of the Lock" or Wilde's *Salomé*, to the inclusion of photographs in some early-twentieth-century multivolume "sets" of English writers like Hardy and James or the multitudinous illustrations in the magnificent Cook and Wedderburn edition of Ruskin's works in thirty-nine volumes,[16] to the combinations of print novels and films of those novels or television versions that have characterized later-twentieth-century forms of mixed media, to the wonderful efflorescence of comic strips such as *Peanuts* or *Pogo*, to graphic novels based on the conventions of comic books (such as Art Spiegelman's *Maus* or the Japanese *manga* graphic novels, many "translated" into English, though that is hardly the word for changing a graphic Japanese word for "Pow!" or "Bang!" into its English equivalent, since the original depends so much on the way the Japanese characters look on the graphic page).

If I want nowadays to write about Imre Kertész's wonderful Holocaust novel *Fatelessness*, or Ian McEwan's *Atonement*, or even works by Austen or James, I am more or less obliged to consider the films and BBC television versions not only of Kertész and McEwan but also of novels by Austen, James, Dickens, Hardy, Conrad, et al.[17] I say "obliged" because in my experience more and more students and faculty around the world will have seen the film but will not have read the book. If you want their attention and understanding in a lecture, you had better say something about the film.

I think part of the reason for the sharp separation between verbal and graphic modes in some people's minds derives from the way novels without pictures tended to be published during a relatively brief period of high modernism (for example, the novels of Conrad in the Dent Edition, or the Hogarth Press edition of Virginia Woolf, or the paperback editions of novels by Faulkner, though those have lurid covers). Virginia Woolf's *The Waves*, for example, has no illustrations beyond the elegant Hogarth Press cover designed by Vanessa Bell; on the other hand, it is available for free in a searchable e-text that turns it to some degree into a graphic presentation, that is, into images on a screen.[18] Older novels—for example, those by Dickens, Trollope, or Hardy—were usually published during the high modernist period without their original illustrations. That led teachers and students (like me, for example) to tend to forget or ignore the role those illustrations originally played in the generation of meaning. I was taught to read and then teach Victorian novels using inexpensive paperbacks like Penguin editions or the older Everyman and Modern Library reprints that totally omitted the original illustrations and thereby hid the way Victorian novels were mixed-media creations with a complex interplay between verbal text and illustration.

In doing this, I was forgetting the children's books that did so much to inform my early sensibility, my pleasure in puns and wordplay in general, and my spontaneous ability to "read" pictures. Such books would include especially, for me, Lewis Carroll's *Alice's Adventures in Wonderland* and *Through the Looking-Glass*, with the John Tenniel illustrations; Kenneth Grahame's *The Wind in the Willows*, with the Ernest H. Shepard illustrations; and A. A. Milne's Winnie-the-Pooh books.[19] I remember as much the glorious pictures of Humpty Dumpty, or of the tea party in which the dormouse is dipped in tea, in the *Alice* books; or, in *The Wind in the Willows*, Rat "messing about in boats," or Toad tearing down the road in an open car calling, "Speed! More speed!," or Piglet terrified by Pooh fallen in a pit with his head stuck in a honey jar and therefore looking to Piglet like a "horrible heffalump" or a "heffable horrilump" in one of the Winnie-the-Pooh books. But I must desist. Henry James, in *A Small Boy and Others*, puts his finger on the truth about these mixed-media creations as read by young people. Speaking of the Cruikshank illustrations for *Oliver Twist*, James, with wonderful astuteness, writes: "It perhaps even seemed to me more Cruikshank's than Dickens's; it was a thing of such vividly terrible images, and all marked with that peculiarity of Cruikshank that the offered flowers or goodnesses, the scenes and figures intended to comfort and cheer, present themselves under his hand as but more subtly sinister or more suggestively queer, than the frank badnesses and horrors."[20] Cruikshank's Sikes, James is saying, looks, paradoxically, wholesome and sane compared to his Mr. Brownlow or his Oliver.

I turn in conclusion to the transformation of literary studies by the Internet. This is a topic that comes up often in these lectures given over the last quarter century in China, partly because the issue deeply concerns me, partly because Chinese academic audiences have wanted me to express my views about it.

Today print culture is fast fading. It is being rapidly replaced by digital culture of all sorts. Most people in the United States do not any longer read Shakespeare or Dickens or Emily Dickinson unless forced to do so in school. As I have said earlier in these essays, they watch Fox News on cable television, or (at best) the PBS evening news, or BBC sitcoms, or (a few people) television adaptations of classic English novels. Today people play collective video games online. They spend hours every day using cell phones, iPods, iPhones, iPads, e-mail, Facebook, Twitter, and wireless laptop computers. They use emoticons and they text, or indulge in "txtng," even while driving a car, to their great peril. They communicate by Skype with the simulacrum of a friend on the screen. Features of the so-called postmodernist sensibility, specialists in it like Fredric Jameson say, are subjective depthlessness, absence of unified selfhood, lack of affect, and the loss of any historical sense. These are results of our society of spectacle. One must be careful, however, not to fall into some naive version of irresistible technological determinism. The new gadgets can be used in all sorts of ways. They limit but do not absolutely determine the use that is made of them.

A concomitant of the digital revolution, which has taken only twenty years to happen, has been great confusion and uncertainty in the humanities. What should we humanists study and teach? If we teach anything like the old curriculum, we are teaching things that have less and less relevance to the actual lives of our students. In Victorian England (my special field), middle-class ideology, beliefs about gender roles, courtship and marriage, class divisions, and so on, were both transmitted and created to a considerable degree by novels—by Jane Austen, George Eliot, Charles Dickens, Elizabeth Gaskell, Anthony Trollope, and a host of other popular novelists. Now such beliefs are passed on and, to some degree, created by films; by radio and television, including talk shows on TV and radio; and by video games. Talk shows have such increasing power in politics that some people say that the actual heads of the Republican Party in the United States are Rush Limbaugh, Glenn Beck, and that other media celebrity, who also worked for Fox News, Sarah Palin. Most people these days have not read Jane Austen at all. They know her work, if at all, only through the latest BBC adaptation. Book publishers, including university presses, appear to have concluded that little or no market exists for old-fashioned literary studies, whereas a book on the cultural history of Botany Bay is assumed to have a market.

One result of these amazingly rapid changes—which, again, I call "prestidigitalization"—has been the overnight change in the humanities from literary study to cultural studies. Younger scholar-teachers, understandably, want to study and teach what really matters to them and to their fellow citizens. This is all to the good. Cultural studies, however, has not yet quite become as well-organized a discipline as once was, for example, the study of British literature, or of medieval European history, or of German literature. Cultural studies straddles the humanities and the social sciences, as do sociology, anthropology, and "media studies." No widespread agreement exists about just what is the best training, the best curriculum, to prepare scholars to do "cultural studies." By contrast, I once could have told you exactly what courses you needed to take to prepare yourself for a career as a specialist in Renaissance literature or in Victorian literature. We knew, or we thought we knew, what you needed to know.

Some amazingly good things, however, have been brought to literary studies by the digital revolution. The ease of writing and revising on a computer is one of them. Moreover, it is no longer necessary to be at a major university with a big library to do serious research and criticism. This is a powerful form of democratization. Much literature is available online, if you happen to want to read it that way (for example, work by all the writers I have mentioned in this essay as well as large amounts of secondary literature about literature—all of Dickens, Henry James, and so on and on). I worked not long ago on, among other things, Franz Kafka and Imre Kertész. More or less all of Kafka's work in German is available online in searchable form.[21] When I wanted to check the Hungarian word for "naturally," and its frequency, as against the English translation of Kertész's *Fatelessness*, I found a searchable version in Hungarian in a minute by Googling it. That website has since mysteriously disappeared, by the way, probably because it was unauthorized or because the sale of printed versions greatly increased after

Kertész received the Nobel Prize in Literature. I ordered the film version of *Fatelessness* from Amazon and had it in my computer's DVD slot in a few days. Recently I could not remember the location in Shakespeare of a phrase I remembered, "the beast with two backs." In two minutes, I found it by way of an online concordance; it is Iago speaking in *Othello*, act 1, scene 1, line 126. The Internet, the World Wide Web, and *Wikipedia* are fantastic resources for even the most traditional forms of humanistic scholarship. I use *Wikipedia* a lot. As with any encyclopedia, one has to be skeptical and check it against other sources, but I have found *Wikipedia* to be amazingly accurate. One "spectacular" result is that I rarely have to borrow a book from the quite comprehensive University of California library system. I can do the scholarly and critical work I want to do just about as well in Sedgwick, Maine, or on Deer Isle, Maine, as I could in Irvine, New Haven, or Baltimore. (I have emphasized this by giving the URLs for many of the online sources I consulted to write this essay.) E-mailing, though I spend an inordinate amount of time doing it, has changed my life. It has put me in more or less instant contact with scholars and students all over the world. Through e-mail, I have created my own *virtual* community. I stress "virtual." Essays and book manuscripts are sent to me by e-mail attachment, though I still have difficulty reading books and essays on a computer screen or on my Kindle for the Mac. [That difficulty, however, is rapidly decreasing.—JHM]

I am certain that using e-mail, the Internet, and the computer has changed my personality as well as the way I write essays and books. I have not, however, found it all that easy to be precise in identifying just what the difference is between doing literary study exclusively with printed books and essays and doing it with the help of the Internet. I think Debord and Baudrillard may help in understanding that difference. If I read a printed book, it ties me to the print epoch, a time when, however problematically, verbal and graphic creations were assumed to be in one way or another representational. They were taken as tied to the real extraverbal and extragraphic world by some form of mimesis. When a given printed text—Woolf's *The Waves*, to repeat that example—is made available online as an e-text, it is subtly transformed into an image. It is transmogrified willy-nilly into one simulacrum among the billions of simulacra floating around in cyberspace in our society of spectacle. That is a huge difference. Whether I can work with such materials and remain true to the McLuhanesque commitments I share with the early editors of *Wired*, or whether I, like the dyer's hand, will inevitably become subdued to what I work in as rapidly as were those in charge of

Wired, is another question. In any case, working with digitized materials as opposed to print materials means submission to a quite different technological or spectacular regime, even though both print and the results of prestidigitalization are different forms of mixed media.

CHAPTER 15

Literature Matters Today

"Matters"! This is an odd word when used as a verb. Of course we know what it means. The verbal form of "matter" means "count for something," "have import," "have effects in the real world," "be worth taking seriously." Using the word as a noun, however, someone might speak of "literature matters," meaning the whole realm that involves literature. The newsletter of the Maine chapter of the Appalachian Mountain Club is called *Wilderness Matters*, punning on the word as a noun and as a verb. We might say, analogously, "Literature Matters," as my title does. In medieval Europe, learned people spoke of "the matter of Rome," "the matter of Arthur," "the matter of Greece," meaning the whole set of stories that lay behind Aeneas's story, the Arthurian romances, or Odysseus's, Achilles's, and Oedipus's stories. The verb "matter" resonates with the noun "matter." The latter means sheer unorganized physical substance. Aristotle opposed unformed matter to form. This suggests that if something matters, its import is not abstract. What matters is not purely verbal, spiritual, or formal. It has concrete effects on materiality, in the form, perhaps, of human bodies and their behavior. Does literature matter in that sense today?

It matters quite a bit, however, what we mean by "literature" when we ask whether literature matters today. I am assuming "literature" means printed books that contain what most people ordinarily think of these days as "literature"—that is, poems, plays, and novels. Just what is "literary" about poems, plays, and novels is another matter, to which I shall return. It is often taken for granted that what most matters about literature, if it matters at all, is the accuracy with which it reflects the real world or functions as a guide to conduct for readers living in that world. The 2,500-year-old mimetic paradigm, going back to the Greeks, in its multitude of permutations has had and still has great power, at least in the Western world. A little reflection, however, will show that this paradigm is extremely problematic. It is easily contested or easily made more complicated, as I shall later on briefly show.

The reader will recognize that adding "today" to "literature matters," as I have done, is a move that matters. Literature's import differs in different times, places, and societies. My interest is in the question of whether literature matters now, today, in the fall of 2012, here in the United States of America (since I know that best) but also in the global here-and-now within which all we human beings, Americans and the rest, more and more live from moment to moment today. I note from the outset that so many journal issues and books about whether literature matters would not be necessary if the mattering of literature today were not in doubt. All who love literature are collectively anxious today about whether literature matters. No such issue of a journal would have likely seemed necessary in Victorian England, for example, my original field of specialization. To middle- and upper-class literate Victorians, the assumption that literature matters quite a lot was so much taken for granted as almost never to be a matter for interrogation.

"Literate" and "literature" have the same root, meaning written "letters." You are literate if you can make sense of written letters. You are then "lettered." Literature is made of letters, marks made on paper by some writing technology or other. The primary technology was the printing press in the epoch from the seventeenth century to the present. That was the period of what we Westerners generally mean by "literature." Victorian readers took it for granted that printed literature, especially in the form of novels, reflected back to them the everyday social world they lived in. Novels, moreover, as I have observed in earlier chapters of this book, taught them how to behave in courtship and marriage as well as in many other regions of everyday life. This way of assuming that literature matters may explain the continued power of the mimetic, "realist" paradigm.

Literature, however, was also the chief way in which Victorians could enjoy the pleasures of entering into an imaginary world invented for them by someone more gifted than they in manipulating language. Those pleasures were often seen as guilty and dangerous, especially for young women but also for young men. Think of Catherine Morland, the heroine of Jane Austen's *Northanger Abbey*, or of Conrad's Lord Jim. Flaubert's Emma Bovary is the paradigmatic example of a fictional character corrupted by reading literature.

These two assumptions about why literature matters were in tension in Victorian culture and in European culture generally. That tension defined the social role the Victorian literate middle and upper classes assumed literature to have. Think of it! The Victorians had no film, no radio, no television, no video games, no DVDs, no Internet, no iPhoto. Such technological impoverishment! They had only printed books, newspapers, and magazines to satisfy their needs both for reflective mimesis and for enjoying the imaginary.

I shall now dare to speak briefly about why literature has mattered to me. Though I am not quite a Victorian, I do go back, believe it or not, to a time when the only forms of telecommunication available to me besides books were radio, telephone, record players, and, quite infrequently, films. I lived in a small village in upstate New York. I was fascinated by literature and read much as a child, though more for the pleasures of the imaginary than for any presumption that reading literature was teaching me how to behave correctly in everyday life. I could not have cared less about that! I also took spontaneous pleasure, as I have elsewhere recounted in detail (see chapter 14 of this volume), in the word play of Lewis Carroll's Alice books and of A. A. Milne's Winnie-the-Pooh books.[1] Though my mother had been a high school teacher of English, and my father was a small-college president who held a Columbia University PhD in philosophy influenced by John Dewey's pragmatism, my literary knowledge was pretty marginal when I went off to Oberlin College with plans to be a physics major.

I shifted from physics to literature primarily because I "loved literature" but also because I found literature extremely puzzling. Literature seemed to me a challenge to explanation, something like strange data from a galaxy (for example, from a black hole). When I got to Oberlin, I discovered that many students there knew immensely more about literature than I did. I had never heard of T. S. Eliot. I'd had one good literature teacher in high school. He taught American literature. But mostly he taught the names of major works and authors of American literature. So I knew that there was somebody called St. Jean de Crèvecœur in the eighteenth century who wrote a book called *Letters from an American*

Farmer, but I had never read it. We did not do any reading of original works in that class, as well as I can remember, and Crèvecœur's book was not in my home library. At Oberlin, the teaching of literature was quite good. It did involve much reading of actual literary texts from all "periods," as I found when I shifted to become an English major. Oberlin had courses in the whole range of English literature, even in now marginalized topics like eighteenth-century poetry after Dryden and Pope and before Wordsworth. I wonder how many such programs still exist in the United States. They seem pretty old-fashioned now.

In spite of that training, I remain to this day puzzled by literary works. I remember the poem that exemplified my puzzlement and still does so. This is a short poem by Tennyson, one of the songs in *The Princess*, called "Tears, Idle Tears." It is a wonderful poem. I looked at this poem when I was still a physics major and found it an exceedingly strange use of language. In my science courses, I was taught to say the truth straightforwardly, to explain anomalies, and to use language in as uncomplicated a way as possible. Tennyson seemed to me to do no such things. The poem begins:

> Tears, idle tears, I know not what they mean,
> Tears from the depth of some divine despair
> Rise in the heart, and gather to the eyes,
> In looking on the happy Autumn-fields,
> And thinking of the days that are no more.[2]

I asked myself, "What in the world does this mean?" What does Tennyson mean by calling his tears idle? In what sense are these tears idle? Why did he write, "I know not what they mean"? I did not know what they mean, either. The poem is very beautiful. There is no doubt about that, but so what? And "tears from the depth of some divine despair"? What does "divine despair" mean? It must mean despair of some god. What god? Gods are not supposed to despair. What is this god in despair about? Why are the "Autumn-fields" happy? I thought they were just inhuman matter. In short, I had dozens of questions about just these few lines. It seems to me that simply to read the poem out loud to students, as teachers often used to do, and to say how beautiful it is, is not enough. Yes, I agree. It is beautiful. But what does it *mean*? I think we are justified in demanding a high degree of "explicability" from literary works and in demanding that our teachers help students in this hermeneutic work.

Why, I continued to wonder, should it matter to me whether I read and understand this poem or not? I wanted to figure out answers to these questions, to account for the poem in the way astrophysicists account for data from outer space. Decades after my shift from physics to literature, I wrote an essay trying, belatedly, to answer those questions I had about "Tears, Idle Tears."[3] What was wrongheaded about my original project took me some years to discover. I am still discovering—that is, still trying to come to terms with—the irreconcilability of hermeneutics and poetics, meaning and the way meaning is expressed.[4] A shorthand description of my mistake would be to say that data from the stars, on the one hand, and the linguistic "matter" that makes up poems, on the other, require fundamentally different methodologies of "accounting for." I have spent my whole life trying to account for various presumptively "literary" works. That is my vocation—reading, teaching, lecturing, and writing about print literature. Literature matters a great deal to me.

Well, how much does literature matter in the world in general today? It is easy to see, as I have already argued in earlier chapters of this book, that literature, in the sense of printed poems, plays, and novels, is mattering less and less. We are in the long-drawn-out twilight of the epoch of print literature. This epoch began less than four centuries ago. It could end without bringing about the death of civilization. Though of course literary works are still widely read all over the world, in different degrees in different places, literature matters less and less to many people, including highly educated ones. The double role of allowing the pleasures of entering imaginary worlds, and of learning about the real world and how to behave in it, is more and more shifting to newer technological devices and platforms for telecommunications—films, video games, television shows, popular music, Facebook, and so on. I include television news broadcasts as forms of the imaginary. The ability or the need to create imaginary worlds out of words on printed pages is less and less an important part of most people's lives. Probably people are becoming less and less adept at doing it. Why go to all the bother to read an extremely difficult novel, such as Henry James's *The Golden Bowl*, when you can so much more easily watch the splendid BBC television version?

The new telecommunications devices and platforms have made a fantastically rapid and sweeping change worldwide in human culture. Literature, too, has been radically and irreversibly changed. Downloading and reading on a computer screen, or on a Kindle or on an iPad, George Eliot's *Middlemarch* or any of the probably millions of other literary texts now floating in cyberspace is, in obvious ways and in more subtle ways, too, greatly different from reading a literary work in a printed book. This is partly because the digital version is searchable and can be cut and pasted; partly because its material base, its "matter," its *subjectile*,[5] is so different; partly because of a digital text's radically different surrounding context (all the unimaginable heterogeneity of cyberspace as against the neat rows of alphabetized books in a library); and partly because of its different form of portability and its different (non)location (the nonspace of cyberspace, or the ghostly letters on a computer screen, as against a printed book in a private or public library, a solid object you can hold in your hands).

The process of inventing literary works has also been radically changed. The underlying matter of literature, its material base, has been revolutionized. No more writing successive drafts by hand on paper with a pen or pencil, then laboriously typing and retyping the text to get a final draft ready to be typeset. This typesetting happened at first, during the early print epoch, letter by letter. Subsequently it was done by Linotype, with successive proofs to be read, marked by hand, reset, and then reset again. Composition of literary works on the computer has changed all that. The ease of revision of a computer file means that a new literary text is never really finished. It can always be further revised, as I am revising this essay at this moment. (I leave it to you to figure out which moment or moments I mean.) The successive drafts of computer files are, for the most part, lost forever. That puts a whole scholarly industry out of business—the study of early drafts of a given text. This new form of literature exists from the beginning in a quasi-disembodied form, as 0's and 1's on a hard drive or in some "cloud memory." Though the "file" may ultimately take print form, that printing is now done flawlessly from a computer file, often a PDF. [PDF stands for Portable Document Format, a standard developed by Adobe.—JHM] More and more, literary works come out simultaneously in print form and as e-texts. More and more, people who still read literature at all choose to read it online. As mentioned several times before, I call this the "prestidigitalization" of literature.

"The medium is the maker."[6] The mode of materialization of a given literary work fundamentally determines its meaning and its performative force. The matter of literature matters. The new computer "medium" makes literature radically different from its old self—different, that is, down to the bottom. "Medium" must be taken here in the sense both of a new material base and of a somewhat spooky, spiritualist, mediumistic, telepathic means of transmission. Something speaks to me through the medium.

Strangely enough, one thinks with one's fingers when writing. I am not a "creative writer," just someone who writes about, and round about, literature, in endless circumlocution. Nevertheless, I have had my own experience of how difficult it is to change from inventing words with a pen in my hand, as I used to do, to inventing them with my fingers on a computer keyboard, as I do habitually now. That is happening right now with the words that are at this moment flowing through my fingers from who knows where in my nervous system onto the keyboard and then magically appearing on my computer screen. Some impersonal inner voice seems to speak them as they are keyed in. They come into being by an inventive bodily process that is more "discovering" than deliberately "making up," to recall the bifurcated meaning of the word "invention."

Jacques Derrida long ago identified literature in our modern sense with the several centuries of print culture and its attendant technologies, with the appearance of modern democracies and modern capitalism, and with the concomitant rise of a literate middle class granted *nominal* (I stress "nominal") freedom to say and write anything in a literary work and not be held accountable for it.[7] An author could always say, even of the narrator of a novel or of the speaker of a lyric poem she or he had written, "That is not me speaking but an imaginary person created out of words." Derrida also long ago prophetically foresaw—in a notable passage in the "Envois" section of *La carte postale*, cited in earlier chapters of this book—that computer technology would bring literature, along with a number of other important cultural institutions, to an end.[8] The technological regime overpowers any political regime, as we can see in the transformations, made possible to a considerable degree by cell phones, of repressive regimes in North Africa. Derrida elsewhere in *La carte postale* writes about how psychoanalysis, as a quasi-science and as a social institution, would have been radically different if Freud and his associates had been able to communicate by e-mail rather than having to depend on the postal system and the telephone. The same thing can be said of literature. Suppose Shakespeare or Fielding, Wordsworth or Dickens, had been able to compose on the computer and self-publish on a personal website or on Facebook! The mind boggles at the thought.

The signs that Derrida was right—that is, the signs of a gradual vanishing of print literature as a cultural force—are everywhere visible, in different degrees and different ways, in each country. Evidence in the United States is the reduction in the number of bachelor's degrees earned in English, humanities, and foreign languages in US colleges and universities along with the huge number of unemployed or underemployed PhDs in literature, the failure of our politicians ever to mention literature in their noble speeches about education (in science, math, and engineering), and the transformation of so many departments ostensibly for teaching literature into departments that actually do "cultural studies," often with minimal attention to literary texts as anything other than one more or less minor cultural form among many others.[9] As I mentioned in chapter 13, I have never heard Barack Obama so much as mention literature in his eloquent speeches about education. His emphasis, and even the emphasis of university presidents like Richard Levin of Yale, is all on improving the study of science, math, and engineering so the United States can become "competitive in the global economy." Richard Atkinson said that was his goal for the then nine-campus University of California when he took up his position some years ago as its president. The old model of a comprehensive liberal arts education as preparation for life as well as for a profession is rapidly being replaced by a concept of higher education as vocational schooling in science, math, and engineering in preparation for some technological or business position (for example, in computer programming). You do not need to have read Shakespeare for such work.

Moreover, worrying about whether literature any longer matters seems a trivial pastime in a globalized and telecommunications-dominated world of financial meltdown; double-dip recessions; unemployment of over 9 percent [Down to 7 percent as of December 2013, and now even lower.—JHM] in the United States (much higher if part-time workers, underemployed workers, and people who have given up trying are included); a 15.1 percent poverty rate and crumbling infrastructure in the United States; political chaos in many countries; and catastrophic human-caused climate change, with, for example, unprecedented wildfires and prolonged heat waves in Australia and Texas, accelerated melting of Arctic ice, looming food wars, and widespread species extinction, including possibly the extinction of that wise (but self-destructive, autoimmune) creature, *Homo sapiens*. The United States is the only Western country that does not have some form of universal health care. As a consequence, health care costs nationally are already 17.6 percent of gross domestic product—that is, $8,000 per person annually and climbing, far higher than in any other country. Almost 50 million Americans do not have any health care insurance at all. That figure rises every year and will rise even faster if the Republicans succeed in repealing the new health care law, so-called Obamacare. [The implementation of the Affordable Health Care Act has already, in a short time, greatly ameliorated the US healthcare situation; 16 million additional citizens now have healthcare. The Republicans still intend to repeal Obamacare if they can.—JHM] We do not have time today, it might well be argued, to worry about whether literature any longer matters. Who cares? How can we justify taking time to care about something so trivial, something that matters so little?

I have elsewhere argued for an anachronistic reading of older literary works.[10] I mean by "anachronistic" a reading of literature in the context of our situation today, not by way of some attempt to put oneself back inside the mind-frame of a Renaissance man or woman in order to read Shakespeare, or that of a middle-class Victorian to read Dickens or George Eliot. The concept of a uniform period mind-set, as in Walter E. Houghton's *The Victorian Frame of Mind* or E. M. W. Tillyard's *The Elizabethan World Picture*, is in any case extremely problematic.[11] Victorian and Elizabethan frames of mind, the evidence shows, were quite heterogeneous. Even if a uniform period mind-set existed, why would identifying oneself with it be an attractive thing to try to do except for literary historians, those putatively impersonal and objective scholars? Why pretend we are still Victorians or Elizabethans? The answer, I suppose, is that it will make us better readers of *Middlemarch* or of Tennyson's *The Princess*, but literary works create their appropriate frames of mind in their readers, a different one for each text, however much explanatory historical footnotes may help. In place of the virtues claimed for the so-called historical imagination, I argue that literature matters most for us if it is read for today, and read "rhetorically," partly as training in ways to spot lies, ideological distortions, and hidden political agendas such as surround us on all sides in the media these days.

I give one example: *NBC Nightly News* on television in the United States ends almost every day with another "Making a Difference" segment. These are typically moving "human interest" stories about how some person, family, or group is helping neighbors. A recent one told the story of a family in Texas that is sending $2,000 a month to a family in Alabama whose breadwinners have lost their jobs and have had their mortgage foreclosed. They were about to lose their home because they could not make the monthly mortgage payments. The father is also being aided in his job search. Who would not admire the charity, the human sympathy, of that family in Texas? The hidden political message, however, drummed in implicitly day after day by ever-new versions of such stories, is that we do not need to have higher taxes on rich people and large corporations; better education; regulation of banks, other financial institutions, and credit card companies; stimulus spending by the federal government to create jobs; universal health care; control of carbon dioxide emissions; and so on. We do not need these because families in Texas or elsewhere will always help the needy.

Teaching people how to read those old poems, plays, and novels "rhetorically" could make such texts the foundation of concentrated training in reading the media. By "rhetorically" I mean reading that is based on the teaching of literature by way of the distinction, already mentioned, between hermeneutics and poetics, between what is meant (*Das Gemeinte*) and the way that meaning is expressed (*Die Art des Meinens*). I borrow these terms from Paul de Man, who borrows them from Walter Benjamin and from the *Hermeneutik und Poetik* series of conferences and conference books from the University of Konstanz.[12] De Man claims, correctly, that hermeneutics and poetics are incompatible. Of course this incompatibility can also be taught by way of items in the new media—for example, by explaining the hidden message in the way the spokespersons in oil, gas, and coal television commercials are consistently women, "minorities," or bearded intellectuals, not the more or less ruthless and greedy white men who actually run Chevron, Halliburton, and the rest. Many of the best "rhetorical" readings, however, are of literary works, or of philosophical and theoretical texts—for example, readings by Paul de Man and Jacques Derrida. Literary works, moreover, offer more concentrated and complex examples of how to read covert ideological implications.

Teaching how to read in light of the distinction between poetics and hermeneutics is a way literature can still be brought to matter. This way of teaching how to read literature is, alas, unlikely to become a widespread program. It is a Utopian dream. This dream may become reality in isolated cases, but most teachers of literature are not trained today to teach in that way. Literature, as I have said, is in any case taught less and less in any way at all, at least in the United States. To many people here, literature does not matter.

Now, it might be argued that satisfaction of human beings' insatiable desire for the literary, for the imaginary—that is, for a certain figurative or fictive use of words or other signs—has simply migrated to other media (to films, for example, including animated films, or to video games, or even to punning newspaper headlines, or to television advertising). What I have called "a certain figurative or fictive use of words or other signs" is an extremely problematic definition of the "literary," by the way, one that warrants extensive commentary. Derrida was right, I believe, to assert, in an interview with Derek Attridge in *Acts of Literature*, that "there is no text which is literary *in itself*. Literarity is not a natural essence, an intrinsic property of the text. It is the correlative of an intentional relation to the text, an intentional relation which integrates in itself, as a component or an intentional layer, the more or less implicit consciousness of rules which are conventional or institutional—social, in any case."[13] "Intentional," here, is a Husserlian or phenomenological word naming the orientation of consciousness toward something or other. Newspaper headlines and television ads are often conspicuously witty and imaginative. If Derrida is right, we might well be justified in "intending" them as manifestations of "literarity." A television commercial often takes the viewer/listener instantly into a conspicuously wacky or slapstick imaginary world, as in the ad for an investment firm that shows a little dog rushing back and forth, trying to find a safe place to hide a bone. This is an analogue, it turns out, for human beings' search for a safe place to invest their money.

Such ads employ an extremely sophisticated set of conventions. They often use animation and other advanced cinematic devices. Most such commercials, by the way, include a large component of outright lies, or at least of ideological distortions, as in my example of NBC's "Making a Difference" series, or in the many ads on behalf of oil, gas, and "clean" coal companies. These ads neglect to mention that use of fossil fuels is bringing about irreversible and catastrophic climate change to the whole planet. Lies are a potent form of the imaginary. If Shakespeare were resurrected today, he might be creating video games or ad spots, not writing plays. The digital world is where the big money is.

The migration of "literarity" is certainly happening, but this movement happens at the expense of literature in the sense in which I think the word is normally meant, as in the phrase "Does Literature Matter?" If printed literature is gradually becoming a thing of the past, something like literature nevertheless lives on in other media. Moreover, printed literature will go on being read (more and more often in e-text form) and taught in schools and universities. For example, the study of English literature is flourishing in China today, as I have found through repeated visits. I have suggested some reasons why studying literature might be a good thing, why literature still matters today. I hope literature will go on being taught worldwide as something of vital importance today, even in these bad times, when global climate change, worldwide financial crises, the threatened breakdown of democratic institutions in the United States, and the other challenges I have mentioned in these essays may seem of more pressing importance. My claim is that reading literature can still be relevant even in such a situation, and I have tried to explain why.

I end by returning to something I mentioned in the introduction to this book—that is, my admiration for all those more or less hidden adjuncts and nontenured faculty who go on faithfully teaching literature, often with great brilliance, and in difficult circumstances.

APPENDIX

J. Hillis Miller in China (1988–2012)

Prepared by Guo Yanjuan

Date	Location	Occasion and/or Activity	Title(s) of Lecture(s)
May 1988	Chinese Academy of Social Sciences	Visit with delegation of the American Academy of Arts and Sciences	
		Lectures	"The Function of Theory in American Literary Studies" (chapter 1)*† "About Henry James's Stories"
	Shanghai Academy of Social Sciences	Discussion with Chinese scholars on American literary studies and deconstruction	
December 1994	Peking University	Acceptance of honorary professorship	
		Lecture	"The Global Tendency in University Humanities Education"
	Institute of Foreign Literature at Chinese Academy of Social Sciences	Lecture	"New Orientations in American Literary Studies" (chapter 2)*†
April 1997	Peking University	Lecture	"The Influence of Globalization on Literary Studies" (chapter 3)*†
	Chinese Academy of Social Sciences	Lecture	"The Influence of Globalization on Literary Studies" (chapter 3)*†
August 1999	Chinese Academy of Social Sciences	Lecture	"Will Literary Study Survive?"

July 2000	Beijing Language and Culture University	International Conference on the Future of Literary Theory: China and the World	
		Lecture	"Will Literary Studies Survive the Globalization of the University and the New Regime of Telecommunications?" (chapter 4)*
	Guilin	International Conference on Marxism and Aesthetics	
		Lecture	"Promises, Promises: Speech Act Theory, Literary Theory, and Politico-Economic Theory in Marx and de Man" (chapter 5)*
August 2001	Liaoning University	International Conference on the Construction of 21st-Century Chinese Literary Theory	
		Lecture	"Literary Studies as Global Area Studies"
	Tsinghua University	Third Sino-American Symposium on Comparative Literature	
		Lecture	"On the Authority of Literature" (chapter 6)*
	Beijing Language and Culture University	Lecture	"On the Authority of Literature" (chapter 6)*
	Beijing Normal University	International Conference on Culture, Literature and Man in the Global Context	
		Lecture	"Literary Studies as Global Area Studies"

September 2003	Tsinghua University	Forum on Globalization and Cultural Studies	
		Lecture	"The (Language) Crisis of Comparative Literature" (chapter 7)*
	Tsinghua University, Department of Foreign Languages	Lecture	"The Indigene and the Internet Surfer" (chapter 8)*†
	Suzhou University	Lecture	"The (Language) Crisis of Comparative Literature" (chapter 7)*
June 2004	Zhengzhou University	International Conference on Globalization and Local Culture	
		Lectures	"The Indigene and the Internet Surfer" (chapter 8)*† "'Material Interests': Modernist English Literature as Critique of Global Capitalism"* (chapter 9)
	China Renmin University	International Conference on the Construction of Literary Theory in a Multidialogic Context	
		Conference on Jameson and China	
		Lecture	"Why I Choose to Study Literature"
	Tsinghua University	International Conference on Critical Inquiry	
		Lecture	"'Material Interests': Modernist English Literature as Critique of Global Capitalism"* (chapter 9)

June 2005	Central China Normal University	International Conference on Literary Criticism and Cultural Critique	
		Lecture	"Postmodern Ethics in Literature: Late Derrida, Morrison, and the Other"
August 2005	Shenzhen University	Eighth Triennial Congress of Chinese Comparative Literature Association	
		Lecture	"On the Position of Theory in Comparative Literature"
	Weihai City, Shandong Province	International Conference on the Orientations of 21st-Century Literary Theory	
		Lecture	"On the Future of Literary Theory"
June 2006	Wuhan University	Forum on Cultural Studies and Modernity	
		Lecture	"Who's Afraid of Globalization?" (chapter 10)*
	Tsinghua University	Forum on Derrida and Deconstructive Criticism	
		Lecture	"Derrida's Remains"
August 2006	Tsinghua University	International Conference on Translating Global Cultures: Toward Interdisciplinary Reconstruction	
		Lecture	"A Defense of Literature and Literary Study in a Time of Globalization and the New Teletechnologies"

November 2008	Nanjing Postal-Telecommunication University	Lecture	"A Comparison of Literary Studies in the United States and China" (chapter 11)*
	Nanjing Normal University	Lectures	"The Function of Literary Theory: Ethical Criticism as Example" "The Future of Literature and Literary Theory: The University with Conditions"
August 2010	Shanghai Jiaotong University	Fifth Sino-American Symposium on Comparative Literature	
		Lecture	"Globalization and World Literature" (chapter 12)*
September 2010	Guangdong University of Foreign Studies	International Conference on Literature Reading and Research	
		Lecture	"Cold Heaven, Cold Comfort: Should We Read or Teach Literature Now?" (chapter 13)*
May 2011	Yangzhou University	Lecture	"Can Novels Work as Testimony?"
June 2011	Nanjing University	Lecture	"Can Novels Work as Testimony?"
September 2012	Beijing Language and Culture University	Lectures	"Romance, Realism, Trauma: Ian McEwan's *Atonement*" "Mixed Media Forever: The Internet as Spectacle; or, The Digital Transformation of Literary Studies" (chapter 14)*
	Peking University	Lecture	"Literature Matters Today" (chapter 15)*
	Tsinghua University	Lecture	"National Literatures in the Context of World Literature Today" (a version of "Literature Matters Today")

* Lecture is included as an essay in this book (chapter number is indicated in parentheses).
† Title has changed since the date of the lecture's presentation.

Notes

INTRODUCTION

1. Guo Yanjuan has been immensely helpful, in a good example of Chinese courtesy to me. She is the author of a dissertation in Chinese on my work, one of several (for example, a recent one by Wang Yue).

2. See Justin Gillis, "The Flood Next Time," *New York Times*, 13 January 2014, available at http://www.nytimes.com/2014/01/14/science/earth/grappling-with-sea-level-rise-sooner-not-later.html?nl=todaysheadlines&emc=edit_th_20140114&_r=0.

3. Throughout this volume, I have in general capitalized the term "World Literature" when I mean the new discipline, as distinct from the collection of various national literatures that might be included in "world literature."

4. Stephen Owen, ed. *An Anthology of Chinese Literature* (New York: Norton, 1966).

CHAPTER 1

1. Matthew Arnold, preface to *Culture and Anarchy* (1869), in R. H. Super, ed., *The Complete Prose Works*, vol. 5 (Ann Arbor: University of Michigan Press, 1965), 233.

2. Gerald Graff's brilliant *Professing Literature: An Institutional History* (Chicago: University of Chicago Press, 1987) is the most recent and best account of the development of teaching and scholarship in literature in the United States. But it is a feature of the profession of literature in the United States today that there has been increasing reflection on the historical and institutional aspects of that profession. Graff's book is only one among an increasing number of books and articles on the topic. For salient examples, see A. Oleson and

J. Voss, eds.. *The Organization of Knowledge in Modern America: 1860–1920* (Baltimore: Johns Hopkins University Press, 1979); G. Webster, *The Republic of Letters* (Baltimore: Johns Hopkins University Press, 1979); Samuel Weber, "The Limits of Professionalism," *Oxford Literary Review* 5 (1982), 59–74; Jonathan Culler, "Criticism and Institutions: The American University," in Derek Attridge, Geoff Bennington, and Robert Young, eds., *Post-Structuralism and the Question of History* (Cambridge: Cambridge University Press, 1987); Vincent B. Leitch, *American Literary Criticism from the Thirties to the Eighties* (New York: Columbia University Press, 1988). Graff has been kind enough to read a draft of the present essay and to make many suggestions here and there for additions or changes. I have adopted most of his suggestions and express herewith my gratitude to him.

3. Wallace Stevens, *Opus Posthumous* (New York: Knopf, 1957), 174.

4. Graff, *Professing Literature*, 30.

5. A. J. Frantzen and C. L. Venegoni, "The Desire for Origins: An Archaeological Analysis of Anglo-Saxon Studies," *Style* 20 (1986), 142–56.

6. Jacques Derrida, "The Principle of Reason: The University in the Eyes of Its Pupils," *Diacritics* 13 (1983), 3–20. See also Jacques Derrida, "Mochlos ou le conflit des facultés," *Du droit à la philosophie* (Paris: Galilée, 1990), 397–438; Jacques Derrida, "Mochlos, or the Conflict of the Faculties," *Right to Philosophy*, vol. 2: *Eyes of the University,* trans. Jan Plug et al. (Stanford, CA: Stanford University Press, 2004), 83–112.

7. Graff, *Professing Literature*, 114.

8. Graff, *Professing Literature*, 81–97.

9. Lionel Trilling, *Matthew Arnold* (New York: Columbia University Press, 1949).

10. Quoted in Graff, *Professing Literature*, 85.

11. Murray Krieger, *The New Apologists for Poetry* (Minneapolis: University of Minnesota Press, 1956); Leitch, *American Literary Criticism.*

12. Cleanth Brooks and Robert Penn Warren, *Understanding Poetry* (1938), 2nd ed. (New York: Holt, Rinehart and Winston, 1950).

13. Cleanth Brooks, *The Well Wrought Urn: Studies in the Structure of Poetry* (New York: Harcourt, Brace and World, 1947).

14. Leitch, *American Literary Criticism*, 35.

15. Northrop Frye, *Anatomy of Criticism* (Princeton, NJ: Princeton University Press, 1957).

16. Richard Macksey and Eugenio Donato, *The Languages of Criticism and the Sciences of Man* (Baltimore: Johns Hopkins University Press, 1970).

17. David Easton and Corinne S. Schelling, eds., *Divided Knowledge: Across Disciplines, Across Cultures* (Newbury Park, CA: Sage, 1991).

18. J. Hillis Miller, "The Triumph of Theory, the Resistance to Reading, and the Question of the Material Base," *PMLA* 102 (1987), 281–291.

19. Paul de Man, "The Resistance to Theory," *The Resistance to Theory* (Minneapolis: University of Minnesota Press, 1986).

20. Leitch, *American Literary Criticism.*

21. Phyllis Franklin, "Literary Scholarship: New Titles, Old Canon," *MLA Newsletter,* 13 February 1988.

22. De Man, "Resistance to Theory," 11.

23. Derrida, "Mochlos, or the Conflict of the Faculties," 101.

24. Steven Greenblatt, *Shakespearean Negotiations: The Circulation of Social Energy in Renaissance England* (Berkeley: University of California Press, 1988).

25. J. Hillis Miller, "Literature and History: The Example of Hawthorne's 'The Minister's Black Veil,'" *Bulletin of the American Academy of Arts and Sciences* 41 (1988), 15–31.

26. J. L. Austin, *How to Do Things with Words* (1962), 2nd ed. (Cambridge, MA: Harvard University Press, 1975).

27. J. Hillis Miller, *The Ethics of Reading* (New York: Columbia University Press, 1987). My remarks about the "triumph of theory" in the foregoing pages are expanded from three paragraphs that appeared in J. Hillis Miller, *Versions of Pygmalion* (Cambridge, MA: Harvard University Press, 1990).

28. Louis Althusser, "Ideology and Ideological State Apparatuses (Notes towards an Investigation)," *Lenin and Philosophy, and Other Essays,* trans. Ben Brewster (London: New Left Books, 1971), 127–86, esp. 127.

29. Louis Althusser, "Marxism and Humanism," *For Marx,* trans. Ben Brewster (London: New Left Books, 1977), 219–48, esp. 231.

30. De Man, "Resistance to Theory," 11.

CHAPTER 2

1. See William Readings, *The University in Ruins* (Cambridge, MA: Harvard University Press, 1996).

2. For a discussion of this move as it was institutionalized in Benjamin Brower's Humanities 6 course at Harvard in the 1950s, see Paul de Man, "The Return to Philology," *The Resistance to Theory* (Minneapolis: University of Minnesota Press, 1986).

3. Jacques Derrida, "Mochlos ou le conflit des facultés," *Du droit à la philosophie* (Paris: Galilée, 1990), 424 (my translation).

4. Richard Kearney, *Dialogues with Contemporary Continental Thinkers* (Manchester: Manchester University Press, 1984), 123.

5. Stefano Rosso, "An Interview with Paul de Man," in Paul de Man, *The Resistance to Theory* (Minneapolis: University of Minnesota Press, 1986), 121.

6. Frank Lentriccia and Thomas McLaughlin, eds., *Critical Terms for Literary Study* (1990), 2nd ed. (Chicago: University of Chicago Press, 1995).

7. Antony Easthope, *Literary into Cultural Studies* (London/New York: Routledge, 1991), 129–30.

8. Conrad Atkinson, "Disney Saves Virginians from More Sprawl; The Lesson of Elvis," letter to the editor, *New York Times,* 16 August 1994.

9. [Tom Cohen is the author of *Hitchcock's Cryptonymies* (Minneapolis: University of Minnesota Press, 2005), among many other works.—JHM]

10. Hypertext is nonlinear because it contains within it links (activated by clicking on the indicated keywords) to other texts, pictures, or sounds. In a hypertext version of Thoreau's *Walden*, for example, when Thoreau mentions a certain New England bird, a click on the bird's name would give you a picture

of the bird, some information about it, and the sound of its song. Hypertext, as is evident, can be read only on the computer. [Amazing that in 1994 I felt it necessary to explain hypertext links! Moreover, the term "hypertext" is now more or less obsolete.—JHM]

11. I have discussed this and other, related issues in J. Hillis Miller, *Illustration* (London/Cambridge, MA: Reaktion Press/Harvard University Press, 1992), 37–43. For the best book so far on hypertext and humanistic study, see George P. Landow, *Hypertext: The Convergence of Contemporary Critical Theory and Technology* (Baltimore: Johns Hopkins University Press, 1992); a hypertext version of the book, '*Hypertext' in Hypertext*, is available from Johns Hopkins University Press on 3.5-inch diskette for either the Microsoft Windows or the Apple Macintosh operating system. [Computers no longer have 3.5-inch diskette slots.—JHM]

12. Marcel Proust, *Remembrance of Things Past,* 3 vols., trans. C. K. Scott Moncrieff and Terence Kilmartin (New York: Vintage Books, 1982–84), 3:1087; Marcel Proust, *À la recherche du temps perdu*, ed. Jean-Yves Tadié, 4 vols. (Paris: Gallimard, 1987–89), 4:608.

13. *Myst*, a multimedia work available on CD-ROM, is quite popular in the United States. It is a strange combination of computer game, interactive detective story, and admirable exploitation of the possibilities of computer graphics. The "player," confronted with a scene on the computer screen, explores the scene by clicking on various objects. The object of the game is to reconstruct a story hidden in the graphics, though in fact there are several different stories, or at least several alternative endings. [*Myst* certainly seems primitive when compared to present-day video games!—JHM]

14. Here, the word "Galaxy" is a reference to the name of one subsection of MacWeb, a widely used Internet browser exclusive to the Macintosh operating system. The implication is that stations on the Internet are distributed in a spatial array like the innumerable stars of a galaxy. MacWeb, the Internet, and the World Wide Web are themselves, of course, also spatial images. (The term "World Wide Web" is [Was initially.—JHM] the name for a hypertext program designed for gaining access to the Internet by way of the linear accelerator laboratory, CERN, in Geneva, Switzerland.) The Internet, however, is not a spatial array but an unimaginable co-presence and superimposition of thousands of sites and millions [Now billions. And who now remembers MacWeb?—JHM] of files that can be brought from all over the world to any computer screen that is connected to the Internet.

CHAPTER 3

1. California Governor Pete Wilson and University of California President Richard C. Atkinson, quoted in press releases dated 3 January 1996.

2. For a discussion of this and other aspects of the changes I am describing, see Bill Readings, *The University in Ruins* (Cambridge, MA: Harvard University Press, 1996).

3. Among books on this change are Nicholas Negroponte, *Being Digital* (New York: Knopf, 1995); Mark Poster, *The Second Media Age* (Cambridge:

Polity Press, 1995); Sherry Turkle, *The Second Self: Computers and the Human Spirit* (New York: Simon & Schuster, 1984); and Sherry Turkle, *Life on the Screen: Identity in the Age of the Internet* (New York: Simon & Schuster, 1995).

4. Jon Katz, "Netizen: Birth of a Digital Nation," *Wired*, April 1997, 49–191. A more recent essay by Katz modifies somewhat, on the basis of a Merrill Lynch forum and a *Wired* poll, some of his generalizations about the "digital young"; see Jon Katz, "The Digital Citizen," *Wired*, December 1997, 68–82, 274–75: "[W]here I had described [the digital citizen] as deeply estranged from mainstream politics, the poll revealed that they are actually highly participatory and view our existing political system positively, even patriotically" (71).

5. Walter Benjamin, *Gesammelte Schriften*, 7 vols., ed. Rolf Tiedemann and Hermann Schweppenhauser (Frankfurt am Main: Suhrkamp, 1974–89), 1:478.

6. Walter Benjamin, "Das Kunstwerk im Zeitalter seiner technischen Reproduzierbarkeit," *Illuminationen: Ausgewählte Schriften*, ed. Siegfried Unseld (Frankfurt am Main: Suhrkamp, 1955), 148–84; Walter Benjamin, "The Work of Art in the Age of Technical Reproducibility," *Illuminations*, trans. Harry Zohn (New York: Schocken, 1969), 217–51.

7. [Recent empirical studies have indicated that the brain of a habitual reader of books is different from the brain of a habitual player of video games. The video game player has a shorter attention span and a higher multitasking ability. He or she, although not as well equipped as those brought up in the printed-book epoch to read a long novel like *Middlemarch* or *Gravity's Rainbow*, is remarkably adept at playing *Grand Theft Auto*.—JHM]

8. Katz, "Netizen," 184.

9. [There is no longer a functioning link to the ARTFL site, but the material the site once provided will, for the most part, be available elsewhere on the Web (for example, by way of a Google search for the relevant French text).—JHM]

10. See J. Hillis Miller, "What Is the Future of the Print Record?," in Modern Language Association of America, ed., *Profession 1995* (New York: Modem Language Association of America, 1995), 33–35.

11. [ASCII stands for American Standard Code for Information Interchange.—JHM]

12. [The link to *Ayada's Angel* has expired. Those who see the Internet as a huge assemblage of fragile and temporary sites that disappear like meteors flashing across cyberspace, as opposed to perdurable printed books remaining solidly there on the library shelves, have some evidence to support their fears. In compensation, however, *Ayala's Angel* is now available from Project Gutenberg as a free e-book in six different formats; see http://www.gutenberg.org/ebooks/33500.—JHM]

13. [Chapter 2 describes the resurgence, in the mid-1980s, of extrinsic criticism and the emergence of a new desire to politicize and rehistoricize the study of literature.—JHM]

14. Alan Liu, "The Future Literary: Literary History and Postmodern Culture," unpublished manuscript, 2.

15. Charles Bernheimer, ed., *Comparative Literature in the Age of Multiculturalism* (Baltimore: Johns Hopkins University Press, 1995).

16. Ibid., 42.

17. In Carlyle's translation, "professor of Things in General at the University of Don't Know Where."

18. René Wellek, *A History of Modern Criticism, 1750–1950*, 8 vols. (New Haven, CT: Yale University Press, 1955–1992).

19. Bernheimer, *Comparative Literature*, 44.

CHAPTER 4

1. Jacques Derrida, "Envois," *La carte postale: De Socrate à Freud et au-delà* (Paris: Aubier-Flammarion, 1980), 212, 219; Jacques Derrida, "Envois," *The Post Card: From Socrates to Freud and Beyond*, trans. Alan Bass (Chicago: University of Chicago Press, 1987), 197, 204.

2. See Avital Ronell, *The Telephone Book* (Lincoln: University of Nebraska Press, 1989); Laurence Rickels, "Kafka and Freud on the Telephone," *Modern Austrian Literature: Journal of the International Arthur Schnitzler Association* 22:3–4 (1989), 211–25; Laurence Rickels, *Aberrations of Mourning* (Detroit: Wayne State University Press, 1988), esp. chaps. 7 and 8; Friedrich Kittler, *Essays: Literature, Media, Information Systems*, ed. John Johnston (Amsterdam: G+B Arts International, 1997), esp. 31–49.

3. See Jacques Derrida, *Glas* (Paris: Éditions Galilée, 1974); Jacques Derrida, *Glas*, trans. John P. Leavey Jr. and Richard Rand (Lincoln: University of Nebraska Press, 1986). See also John P. Leavey Jr., *Glassary* (Lincoln: University of Nebraska Press, 1986), a companion to Leavey and Rand's English translation of *Glas*, which features a foreword by Derrida and an essay, "Sounding the Unconscious," by Gregory L. Ulmer.

4. See Jacques Derrida, "Télépathie," *Furor* 2 (1981), 5–41; the essay also appears in Jacques Derrida, *Psyché: Inventions de l'autre* (Paris: Galilée, 1987), 237–70, and in the first volume of Jacques Derrida, *Psyché: Inventions de l'autre*, 2 vols. (Paris: Galilée, 2003). See also Jacques Derrida, "Telepathy," trans. Nicholas Royle, *The Oxford Literary Review* 10:1–2 (1988), 3–41; Jacques Derrida, *Psyche: Inventions of the Other*, vol. 1, ed. Peggy Kamuf and Elizabeth Rottenberg (Stanford, CA.: Stanford University Press, 2007), 226–61.

5. [Essentially all of James's writings are now available for free at http://www.onlinc-literature.com/henry_james.—JHM]

6. See Karl Marx and Friedrich Engels, *The German Ideology: Parts I & II*, ed. R. Pascal (New York: International Publishers, 1963).

7. Paul de Man, "The Resistance to Theory," *The Resistance to Theory* (Minneapolis: University of Minnesota Press, 1986), 11.

8. Louis Althusser, "Ideology and Ideological State Apparatuses (Notes towards an Investigation)," *Lenin and Philosophy, and Other Essays*, trans. Ben Brewster (New York: Monthly Review Press, 1972), 163.

9. Ibid., 143.

10. Kittler, *Essays*, 37.

11. See Bill Readings, *The University in Ruins* (Cambridge, MA: Harvard University Press, 1996); Giorgio Agamben, *La comunità che viene* (Turin: Einaudi, 1990); Giorgio Agamben, *The Coming Community*, trans. Michael Hardt (Minneapolis: University of Minnesota Press, 1993).

12. G. W. F. Hegel, *Vorlesungen über die Ästhetik: Theorie Werkausgabe*, 20 vols. (Frankfurt am Main: Suhrkamp, 1970), 13:25. I am grateful to Andrzej Warminski for providing this reference.

13. I thank Andrzej Warminski for suggesting an interpretative translation to me on the Hegel-less Maine island where I am writing this. I also thank him for an e-mail interchange about the meaning of Hegel's sentence.

CHAPTER 5

1. Karl Marx, *Grundrisse: Foundations of the Critique of Political Economy*, trans. Martin Nicolaus (New York: Vintage Books, 1973).

2. Jacques Derrida, *Specters of Marx*, trans. Peggy Kamuf (New York and London: Routledge, 1994), 34; Jacques Derrida, *Spectres de Marx* (Paris: Galilée, 1993), 65.

3. [Her revised dissertation has now been published; see Jennifer Bajorek, *Counterfeit Capital: Poetic Labor and Revolutionary Irony* (Stanford, CA: Stanford University Press, 2008).—JHM]

4. See Derrida, *Spectres de Marx*; Derrida, *Specters of Marx*. See also Werner Hamacher, "*Lingua Amissa*: The Messianism of Commodity-Language and Derrida's *Specters of Marx*," *Ghostly Demarcations: A Symposium on Jacques Derrida's Specters of Marx* (London and New York: Verso, 1999), 168–212; Andrzej Warminski, "Hegel/Marx: Consciousness and Life," in Jacques Lezra, ed., *Depositions*, special issue, *Yale French Studies* 88 (1995), 118–41.

5. Karl Marx, *Das Kapital* (Berlin: Kiepenheuer, 1932), 86.

6. Karl Marx, *Capital*, trans. Ben Fowkes, 3 vols. (London: Penguin, 1980), 1:167.

7. Paul de Man, *Allegories of Reading: Figural Language in Rousseau, Nietzsche, Rilke, and Proust* (New Haven, CT: Yale University Press, 1979), 205.

8. Paul de Man, "The Resistance to Theory," *The Resistance to Theory* (Minneapolis: University of Minnesota Press, 1986), 7.

9. Stefano Rosso, "An Interview with Paul de Man," in Paul de Man, *The Resistance to Theory* (Minneapolis: University of Minnesota Press, 1986), 121.

10. Karl Marx and Friedrich Engels, *The German Ideology: Parts I & II*, ed. R. Pascal (New York: International Publishers, 1963), 199.

11. Derrida, *Specters of Marx*, 51.

12. Paul de Man, "The Concept of Irony," *Aesthetic Ideology* (Minneapolis: University of Minnesota Press, 1996), 165.

13. J. L. Austin, *How to Do Things with Words* (1962), 2nd ed., ed. J. O. Urmson and Marina Sbisà (Oxford: Oxford University Press, 1980), 14–15.

14. Marx, *Kapital*, 83; Marx, *Capital*, 1:163.

15. Marx, *Kapital*, 65.

16. Marx, *Capital*, 1:143–44.

17. See Hamacher, "*Lingua Amissa*."

18. Walter Benjamin, "Zur Kritik der Gewalt" (1921), *Gesammelte Schriften* 2:1 (Frankfurt am Main: Suhrkamp, 1977), 179–203; Walter Benjamin, "Critique of Violence," *Selected Writings*, ed. Marcus Bullock and Michael W. Jen-

nings, trans. Edmund Jephcott, vol. 1: *1913–1926* (Cambridge, MA: Belknap Press of Harvard University Press, 1999), 236–52.

19. For his focus on Kant and Schlegel, see de Man, *Aesthetic Ideology*, 90, 181. See also Paul de Man, *The Rhetoric of Romanticism* (New York: Columbia University Press, 1984), 290, for de Man's focus on Kleist.

20. Paul de Man, *Allegories of Reading*, 277.

21. Marx, *Kapital*, 65; Marx, *Capital*, 1:144.

22. Marx, *Kapital*, 65–66.

23. Marx, *Capital*, 1:144.

24. Marx, *Kapital*, 83.

25. Marx, *Capital*, 1:163.

26. Marx, *Kapital*, 83.

27. Marx, *Capital*, 1:163–64.

28. Marx, *Kapital*, 83.

29. Marx, *Capital*, 1:164.

30. Marx, *Capital*, 1:164.

31. Marx, *Kapital*, 83; Marx, *Capital*, 1:164.

32. Marx, *Kapital*, 84–85.

33. Marx, *Capital*, 1:165.

34. De Man, "Resistance to Theory," 11.

35. De Man, *Rhetoric of Romanticism*, 122.

36. De Man, "Resistance to Theory," 7.

CHAPTER 6

1. Marcel Proust, *À la recherche du temps perdu*, 4 vols., ed. Jean-Yves Tadié (Paris: Gallimard, 1987–89), 3:721; Marcel Proust, *Remembrance of Things Past*, 3 vols., trans. C. K. Scott Moncrieff and Terence Kilmartin (New York: Vintage Books, 1982–84), 3:213 (translation slightly modified). The next two paragraphs of this essay have been adapted, in compressed and somewhat changed form, from my portion of J. Hillis Miller and Manuel Asensi, *Black Holes / J. Hillis Miller; or, Boustrophedonic Reading* (Stanford, CA: Stanford University Press, 1999).

2. Proust, *Recherche*, 3:761; Proust, *Remembrance*, 3:258.

3. Proust, *Recherche*, 3:761; Proust, *Remembrance*, 3:259.

4. Proust, *Recherche*, 3:762; Proust, *Remembrance*, 3:260.

5. Proust, *Remembrance*, 3:263–64.

6. Proust, *Remembrance*, 3:265.

7. See Henry James, preface to *The Golden Bowl*, in *The Novels and Tales of Henry James: New York Edition*, 24 vols. (Fairfield, NJ: Augustus M. Kelley, 1976), 23:xiii–iv (volumes 1 and 2 of *The Golden Bowl* are volumes 23 and 24 of the *New York Edition*). See also Jacques Derrida, "Ponctuations: Le temps de la thèse," *Du droit à la philosophie* (Paris: Galilée, 1990), 443–44; Jacques Derrida, "The Time of a Thesis: Punctuations," trans. Kathleen McLaughlin, in Alan Montefiore, ed., *Philosophy in France Today* (Cambridge: Cambridge University Press, 1983), 34–50. I have discussed both of these elsewhere, the first in J. Hillis Miller, "Re-Reading Re-Vision: James and Benjamin," *The Ethics of*

Reading (New York: Columbia University Press, 1987), 110–22, the second in J. Hillis Miller, "Derrida's Topographies," *Topographies* (Stanford, CA: Stanford University Press, 1995), 297–301.

8. William Blake, *The Poetry and Prose*, ed. David V. Erdman (Garden City: Doubleday, 1970), 38.

9. Charles Dickens, "Author's Preface to the Third Edition," *Oliver Twist*, ed. Kathleen Tillotson (Oxford: Clarendon Press, 1966), lxv: "It is useless to discuss whether the conduct and character of the girl seems [*sic*] natural or unnatural, probable or impossible, right or wrong. IT IS TRUE." See also Charles Dickens, preface to *Bleak House*, ed. Nicola Bradbury (London: Penguin, 1996), 6–7.

10. Plato, *Ion*, sec. 334b, *Plato: The Collected Dialogues,* ed. Edith Hamilton and Huntington Cairns (Princeton, NJ: Princeton University Press, 1973), 220.

11. Percy Bysshe Shelley, "A Defence of Poetry," *Shelley's Poetry and Prose*, ed. Donald H. Reiman and Sharon B. Powers (New York: Norton, 1977), 503–4.

12. Ibid., 508.

13. W. B. Yeats, "The Symbolism of Poetry," *Essays and Introductions* (London: Macmillan, 1961), 158–59.

14. Anthony Trollope, *An Autobiography*, ed. David Skilton (London: Penguin, 1996), 119.

15. Plato, *Republic*, book III, secs. 395b–396b, *Plato: The Collected Dialogues,* Edith Hamilton and Huntington Cairns, eds. (Princeton, NJ: Princeton University Press, 1973), 640–41.

16. James Joyce, *A Portrait of the Artist as a Young Man* (New York: Viking, 1964), 252–53.

17. Henry James, *The Tragic Muse*, in *The Novels and Tales of Henry James: New York Edition*, 24 vols. (Fairfield, NJ: Augustus M. Kelley, 1976), 7:188–89 (volumes 1 and 2 of *The Tragic Muse* are volumes 7 and 8 of the *New York Edition*).

18. Jacques Derrida, *Points de Suspension* (Paris: Galilée, 1992).

19. Mel Gussow, "An Explorer of Human Terrrain," *New York Times*, 26 December 2000.

20. Ibid.

21. Ibid.

22. I paraphrase Derrida's argument. See Jacques Derrida, *Passions* (Paris: Galilée, 1993), esp. 67–68; Jacques Derrida, *On the Name*, ed. Thomas Dutoit, trans. David Wood (Stanford, CA: Stanford University Press, 1995), 3–31, esp. 28–30.

23. Trollope, *An Autobiography*, 140.

24. Henry James, preface to "The Lesson of the Master," "The Death of the Lion," "The Next Time," "The Figure in the Carpet," and "The Coxon Fund," *The Novels and Tales of Henry James: New York Edition*, 24 vols. (Fairfield, NJ: Augustus M. Kelley, 1976), 15:viii, x.

25. Ibid., ix.

26. Proust, *Remembrance*, 3:187 (translation slightly modified); Proust, *Recherche*, 3:694.

27. Proust, *Remembrance, 3*:186–88; Proust, *Recherche,* 3:693–96.

28. Henry James, preface to "The Lesson of the Master" et al., *The Novels and Tales of Henry James,* xii.

29. Ibid.

30. See my discussion of this in J. Hillis Miller, *Speech Acts in Literature* (Stanford, CA: Stanford University Press, 2002).

31. Paul de Man, *Allegories of Reading: Figural Language in Rousseau, Nietzsche, Rilke, and Proust* (New Haven, CT: Yale University Press, 1979), 299–300.

32. See J. L. Austin, *How to Do Things with Words* (1962), 2nd ed., ed. J. O. Urmson and Marina Sbisà (Oxford: Oxford University Press, 1980), 10. That Austin a few pages later welshes on this commitment, making sincerity a condition of a felicitous performative, is a major crux or contradiction in his speech act theory. He has to have it both ways, but of course he cannot logically have it both ways.

33. Derrida, *Passions.*

34. This is Derrida's example; see Jacqus Derrida, *Donner le temps. 1. La fausse monnaie* (Paris: Galilée, 1991); Jacques Derrida, *Given Time: 1. Counterfeit Money*, trans. Peggy Kamuf (Chicago: University of Chicago Press, 1992).

CHAPTER 7

1. René Wellek, "The Crisis of Comparative Literature," *Concepts of Criticism* (New Haven, CT: Yale University Press, 1963), 282.

2. Ibid., 282–83.

3. Ibid., 295.

4. René Wellek, "Destroying Literary Studies," *The New Criterion*, December 1983, 1–8.

5. Henry James, *The Wings of the Dove*, in *The Novels and Tales of Henry James: New York Edition*, 24 vols. (Fairfield, NJ: Augustus M. Kelley, 1976), 20:57 (volumes 1 and 2 of *The Wings of the Dove* are volumes 19 and 20 of the *New York Edition*). [I discuss "Oh!" in *The Wings of the Dove* at greater length in J. Hillis Miller, *Literature as Conduct: Speech Acts in Henry James* (New York: Fordham University Press, 2014), 199–202.—JHM]

6. Marcel Proust, *À la recherche du temps perdu*, 4 vols., ed. Jean-Yves Tadié (Paris: Gallimard, 1987–89), 3:693–96.

7. Marcel Proust, *Remembrance of Things Past*, trans. C. K. Scott Moncrieff and Terence Kilmartin (New York: Vintage Books, 1982–84) 3:186–88.

8. René Wellek: *A History of Modern Criticism, 1750–1950*, 8 vols. (New Haven, CT: Yale University Press, 1955–1992).

9. Thomas Wyatt, "Whoso List to Hunt," available at http://www.luminarium.org/renlit/whosolist.htm.

10. Francesco Petrarch, *Sonnets & Songs*, trans. Anna Maria Armi (New York: Pantheon, 1946), 282–83.

11. Wyatt, "Whoso List to Hunt."

12. Ibid.

13. Ngugi wa Thiong'o, *A Grain of Wheat*, rev. ed. (Oxford: Heinemann, 1986), 2.

14. Ibid., 152; see 172 and 176 for additional examples of untranslated sayings in Gikuyu.

15. Ibid., 148.

16. Ibid., 218.

17. Stephen Owen, ed., *An Anthology of Chinese Literrature* (New York: Norton, 1996).

18. Thomas De Quincey, "The Last Days of Immanuel Kant," *Collected Writings*, 14 vols., ed. David Masson (London: A. & C. Black, 1896–97), 4:375–76.

19. Jacques Derrida, *Le toucher, Jean-Luc Nancy* (Paris: Galilée, 2000), 339.

20. Ibid., 327–28.

21. Owen, ed. *Anthology of Chinese Literature.*

22. [For the revised dissertation, see Simona Sawhney, *The Modernity of Sanskrit* (Minneapolis: University of Minnesota Press, 2008).—JHM]

23. [The two essays have now been published. See Simona Sawhney, "Ethics and the Writing of Experience: Kalidasa in the work of Mohan Rakesh," *Journal of Contemporary Thought (India)* 14 (2001), 41–53; Simona Sawhney, "Who is Kalidasa? Sanskrit Poetry in Modern India," *Postcolonial Studies* 7:3 (2004), 294–312.—JHM]

CHAPTER 8

1. "The unavowable of the community is also a sovereignty that can only pose itself and impose itself in silence, in the non-said" (my translation).

2. Fengzhen Wang and Shaobo Xie, "Globalization and Indigenous Cultures: Proposal for *ARIEL* Special Issue 2003," call for papers, 1; see also Fengzhen Wang and Shaobo Xie, eds., *Globalization and Indigenous Cultures*, special issue, *ARIEL* 34:1 (2003).

3. On the term "rogue," see the characteristically brilliant and forceful work by Jacques Derrida, *Voyous: Deux essays sur la raison* (Paris: Gallilée, 2003); Jacques Derrida, *Rogues: Two Essays on Reason*, trans. Pascale-Anne Barault and Michael Nass (Stanford, CA: Stanford University Press, 2005).

4. See Maurice Blanchot, "L'homme au point zero," *L'Amitié* (Paris: Gallimard, 1971), 87–97; Maurice Blanchot, "Man at Point Zero," *Friendship*, trans. Elizabeth Rottenberg (Stanford, CA: Stanford University Press, 1997), 73–82. See also Claude Lévi-Strauss, *Tristes Tropiques*, trans. John Russell (New York: Atheneum, 1970).

5. W. B. Yeats, "A Prayer for My Daughter," *The Variorum Edition of the Poems*, ed. Peter Allt and Russell K. Alspach (New York: Macmillan, 1957), 405.

6. Wallace Stevens, *The Collected Poems* (New York: Vintage, 1990), 418–19.

7. Ibid., 76.

8. Ibid., 356, 128–30, 93, 235.

9. See http://en.wikipedia.org/wiki/Damariscotta,_Maine.

10. Stevens, *Collected Poems*, 66–70.

11. Ibid., 37.

12. See Martin Heidegger, "Bauen Wohnen Denken," *Vorträge und Aufsätze*, 2 vols. (Pfullingen: Neske, 1967), 2:19–36; Martin Heidegger, "Building Dwelling Thinking," *Poetry, Language, Thought*, trans. Albert Hofstadter (New York:

Harper & Row, 1971), 145–61; Martin Heidegger, "Heimkunft/An Die Verwandten," *Erläuterungen zu Hölderlins Dichtung*, 2nd ed. (Frankfurt am Main: Vittorio Klostermann, 1951), 13–30; Martin Heidegger, "Homecoming/To Kindred Ones," *Elucidations of Hölderlin's Poetry*, trans. Keith Hoeller (Amherst, NY: Humanity Books, 2000), 23–49; Martin Heidegger, ". . . dichterisch wohnet der Mensch . . . ," *Vorträge und Aufsätze*, 2 vols. (Pfullingen: Neske, 1967), 2:61–78; Martin Heidegger, ". . . Poetically Man Dwells . . . ," *Poetry, Language, Thought*, trans. Albert Hofstadter (New York: Harper & Row, 1971), 213–29; Friedrich Hölderlin, "Heimkunft/An Die Verwandten" ("Homecoming/To the Relatives"), *Poems and Fragments*, bilingual ed., trans. Michael Hamburger (Cambridge: Cambridge University Press, 1980), 254–61.

13. Stevens, *Collected Poems*, 420.

14. Ibid., 418.

15. Ibid., 419.

16. Jennifer Bajorek, "The Offices of Homeland Security, or, Hölderlin's Terrorism," *Critical Inquiry* 31:4 (2005), 874–902.

17. George W. Bush, "We Are a Country Awakened to Danger and Called to Defend Freedom," available at http://www.hum.uu.nl/medewerkers/a.j.boekestijn/historisch%20ambacht/Bush%20speech.htm.

18. Bajorek, "Offices of Homeland Security," 894.

19. Benedict Anderson, *Imagined Communities: Reflections on the Origin and Spread of Nationalism* (New York: Random House, 1983).

20. Georges Bataille, *L'apprenti sorcier du cercle communiste démocratique à Acéphale: Textes, lettres et documents (1932–1939)*, ed. Marina Galletti (Paris: Éditions de la Différence, 1999); Maurice Blanchot, *La communauté inavouable* (Paris: Éditions de Minuit, 1983); Maurice Blanchot, *The Unavowable Community,* trans. Pierre Joris (Barrytown, NY: Station Hill Press, 1988); Jean-Luc Nancy, *La communauté désoeuvrée* (Paris: Christian Bourgois, 1990); Jean-Luc Nancy, *The Inoperative Community*, ed. Peter Connor, trans. Peter Connor, Lisa Garbus, Michael Holland, and Simona Sawhney (Minneapolis: University of Minnesota Press, 1991); Jean-Luc Nancy, *Être singulier pluriel* (Paris: Galilée, 1996); Jean-Luc Nancy, *Being Singular Plural*, trans. Robert D. Richardson and Anne E. O'Byrne (Stanford, CA: Stanford University Press, 2000); Giorgio Agamben, *La comunità che viene* (Turin: Einaudi, 1990); Giorgio Agamben, *The Coming Community*, trans. Michael Hardt (Minneapolis: University of Minnesota Press, 1993); Alphonso Lingis, *The Community of Those Who Have Nothing in Common* (Bloomington: Indiana University Press, 1994); Jacques Derrida, with Maurizio Ferraris, *A Taste for the Secret*, ed. Giacomo Donis and David Webb, trans. Giacomo Donis (Cambridge: Polity Press, 2001); Derrida, *Voyous*; Derrida, *Rogues*; Jacques Derrida, "Foi et savoir: Les deux sources de la 'religion' aux limites de la simple raison," *La religion*, ed. Jacques Derrida and Gianni Vattimo (Paris: Seuil, 1996), 9–86; Jacques Derrida, "Faith and Knowledge: The Two Sources of 'Religion' at the Limits of Reason Alone," trans. Samuel Weber, *Acts of Religion*, ed. Gil Anidjar (New York: Routledge, 2002), 42–101.

21. Blanchot, *The Unavowable Community*, 1; Blanchot, *La communauté inavouable*, 9.

22. L. Austin, *How to Do Things with Words* (1962), 2d ed., ed. J. O. Urmson and Marina Sbisà (Oxford: Oxford University Press, 1980), 14.

23. Ibid., 44.

24. Nancy, *The Inoperative Community*, 14–15; Nancy, *La communauté désoeuvrée*, 41–42.

25. Maurice Blanchot, *L'écriture du désastre* (Paris: Gallimard, 1980); Maurice Blanchot, *The Writing of the Disaster*, trans. Ann Smock (Lincoln: University of Nebraska Press, 1995).

26. Nancy, *The Inoperative Community*, 81.

27. Jean-Luc Nancy, *Le partage des voix* (Paris: Galilée, 1982).

28. Nancy, *The Inoperative Community*, 1.

29. Ibid., 29.

30. Ibid., 80–81.

31. Matthew Arnold, *The Poems*, ed. Kenneth Allott (London: Longmans, 1965), 242.

32. Jean-Luc Nancy, *L'expérience de la liberté* (Paris: Galilée, 1988); Jean-Luc Nancy, *The Experience of Freedom*, trans. Bridget McDonald (Stanford, CA: Stanford University Press, 1993).

33. Charles Baudelaire, *Oeuvres Complètes*, ed. Yves-Gérard le Dantec (Paris: Gallimard, 1954), 82.

34. Blanchot, *The Unavowable Community*, 42–43, and see 41, where a longer passage can serve as a gloss or preparation for the paragraph about Tristan and Isolde; here, Blanchot is speaking about the relation between the two lovers in Marguerite Duras's *La maladie de la mort* (*The Malady of Death*):

> . . . in the homogeneity—the affirmation of the Same—understanding demands that the heterogeneous appear suddenly, i.e., the absolute Other in terms of which any relationship signifies: no relationship, the impossibility that willing and perhaps even desire ever cross the uncrossable, in the sudden and clandestine meeting (outside of time) that annuls itself with the devastating feeling that is never certain to be experienced by the one whom this movement consigns to the other perhaps by depriving him of his "self." A devastating feeling that is, in truth, beyond all feeling, ignoring pathos, overflowing consciousness, breaking with self-involvement and demanding—without rights—that which removes itself from all demands, because in my request there is not only the beyond of what could satisfy it, but the beyond of what is requested. An overbidding, an outrage of life that cannot be contained within life and which thus, interrupting the pretension of always persevering in being, opens to the strangeness of an interminable dying or of an endless "error."

See also Marguerite Duras, *La maladie de la mort* (Paris: Éditions de Minuit, 1982); Marguerite Duras, *The Malady of Death*, trans. Barbara Bray (New York: Grove, 1986).

35. Derrida, *Rogues*, 60.

36. Derrida, *Voyous*, 90. I have cited the entire passage in French so the reader can see the complex plays on words that Derrida employs in the original. This wordplay is, for the most part, carried over into the translation.

37. Lingis, *The Community of Those Who Have Nothing in Common.*

38. Fengzhen Wang and Shaobo Xie, "Globalization and Indigenous Cultures," 1.

39. Martin Heidegger, *Sein und Zeit* (Tübingen: Max Niemeyer, 1967), 235–67; Martin Heidegger, *Being and Time*, trans. John Macquarrie and Edward Robinson (London: SCM Press, 1962), 279–311.

40. Mark Warschauer, "Demystifying the Digital Divide," *Scientific American,* August 2003, 42–47.

CHAPTER 9

1. See Nicholas Royle, "The 'Telepathy Effect': Notes toward a Reconsideration of Narrative Fiction," *The Uncanny: An Introduction* (Manchester: Manchester University Press, 2003), 256–76; see also Nicholas Royle, "The 'Telepathy Effect': Notes toward a Reconsideration of Narrative Fiction," in Carol Jacobs and Henry Sussman, eds., *Acts of Narrative* (Stanford, CA: Stanford University Press, 2003), 93–109.

2. The best interpretation of Conrad's work from a narratological perspective is Jakob Lothe, *Conrad's Narrative Method* (Oxford: Clarendon Press, 1989).

3. [See the previous chapter for my discussion of these authors.—JHM]

4. Joseph Conrad, *Nostromo* (New York: Modern Library, 1951), 157. All references to *Nostromo* are to this edition, which I have used because it reprints the first version of the book and has some passages that Conrad later cut.

5. Benedict Anderson, *Imagined Communities: Reflections on the Origin and Spread of Nationalism* (New York: Random House, 1983).

6. Conrad, *Nostromo*, 529.

7. For a succinct account of Conrad's sources, see Cedric Watts, "A Note on the Background to 'Nostromo,'" in Cedtric T. Watts, ed., *Joseph Conrad's Letters to R. B. Cunninghame Graham* (Cambridge: Cambridge University Press, 1969), 37–42. A fuller account is given in Cedric T. Watts, *Conrad's 'Nostromo'* (London: Penguin, 1990).

8. Raymond Williams, *The Country and the City* (New York: Oxford University Press, 1975).

9. Conrad, *Nostromo*, 5.

10. Ibid., 206.

11. Watts, ed., *Conrad's Letters*, 57.

12. Jean-Luc Nancy, *The Inoperative Community*, ed. Peter Connor, trans. Peter Connor, Lisa Garbus, Michael Holland, and Simona Sawhney (Minneapolis: University of Minnesota Press, 1991), 1.

13. Conrad, *Nostromo*, 98.

14. Ibid., 99.

15. For a discussion of Nancy's ideas about community, see chap. 8 of the present volume.

16. Joseph Conrad, *A Personal Record* (London: Dent, 1923), 98.

17. Conrad, *Nostromo*, 111; the text has "roots," as does the 1918 Dent edition, but surely that is a misprint for "roofs." The phrase "palm-leaf roots" doesn't make sense. I have changed the word to "roofs."

18. Ibid., 92–93.

19. Ibid., 84.

20. Ibid.

21. Ibid., 84–85.

22. Ibid., 89.

23. [Enron has now vanished. It was found to be a spectacular house of cards built on fraud; see https://en.wikipedia.org/wiki/Enron_scandal.—JHM, 2015]

24.Conrad, *Nostromo*, 85.

25. Ibid., 85–86.

26. Ibid., 254.

27. Watts, ed., *Conrad's Letters*.

28. Aristotle, *Poetics*, sec. 1451b, in S. H. Butcher, ed. and trans., *Aristotle's Theory of Poetry and Fine Art*, 4th ed. (New York: Dover, 1951), 35.

29. F. R. Leavis, in *The Great Tradition,* first published in 1946, makes a strikingly similar claim for the relevance of *Nostromo* to understanding the history of Leavis's own time. Speaking of "Charles Gould's quiet unyieldingness in the face of Pedrito's threats and blandishments," Leavis says this episode "reinforce[s] dramatically that pattern of political significance which has a major part in *Nostromo*—a book that was written, we remind ourselves in some wonder, noting the topicality of its themes, analysis, and illustrations, in the reign of Edward VII [1901–1910]"; see F. R. Leavis, *The Great Tradition* (Harmondsworth: Penguin, 1962), 218. I owe this reference to Jeremy Hawthorn. I am no Leavisite but am nevertheless always happy to find myself in agreement with Leavis, who would no doubt have had little sympathy with my insistence on the way *Nostromo* is "parabolic"—that is, "imaginary (but true)"—as opposed to being realistic representation.

CHAPTER 10

1. Thomas L. Friedman, *The World Is Flat: A Brief History of the Twenty-First Century* (New York: Farrar, Straus and Giroux, 2005).

2. Karl Marx and Friedrich Engels, *The Communist Manifesto*, chap. 1, available at http://www.marxists.org/archive/marx/works/1848/communist-manifesto/ch01.htm.

3. Ibid.

4. Jacques Derrida, *Specters of Marx*, trans. Peggy Kamuf (New York and London: Routledge, 1994), 85.

5. Friedman, *The World Is Flat.*

6. Jacques Derrida, *The Politics of Friendship,* trans. George Collins (London: Verso, 2006); Jacques Derrida, *Politiques de l'amitié* (London: Verso, 1997). See also Jacques Derrida, *The Gift of Death; and Literature in Secret,* 2nd ed., trans. David Willis (Chicago: University of Chicago Press, 2008); Jacques Derrida, "Donner la mort," in Jean-Michel Rabaté and Michael Wetzel, eds., *L'éthique du don: Jacques Derrida et la pensée du don* (Paris: Métailié-Transition, 1992).

7. Anthony Trollope, *The Last Chronicle of Barset* (London: Penguin Books, 2002), 595.

8. Derrida, *Specters of Marx*, 80.

9. See Adam Cohen, "A Small-Time Crime with Hints of Big-Time Connections Lights Up the Net," *New York Times,* 17 April 2006, available at http://www.nytimes.com/2006/04/17/opinion/17mon4.html?th&emc=th.

10. "AT&T and Domestic Spying," editorial, *New York Times,* 17 April 2006, available at http://www.nytimes.com/2006/04/17/opinion/17mon2.html?th&emc=th.

11. Tom Cohen, unpublished paper.

12. Alan Liu, *The Laws of Cool: Knowledge Work and the Culture of Information* (Chicago: University of Chicago Press, 2004).

13. [The information about the number of *World of Warcraft* subscriptions in China in 2005, found in 2006 at http://blizzard.com/press/050720.shtml, is no longer available at that site; more recent and fuller information, including details about changes in the game imposed by the Chinese government (for example, the addition of flesh to skeletons), is available at http://en.wikipedia.org/wiki/World_of_Warcraft. Today the example of immense initial sales would not be *World of Warcraft* but rather *Grand Theft Auto V* (US $800 million in the first twenty-four hours after its release, and $1 billion in the first three days). *World of Warcraft* is played on a computer, whereas *Grand Theft Auto* requires a Sony PlayStation device, though an online version exists, too; see http://en.wikipedia.org/wiki/Grand_Theft_Auto_V. In any event, my granddaughter, Jessica Maryott, no longer spends so much time playing computer games. She is employed full-time by the neuroscience department at Brandeis University.—JHM]

14. Karl Marx and Friedrich Engels, *The German Ideology: Parts I & II*, ed. R. Pascal (New York: International Publishers, 1963); Derrida, *Specters of Marx*.

15. Tom Cohen, *Hitchcock's Cryptonymies* (Minneapolis: University of Minnesota Press, 2005).

CHAPTER 11

1. [See the appendix to this chapter for the Ministry of Education's list of "extracurricular" and selected additional readings for English majors. The list is remarkably conservative and comprehensive. It does not differ greatly in spirit from something like the *Norton Anthology of English Literature,* though many novels are included in the Chinese list, whereas they are not present in the Norton anthology. What my informant told me about how English language and literature are taught in China, and the lists in this chapter's appendix, invite comparison with the so-called Common Core, recently adopted by many US states. The Common Core did not yet exist in 2008, when I wrote this essay, or at any rate I was not yet aware of it. A thorough and detailed comparison of the two curricula would take a good many pages but would be well worth doing. The differences are as important as the similarities. The Chinese lists and procedures are only for English majors there, whereas the Common Core is intended for all undergraduates in US colleges and universities. My Chinese

informant did not tell me whether there are standardized tests in the People's Republic, as there are, controversially, in connection with the Common Core. In both China and the United States, however, a good bit of freedom exists, at least in principle, regarding just how and what to teach in a given classroom, within the established parameters.—JHM]

2. The remarks that follow in this essay are adapted from J. Hillis Miller, "Reading (about) Modern Chinese Literature in a Time of Globalization," in Wang Ning, ed., *China in the Twentieth Century*, special issue, *Modern Language Quarterly* 69:1 (2008), 187–94.

3. Douwe Fokkema, "Chinese Postmodernist Fiction," in Wang Ning, ed., *China in the Twentieth Century*, special issue, *Modern Language Quarterly* 69:1 (2008), 141–65.

4. See Ming Dong Gu, "The Art of the *Hongloumeng*: Poetic Fiction and Open Fiction," *Chinese Theories of Fiction: A Non-Western Narrative System* (Albany: State University of New York Press, 2006), 153–80.

5. Ming Dong Gu, "Lu Xun and Modernism/Postmodernism" in Wang Ning, ed., *China in the Twentieth Century*, special issue, *Modern Language Quarterly* 69:1 (2008), 29–44.

6. Fokkema, "Chinese Postmodernist Fiction."

7. Chen Yongguo, "Becoming-Obscure: A Constant in the Development of Modern Chinese Poetry," in Wang Ning, ed., *China in the Twentieth Century*, special issue, *Modern Language Quarterly* 69:1 (2008), 81–96.

8. Fokkema, "Chinese Postmodernist Fiction."

9. Harold Bloom, *The Anxiety of Influence: A Theory of Poetry* (New York: Oxford University Press, 1973).

10. Fokkema, "Chinese Postmodernist Fiction."

11. Ibid.

12. Chen Yongguo, "Becoming-Obscure."

13. Ibid.

14. See *Lu Xun (Lu Hsun) Reference Archive,* available at http://www.marxists.org/archive/lu-xun/index.htm.

15. Fokkema, "Chinese Postmodernist Fiction."

16. Ming Dong Gu, *Chinese Theories of Fiction.*

CHAPTER 12

1. Karl Marx and Frederich Engels, *The Communist Manifesto*, available at http://www.marxists.org/archive/marx/works/1848/communist-manifesto.

2. Claire Colebrook, in an essay titled "A Globe of One's Own: In Praise of the Flat Earth," *SubStance* 41.1 (2012): 30–39, sent me back to Satan's space travel in Milton. Her essay has been provocative for me in other ways, too, as have recent unpublished papers on critical climate change by Tom Cohen.

3. Gilles Deleuze and Félix Guattari, *Kafka: Toward a Minor Literature*, trans. Dana Polan (Minneapolis: University of Minnesota Press, 1986).

4. David Damrosch, *What Is World Literature?* (Princeton, NJ: Princeton University Press, 2003), 5.

5. Ibid., 4–5.

6. Johann Wolfgang von Goethe, *Conversations with Eckermann*, ed. J. K. Morehead, trans. John Oxenford (London: Everyman, 1930), 132.

7. William Shakespeare, *King Lear*, 4.6.116.

8. Paul de Man, "Genesis and Genealogy (Nietzsche)," *Allegories of Reading: Figural Language in Rousseau, Nietzsche, Rilke, and Proust* (New Haven, CT: Yale University Press, 1979), 79–101; Andrzej Warminski, "Reading for Example: A Metaphor in Nietzsche's *Birth of Tragedy*," *Readings in Interpretation: Hölderlin, Hegel, Heidegger* (Minneapolis: University of Minnesota Press, 1987), xxxv–lxi; Andrzej Warminski, "Terrible Reading (Preceded by 'Epigraphs')," *Responses: Paul de Man's Wartime Journalism* (Lincoln: University of Nebraska Press, 1989), 386–96; Carol Jacobs, "The Stammering Text: The Fragmentary Studies Preliminary to *The Birth of Tragedy*," *The Dissimulating Harmony: The Image of Interpretation in Nietzsche, Rilke, Artaud, and Benjamin* (Baltimore: Johns Hopkins University Press, 1978), 1–22; Thomas Albrecht, "A 'Monstrous Opposition': The Double Dionysus and the Double Apollo in Nietzsche's *Birth of Tragedy*," *The Medusa Effect: Representation and Epistemology in Victorian Aesthetics* (Albany: State University of New York Press, 2009), 51–70.

9. Warminski, "Reading for Example," xliv–xlv.

10. Friedrich Nietzsche, "Vom Nutzen und Nachtheil der Historie für das Leben," *Sämtliche Werke: Kritische Studienausgabe*, ed. Giorgio Colli and Mazzino Montinari, vol. 1: *Die Geburt der Tragödie* (Munich: Walter de Gruyter, 1988), 243–334; Friedrich Nietzsche, "On the Utility and Liability of History for Life," *The Complete Works of Friedrich Nietzsche*, trans. Richard T. Gray, vol. 2: *Unfashionable Observations* (Stanford, CA: Stanford University Press, 1995), 83–167 (this is now the best translation; the older translation I cite uses a different title).

11. Friedrich Nietzsche, *'The Birth of Tragedy' and 'The Case of Wagner,'* trans. Walter Kaufmann (New York: Vintage Books, 1967), 110; Friedrich Nietzsche, *Sämtliche Werke: Kritische Studienausgabe*, ed. Giorgio Colli and Mazzino Montinari, vol. 1: *Die Geburt der Tragödie* (Munich: Walter de Gruyter, 1988), 9–156, esp. 116.

12. Harold Bloom, *The Anxiety of Influence: A Theory of Poetry* (New York: Oxford University Press, 1973).

13. Nietzsche, *Birth of Tragedy*, 111; Nietzsche, *Geburt der Tragödie*, 116.

14. Nietzsche, *Birth of Tragedy*, 143; Nietzsche, *Geburt der Tragödie*, 155.

15. Ibid.

16. Ibid.

17. Nietzsche, *Birth of Tragedy*, 143; Nietzsche, *Geburt der Tragödie*, 155.

18. T. S. Eliot, "Burnt Norton," *Four Quartets: The Collected Poems and Plays, 1909–1950* (New York: Harcourt, Brace, 1952), 118.

19. Jacobs, "Stammering Text."

20. Nietzsche, *Birth of Tragedy*, 143; Nietzsche, *Geburt der Tragödie*, 154.

21. Nietzsche, *Birth of Tragedy*, 143; Nietzsche, *Geburt der Tragödie*, 155.

22. Jacobs, "Stammering Text," 20–22; Friedrich Nietzsche, *Sämtliche Werke: Kritische Studienausgabe*, ed. Giorgio Colli and Mazzino Montinari, vol. 7: *Nachgelassene Fragmente, 1869–1874* (Munich: Walter de Gruyter, 1988), 1.

23. Warminski, "Reading for Example," liii–lxi, discusses catachresis in his reading of a metaphor in *The Birth of Tragedy*.

24. Here, I have used Beebee's unidentified translation. For the German, see Friedrich Nietzsche, *Sämtliche Werke: Kritische Studienausgabe*, ed. Giorgio Colli and Mazzino Montinari, vol. 5: *Jenseits von Gut und Böse* (Munich: Walter de Gruyter, 1988), 9–243.

25. Nietzsche, *Birth of Tragedy*, 110–11; Nietzsche, *Geburt der Tragödie*, 116.

26. Nietzsche, *Birth of Tragedy*, 113–14; Nietzsche, *Geburt der Tragödie*, 119–20.

27. Here appears again the figure of the tame shore as against the dangerous ocean of universal knowledge, or, in this case, the icy current of existence. "Knowledge" and "existence" are by no means the same, however. The import of the metaphor is reversed in the second example, as happens with so much else in the language of *The Birth of Tragedy*. In the first citation, universal Socratic knowledge is seen as bad, debilitating, like a too vast ocean. In the second citation, man is seen as too timid to entrust himself, as he should, to the icy waters of existence. See Nietzsche, *Birth of Tragedy*, 113; Nietzsche, *Geburt der Tragödie*, 119.

28. Nietzsche, *Birth of Tragedy*, 113–14; Nietzsche, *Geburt der Tragödie*, 119–20.

29. Nietzsche, *Birth of Tragedy*, 144; Nietzsche, *Geburt der Tragödie*, 155–56.

30. Nietzsche, *Birth of Tragedy*, 144; Nietzsche, *Geburt der Tragödie*, 156.

31. George Eliot, *Middlemarch* (Harmondsworth: Penguin, 1974), 229. The Cabeiri were a group of Samothracian fertility gods, the notes to the Penguin *Middlemarch* tell me, with Casaubon-like learning. That Casaubon himself needs help from fertility gods is a characteristic sly ironic joke by Eliot.

32. Ibid., 96.

CHAPTER 13

1. Jacques Derrida, *L'Université sans condition* (Paris: Galilée, 2001); Jacques Derrida, "The University without Condition," *Without Alibi*, ed. and trans. Peggy Kamuf, 202–37 (Stanford, CA: Stanford University Press, 2002).

2. See Marc Bousquet, *How the University Works: Higher Education and the Low-Wage Nation* (New York: New York University Press, 2008); Christopher Newfield, *Unmaking the Public University: The Forty-Year Assault on the Middle Class* (Cambridge, MA: Harvard University Press, 2008); Frank Donoghue, *The Last Professors: The Corporate University and the Fate of the Humanities* (New York: Fordham University Press, 2008); Jeffrey J. Williams, "The Post-Welfare State University," *American Literary History* 18:1 (2006), 190–216. All four of these works have extensive bibliographies. See also Peggy Kamuf, "Counting Madness," in Timothy Clark and Nicholas Royle, eds., *The Future of the Humanities: U.S. Domination and Other Issues*, special issue, *Oxford Literary Review* 28 (2006), 67–77.

3. Quoted in Frank Donoghue, "Prestige," in Modern Language Association of America, ed., *Profession 2006* (New York: Modern Language Association of America, 2006), 156.

4. Richard Levin, "The Rise of Asia's Universities," lecture presented to the Royal Society, London, 31 January 2010, available at http://communications.yale.edu/president/speeches/2010/10/01/rise-asia-s-universities.

5. According to Frank Donoghue, "between 1970 and 2001, bachelor's degrees in English have declined from 7.6 percent to 4 percent, and degrees in foreign languages have even more dramatically declined (2.4 percent to 1 percent)"; see Donoghue, *The Last Professors*, 91.

6. Robert Scholes, quoted in ibid., 20.

7. John Keats, "On Sitting Down to Read King Lear Once Again," available at http://www.poemhunter.com/poem/on-sitting-down-to-read-king-lear-once-again.

8. Matthew Arnold, *The Letters of Matthew Arnold to Arthur Hugh Clough*, ed. Howard Foster Lowry (London/New York: Oxford University Press, 1932), 96.

9. For a proposal for such courses, see David Pogue, "Q&A: Rumors, Cyberbullying and Anonymity," *New York Times*, 22 July 2010, available at http://www.nytimes.com/2010/07/22/technology/personaltech/22pogue-email.html?pagewanted=all.

10. W. B. Yeats, *The Variorum Edition of the Poems of W. B. Yeats*, ed. Peter Allt and Russell K. Alspach (New York: Macmillan, 1957), 316.

11. J. Hillis Miller, "W. B. Yeats: 'The Cold Heaven,'" *Others* (Princeton, NJ: Princeton University Press, 2001), 170–82.

12. The proverb ("Die Rose ist ohne warum; sie blühet weil sie blühet") is cited in the original German by Jorge Luis Borges, "La cábala," *Siete Noches* (Mexico City: Fondo de Cultura Económica, 1980), 120–21; Jorge Luis Borges, "The Kabbalah," *Seven Nights*, trans. Eliot Weinberger (New York: New Directions, 1984), 94. See also Angelus Silesius, *The Cherubnic Wanderer*, trans. Maria Shrady (New York: Paulist Press, 1986).

13. David Damrosch, *What Is World Literature?* (Princeton, NJ: Princeton University Press, 2003).

14. A. Norman Jeffares, *A Commentary on the Collected Poems of W. B. Yeats* (Stanford, CA: Stanford University Press, 1968), 146.

15. W. B. Yeats, *Variorum Edition*, 269.

16. See Pogue, "Q&A: Rumors, Cyberbullying and Anonymity."

17. Paul de Man, "The Resistance to Theory," *The Resistance to Theory* (Minneapolis: University of Minnesota Press, 1986), 11.

CHAPTER 14

1. See Guy Debord, *La société du spectacle* (Paris: Gallimard, 1992); Guy Debord, *The Society of the Spectacle*, trans. Donald Nicholson-Smith (New York: Zone Books, 1994), available at http://antiworld.se/project/references/texts/The_Society%20_Of%20_The%20_Spectacle.pdf. See also Jean Baudrillard, *Simulacra et simulation* (Paris: Galilée, 1981); Jean Baudrillard, *Simulacra and Simulation*, trans. Sheila Glaser (Ann Arbor: University of Michigan Press, 1994). Finally, see Maurice Blanchot, "Les deux versions de l'imaginaire," *L'espace littéraire* (Paris: Gallimard, 1955), 266–77; Maurice Blanchot, "Two

Versions of the Imaginary," *The Gaze of Orpheus and Other Literary Essays*, trans. Lydia Davis (Barrytown, NY: Station Hill Press, 1981), 79–89; Maurice Blanchot, "Le chant des Sirènes," *Le livre à venir* (Paris: Gallimard, 1959), 7–34; Maurice Blanchot, "The Song of the Sirens," *The Book to Come*, trans. Charlotte Mandell (Stanford, CA: Stanford University Press, 2003), 1–24.

2. See http://www.ubu.com/film/debord_spectacle1.html. (In this chapter, I give a number of citations and references to sources in the form of URLs, to exemplify one version of our present-day society of multimedia spectacles and simulacra.)

3. See https://en.wikipedia.org/wiki/Guy_Debord.

4. See http://en.wikipedia.org/wiki/Simulacra_and_Simulation.

5. For the replica of the Eiffel Tower, see http://www.vegas.com/attractions/on_the_strip/eiffeltower.html.

6. Blanchot, "Song of the Sirens," 14; Blanchot, "Chant des Sirènes," 22.

7. Here I let Blanchot, now a voice from the grave, speak for himself, or "itself" (Blanchot, "Song of the Sirens," 6–7, transation slightly modified; Blanchot, "Chant des Sirènes," 12–13):

> The narrative [*récit*] begins where the novel [*le roman*] does not go but still leads us by its refusals and its rich negligence. The narrative is heroically and pretentiously the narrative of one single episode, that of Ulysses' meeting and the insufficient and magnetic song of the Sirens. [As I indicated earlier, Blanchot alludes elsewhere in these essays to the ambiguous ending of Proust's great novel and to Ahab's climactic mortal re-encounter with Moby Dick as further examples of the *récit* as approach to the image as "point."—JHM] Narrative is not the relating of an event but this event itself, the approach of this event, the place where it is called on to unfold, an event still to come, by the magnetic power of which the narrative itself can hope to come true [*par la puissance attirante duquel le récit peut espérer, lui aussi, se réaliser*]. . . . Narrative is the movement toward a point—one that is not only unknown, ignored, and foreign, but such that it seems, before and outside of this movement, to have no kind of reality; yet one that is so imperious that it is from this point alone that the narrative draws its attraction, in such a way that it cannot even "begin" before having reached it; but it is only the narrative and the unforeseeable movement of the narrative that provide the space where the point becomes real, powerful, and alluring.

8. Wallace Stevens, "Anecdote of the Jar," lines 2, 8, *Collected Poems* (New York: Knopf, 1954), 76; available at http://www.poemhunter.com/poem/anecdote-of-the-jar.

9. Paul de Man, "The Resistance to Theory," *The Resistance to Theory* (Minneapolis: University of Minnesota Press, 1986), 11.

10. For an informative brief talk about *New Yorker* covers, see Françoise Mouly, Daniel Clowes, R. Crumb, and Chris Ware, "Talk on *Blown Covers*," in Hillary L. Chute and Patrick Jagoda, eds., *Comics & Media*, special issue, *Criti-*

cal Inquiry, Spring 2014, 186–97. Mouly has been art editor of *The New Yorker* since 1993. See also Françoise Mouly, *Blown Covers:* New Yorker *Covers You Were Never Meant to See* (New York: Abrams, 2012). With respect to the second example, *Wired*, for reasons of its own, does not indicate page numbers for its multiudinous advertisements. The one I am discussing appeared near the front of the issue, just between the two pages giving, in long lists, information about editors, publishers, and so on. The Coca-Cola Company, owner of the brand of water in question, must have paid a bundle for this ad. The ad has not reappeared, to my knowledge, in subsequent issues of *Wired*. My request to reproduce the ad was refused, and the online edition of *Wired* does not include the ads in any given issue, so the only way for you to see the ad is to get a printed copy of that issue of *Wired* in a library or to order it online. I greatly regret that. The ad is well worth a thoughtful look.—JHM]

11. See Marshall McLuhan, *The Gutenberg Galaxy: The Making of Typographic Man* (Toronto: University of Toronto Press, 1962); Marshall McLuhan, *Understanding Media: The Extensions of Man* (New York: McGraw-Hill, 1964). See also http://en.wikipedia.org/wiki/Marshall_McLuhan and http://en.wikipedia.org/wiki/The_medium is_the_message.

12. Blanchot, "Song of the Sirens," 14; Blanchot, "Chant des Sirènes," 22.

13. See the fascinating *Wikipedia* entry about the history of *Wired*, available at http://en.wikipedia.org/wiki/Wired_(magazine).

14. See http://www.wired.com.

15. De Man, "Resistance to Theory," 11.

16. See John Ruskin, *The Works*, 39 vols., ed. E. T. Cook and Alexander Wedderburn (London/New York: G. Allen/Longmans, Green and Co., 1903–1912). This wonderful mixed-media edition is now available in its entirety at http://www.lancaster.ac.uk/users/ruskinlib/Pages/Works.html. This is a good example of the Web's amazing resources for literary study: the Cook and Wedderburn edition used to be available only in relatively rare printed copies that cost thousands of dollars; now anyone with a computer and an Internet connection can download it for free. Ah, the wonders of the Internet! See also Art Spiegelman, *Maus: A Survivor's Tale* (New York: Pantheon Books, 1986).

17. Imre Kertész, *Fatelessness*, trans. Tim Wilkinson (New York: Vintage International, 2004). See also Ian McEwan, *Atonement* (New York: N.A. Talese/Doubleday, 2002).

18. See Virginia Woolf, *The Waves*, available at http://gutenberg.net.au/ebooks02/0201091h.html.

19. Lewis Carroll, *'Alice's Adventures in Wonderland' and 'Through the Looking-Glass'* (New York: A. L. Burt Company, n.d.). I still have that book, much battered and entirely missing its spine; it has my younger brother's *ex libris* on the back of the cover, which must mean that he appropriated it after I was older. See also Kenneth Grahame, *The Wind in the Willows*, illus. Ernest H. Shepard (New York: Scribner, 1933), available at http://en.wikipedia.org/wiki/The_Wind_in_the_Willows and http://www.online-literature.com/grahame/windwillows/1 (the second of these two URLs links to an e-text that has the original illustrations of 1908 by Paul Bransom, not the Shepard ones; I have not been able to find the 1933 edition online). Finally, see A. A. Milne, *Winnie-*

the-Pooh, illus. Ernest H. Shepard (London: Methuen, 1926); A. A. Milne, *The House at Pooh Corner*, illus. Ernest H. Shepard (London: Methuen, 1928). I no longer know which editions of the two Milne books I had as a child in the early 1930s, but they had the Shepard illustrations.

20. Henry James, *A Small Boy & Others* (New York: Scribner, 1962), 120.

21. See Mauro Nervi, *The Kafka Project*, available at http://www.kafka.org/index.php?project.

CHAPTER 15

1. J. Hillis Miller, *On Literature* (London: Routledge, 2002), 156–59.

2. Alfred, Lord Tennyson, "Tears, Idle Tears," available at http://www.poemhunter.com/poem/tears-idle-tears.

3. J. Hillis Miller, "Temporal Topographies: Tennyson's Tears," *EurAmerica* 21:3 (1991), 29–45.

4. Paul de Man, "'Conclusions': Walter Benjamin's 'The Task of the Translator,'" *The Resistance to Theory* (Minneapolis: University of Minnesota Press, 1986), 87–88.

5. Jacques Derrida, "Forcener le subjectile," in Paule Thévinin and Jacques Derrida, *Artaud: Dessins et portraits* (Paris: Gallimard, 1986), 55–108; Jacques Derrida, "To Unsense the Subjectile," in Jacques Derrida and Paule Thévenin, *The Secret Art of Antonin Artaud,* trans. Mary Ann Caws (Cambridge, MA: MIT Press, 1998), 59–157.

6. J. Hillis Miller, *The Medium Is the Maker: Browning, Freud, Derrida, and the New Telepathic Ecotechnologies* (Brighton: Sussex Academic Press, 2009).

7. Jacques Derrida, *Passions* (Paris: Galilée, 1993), 64–68; Jacques Derrida, "Passions: 'An Oblique Offering,'" *On the Name*, ed. Thomas Dutoit, trans. David Wood (Stanford, CA: Stanford University Press, 1995), 28–30.

8. Jacques Derrida, "Envois," *La carte postale: De Socrate à Freud et au-delà* (Paris: Aubier-Flammarion, 1980), 114–15; Jacques Derrida, "Envois," *The Post Card: From Socrates to Freud and Beyond*, trans. Alan Bass (Chicago: University of Chicago Press, 1987), 104.

9. On the reduction in the number of bachelor's degrees earned in English and foreign languages at US colleges and universities between 1970 and 2001, see Frank Donoghue, *The Last Professors: The Corporate University and the Fate of the Humanities* (New York: Fordham University Press, 2008), 91.

10. J. Hillis Miller, "Anachronistic Reading," *Derrida Today* 3 (2010), 75–91.

11. Walter E. Houghton, *The Victorian Frame of Mind, 1830–1870* (New Haven, CT: Yale University Press, 1957); E. M. W. Tillyard, *The Elizabethan World Picture* (London: Chatto & Windus, 1943).

12. De Man, "'Conclusions,'" 87–88; Walter Benjamin, "Die Aufgabe des Übersetzers," *Illuminationen: Ausgewählte Schriften*, ed. Siegfried Unseld (Frankfurt am Main: Suhrkamp, 1955), 56–69; Walter Benjamin, "The Task of the Translator," *Illuminations*, trans. Hannah Arendt (New York: Schocken Books, 1969), 69–82.

13. Jacques Derrida, "This Strange Institution Called Literature," *Acts of Literature*, ed. Derek Attridge (London: Routledge, 1992), 33–75.

Index

FLASHPOINTS

1. *On Pain of Speech: Fantasies of the First Order and the Literary Rant*, Dina Al-Kassim
2. *Moses and Multiculturalism*, Barbara Johnson, with a foreword by Barbara Rietveld
3. *The Cosmic Time of Empire: Modern Britain and World Literature*, Adam Barrows
4. *Poetry in Pieces: César Vallejo and Lyric Modernity*, Michelle Clayton
5. *Disarming Words: Empire and the Seductions of Translation in Egypt*, Shaden M. Tageldin
6. *Wings for Our Courage: Gender, Erudition, and Republican Thought*, Stephanie H. Jed
7. *The Cultural Return*, Susan Hegeman
8. *English Heart, Hindi Heartland: The Political Life of Literature in India*, Rashmi Sadana
9. *The Cylinder: Kinematics of the Nineteenth Century*, Helmut Müller-Sievers
10. *Polymorphous Domesticities: Pets, Bodies, and Desire in Four Modern Writers*, Juliana Schiesari
11. *Flesh and Fish Blood: Postcolonialism, Translation, and the Vernacular*, S. Shankar
12. *The Fear of French Negroes: Transcolonial Collaboration in the Revolutionary Americas*, Sara E. Johnson
13. *Figurative Inquisitions: Conversion, Torture, and Truth in the Luso-Hispanic Atlantic*, Erin Graff Zivin
14. *Cosmopolitan Desires: Global Modernity and World Literature in Latin America*, Mariano Siskind
15. *Fiction Beyond Secularism*, Justin Neuman
16. *Periodizing Jameson: Dialectics, the University, and the Desire for Narrative*, Phillip E. Wegner
17. *The Practical Past*, Hayden White
18. *The Powers of the False: Reading, Writing, Thinking Beyond Truth and Fiction*, Doro Wiese
19. *The Object of the Atlantic: Concrete Aesthetics in Cuba, Brazil, and Spain, 1868–1968*, Rachel Price
20. *Epic and Exile: Novels of the German Popular Front 1933–1945*, Hunter Bivens
21. *An Innocent Abroad: Lectures in China*, J. Hillis Miller
22. *Form and Instability: East Europe, Literature, Postimperial Difference*, Anita Starosta
23. *Bombay Modern: Arun Kolatkar and Bilingual Literary Culture*, Anjali Nerlekar